DATE DUE

DEC 1 6 2010		
DEC 2 7 2011		
MAR 2 2 2012		
AUG 0 5 2014		

NEXT YEAR COUNTRY

Next Year Country

Dust to Dust in Western Kansas,
1890–1940

CRAIG MINER

 University Press of Kansas

The photograph on pages ii–iii, courtesy of Mary Wettig collection, depicts harvest of Elliott and Holmstrom, near Copeland, Gray County, Kansas, 1920s.

Published by the University Press of Kansas (Lawrence, Kansas 66045), which was organized by the Kansas Board of Regents and is operated and funded by Emporia State University, Fort Hays State University, Kansas State University, Pittsburg State University, the University of Kansas, and Wichita State University

Library of Congress Cataloging-in-Publication Data

Miner, H. Craig.
   Next year country : dust to dust in western Kansas, 1890–1940 / Craig Miner.
       p.   cm.
   Includes bibliographical references and index.
   ISBN 0-7006-1476-1 (cloth : alk. paper)
       1. Kansas—History—19th century.   2. Kansas—History—20th century.   3. Frontier and pioneer life—Kansas.   4. Kansas—Environmental conditions.   5. Human ecology—Kansas—History—19th century.   6. Human ecology—Kansas—History—20th century.
I. Title.
   F686.M55 2006
   978.1′02—dc22

                                                                              2006011227

British Library Cataloguing-in-Publication Data is available.

Printed in the United States of America

10 9 8 7 6 5 4 3 2 1

The paper used in this publication meets the minimum requirements of the American National Standard for Permanence of Paper for Printed Library Materials z39.48-1984.

For two Hal Miners

Contents

Illustrations

Preface

Jess Denious, the editor of the *Dodge City Globe*, was an active supporter of the Kansas Author's Club. In 1939, at the end of a hard time in his area, he spoke to a representative group from that club on the theme of the importance of good writing about Kansas to developing, maintaining, and enhancing the spirit of the place. What would Kansas be, he said, without William Allen White, Dr. Charles Sheldon, May Williams Ward, or Tom McNeal? "We all know," Denious said, "that these persons made no new plows, no airplanes, no automobiles, none of the gadgets which relieve us of drudgery. All they did was to keep the flag of Kansas waving, to hold aloft the ideals of our people, to strengthen our faith, to make our minds more alert, to awaken our interest in the beautiful things about us, and to make us better acquainted with the race of men to which we belong."[1] No regional historian could ask for a better statement of mission.

My understanding of the history of Western Kansas has been much informed by the vivid writing and deep insights of writers who have gone before. Most especially, these have been journalists—editors of newspapers in small and medium-sized towns across the Kansas High Plains. Some left letters and reminiscences. All left their day-to-day reactions to the events in the communities to which they and their business enterprises were intimately tied. Scholars have at times criticized newspapers as sources, and to be sure they must be used with the same care and alertness to bias as other sources. But it is hard to fool local readers about yesterday's events in their own town. And it would be equally hard to manufacture

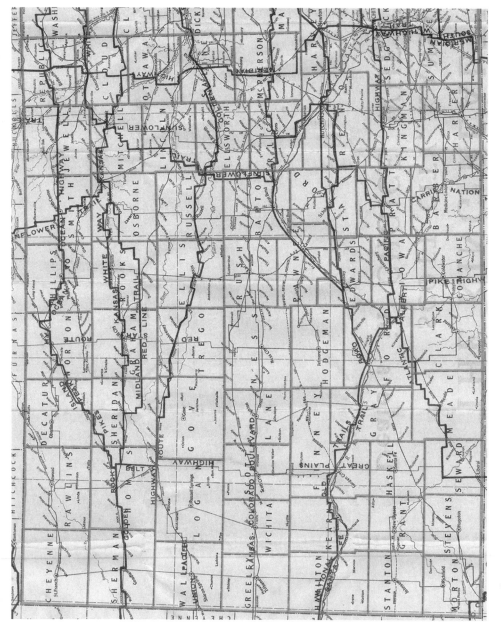

Map of Western Kansas in 1920 emphasizing highway development (courtesy of Wichita State University Special Collections)

some consistent slant over so many thousands of individual newspapers issued in dozens of towns over a period of fifty years. Therefore, it is with no embarrassment that I acknowledge that my core source for this book is a detailed study of the newspapers of a number of towns in Western Kansas. These were chosen for geographical spread, for a penchant for community news well reported, and for a certain style on the part of certain editors in reporting and interpreting what they experienced.

Kansas is famous for newspapers and editors. The Kansas State Historical Society, founded by a group of editors, has a fine newspaper collection. The names of William Allen White of the *Emporia Gazette*, Ed Howe of the *Atchison Globe*, Sol Miller of the *Troy Chieftain*, Marshall Murdock of the *Wichita Eagle*, or Rolla Clymer of the *El Dorado Times* are recognizable to students of Kansas history. But those editors all hail from east of Highway 81. The contributions of the west have been less well studied, and the names of the giants of the place in so many fields are less well known. Names to be reckoned with in twentieth-century Western Kansas are Jess Denious of the *Dodge City Globe*, Frank Motz of the *Hays News*, Will Townsley of the *Great Bend Tribune*, W. F. Hubbard of the *Hugoton Hermes*, Ben Hibbs of the *Goodland Republic*, Joseph Bristow and Roy Bailey of the *Salina Journal*, Ray Millman of the *Liberal News*, Herb Fryback of the *Colby Free Press*, W. Y. Morgan of the *Hutchinson News*, J. K. Barnd of the *Ness County News*, A. Q. Miller of the *Belleville Telescope*, and a host of other memorable and quotable writers.

William Allen White founded a school of journalists who felt it was their duty to feel the pulse of the community and reflect its aspirations—and also to help form its unique, pragmatic values. If the salt of the earth in Western Kansas has lost any of its flavor, it is not for lack of effort by these editors to maintain a sense of place against a "chain store" culture and to enforce a discipline of appropriate behavior for its regional citizens.

Western Kansas editors often wrote about their job. "The comings and goings of our people have been noted," wrote the editor at Ness City, "the joy bells have been rung for hundreds of happy couples, and their notes have mingled with funeral dirges for those who have crossed the dark and silent river; tidings of the gospel have mingled with gossip of the neighborhood; pleasure and politics have each had a due share of attention; but the principal effort has been to give a correct and unexaggerated mirror of events as they transpired."[2] An editor in Garden City expressed himself in a similar way, stating that the "coming and going of the people of the town" was "grist that comes to the hopper of the live local paper. If you were to write a letter to your absent friends and undertake to tell them half the news that your local paper does, you would soon give up in despair."[3] Denious made a broad claim: "A newspaper is the best historical text a state can have and the histories of Kansas which are to come will be written largely from the facts bound in the back files of newspapers."[4]

The division of historians into "schools" is artificial. There is all too much trendy technique, too much upsetting the applecart of what has gone before with minimal justification. However, I should say something about my philosophy and approach as reflected in this book and others.

I admire the Realist school in nineteenth-century art and fiction. These writers and artists shared some of the interest of contemporary historians in documenting the lives of ordinary people, and they eschewed anomalous drama, exaggerated significance, and the kind of simplification of real events that led to romantic contrast between good and evil, light and darkness, in an almost Manichean sense. Oliver Wendell Holmes once observed that the average person spent more time thinking about his breakfast than about world events. There was drama in a divorce that was more interesting in many ways than a cavalry charge. But it developed slowly and required of the reader patience in understanding the evolving character of the players as well as the circumstances, real and imagined, in which they acted. Local history has often been the domain of amateurs of more enthusiasm than skill, but done properly it is no amateur undertaking. The closer one gets to things, the harder it is to impose pattern. The complexities of the things in themselves and their relations, the multiplicity of characters and motives when seen close up, play havoc with stepwise exposition.

My purpose is to shed light on the situations of people of mixed motives and a range of backgrounds and abilities responding over time in certain places to conditions that were neither simple nor stable. They made decisions in conditions of uncertainty without the benefit of hindsight, omniscience, or a lofty perspective. And they did it where they lived with the materials in front of them, using what they brought and what they found. Therefore I think it is important for the reader to be on the ground in the field among them as much as time and chance allow, to hear their voices with their words and style, and to avoid distortion of selection or interpretation imposed by an orientation too much tied to present tendencies or priorities. The relevance of a shared human enterprise in a similar place will become obvious without being forced into overbroad paradigms. People do not act upon "general ideas" so much as locked in a welter of detail from which they are trying to make sense. Our sources strip away enough of the richness of real experience without the historian's purposefully trying to render it more suitable for pedagogical purposes and thus distancing it from the quotidian feeling one gets from reading primary sources.

Walt Whitman expressed the sentiment—echoing Ralph Waldo Emerson and William Blake—that in anything is everything, that the insurance office and the railroad train, modern in his time, lacked no drama or dignity for an interpreter with imagination, and that when we write good history there will be no need for romance. The nearby gnat, Whitman thought, could tell us all we need to know. The English historian Thomas Macauley wrote: "I do, indeed, greatly disapprove of those notions which some writers have of the dignity of history. For fear of alluding to the vulgar concerns of private life, they have no notions of the circumstances which deeply affect the happiness of nations."[5]

It is with those preconceptions and methods that I approach the history of an "ordinary" region, circumscribed narrowly, geographically and chronologically, with a seemingly limited cast of characters and options. I hope, by diving deep, to reveal some of the fascination, interleavings, and stark profundities of the struggles of people trying to make an unpublicized living at home. Having written before about Western Kansas, having over a century of family roots there, and having a strong personal sense of the intrinsic interest and value of events there, my choice of setting for such an experiment in the writing of local history was easy.

Where is Western Kansas exactly? Almost any native would agree that, west of old Highway 81, now Interstate 35, there is a second Kansas. At about the 96th meridian, this makes Western Kansas into a territory of 60 counties of the 105 in the state as a whole. It is an almost square region, measuring approximately 250 miles by 200 miles and incorporating about two-thirds of the state's 50 million acres but considerably lesser percentages of its population or annual rainfall.

Sometimes the physical transition is more obvious than at other times. Driving west from I-35 up the Solomon River Valley, one would not question that the landscape and the culture is that of Western Kansas. The same would hold at the south end of the district for a drive west from Wellington on Highway 160 into the Gyp Hills of Barber County. The rolling hills west of Salina represent a similarly obvious break, and few would question that Ellsworth is a Western Kansas town. But to say that Wichita, which is barely more than a third of the way west into Kansas and is its largest and most industrialized city, is in Western Kansas is a stretch.[6] The same might be said about other "borderland" cities like McPherson, Salina, Hutchinson, or Concordia. A movement in 1892 to divide Kansas in two suggested that the new state of West Kansas might begin at the west boundary of Kingman County, or just beyond the 98th meridian.[7] When a group of University of Kansas students formed a shortgrass club in Lawrence in 1912, they defined their Western Kansas interest group as consisting of those hailing from west of the 99th meridian. This would be one county further west yet and would be a point just west of Great Bend and east of Hays.[8] The true High Plains physical subdivision of Kansas begins at the 100th meridian, or about the longitude of Dodge City. That would have it incorporate only about the western one-third of Kansas, a definition Kansans in the past would have accepted as delimiting the extreme of the climatic challenge, but not as by any means representing the whole of the Western Kansas identity and interest. It would be odd to be forced by that definition to locate such icons of Western Kansas as Dodge City, Garden City, or Hays in the region's eastern suburbs.

There is shading at the limits. Just as people in Colby or Tribune ran on Mountain Standard Time and perhaps felt more affinity with Denver than with Topeka, the border cities on the east were more feeders to and jobbers for the western region than typical parts of it. They had terminal elevators, multistory wholesale warehouses, fancy union terminals, and substantial railroad yards. The more typical Western Kansas town had country elevators, general stores, a railroad depot of standard design. Many were on a "bobtail" branch line where the irregular schedule shared more with the rhythm of the seasons than the precision of the factory. In the twentieth century, the west part of Kansas was less isolated than before and had its radios, its autos, its farm machines, its paved streets, its public libraries, its electric light plants, its civic clubs, and its oratorios. But before 1940, it was still distinctly rural in a way that one might argue became more blurred in the late twentieth century when packing plants and feed lots gave an industrial look to Garden City and Dodge City.

The independent history of the central Kansas towns and cities is too complex to be treated well as an attachment to a subregional study. Also, the diversity of the economies and the size of the daily papers in these border cities tend to dilute the focus and diffuse the homogeneity of interest and attitude that gives a subregion character and its history verve and depth. Therefore I confess that I give the eastern edge of the region shorter shrift— shorter than the swatch it has cut in percentages of population and product in the Western Kansas region most broadly defined would seem to justify. Wichita looms to the east always for this region, in its psyche if not in its sights, as Kansas City does for towns in eastern Kansas. People in the west often read the *Wichita Eagle* along with their local sheets. But travel to Wichita for a pre-1940 High Plains resident was almost a visit to another planet.

Despite some problems of definition, however, there is much to be said for making what William Least Heat-Moon has called a "deep map" of such a subregion.[9] One advantage is to allow a cast of characters to emerge that extends beyond the "famous" and even beyond those people usually covered in the broader scope of state history.

Pamela Riney-Kehrberg, in presenting the diary of a woman with only a fourth-grade education residing in Hamilton County, Kansas, during the Dust Bowl, makes a case that that single woman's experience preserving one farm home has implications beyond herself—lessons that may well be missed in the study of incorporated masses. There is purpose, Riney-Kehrberg notes, in examining historical phenomena like the Dust Bowl from the inside out, "from the perspective of the individual living the moment, and perhaps not perceiving themselves as engulfed in historical cataclysm."[10] There is little editing from hindsight or filtering of abstraction in such accounts.

Far from an exercise in the collection of trivial or mythological anecdote from an interpretive backwater, the careful study of local history, through use of representative detail, and through the documentation of the "holistic" lives of specific individuals, enriches and fine-tunes the "big picture."

The tools for doing any historical research are documents. The collectors of those have been universities and historical societies. I continue to be awed by the depth of resources on the history of Kansas available at regional archives. The Kansas State Historical Society (KSHS), which has been collecting documents on the history of Kansas seriously since the 1870s, is unmatched anywhere for my purposes. Without its collections, a book like this might well be impossible; it would certainly be far less satisfactory. Leaving its world-class genealogical collection aside, newspapers are clearly the strength of the KSHS. But it is outstanding also in manuscript collections. The Special Collections at Kansas State University were particularly important, too, because of the large role the Kansas State Agricultural College played in advising the people of Western Kansas on new modes of agriculture in the twentieth century. I also was able to make significant use of collections at the University of Kansas and at Wichita State University.

Fred Woodward at the University Press of Kansas has encouraged me over the years and has especially supported my work on Western Kansas. The staff of the KSHS has been a great help, particularly Patricia Michaelis, Virgil Dean, Debbie Greeson, and Nancy Sherbert. My interlibrary loan requirements on this project were especially challenging and well met. My wife, Susan, now living alone with an eccentric professor without the buffer or diversion of our children, should be honored for forbearance and thanked for a keen editorial eye and for a humanizing, if sometimes deflating, wit. Last, I acknowledge my family who came to Kansas in the 1880s and stayed. Appreciation of Kansas is an acquired taste, and it sometimes takes a generation or two to acquire it fully.

Introduction:
Blood Ties

As this book is finished in 2005, I am sixty years old, a college professor living in Wichita, a city set in a shallow river valley between the rolling tallgrass Flint Hills prairie to the east and the shortgrass High Plains of Kansas to the west. It has taken me a long time to feel truly at home here, but it really should not have.

My father's name was Stanley. He was born in February of the war year 1917 on his own father's birthday in a big stucco-clad house on Topeka Street in Ness City, Kansas, altitude 2,251 feet, longitude 99 degrees, 54 minutes, 22 seconds, west. Stanley's father's name was Hal. He was an 1899 graduate of Ness City High School, who married a girl from upstate New York in 1907 and brought her west to share his life in the real estate and loan business. Mabel Pinkney's parents were so unsure about the "cowboy" from Ness County who was building their daughter a little house in the Wild West that they refused to attend the wedding or have their names placed on the invitations. My grandfather said people might think he was marrying an orphan. Grandma used to joke when I visited her in her house, smelling of fine dust, in the 1950s, that she was glad the family didn't go further west—Dighton was worse.

Hal's father was William Dennis. He came to Ness City in 1885 from Corning, Iowa, where he had been a banker. He served as mayor of Ness City, promoter of the Ness City and Sidney Street Railway, county treasurer, attorney, and proprietor of Miner's Cash Store. It was he who imported a Russian man, a worker on the trans-Siberian railroad, to be a tenant on some of the farmland he had accumulated. The family story is that Casper Frank arrived at the Ness City railroad depot about 1905 with a sign around his neck

Stanley Miner (left), early 1920s, in Ness County (author's collection)

addressing him to William D. Miner, Ness City, pretty much like a package. Another fragment of oral tradition is more racy. Once, it seems, great-grandpa had gone in person to collect rent. A woman answered the door completely nude. Not in the least flustered, Miner is supposed to have said: "Madam, I came to collect the rent, but I see you do not have it on you."

William D. had been in the state of New York for a time in early life, where his father William D. Sr. was postmaster at Warsaw. Before that the family had hailed from Connecticut for the 250 years since Thomas Miner, baptized in 1605 at Chew Magna, Somerset County, England, had in 1653 planted his home on a sea cove near Stonington, Connecticut. The second William D., my great-grandfather, on whose ninety-five-year-old lap I sat as a four-year-old listening to his 1877 model gold pocket watch tick, was the biggest mover among my line of people since then. I have the watch. I have the heritage. And the blood is only part of it.

One of the towns I chose to research in depth for this history was, naturally, Ness City. It represented a regional also-ran and was a place with which I was familiar, a kind of test of the authenticity of everything else. Even one who has spent a lifetime writing history, and who is perfectly aware that we are talking about real people here, can be taken aback when reeling through the microfilm of the *Ness County News* for 1921 to read that H. D. Miner, wife, and small son, Stanley, had departed for Battle Creek, Michigan, where Hal was to check into a sanitarium. That trip was my dad's earliest memory, and he told me several times how strange it was as a four-year-old to go to that northern city where his father's diabetes, which would kill him nine years later, was diagnosed and my grandmother was trained in providing the right diet and in giving insulin injections.

Stanley was always small, though he gamely played quarterback in the 1930s at Ness City High School. He got pneumonia nearly every winter as a young boy and sometimes was placed in the warm oven until the crisis passed. He tended fancy roosters with which his dad indulged him and had a pony and a bicycle. He drove his mother, who had had an eye put out by an arrow as a girl and never learned to drive, to the Chicago Century of Progress Exhibition in 1933. He was sixteen then, and sat on a pillow to see over the wheel. They went west to California later, the widow and the youngest son, and saw men camping along Highway 66.

Stan married Marybel at the Tri-Delta sorority house at Kansas State Agricultural College in 1939. There was a tradition of house weddings. His own father and mother had been married in front of the fireplace at the home in Castile, New York, called Ivywild, where she had been a governess. There was a tradition of name changes too. Grandma Miner had been Mabel, then Maybelle. Mom was born Mary Isabel Smith, incongruously into a plain-dressing Church of the Brethren family suspicious of all things Roman Catholic. In terror of going through life as Mary Smith, not to mention Isabel, she had decided to call herself Marybel. The little house my parents built in Ness City as World War II was breaking out in Europe is still there. I can imagine the windy, dusty day after they returned there following a stint in the navy in Chicago, where I was born, when dad said, "I don't care if I never see this God-forsaken place again." My mother responded in one of the odd juxtapositions for which she was famous: "Et tu Brute." Anyway they moved. He became an attorney in Wichita and my Old Settler status at the Ness County reunions is based on only a year's residence.

But we always returned, always went home again, and dad became my link to the magic of a place set in time. Driving west with me in the heat and the color of harvest time in a 1950s-era Buick or Oldsmobile, he talked about those times when he was a boy and about what a big and impressive industry growing wheat on the High Plains was. He would talk of people with what seemed to me exotic names: Harold Humburg, Chesney Floyd, Casper Frank, Gilbert Arnold. Sometimes we would stop at the farmhouse of a tenant farmer, as he had stopped with his dad years before, and as his dad had stopped with his dad before that in the same country. Sometimes it was only a basement with a grade-level entrance—always it seemed a small and simple shelter with just a few trees between the man, wife, and kids and the very hot or very cold wind. In November, I would hunt pheasants in those fields, at first hardly more than a toddler, armed with a BB gun. Later I had a .22 caliber rifle, then a 4-10 shotgun, which made me cry when first I fired it, a 20-gauge bolt action, and finally a 12-gauge automatic with which I could get off almost as many shots at a whirring flight as my cousin Gary. There were those cold mornings with the frost on the land and the steaming coffee and cigarettes and ammunition and dead fowl, whose gamey taste reminded you of wringing the necks of the thrashing birds in the grass (a boy's job when there were no dogs), and of man-talk of men mostly dead now. It was a foreign country with different colors and different air, where it was cool in the shade even in the heat of harvest and you could sleep on a summer night with the windows open. I played with cast-iron toys from the early twentieth century in an unfinished storage room at the top of oaken stairs at my grandmother's house and read books about Billy Whiskers the goat and stacked-up comic strips, still fragrant of old inks and dust, concerning Joe Palooka and Jiggs and Maggie. "Time of my father's time," wrote Thomas Wolfe after some conversations with his dad, "blood of his blood," yet as remote somehow as "the buried city of Persepolis."

Grandma was a reader and took me on her lap near the mahogany radio in her living room to show me the latest offering from her book club. She had a little watch pinned on her dress (she favored purple in dresses), and I listened to it tick until she died in 1964.

In the 1980s, I spent some time in Ness again. On a two-acre piece of rough land in a rough draw there was the ruin of a post rock house, which, such as it was, was owned by my dad. I had an interest in amateur astronomy, and that little prairie grass corner was the darkest deep-sky site I had ever seen. The Andromeda galaxy seemed as bright and large to the unaided eye as the moon. The Milky Way was granulated, and sixth-magnitude globular clusters were easily visible. My telescope seemed to grow when transported there from Wichita and find new capabilities. Some friends and I put a roof on the house, makeshift windows, and a concrete floor. Once I took my wife there. There was about a 50-mile-per-hour straight wind that day. She almost blew over as I took her to the restored pump and showed off the cool clear water. Upon entering the house we saw a snake in the middle of the floor. She told me I need not proceed with the house restoration on her account.

I thought about how many kids had grown up in that rock house in the early twentieth century. My cousin told me that the dirt road that went by it was actually an extension of Tenth Street in Great Bend 70 miles to the east and that I ought to calculate how far west I was on Tenth Street and put up an address marker. I never did. My friends went on to other things and I got busier. One night the wood shingles blew off in a storm. People took most of the rock fence post that had once been piled up there, and then a combination of storms and vandals took down a good deal of the house, leaving it an unrecognizable pile of stone.

There were other comings and goings that I watched from a distance, a backdrop to my life that gave it style and continuity. The Kansas High Plains region was the kind of place that was special because one could and did re-call it with emotion. My Aunt Arline, whom we stopped to see for so many years in Great Bend, was killed on the road between Great Bend and Ellinwood. She is buried at the Ness City cemetery next to Uncle Dud and near the infant they lost when they were newly married and hardly out of their teens. My grandma and grandpa and great-grandma and great-grandpa are there also. The very land on which the cemetery is located once be-longed to great-grandfather William. Ness City and the local township brought a suit against him in 1926, arguing that the plot was not worth as much as he was asking for it, which was $500 less than the appraisal. Two years later the land appraised 50 percent higher than he had asked for it originally, and he had made his point. At that juncture, he did what he had always intended to do and gave it to the city free of charge.[1] When I stand there or in many other places in that country, I stand in a lot of personal story, not escaping the sad beauty of time and death and family and be-longing, and not wishing to.

Dad died in 1996. Mom is in the Alzheimer's wing of a local nursing home and has forgotten my name. Ness City is still there, though, and the blue hills to the west and the mysteries and the challenges abiding for new generations.

So the history of Western Kansas is personal to me. I can't exactly live there. When I threaten to move my wife says, "I'll miss you." But it's "almost heaven" here in Wichita at the edge of that world, and as an academic re-searcher I have clear and unlimited license to delve into vicarious experiences there far beyond the reaches of my life and time. It is not the first time. In 1986, I investigated the settlement period of Western Kansas in my book *West of Wichita: Settling the High Plains of Kansas, 1865–1890*. Fred Woodward, at the University Press of Kansas, which published that book, claims now that he first started suggesting in 1989 that I write a sequel.

I had a title early but turned to other things. I had some concern that after that dramatic story of sod houses, railroad-building, and town-booming, the twentieth-century part might be anticlimactic. In that I shared the naïveté of so many who mistake their ignorance of the details for pallor in the actual events.

But then I thought of those stories my dad told me on those long car rides. The one about the politician pulling into Ness City in a 16-cylinder Hispano-Suiza and having to get the oil changed at a tractor shop. Or the local boys imitating the Tom Mix movie at the Doris theater on their ponies at the railroad trestle west of town. Or the family's packing up their car with trunks strapped to the running boards and braving the corrugated roads to make it to cool Colorado in the summers. It would rain, the side curtains would go up, it would get sticky, and Aunt Margaret would throw up. Or the mix of trucks and trains at the elevator, and combines, like big insects, running in the fields late under electric lights. Those were all things of the 1920s and 1930s, new things, but dramatic too. I found with some research that the early twentieth century on the Western Kansas plains involved the same struggle among the "stickers" and the "kickers," the weather and the machines, thought and deed, as had characterized the settlement era. It would be interesting beyond just the collecting of forgotten facts to write that story and to bring another generation, the sons and daughters of the pioneers in their carriages and wagons, onto the stage with their automobiles and tractors, irrigation pumps, and electric schemes. It was still about how man and Nature could best coexist and cosupport in that ancient, challenging, high, magical, semiarid place.

My friend Pat Rowley was telling me one day about his childhood in Wichita under the weird red light of a dusty sky. Reading J. R. Tolkien's Ring Trilogy shortly thereafter, I thought of the dark land of Mordor, times of the 1890s depression and drought where the new book would begin, and how those ghostly, desperate scenes could be book-ended by the dusty times of the 1930s that came at its end, with all the "next year country" native optimism in between. There would have been learning, but there would have been chastising too, glory and judgment.

In the new research, as had been true with *West of Wichita*, I was amazed by the intelligence, courage, and articulate common sense of hundreds of ordinary people and local leaders working out the destiny of small communities amid great challenges. There were many dazzling scenes in the high boom 1880s in Western Kansas, but nothing more interesting than the Atchison, Topeka & Santa Fe "Opportunity Special," carrying Vada Watson, the Wheat Girl, and a bevy of professors and demonstrations to crowds of thousands, in town after town across the region in 1925.

Some things about my own family our oral tradition did not tell me, but old newspapers did. My Great-Uncle John, for instance, whose picture I had seen wearing his Spanish American War uniform and carrying a bugle, was in fact in Manila with the company band those years, writing letters back to the *Ness County News*. But I had not known about the August night in 1896 when as a high school student he tried to drive a buggy back from a picnic out of town with three friends, Curt Redd, Louette Jacobs, and Ella Barnd. They lingered longer than the others, long enough that the kind of pitch darkness fell that can only happen in Western Kansas when the moon is down. John, with an eye on the lightning and concern for spitting rain, gave the team its head to find the way home. He did not know that they left the wagon road and started along the furrows of the railroad fireguard, fifty yards to one side.

All over the country in the wake of the Kansas boom were abandoned farmsteads, left hastily by the discouraged, who often salvaged the materials and left gaping holes in the ground where the cellar and the well had been as markers of their passing. John Miner's team fell into one of those cellars, leaving the erstwhile picnickers stranded in the surrey at the edge. While Miner helped the horses out of the hole, Redd took hold of the buggy pole to guide it around the obstacle and the girls pushed from the back. Miss Jacobs, however, changed to a position in front of Redd on the pole, and therefore was the first to reach the open well. The friends heard her hit the bottom, thirty feet down. They called—nothing. They did not know where they were, and as Ella Barnd's father, the editor of the *Ness County News*, put it the next day, "The awfulness of the situation naturally paralyzed their faculties and confused them as to their surroundings."

They lowered the driving lines, but they would not reach the bottom. John then started in the direction of the nearest light, the farmhouse of William Balfour. Balfour had no rope, no lantern. John went on to John Gardner's house and got rope. Ella Barnd said she was the lightest and volunteered to be lowered, but the boys would have none of it. John, the lighter of the boys, went, but had scarcely reached the bottom before he passed out in the close atmosphere of the well and could not respond to calls. By then Mr. Gardner had arrived and had the presence of mind to attach a rain slicker to the rope and move it, forcing a current of fresh air into the well. Curt Redd, oriented by the farmers, went to the town depot to sound the alarm, and Gardner went in search of a ladder, leaving Miss Barnd alone with her two unconscious friends in the dark.

Miner shortly revived and tied the rope around Miss Jacobs. Both were pulled up as help arrived. Miner was "semi-dazed," but Jacobs was dead. The body, "the form of the beautiful and bright girl of yesterday," went to the undertaker, probably at Miner's Cash Store, to start its journey into the unknown.

J. K. Barnd, editor of the *Ness County News* (courtesy of Kansas State Historical Society)

There was an editorial about the dangers of abandoned homesteads and an extra edition about the events. Unquestionably there was some discussion around the Miner family table to which my grandfather was at least a witness and in which my great-grandfather was doubtless an active participant. And then, even among the descendants of those most intimately involved, the event was forgotten. But a compositor had set it in type, even as the body lay in the town. It stayed there for me to recover among so many stories that were its kin except not about my kin.[2]

This is not a particularly unusual story. My personal connection to it only served to emphasize to me the connection we all should by rights feel to the human experience generally, and particularly to that of the pioneers on our home ground. I place it here—a matter of a half hour's note taking—because otherwise it would be among those thousands of notes that simply remain on my computer files, not worth a mention in a book that, while seemingly so local and narrow and detailed, is really impossibly, irresponsibly broad and vague.

But to know something about it anyway, and in the interest of being less unfocused than some who sweep across time and the globe, I have returned to the past of this loved landscape a second time. I did so for readers with a serious interest, for scholars, and for ordinary Kansans. But, truth be told, I did it for myself too.

I

Foreclosed

Some thought it was a miscalculation; others called it a calamity.

What was certain was that the year 1890 introduced Western Kansas to a long dark time in the variegated history of the struggles of its people with and against the changeable environment of the High Plains. The famous Kansas boom of the 1880s, which the western section of the state had not only shared, but also perhaps engendered, was over. The 1880s had been a decade of frequent rains, heavy emigration, prosperous towns, and industrial and political panaceas. Now came unremitting drought and a "calamity howler" politics of protest. Once-impressive rivers disappeared from the surface and went underground. There were mortgage foreclosure suits; dust and static electricity in the air; hot winds; Russian thistles rolling across long flats, sometimes lit at their tips from prairie fires blackening whole counties; wizards abroad with fraudulent schemes and promises; a shortage of seed wheat, cash, and basic staples; abandoned canals and ditches; near-biblical attacks by insect hosts; enormous and crippling losses of population; smallpox epidemics; crumbling limestone walls on the prairie, where had lately been towns with newspapers and hope; a plague of jackrabbits and prairie dogs, multiplying and eating the substance of the people; and railroads with distant shoreline terminals in their names that now either struggled to meet their reduced payrolls or remained dotted lines on a map of projections. The landscape, bleak again, sere as it had been in the earliest frontier times before the desert had bloomed, was littered with cellar holes and abandoned wells. Steam traction engines belching smoke crawled like enormous black mechanical monsters through fields where the sown grain was anything but sure to be reaped.

The heat and the dust were enervating, depressing, unhealthy. They transformed the familiar landscape into something weird, even demonic. The mirages arising when the sun baked the plains showed distant towns floating above the horizon and heightened the sense of loss and betrayal at the thought that the real towns might prove as much illusions as their wavering images.

It seemed a transmogrified environment, a sort of black mass, a reversed land, once fine and full of promise, on which an evil spell had been cast. There was something in it of Tolkien's land of Mordor and also of the opening Kansas scenes from Frank Baum's 1900 novel *The Wonderful Wizard of Oz*. Baum was thinking of 1890s Kansas, perhaps the west especially, when he wrote of that flat, hot, gray country of doom and dust from which Dorothy and her house were lifted away toward Oz, never imagining that Kansas could be home again. The author made the point that his little everywoman from Kansas did mature and adapt, that she learned to bloom where she was planted and not always to imagine that the emerald city was real life. But the iconography of *Wizard*, which has stuck so tenaciously to the state, does not have to do with the conclusion of the book but with its cyclonic and witch-haunted 1890s beginning.[1]

It was as painful for residents of that "glorious upland" to reflect on what had been as it was to speculate on what was to be. It was as though the earlier brightness was only an adumbration of this gloom, a trap for the naïve now confronted by the stale leftovers of enthusiasms turned sour. "We are disgruntled, mad," wrote the editor of the *Wichita Eagle*. "Everything seems wrong. Times are hard."[2]

Eastern Kansas blamed the western section for the state's "black eye." William Allen White of Emporia wrote in 1895, "They talk about 'Kansas sufferers,' as though western Kansas is really a part of Kansas."[3] It was a long way from Topeka to Goodland, in more ways than mere miles.

Late in August of 1890, a reporter from the *Ness County News* poked around in the charred remains of the torched sorghum sugar mill at Ness City, ruminating no doubt on the paths of glory. The county had appropriated $60,000 in 1889 to assist the mill.[4] There were plans to add a foundry, a creamery, a paper mill, a windmill factory, and a sash and door plant.[5] When the mill machinery arrived and the 64-foot-tall, 8-foot-diameter, smokestack went up beside the 242-foot-long, 5-story factory, there seemed to be sure permanence and predictability in the economic future of Ness City.[6] There were contracts with farmers to grow sorghum, there was major eastern capital committed, and there was a huge potential market if cane sugar could be replaced with the sorghum product.

To be sure, there were signs that the mill was not working as planned.[7] But no one expected the sudden shock that came when it was reduced to nothing in two hours in the middle of one Saturday night in the summer of 1890. Perhaps it was an arsonist aiding an insurance fraud. There were lawsuits for years dredging the thing up in briefs and arguments. But whatever the reason, with terrifying swiftness, and as though to underscore the change in the whole country, the great sugar mill went from everything to nothing. It became blackened walls "enclosing a mass of dismantled machinery and gnarled and twisted pipe and shafting, and shapeless tanks, defecators and sugar wagons." The strike pan on iron columns and the stone foundations rearing up 40 feet no longer had any context. The boiler house, which was undamaged because a strong south wind drove the flames away from it, no longer had anything to power. What the fire did not destroy a heavy storm of wind and hail the next day did. The storm blew the ruins of the south wall into the north wall, "giving the wind egress to the building."[8]

What did they get from the whole thing, Ness Citians asked? There was a pond stored up from creek water behind a dam the Kilby Manufacturing Company had built for its mill. Farmers in a year were growing wheat on some of the land that had been broken to grow sorghum for the mill. But even the spur to the mill laid from the branch line of the Santa Fe railroad that served Ness City was taken up by the summer of 1891.[9] It was not much of a silver lining.

The sense of loss in the first post-boom dark decade was perhaps greater than the actual losses. But the real losses, conveyed by bland statistics, were tremendous. The population of many western counties was greater in the late 1880s than it has ever been since. The counties west of Wichita had a population of 629,982 in 1888, about 40 percent of the total population of Kansas. Although the population of the state as a whole remained steady in the 1890s, Western Kansas dropped to 471,065 by 1898, a loss of over 150,000 people, or more than 25 percent of the regional population. The region's share of the Kansas population dropped to about 30 percent. Assessed valuation in Western Kansas declined in the 1890s from $152,810,433 to $127,356,433, down over $25 million or around 16 percent.[10]

"Vacation" in the 1890s did not mean a holiday. In 1890, in the WaKeeney land office district there were great tracts of vacated lands, where the would-be purchasers had given up on their payments. People walked away from

2,000 acres in Rooks County, 10,000 in Trego, 1,480 in Ness, 10,000 in Greeley, 41,000 in Wallace, and 6,500 in Lane.[11] Land prices were low, but there were no bargain hunters to buy it.

The regional economy, based heavily on agriculture, declined apace. Planted acreage decreased as people moved away, yields deteriorated in the harsh weather, prices declined in the national depression, while mortgage debt soldiered on with a crushing regularity. No wonder those who stayed "howled." An editor in Colby listened to people coming in to settle their bills and renew their newspaper subscriptions early in the year 1890. "They all have the same story," he wrote. "Pressed with debts, no prices for anything. Never saw the like. Don't know what will become of them."[12]

Newspaper operations cut back, so much so that several editors on the Plains of Kansas in the 1890s published newspapers all by themselves, playing all the roles from reporter, to writer, to compositor, to pressman.[13] Local advertising all but disappeared. One looked in vain in the pages of the *Hays Sentinel*, the best-circulated paper in Ellis County, for evidence that there was a dry goods store, a boot and shoe store, a clothing store, or a bank in Hays. "The only people who can afford to advertise are the 'liver pad' and 'lost manhood' manufacturers," the Hays editor complained.[14] The *Oberlin Herald* joked in 1890 that the Farmers' Alliance Party paper was moving to Oberlin. The editor, with heavy irony, wrote he was glad to hear it, as Oberlin much needed another newspaper. The three it already had "cannot possibly handle the great volume of business being thrust upon them." If the new paper came, the editor of the *Herald* could get back to clipping "the interest coupons on our rapidly accumulating government bonds—a duty long neglected."[15] When F. C. Montgomery, who had cleverly edited the *Hays City Sentinel*, moved to Topeka in 1894 to work on the *Mail and Breeze*, the *Lawrence Gazette* commented that it was a good thing. Montgomery was another "bright writer who has been wasting his genius on the desert air."[16]

On all sides was a tone of emergency. The Kansas State Board of Railroad Commissioners warned Governor Lyman Humphrey in January 1891 that the situation in Western Kansas was critical. "This office is in almost daily receipt of incontestable evidence that great destitution and suffering exists upon our frontier. . . . The situation is painful. Many people are absolutely destitute and helpless. They are cold and hungry and deep snow covers the ground." The board had received a communication from Rawlins County, where 12 inches of snow had fallen, that families were burning their furniture to keep themselves from freezing.[17] Could the state not do something to regulate county taxes? The mill levy to pay off the boom bonds rose as values and population declined.[18] Personal debt was unbearable in the unprecedented, unexpected, reverse. "We could stand the dry seasons much better," wrote a man in Ransom, Ness County, if there were some provision for a moratorium on mortgage debt.[19] "In the name of God and humanity," wrote another, "can't you stay the hands of these oppressors and give us poor people a chance to save our homes and families. . . . I don't want to leave my home and be drove out without anything."[20]

People lacked cash, and they paid for their supplies and their newspaper subscriptions by bartering farm produce. "Give us a pig, chicken, turkey or watermelon on subscription," wrote the editor at Colby in 1892. "Anything to stay the pangs of hunger."[21] Some lacked even that. The county commissioners in Scott County estimated that in 1893 not more than fifty men had any money to keep themselves and their families over the winter.[22] I "take my Pen in hand," wrote a woman at Mendota, Decatur County,

> to let you know that we are starving to death. It is pretty hard to do without anything to eat hear [sic] in this God forsaken country. We would have had plenty to eat if the hail hadn't cut our hay down and ruined our corn and potatoes. I had the prettiest garden that you ever seen and the hail ruined it and I have nothing to look at. My husband went a way to find work and came home last night and told me that we would have to starve. . . . It is pretty hard for a woman to do without anything to eat when she doesn't no [sic] what minute she will be confined to bed. If I was in Iowa I would be all right. . . . I haven't had nothing to eat to day and it is three o'clock.[23]

A "prophetess" in Wichita in 1894 said, "The world will wind up its business and adjourn *sine die* very soon."[24] Wrote one poet: "Our horses are of bronco race, / Starvation stares them in the face; / We do not live, we only stay, / We are too poor to get away."[25]

Begging for aid was inevitable in the short run, but embarrassing, even degrading, for many residents who had moved to family farms on the Plains partly for the independence it promised. It also led to exaggeration of the disaster by the eastern press, with consequent negative effects on future emigration to the region. The *Kansas City Times* reported in 1891 that people in the western counties were living on mule and dog meat.[26] A man in Wallace County felt that having to ask government or charities for aid was a

A Sherman County family farm (courtesy of Kansas State Historical Society)

"deplorable state of affairs to contemplate." Many were deserving of the aid, "yet the practice of distributing alms is the most degrading and unjust to our present social ethics. It injures the giver by robbing him and teaches the receiver the habits of indolence and dependence."[27]

Even the pittance came with strings and strains. In Russell, there was a campaign in 1891 to tighten up on the distribution of aid by township trustees on the grounds that the taxpayers could no longer afford the extravagance. There was too much sympathy and too little investigation of the real need. Perhaps it would be better to have a county farm where supplies could be purchased in bulk, and the poor supervised in a single place while working for their keep.[28] The editor in Sharon Springs thought that was a good idea, since "our paupers live high," on the $8 a week distributed to poor persons.[29]

It was difficult, however, to avoid charity. Wheat was 35 cents a bushel in Scott County in 1894.[30] Since the boom excesses had "filled the . . . country with terror at the sight of a Kansas mortgage," even small improvement loans were hard to get.

Perseverance and innovation to avoid the dole were considered virtues. "You must have a brave heart and enter each year with the same fiber and hope that you did the prior one." Lands were cheap, even prime railroad land going for $4 to $7 an acre.[31] Perhaps one could live temporarily somehow. There were 2- to 5-cent bounties paid by counties on jackrabbit scalps.[32] Or the rabbits could be eaten. A Scott County woman remembered a hunt in

December 1894 when 700 rabbits were killed, which provided the fare for 120 dinners at the Scott City Hotel. Families made the jacks into mincemeat or pies. They stewed rabbits and served them over a stove fired with "prairie coal" (cow chips) with raised dough dumplings. Hunting of other game, including the increasingly scarce antelope, became an avocation rather than a pastime for people who had never hunted before. Some took railroad jobs, although the pay in the late 1890s was only about 11 cents an hour and workers were limited to eight hours a day. They plowed tree claims for nonresident owners. They fenced and filled old wells on abandoned claims for 50 cents a well. They sold coyote pelts for $1.50. They petitioned for better pensions from their Civil War service. Wives churned butter, made their family's clothes, sold eggs, gave music lessons, provided meals for sale to people coming through towns on trains, or taught at the school, where they sometimes slept during the week to save a commute home. They hoarded coffee at 15 cents a pound and brewed it only for company. They put away kerosene lamps, as kerosene cost 20 cents a gallon. Candles were too expensive also, so people used melted lard in a saucer with a soft rag as a wick. They used limewater in place of laundry soap. Flour sacks served for everything from dishtowels to underwear to a source of thread. When the family went to town, they either would not eat for the whole day or would take a sack lunch. They could not afford to eat at a restaurant that charged 25 cents a meal. Christmas presents came in ordinary store wrapping paper, and the Christmas tree was likely a hackberry cut along a local stream.[33] Itinerant peddlers marketed inferior groceries or wild fruits gathered from the landscape at rock-bottom prices. Many families lived on cooked wheat and parched corn. Women drove 10 or 15 miles to town in winter in lumber wagons with their faces and heads swathed in dark brown or black woolen veils.[34]

It was too much for some. Henry Monson, living 10 miles north of Hoxie, committed suicide in May 1894 by hanging himself from a tree. He had taken a high dose of morphine the week before, but it had failed to kill him.[35] Charles Peck, who lived 3 miles northwest of Garden City, went around town on a Tuesday morning in the fall of 1896 settling his accounts. He transferred a certificate of deposit into his wife's name, and that night, with his nightclothes on, hanged himself in his barn with a halter strap.[36]

But most of the depressed did not take leave of the world, only the region. The ones who stayed were of a steady psychological makeup, made tougher by their challenges. With such people, Western Kansas would get by, her residents said. It was "a good country to go hungry in."[37] The region, her spokespersons insisted, was not "on the verge of material, moral or political ruin," and the inhabitants were "not beggars or tramps."[38] Surely things would improve.

At base the problem was the elements; it was elemental, "primeval and unfavorable conditions," one editor wrote.[39] It was dry, it was hot, and it was windy.

Drought was perhaps the most damaging environmental hazard. In small-town papers on the High Plains, modest rains were front-page news. Some complained with typical hyperbole that they felt like the people in a remote part of Egypt where it had never rained and where people refused to believe travelers who told them that water could fall from the sky. "When it gits dry in Kansas," wrote a local poet in 1901, "the catfish go and hide / Away down in the mucky mud / To keep from being dried. . . . When it gits dry in Kansas / The chinch bugs multiply / N' hopers fly up in yer face / When you go passin' by; / N' dust gits seven inches thick / N' hot winds start to blow. . . . / When it gits dry in Kansas / There's nothin' has a show."[40]

It has been said that the Great Plains experiences a major drought about once every twenty-one years. The midpoints of the three serious ones for the period of this book were 1892, 1912, and 1934. But Western Kansas experienced patterns in given years that were too localized to show in the records of the regional weather station or in the statistics kept at Kansas State Agricultural College in Manhattan. "Normal" precipitation for the region ranged from 28 inches annually near Wichita to 18 inches near the Colorado border. However, as geographer Huber Self put it once, "Average weather has little practical meaning to a person living in Kansas."[41]

What is one to think of averages, or even of the concept of a general drought, in looking at the rainfall record for Goodland, a principal town in that zone, during the 1890s? Goodland got 26 inches of rain in 1889, 12 in 1890, 26 in 1891, 38 in 1892, 20 in 1893, 8 in 1894, and 42 in 1895.[42] Dodge City got 11.7 inches in 1890 and 32.3 in 1891.[43] All that was certain was that the more westerly areas were drier and that for Western Kansas there were some disastrous 1890s crop years.

Timing was also a consideration. Often the rain that did fall did not fall at the ideal time or in the right form for the maturation of the crops farmers were trying to grow. For example there was an eight-month period in 1892–93, from October 1 to June 1, the winter wheat season, when Colby had fewer than 4 inches of rainfall.[44] The seeming good effect of the wet seasons could be compromised by the fact that sometimes the rains brought on the Russian thistles and the grasshoppers. In some years, untimely frost killed the thistles and hopper eggs but killed the wheat also. Chancellor Francis Snow of the University of Kansas noted that there was a "periodical oscillation" in rainfall in the western part of the state, maybe in seven-year cycles. Not every year in every place was a meteorological disaster, and that accounted partly for the surprising persistence, or delusion, of farmers. The rains in Western Kansas, Snow observed, were "generally quite local, and consist of a heavy downpour in a comparatively short time. Long-continued moderate or drizzling rains are almost unknown in this part of the state."[45] With those sudden heavy rains could come hail and wind. Usually one could adjust. But in the dry, hard times, given the high altitude, high evaporation rate, and short growing season of the High Plains "steppes," there was no room for error.[46]

The dryness was complicated by heat. The Garden City paper described one July day when it had "been a little bit warm in western Kansas, in fact warm enough to melt tin roofs, render lard out of living hogs, and to boil steak," but there had been no sunstrokes and it cooled off nicely at night.[47] "A man boring a well at Bird City struck six feet of cinders at a depth of 270 feet," a newspaper reported. "Bird City had better plug that hole and quit pestering with the infernal regions. First thing she knows there will be hell fire and spike-tailed devils running all over Cheyenne County."[48] Humidity at 20 percent, temperatures above 100 degrees, and gritty winds steady at 30 to 40 miles per hour with gusts burned and strafed crops to death in a matter of days. A resident of Dodge City recorded in 1891 that people seemed to have given up on southwest Kansas. It was held up as a place where farming was not profitable, "where nothing exists but coyotes, jack rabbits and prairie dogs, and that the few human beings who do reside in Southwestern Kansas cannot afford to wear socks, and cannot find enough water to wash the plow dirt off their shins."[49] A poet at Hays three years later took a similarly dim view: "We're in the land of drought and heat / Where nothing grows for man to eat / The winds do blow with burning heat / And O! this land is hard to beat."[50]

"It's too blamed hot to live," wrote Alpha Hansen of Logan, Phillips County, in 1910 during a later dry spell, "let alone be so cruel as to send a recital of one's sufferings to worry one's friends and relatives. The weather man has certainly taken a violent dislike to our country or else he is taking this method of showing his special esteem. At any rate, he is preparing us for the brimstone lake if we allow ourselves to be led to 'cussation' by it." If the 100- to 110-degree weather continued, she thought, "I fear all of us will return to the Adam and Eve styles in dress."

Alpha was seated in front of the door of her home "in the vain hope that I may intercept some stray, cool breeze—but alas, they are not! The chief view presenting itself to my weary gaze is the screen filled with several million buzzing, droning, crawling flies." Her hands stuck to the paper as she wrote, and she reported the family slept outdoors at night. The city pump had broken down and they might have no water for two weeks. "We'll all be dried up and blown away by then, anyway, so we won't notice the dead lawns. . . . Dust! Heat! Flies! Cloudless Skies! Oh, this is Sunny Kansas with a vengeance!"[51]

Winter cold could be as disturbing as summer heat. A Colby man commented in February 1890 that the thermometer "registered 795 degrees below zero, more or less," as men at the post office tried to fix the stovepipe before body parts froze.[52] "We desire to apologize for having applied the term 'Italian climate' to this part of Kansas," a Dodge City reporter wrote in 1895. "This winter has disbursed us of the hallucination."[53]

Perhaps the most ubiquitous evidence of the threat that being close to Nature on the High Plains could bring was the strong winds. Snow, of the University of Kansas, calculated at the beginning of the twentieth century that the wind in Kansas had traveled 2,039,113 miles during the first 15 years of his observations, but only 1,874,941 in the next.[54] The poor farmer on the Plains hardly noticed the difference. Bonnie Bailey Vaughn remembered that in a strong wind her family would see various things "go sailing along in the air, or bumping along the ground" and piling up along fencerows. These included wash boilers, hats, and tumbleweeds. These last "looked as if they were alive, going somewhere in a great hurry." The winds wore at a person, especially someone alone in a claim shanty where it sounded "mournful and depressing."[55] Almost as they do in the "roaring forties" near Antarctica with no continents to block them, so here on the treeless level plains the winds had full scope to turn the farmer's windmill rotor productively or tear the tower apart and dump it in the next county.

Kansas people do not mind the dust and wind any more," wrote an editor in Colby in the spring of 1895; "it is second nature to their very existence." So they sometimes said, but more grim smiles appeared on more wan faces with each tree killed, each garden flattened, each hat blown away, each passing poor season. "Monday was a holy terror!" wrote a resident. "Wind, dirt and rain." The tin roof of the O'Pelt hotel in Colby blew off "and is probably in Oklahoma somewhere," and many windmills leaned on three legs. "It was a very difficult task to stir out Monday forenoon. Small rocks, tin cans, scraps of iron, tin roofs, wagon wheels, boards, barrel hoops, shingles, fence palings and town lots were very promiscuous in the atmosphere which was moving at the rate of 3,000 miles per hour."[56]

One evening in June 1895, the night operator at the Garden City depot placed the consignment for the express from that place on carts. The wind was blowing hard, and when the man turned his back a moment, the zephyr "started the trucks down the platform at a seventy mile gait." When the load got out from the shelter of the depot, boxes and packages flew off. The agent chased them and found several packages blocks from the station.[57] A Garden City editor averred that wind made it imperative to clean up the city. "It is not at all pleasant on a windy day to have your eye almost put out by a tomato can or have your ears plugged up with empty bottles or old newspapers."[58]

It did not take a tornado to create tragedy. In a day of 50-mile-per-hour winds at Garden City in April 1895, three children—Cora and Charley Dick, 10 and 8 years old, and Bertie Orth, age 13—died. Cora and Charley left home, both riding one horse, to retrieve some cattle. They were found lying in the road, dead, with their arms around each other. The horse was standing with them, where he had stayed through forty hours. Bertie Orth went on the same sort of mission. He was handicapped and carried his crutches on his saddle. He was either thrown or fell from the horse. This time the horse ran. Bertie could not walk, but wear on his pants showed he had crawled for some distance. The paper reported, "His face showed the terrible struggle he had made for life."[59]

The drama of the wind was not lost on the residents. An editor in Garden City wrote in May 1896: "Finney county is strewn with the wreck of windmills, small buildings and barns as the result of the hard wind Tuesday. . . . All day long the air was filled with sand and gravel, brick bats, lumber, and everything that was loose. The day was most disagreeable and business was almost at a stand still; people stuck close to their houses and only went out when it was absolutely necessary." A farmer and his hired man fell over with a windmill they had climbed to try to stabilize it with ropes. When the roof blew off the Lincoln block in Garden City and struck a frame store building, a team tied nearby were so badly frightened that the horses climbed into the wagon to which they were hitched. The high school class was just starting its commencement, listening to Walter Lawrence's oration, "The Dying Century," but was distracted some.[60]

When William Allen White visited Western Kansas in 1897, the wind was not to be ignored. "At the Bucklin station, when the wind was blowing so hard that a man had to turn the other way to cough or it would be blown back down his throat, a stranger looked across the prairie at the dust that filled the air like a cloud and said: 'What is land worth out here?' A bystander replied: 'Hell, man, land is free out here—free as the air. But after a man's been to the trouble of catching a loose quarter section, the trouble is to find a good cool damn place to put it on.'"[61] There were only two things wrong with Liberal, commented the local paper in 1896, "one is it gets too dry sometimes, another is that the wind blows too long and too hard."[62]

Rainfall, wind, and temperature statistics were kept and published erratically in the 1890s by the Kansas Board of Agriculture. And, as has been seen, the variability by year and within years was so great as to make analysis of actual effects difficult. But crop statistics and value were recorded religiously, county by county, even township by township. It was harvested crops and the cash for which they sold that determined survival. Therefore, crop yields combined with price data gives the most realistic picture of the impact in the region of the combination of drought, heat, insects, rain timing, and the ups and downs of the market. Much may be learned by looking at the situation concerning winter wheat, the crop about which dreams of fortune for farmers most revolved.

The trend in wheat prices in the decade made the shortfalls in yield more damaging than they otherwise might have been. The price was fair at the opening of the decade—85 cents a bushel in 1890 and 75 cents in 1891, compared to 55 cents in 1889 and about 75 cents in 1885 in what were considered boom times. However, it deteriorated to 55 cents the next year, reached a low of 37 cents in 1893, and remaining at around 50 cents at the end of the decade.[63]

The local press was too optimistic—in an upward direction about wheat prospects and in a downward direction about the costs of farming. In the spring of 1891 the *Hays City Sentinel* published an article on the subject "Does Wheat Pay?" with the typical answer, "Very well, thank you." There had been only a 9-bushel-per-acre average in Ellis County in 1890, but surely that was an anomaly. The paper used Kansas State Board of Agriculture statistics showing that the cost of raising an acre of wheat in Western Kansas was about $6.49. The reporter said there were 80,000 acres of good winter wheat growing in Ellis County and that this crop would average 20 bushels to the acre. Since the price at Hays was about 75 cents a bushel, the calculation went that the county wheat lands would yield $15 an acre, or a clear profit of about $8.51.[64]

There were several problems with this rosy scenario. First, the expected crop was not often the harvested one. The actual Ellis County average in 1891 was only 12 bushels per acre, not the 20-bushel prediction of the newspaper. Second, the Board of Agriculture cost calculations included operating expenses only, not capital costs. There was no provision in the cost estimates for mortgage payments, purchase of machinery, or payment of taxes. An estimate published in the *Kansas Farmer* early in 1893 included $3.00 per acre for rent, and estimated a cost of $9.95 per acre for wheat raising in south central Kansas.[65] This estimate still was less than inclusive of all real costs. Cash-poor farmers were hurt by the dry years.

Production, any production, was not something on which one could depend. In 1892, Ellis County did raise 20-bushel wheat on over 90,000 acres.[66] The price was down to 49 cents, profitable perhaps for one with no debt and minimal expenses. In 1893, however, the wheat crop in Ellis was a total failure, and in 1894, it was effectively so, yielding only about a 2-bushel average for the county, while the price deteriorated further. The 1895 crop averaged about 4 bushels per acre, with 1896 still under 5. It was not until the last years of the decade that Ellis County farmers returned to anything like the yields that might allow the frugal to break even.

Ford County, further south and west than Ellis County, provides another example of the economics of depression wheat growing in Western Kansas. The 1890s there also started out tolerably well. Wheat acres planted in 1890 was 7,297, up from 2,911 the year before. The yield was 105,075 bushels, or a little over 14 bushels per acre. In 1891, the acreage was about 18,000 and the yield was 12 bushels; in 1892, the acreage was about 22,000 acres with a yield of 20 bushels. These were all at least fair crops.

However, as in Ellis County, things then turned unarguably grim. In 1893, over 38,000 acres planted yielded only about a half-bushel-per-acre average. In 1894 the acreage went up to 47,209 acres. The harvest was less than one bushel per acre. In 1895, caution in planting prevailed. There was acreage of 36,617 and a yield of 3 bushels per acre. In 1896, planting was conservative again, with 29,549 acres planted, yielding 4 bushels, a fourth failure in a row. The next year, acres went down again to 20,772, but there was a slightly better crop of 14 bushels per acre. In 1898, Ford County planted 29,855 acres, yielding a poor 9 bushels per acre. The next year was worse—29,608 acres planted and a 6-bushel-per-acre crop, with a price of 50 cents a bushel.

Yields were a little better to the east of Dodge City, and worse to the west.[67] There was a net outflow of cash. Many wheat farmers had to increase their borrowing, a difficult thing to do in such times and with such prospects, or default on debt or taxes they owed. They proclaimed that they were not "repudiators," but struggled to make payments. Mortgage debt in Kansas was $240 million, or nearly equal to the total property valuation.[68] There were mortgage foreclosures by the thousands (an estimated 2,600 in Kansas in the first six months of 1890) and long lists of tax delinquents in the local newspapers.[69]

People who lived in Western Kansas at the time, however, could sometimes laugh about the weather and the crop conditions, and their laughter was part of what boded well to make them whole again. Sometimes their humor took the form of tongue-in-cheek reporting about people who took themselves too seriously. Sometimes it was hilarious exaggeration of such things as wind speeds and temperature. Often it was an evocative joke or story with both a barb and a lesson in it.

There were jokes about their hopes. At Great Bend they looked forward to a big crop in 1894, one where $20 gold pieces would grow on stems and where, at harvest time, silver dollars would be so plentiful they would have to be cleared from the railroad tracks with snow plows. The locals would ride jackrabbits that would "back up to us ready saddled" and let down a ladder for a ride.[70] The *Goodland Republic* reported, "A farmer of this county has put green goggles on his cows and reports that it is a success. They eat everything that comes in their way, from fence posts to last year's sunflower stalks."[71]

They laughed about their illusions. It seems a man raised 1,000 bushels of popcorn and stored it in a barn. The barn caught fire, and the corn popped, filling a 10-acre field. An old cow in the neighborhood with defective eyesight saw the corn, thought it was snow, and lay down and froze to death.[72] "According to the latest accounts," wrote the *Garden City Herald* in 1895, "there are only four places in the world where the light of civilization does not shine, viz: China, Turkey, Mississippi, and Finney county."[73]

They made fun of their difficulties. "Professor Snow reports that there are 250,000 different insect enemies to wheat. A well posted Rush county farmer reports every one of these individuals this year have been working in his wheat. Calamity enough."[74]

Humor was a way of adapting to hard times. Those who laughed at themselves and their troubles were more likely to make it through than those who could not. Their optimism, reflected in jokes and exaggerations, created a perverse pride. A story circulated about an old man who came to Kansas and began to grow young and strong. He was, however, lonely and felt he had outlived his time. Therefore he went back east and became a feeble old man and died in a week. He was laid to rest near his childhood home. However, his 75-year-old son, living in Kansas, brought his father's body back to that state. The Kansas wind blew across the frozen face and the dead woke up. "The old man was hot and gave the boy a piece of his mind to the effect

Foster D. Coburn, secretary of the Kansas State Agricultural Society, 1893 (courtesy of Kansas State Historical Society)

that when he went away from Kansas again to die, he didn't want anybody idling around and cart his body back to Kansas where he couldn't stay dead when he wanted to."[75]

And amid all the bad times there were good times—good times that the persevering treasured and drew from against a better future. A writer in Hugoton opined in 1896:

> The man who has never lived through one of our winters nor tasted the delights of a western Kansas spring or autumn; who has not even enjoyed the halcyon bliss of one of our long summers, might pass over these broad plains and look in pity down upon the poor deluded denizens of a seeming barren waste. But he who has tasted the sweets of life where to merely exist is happiness; where keen appetite makes the simplest repast a feast fit for the gods; where to breathe is ecstasy, looks upon those who dwell elsewhere as

self-inflicted martyrs to willful blindness or sordid devotees at the shrine of Mammon. He who but passes by, and in passing judges that this land must be given over to the eternal hush of utter desolation, whose awful stillness will be broken only by the lowing herds of wandering cattle or the uncanny cry of the coyote, misjudges the land and its people.[76]

2

Fooled

There were effective responses in the early twentieth century to the drought and wind problem—for example, irrigation with wind-driven pumps, the development of drought-resistant crops, and education in farming techniques that conserved moisture. However, initial suggestions about how to deal with the environmental turn in the early 1890s were chimerical. The failure of several "schemes" for dealing with the weather crisis only served to deepen the malaise and insularity of High Plains farmers trying to survive it.

One suggestion was to give up trying to develop Western Kansas as an agricultural area with any sort of population density. There were those who still subscribed to the theory that the native buffalo grass pastures made it hotter and shed water, which ran off into the streams, sending precious moisture where it was less needed.[1] Others thought it a "dire calamity" that the future of Western Kansas should be "turned over to the care of the 'cowboy' under the direction of the loan companies."[2] But many more looked at the series of failed wheat crops and thought that the salvation of the region was in leaving grass where it was and returning many of the plowed fields to their natural state of grazing country for animals.

Captain J. H. Churchill of Dodge City addressed the Kansas Improved Stock Breeders Association in 1897 on the virtues of a regional cattle economy. Western Kansas, he said, had learned "from experience sorrowful and severe" the business "for which the country is naturally adapted." The business had been modernized with sheds for storms and better water supplies and was operating free of opposition. "The objectors—the farmers who could not endure to see cattle around—have moved away, starved out."[3] A night herd law went into effect at Liberal in 1896 to keep calves from chewing the washing of citizens hung out on the line at night, since fences were absent on the reconstituted free range there.[4] "A spirit of economy and business has taken possession of our people," the newspaper there said, "and they have quit their foolishness and extravagance."[5]

There was a realization that the dreams of "rain follows the plow," so ballyhooed in the 1880s, were dreams indeed—pseudoscience or superstition. A Garden City analyst thought it was no longer credible to say that "in time as population forces itself westward, and as trees and grasses get rooted, little by little, further and further out towards the foothills of the mountains, that the wetting process will also extend itself in the same direction. Time and observation have dispelled that long cherished delusion, hugged and held to so tenaciously hitherto, by the settlers of Western Kansas."[6]

Some reasoned that the failure of the boom was related to the lack of self-sufficiency created by specialization in crops depending upon transportation, processing, and nonregional markets. It might be better to pursue diversified agriculture. Chickens and garden crops would provide subsistence for the family, and livestock raising would create a use for forage crops grown on one's own land, as well as provide meat even in the driest years.

There was little science required. "There were no warm chicken houses," a resident of Decatur County remembered of those times, "nor scratching pens nor carefully balanced diets. The chickens ran out in all but the very severe weather and hustled their own food from bugs, grasshoppers and plant seeds or waste grain." When there was danger of predators, the valuable birds were brought into the house with the family at night.[7] F. D. Coburn, head of the Kansas State Board of Agriculture, remarked in 1897 that the hen was a miracle worker in hard times. She produced "while everything else was going to wreck and ruin, supporting herself and the family too; the very insects which would have despoiled the farm she fattened upon, laying her daily egg—the blessed egg that took the place of beef and milk, mutton and pork—and in good time, after all these services, surrendered her toothsome body to the cause of humanity."[8]

The *Wichita Eagle* asserted in December 1896 that there would be no cries for aid that winter. The reason, the paper thought, was that Western Kansas had "passed from the function of trying to raise breadstuff to the province of furnishing the world with meat." That latter role was more appropriate:

Garden City, looking northwest from the Windsor Hotel, c. 1895 (courtesy of Kansas State Historical Society)

> The simple steer with his indolent eyes is doing for Western Kansas something that the complicated and high-priced mechanism-binder, thresher or reaper—could not do. The gentle clucking hen is bringing shekels into the pockets of the Western Kansan where the vaunted "steam plow" fell down ignominiously. Kansas will ask for no aid, not because her western third has all it wants, but because it has come to understand what the western third is capable of.[9]

A related piece of advice was that farmers in these hard times should eschew equipment purchases and the accompanying debt. Machinery was "desirable and convenient," but, said a Ness County editor, "your golden grain had better fall to the ground and rot than that you should burden yourself with a debt you do not know how to pay, or that will take the entire produce of your fields for its liquidation." Having fine equipment was as much a "boom" habit as purchasing town lots or adjoining quarters had been "and the results may be just as disastrous."[10] A header selling for $170 made the agent $34 clear profit and the farmer paid the freight. The agent's profit was "made in the shade, while we as farmers get our hard earned money by slaving beneath the boiling sun." It would be better to take more care of the old machinery and to make certain tools.[11] There were examples of farmers going back to hand methods. The Bailey family in Scott County used a walking plow in the 1890s. Although one could hire steam threshing machines, people could not afford to, so sometimes Western Kansans would cut their wheat with a scythe, rack it by hand, and thresh it with a flail, as had been done in biblical times.[12] Even the most sanguine theorists of the 1890s thought that perhaps only the river valleys of Western Kansas could support intensive agriculture, and then only with the help of irrigation. The uplands would have to go back to grass.[13]

Much of it did. A Pennsylvania man who visited Clark County in 1898 heard that farming there was a thing of the past.[14] A rancher from Clark County visiting Seward County a year later found few of the "granger element" hanging on there. At the Will Stout ranch near Arkalon he saw 400 head of whitefaces and observed that "the narrow, silvery Cimarron winds through his meadow, grass to the water's edge, not an acre plowed."[15]

This retrograde movement was a form of passive adaptation, a sort of learning from the land. Naturally, however, there were fundamentally different sorts of responses to the crisis, much more activist and controlling in orientation. The two most prominent types were scientific and political. The earliest scientific response was a fraud. It was based on the idea that if the plow and the town could not create rain perhaps a rainmaker could. So-called pluviculture as a supposed science was abroad in the American West from about 1890 to 1930, playing on the popular fascination with a confidence in the ability of science to analyze and control conditions.

In Kansas, the most attention came to Frank Melbourne, a tall, bearded Irishman who came to the United States by way of Australia and was "never modest in his pretensions before the public." He carried his equipment in several black gripsacks and operated his machinery in secret in a building where magic gases emerged from a pipe through the roof while spectators heard a "rumbling, fluttering sound." Melbourne, ensconced in a locked stable with a revolver, made it rain in Cheyenne, Wyoming, in 1891 and moved on in September of that year to Goodland, Kansas. According to historian Clark Spence, the rainmakers were "flimflam men . . . who cropped up like weeds in the spring to make a profit out of hard luck."[16]

The Kansas state government took the thing seriously. Governor Humphrey received a letter in 1889 from Thearie and Cooper, Chicago, "Pyrotechnists," offering to make it rain in Kansas "by concussion or otherwise."[17] The next year, Michael Cahill, M.D., offered the governor his theories of the "cause and remedy" of drought "as studied out by myself in the Hands of Providence." He also claimed to be able to solve the cyclone problem through his knowledge of ice around the poles and the habits of high-flying birds.[18]

Melbourne's Goodland experiment, which cost the town $500, seemed tantalizingly and vaguely successful, bringing a misty rain some days after the deadline. In any case, it was enough to encourage the formation of several

Goodland, Kansas, about 1890, looking north from Eleventh and Main (courtesy of High Plains Museum, Goodland)

local companies, the most prominent of which was the Inter State Artificial Rain Company. It also was the basis for the Chicago, Rock Island & Pacific railroad company (CRI&P) to invest considerable money in rainmaking and to outfit a special car for the rainmaking equipment of Clayton B. Jewell, a railroad dispatcher from Goodland. Jewell went about the state from 1892 to 1894, eventually fitting out three cars. He made contracts with several towns, promising, "I'll have Douglas Avenue in Wichita turned into a canal by tomorrow." At Dodge City, before a huge crowd, he fired chemical bombs from a "monster mortar" mounted on a flatcar. These exploded with streams of yellow smoke. Jewell's standard procedure, however, was the generation of an exotic gas from equipment that was as mysterious to most who saw it "as if they had been the stock in trade of a necromancer." Jewell mixed sulfuric acid, zinc, ammonia, common salt, and muriatic acid and then ran a telegraph wire through the liquid to generate a gas. Observers said that the young men in the car did not have bald heads or long beards, like wizards, but looked quite ordinary. So did the three earthenware churn jars with the chemicals, although the jars were hot enough to burn one's hand and the air in the car was hard to breathe. Acrid smoke came out of a stack at the top of the railroad car and supposedly formed clouds.[19] Jewell made nine attempts at rainmaking in Kansas in the spring of 1893 and each time reportedly produced at least one inch of rain within forty-eight hours.[20]

There were other attempts. Judge C. W. Woodman of Chicago addressed a public meeting at Larned in the summer of 1891 on rainmaking. That resulted in a petition from the city to the U.S. Department of Agriculture requesting information.[21] In 1893, a newspaper reporter from Salina interviewed E. F. Murphy, who represented one of the rainmaking companies of that city. The reporter got a "creepy" feeling talking to Murphy but thought he earnestly believed in what he was doing.[22] In 1894, a group tried rainmaking at Garden City by shooting anvils into the air. After an hour of this the clouds rolled away and the sun came out. "All the firing squad accomplished was to jar the chimney off a neighboring house and to scare the life out of a widow."[23]

Western Kansas had seen schemes before, and a common reaction there to all this was deep skepticism. A professor told readers of the *Saline County Journal* shortly after the Melbourne experiments that "while legitimate attempts at rain-making are engrossing the public attention, it is not to be wondered that frauds and humbugs should arise; and some of these may be self-deceived." After two weeks at Goodland "there was no evidence that the rain-maker had any influence whatever."[24] Goodland, a Colby editor thought, had "expensive notoriety" from paying Melbourne and not much rain.[25] In 1893, the Hays newspaper commented that the price of rainmaking had gone to $10,000. "We had a rain . . . free of cost, night before last. These are the rains we depend on."[26] There was "considerable hard feeling" among the farmers of Sherman County in the Goodland area by 1894 against the rainmakers. "They believe that the long continued drought is caused by the anger of the Almighty at their claims of making rain whether he wills it or no."[27] At Garden City, in 1894, some in a crowd watching a rainmaker were so contemptuous that they bet cigars he would fail. They came to his speech wearing slickers and gumboots and carrying umbrellas, just to mock him.[28] In 1895, the Kansas state legislature, which had appropriated some money for rainmaking experiments through the first half of the decade, cut off all support. A University of Kansas professor had experimented in making rain by seeding the air with dust, but a professor at the Kansas State Agricultural College was contemptuous of the balloons, the dynamite, and the magic chemicals. He thought the rainmakers only appeared when natural conditions were favorable for rain.[29] Most people agreed with Joseph Bristow of Salina that it was time for real science, not pseudoscience, in solving Western Kansas' water problems. The rainmaker, Bristow wrote, was "a thing of the past; he was a fraud; an ingenious tramp who played upon the cupidity and superstitions of the people and who worked them the same as a sleight-of-hand performer."[30]

It could be argued that the earliest political responses to the regional agricultural crisis turned out to be frauds also. The political threat of the "disorganization" of Western Kansas and the consequent counterthreat of the

Small-town gothic, Goodland, c. 1910 (courtesy of High Plains Museum, Goodland)

diminished population there to secede from the state was mostly bluster on both sides. The People's Party movement was something taken more seriously, but it proved a flash in the pan as well. "With population declining and wealth decreasing," commented the *New York World*, "Kansas chases more furiously than ever the delusions that are ruining her."[31]

The People's Party (Populists), one of the most successful third-party movements in American history, originated in Kansas in 1890. Although it had a long list of proposals, ranging from government ownership of transportation and communication, to secret ballots, to remonetization of silver in the currency supply, it is best known as a farmers' movement focused on political relief for suffering grangers. After a spectacular and controversial run, it failed, being largely absorbed by the major parties before 1900. Some have regarded it as a "sour grapes" reform and have seen the party's "subtreasury" idea of low-interest, federally backed farm loans as nothing more than the dying gasp of businesspeople who had failed to adapt to new market realities.[32]

   A deep analysis of the complex and ambiguous political effects of Populism on Western Kansas at the local level would require another book. However, at least two surprising conclusions may be drawn here about the phenomenon. First, Populism in Western Kansas was anything but homogeneous, and, second, Western Kansans reacted to the politics of Populism in a pragmatic and local rather than an ideological and regional or national way.

Western Kansas in the 1890s, suffering as it was from hard times, would seem an ideal People's Party recruiting area. Yet, while certainly some western counties elected local and state Populist officials and voted for People's Party candidate James Weaver for president in 1892, most did not. The region as a whole remained Republican throughout the period. It was actually the most solidly and dependably Republican area in a Kansas that for a time had a Populist governor and a Populist majority in the legislature.[33] This suggests the truth of the maxim, "all politics is local." Although there was some general attraction in the rhetoric and the camaraderie of the Populist cause, and particularly in the attention it paid to the problems of small farmers, the solutions to the local problems of Western Kansans were not perceived by residents there as likely to come out of Topeka or from the Populists. Also, the overall leftist ideology of the People's Party, particularly as expressed by some of its more radical spokespersons in Kansas, did not appeal to the fundamentally conservative capitalists of the western plains. They did not want a new world: they wanted their old world back.

The sources of People's Party appeal were the ones one would expect. Populists were conspiracy theorists who blamed the problems of Kansas on outside influences, primarily the middlemen, bankers, and speculators of the eastern establishment. They agitated for a moratorium on mortgage debt, for reforms in the political system that would give the small farmer more voice while diminishing the political influence of railroads and other corporations, and for limiting the size of farming operations and their ownership by nonresidents. Kansas' Populist senator, William Peffer, said in 1891 that the average net return on Kansas farms was only about 1 percent on their value and that that value was low and declining. If the farms of the state were put up for sale, Peffer said, they would not bring half the amount of the mortgages on them.[34] The Republican press hooted at that, but the farmers on the ground knew that Peffer was close to the truth. They appreciated party spokespersons saying that farm problems might be systemic and not due to the shortcomings of the inferior beings that farmed.

That appeal was reinforced at rallies, speeches, and parades. Bonnie Bailey Vaughn recalled going to town as a girl in Scott City to listen to Independence Day orators. The family nailed up a flag at their house, and Eva Freed stood on a float dressed as the Goddess of Liberty. "Sometimes if a strong, hot wind was blowing no one could hear the speech except those close to him, but everyone remained sitting on the benches under the trees in the Court House Park, and listened respectfully." The speeches were followed by a public dinner, then sack races, a bun-eating contest, fireworks, and a dance.[35]

Scott City, Kansas (courtesy of Wichita State University Special Collections)

"The farmers are ridiculed, called demagogues, cranks, calamity howlers, sorghum lappers, croakers, ignoramuses, blind fools, etc.," said the *Colby Free Press*, "and all because they have the manhood and moral courage to stand up and assert their undisputed rights."[36] A lecture by Ben Terrell on farm politics held in Larned in July 1890 drew the largest crowd ever assembled in that city, 1,500 people. A picnic dinner took place in Bright's grove where wagons were plastered with paintings and banners emblazoned with slogans.[37] A rally in Colby in October 1892 advanced similar sentiments. One hundred teams "facing the dust and wind" marched down the streets headed by the Menlo band and carrying banners reading, "Dear Gold Means Poverty for the Masses," "Benny and Grover Are Not in It," "Good Bye Old Parties, Good Bye."[38] Western Kansans of the 1890s did need direct relief. "We are worried over what our Poor People of our county will do for fuel to keep warm this winter," wrote a man in Jetmore, Hodgeman County, in December 1894. The temperature the morning he wrote was 16 degrees below zero. There were 5 inches of snow, and the coal dealers had fewer than 100 bushels on hand. "Under those circumstances what are the people to do?"[39] Occasionally, there was a suggestion that the state ought to provide work building dams or reservoirs to employ the indigent.[40] Most often, however, the aid requested was seed wheat, which farmers asked that the state provide on a loan basis and that the railroads haul for free. The Lane County commissioners wrote in 1893 that the people there were "not mendicants, and many of them would rather move in search of labor than ask for a loan." But they were "our best people, and can illy be spared."[41] In 1894, a man from Rush County wrote:

> For the past 2 days roasting hot winds have prevailed in West Kansas. The wheat crop may yield 2 Bu. Per acre. Corn is practically ruined. No potatoes. No vegetables. Nothing in Grainery . . . and while it's true that this people whose pluck, endurance, and natural pride would deter them from admitting the truth that they must have aid and that quickly[,] nevertheless it's all too true for even now there are people in the west 1/2 of Kansas actually suffering for the necessities of life and the state owes it to this brave & unfortunate people who are part of her existence and extend to them without stint or delay seed wheat.[42]

The People's Party charged that the aid programs under the Republicans had been corrupt, and it proposed increasing government spending both on direct relief and on seed wheat for future crops.[43] There had to be some sort of political action on the aid question. It would be to the advantage of the party to act on aid, wrote a Populist from Menlo, Thomas County, to Governor Lewelling: "I now see the greatest chance for us to do an act that will win hundreds of backsliders back to the fold solid & make hundreds . . . vote with us. . . . We must hold the fort in Kans at all Hazards, our cause must hold the reins of this Government."[44] An Oakley man agreed that a wheat loan would be "a splendid opportunity for the application of practical politics. . . . By the means indicated we may be enabled in this county [which had gone Populist by only a seventy-five–vote majority] not only to *endorse*, but to *sustain* the present administration."[45] Relief was critical. "Two things are possible," said a petition from Sheridan County calling for an extra legislative session in 1893: "We must have some arrangements made, or Western Kansas will practically be abandoned."[46]

Corruption was easy to uncover. County "rings" manipulated taxation to favor cronies.[47] Railroads were easy targets, as they struggled with reduced revenue and limited ability to pay their county taxes or to haul seed grain for free. The political rhetoric against speculators and outsiders had its local and specific application. It was not the man who followed the plow that had caused the failures, wrote a Larned resident, but he "who came here and wanted to get rich without work. . . . It is the fellow who tried to buy a controlling interest in the earth without any capital."[48] In every county were large nonresident local landowners for whom tenant farmers worked and who were easily painted as the enemies of the virtuous family farmer. To counties struggling with debt, down on assessed valuation, down on population, and overburdened with local tax, the People's Party cry to throw the rascals out and examine the books made sense.

But even the issues on which the People's Party seemed strong in the region could receive a negative local twist. In several western counties there was open talk that Governor Lewelling's seed wheat plant was only "a shrewd political scheme" and that farmers had to take a secret oath and become party supporters before they could apply for seed wheat. "Farmers should steer clear of this hollow mockery termed 'reform.'"[49] A story circulated in Barton County that a farmer in 1892 made a banner saying, "Vote for Jerry Simpson [the People's Party congressman] and get one dollar a bushel for your wheat." In the fall of 1894 he learned that wheat was selling for 40 cents. He brought out his banner again, to which he now added, "I find there is 40 cents worth of truth and 60 cents worth of lies in it."[50] The *Hugoton Hermes* editorialized in 1896 that "the rainmaker came with the Populistic aberration; a fitting swindle for a locoed populace."[51] There were charges that Populist candidates were not really farmers but "political acrobats, adventurers and malcontents[,] . . . jacks-at-all-trades, broken-down tradesmen, speculators, loan agents and the like," who had failed in the boom and were looking for something to do.[52] For every local issue or concern that seemed to fit with the Populist program, there was another that did not. Often when the speechifying and the banners got translated into specific local programs, the cheering crowd fractured.

Western Kansans were fiscally and socially more conservative than the Populists. They were down on their luck, but to them that did not justify either anarchy or socialism. They did not like the Populist gas and water socialism applied locally because they were not sure they trusted their city councils enough to want municipal ownership for the light and power plants they were starting to build.[53]

There were differences in attitudes on gender, race, and class. Regional humor was not above kidding Mr. Diggs, husband of Populist Annie Diggs, for staying home with a "clean gingham apron on," washing potatoes and embroidering while she reformed the world.[54] Although Western Kansans later took pride in sending women representatives to the state legislature, the woman's movement, which had a strong place in the People's Party, did not exactly sweep the Western Kansas region in the 1890s. The *Larned Chronoscope* quoted Kate Field on Populist Mary Lease to the effect that she had done great damage to her sex. "We are told that woman suffrage will purify and refine politics; if Mrs. Lease is a sample of what is in store for us, heaven help conventions and everything else. The gift of gab, uncontrolled by reason and delivery, is about the most dangerous thing a woman can wield." When Lease said that the Alliance would pursue its fight "from the banks of Wall street to the gates of hell," it could only "disgust thinking Americans." And those Americans, Field thought, included farmers who would be capitalists if they could be.[55]

The earlier liberal frontier attitudes toward blacks turned toward clannishness and exclusion as segregation clamped down on the nation and Western Kansas. The *Ness County News* reported in the summer of 1891:

> During the past week, our town has looked very much as if it had dropped down into Darkest Africa or a section of Great Bend, judging from the number of colored gentlemen promenading our streets after six o'clock in the evening. The cause of the unwonted cloudiness is the tarrying here of a construction train on the railroad manned by a crew of about seventy, engaged in putting the track in repair, cutting weeds, cleaning ditches and cuts and widening fills. So many colored persons are particularly noticeable in this city from the fact that one is rarely seen on our streets, there not being a single colored resident in Ness county.

These laborers, it was reported, "behaved themselves well" and "have afforded considerable amusement to our people by the games, races and singing after work hours." But the townspeople seemed glad when, after beating the city scrub nine at a game of baseball, the black men moved on.[56]

The 1890s era was the high tide for lynching, often of African Americans, in Western Kansas. Salina mobs lynched two black men within a year in 1892 and 1893.[57] Although the newspaper condemned the crowd for jeering and plucking souvenirs as Dana Adams, the second victim, breathed his last, it seemed unwilling to condemn the extralegal action against "a well-known Negro tough."[58] Law and order was an important conservative value, and Adams had attacked a white man with a razor.

A petition to the governor from African Americans residing in Topeka and Shawnee County pointed out that, while Adams had certainly made a "vicious assault," the legal processes were working. He had been arrested and had pled guilty and was sentenced to the state penitentiary for seven years, the maximum sentence. While in the custody of the sheriff and on his way to prison, he was "dragged from the railway car in which he was seated by a vile, brutal, lawless and debased set of miscreants, and hanged to a telegraph pole." The mob tore away his clothing and distributed it among themselves. There had to have been support in the community to raise such a mob, and the community was not, through its sheriff or prose-

Steam harvest, John Miek property, Ness County (courtesy of Kansas State Historical Society)

cuting attorney, taking any action against the perpetrators. The mob members or their abettors, the petition claimed, "have attempted to bulldoze, terrorize and drive from their homes those who have been brave enough to denounce their act." The lynching, the petitioners said, was "a burning and lasting disgrace upon the people of Salina" and the state of Kansas and was "a painful manifestation of a wave of increasing prejudice, hatred and injustice now sweeping over the entire country against the Negro race." Cowboy independence, or a feeling that there was a frontier heritage of direct justice, should not lead to a "sympathy with the mob" that was no more appropriate to Western Kansas than it would be anywhere else.[59] Western Kansas people lynched whites as well as blacks in the era, but the rhetoric about blacks was different.[60] The paper at Hays in 1895 reported on the case of *State v. Fran Nevels*. Nevels was a black man charged with the murder of a white woman. Eleven jurors stood for conviction, and one, a black man named Jordan, held for acquittal. The reporter commented: "Here is another glaring showing of the defects of our jury system."[61]

Class worries did not always involve race. A well-known People's Party weakness was an inability to create solidarity among farmers and urban laborers, two potentially powerful constituencies for them. Jacob Coxey, an Ohio businessman, proposed a plan of federal work relief on public roads. He organized a march of the unemployed on the capital to advance his plan. Although in the end only about 500 men actually arrived there, wild rumors of several huge "armies" converging on the city caused fear among conservatives of a violent revolution and damaged what little progress the People's Party was making with labor.

In June 1894, elements of Coxey's army under the leadership of an electrician named J. S. Sanders commandeered a Missouri Pacific train in Colorado and headed for Washington, D.C., by way of Western Kansas. The Colby papers reported that the approach of the train many miles to the south of the town threw things there into "a fever of excitement." City authorities and the railroad appointed five marshals "to keep these hungry men from falling upon the mayor and city council and devouring them."[62] Those on the track had greater fears. The sheriff at Tribune tried to raise a contingent of 200 men to intercept the train but, in awaiting reinforcements from Topeka, allowed it to get away.[63] After working their way around three road blocks, the 450 "Commonwealers" aboard the train surrendered without resistance at Scott City to a U.S. marshal and a posse of 50 from Leavenworth.[64] Governor Lewelling, Annie Diggs, and others issued a call for a meeting on how to help these and other unemployed people on their way to Washington, D.C. The Salina paper thought the reporters were disappointed to have traveled so far only to miss any violence. The most radical banner the men on the train displayed said, "Vote for Weaver and Get $1.00 for Your Wheat." But there were among them, a Western Kansas editor wrote, "many desperate looking characters."[65]

Governor Lewelling issued the famous "tramp circular," blaming society for the condition of the unemployed who were riding the rails in the 1890s and begging for food at the back doors of Western Kansas homes. But local residents were not so sure how they regarded the tramps, or even their near kin, the itinerant harvest hands who arrived in their communities every summer and camped in the park or at the railroad yards. There was still a strong element of Social Darwinism present, and the "poor but proud" rural types thought of these people as vagabonds whose condition reflected the defects in their characters. Probably they drank and were not members of a church. There was no local feeling that the men who robbed a Santa Fe train at Cimarron in 1893 were romantic Robin Hood figures. Rather there was emphasis on their slovenly appearance and the crude violence with which they handled the brave express man and on the courage of the law enforcement officials who tracked them down.[66] Poverty and pain were no excuse for dishonesty or illegal action.

Western Kansans also parted with the Populists because the local people were eternal optimists, local patriots with pride in their state and region.

As such, they disliked a vision consisting so largely of "whine." Republican Kansas often commented that the Populists exaggerated problems. William Allen White famously criticized them in his essay "What's the Matter with Kansas?" In the year of the composition of that classic, he wrote: "What an awful thing it must be to stand on a high point of ground in Kansas and 'look away across the sea' of corn, ripening grass and the fields just plowed for wheat, and then pause, with the picture of prosperity and plenty upon the heart, to reflect that you are a Populist and hate God and man."[67] Wrote a Salina critic: "This party has lived upon the magnified misfortunes of the times. It opens its meetings by singing a song of despair, then preaches a sermon from the gloomiest text found in the book of Lamentations and closes its services with the litany of human despondency and desolation."[68] Western Kansans were not sure they wanted reform points made at their expense, by pointing out how oppressed and downtrodden they were. "Every union laborite," wrote a columnist at Larned in 1890, "who sits around the corners of the streets blowing from morning till night[,] . . . every self-constituted reformer who travels around the country sowing the seed of discontent and making those 'poor down-trodden people' pay him a good salary, has preached this stuff to the people until too many of them believe that half of the people are all but in the poor house."[69] A critic at Hays summed it up. If you are going to a Populist speech, he wrote, best to walk around in the cemetery for a time reading epitaphs first to prepare yourself. "No man who has persuaded himself to believe this unbosomed woe has the heart to throw corn to his hogs the morning afterwards, or ask grace at the breakfast table for mercies spared. . . . These men have worms."[70]

And the People's Party had no solutions. They were impractical, newspapers of the region often said. "They add nothing to our stock of useful knowledge. It is simply fault-finding."[71] Capital had been required by Western Kansas and it would be required in the future. "It is worse than idle," wrote a critic of Populism; "it is simply idiotic to brand every eastern man who has sent money to the state to be invested, as a robber and an enemy."[72] The same was true of elected representatives of the region. "Granger" from Hays wrote in 1890 that there was no reason, as some seemed to think, to throw a candidate out because he was successful and lived in a $7,000 house. "If successful men . . . are not the proper men to represent their neighbors . . . let us abandon every plea of capacity, intelligence and experience and . . . go on down the scale . . . and pick out for our representative some of the financial and moral wrecks who quite thickly bestrew the shores of Ellis county politics."[73] The pioneers of Western Kansas, wrote W. Y. Morgan of the *Hutchinson News*, had suffered from three evils: "Those blights, those horrors, those nightmares, those jim jams, those delerium tremens, drouth, hot winds, and Populists."[74]

Then there was socialism. The western papers were filled with the socialism issue, and it was generally treated negatively, even among those editors who supported the Populist cause. Local People's Party speakers such as Noah Allen, C. G. Clemens, Mary Lease, and Judge Frank Doster, as well as national figures in the party like Edward Bellamy, appeared to support a system where private property was not well respected and "where inequalities would be impossible." Senator William Peffer, it was said, thought that the duty of government was to provide a home for the homeless and to give the idle laborer work.[75] That did not set well among the hardy yeomen of the west. By the middle of the decade, some of them were embarrassed to admit they had ever sympathized with the People's Party. Perhaps they had temporarily lost their wits, like the Armenian mother who went mad and thought that "maniacs and demons incarnate were stalking about the world."[76]

"Socialism," opined the *Hays City Sentinel*, "is the wildest flight that impracticality has ever essayed upon earth. It endeavors to make all men equal; to possess all property in common; to make no distinction between intelligence, mediocrity and ignorance. . . . It fastens the drunkard, the sluggard and the criminal upon the sober, the energetic and the honest. It proposes a Utopia which can only exist in fancy-cracked brains of irresponsible lunatics. . . . How many of the Populist farmers of western Kansas fully realize the end to which their party is leading them. Socialism and anarchy!"[77]

The only effective counter to these doubts was the reminder that the alternative to Populist politics was Republican business as usual, and that that might not relieve the pressure. The *Alliance Echo*, in Wallace County, right on the Colorado border, responded in 1890, at the enthusiastic dawn of the protest and at the first fall of the drought hammer, to *Topeka Capital* charges that Populists were "socialistic-communistic hair-brained reformers" with the reminder to area farmers that there was such a thing as oppression:

> What do you call the contraction of currency, the railroad pools, the manufacturing . . . combines and the dozens of other cases of class legislation?. . . . [You farmers] come to town in lumber wagons and haven't hardly clothes sufficient to shield you from the winter's storm, and your wife works from four o'clock in the morning until nine o'clock at night and then can't go to church on Sunday because you are too poor to buy her a decent dress to wear, and your children have to stay at home from school because you can't buy them clothes and books.

They did not need to be told by free-market thinkers, "You have no brains, you are fools, you, your wife and little children deserve to starve or go to the asylum for idiots."[78] That view was present, but the majority felt confident it would rain again and that their fertile, sunny country would make them prosperous one day.

There were two highly regional and immediate political threats to Western Kansas in the early 1890s, which would not benefit any party in power at Topeka and certainly did no good for the thin People's Party support there. One was the so-called disorganization issue. Given the population decline in the area, and given the expense of maintaining the machinery of the numerous counties that had been organized there during the boom, there was agitation in the state legislature to eliminate some western counties, combine some administratively with others, and reduce the representation in the legislature from Western Kansas. The other threat was that the state government at Topeka would simply ignore the western region, as the western region claimed it had been doing for years. So strongly did Western Kansas feel about this, and about being taxed while getting few benefits from the state, that residents talked of seceding and forming a state of Western Kansas.

Disorganization was universally opposed in the western part of the state. The argument was that taxes would not be reduced by consolidation. The existing counties would be more likely to collect delinquent taxes on large landowners and so relieve the tax burden on the small man than would a larger unit. "Disorganization," said a paper in Johnson City, Stanton County, "is only a step toward repudiation. It means the exodus from this county of 30,000 brave men with their families, who have spent from 10 to 15 years of their lives enduring hardships in the upbuilding of their homes. It means the confiscating of their property, in order that a few syndicate land owners and cattle barons may be benefited." Consolidate some of the county offices, the editor recommended, "but let the county boundaries alone."[79] Combining counties might reintroduce the county seat wars that had been so damaging to Western Kansas in the 1880s. "We have gotten rid of that reckless and extravagant element which brought us so much trouble in our early days," wrote a Liberal man. "The county affairs are now in the hands of capable, honest, business men, who are running our business as cheaply as it could be done under any circumstances."[80]

There were headlines in the eastern Kansas papers in 1896 that J. W. Davis, a Western Kansas attorney, was suggesting that forty counties in Western Kansas could be consolidated into five. A Garden City editor noted that Davis was "an egotistical ass" and that those who knew him would give no thought to his "idiotic proposition." Western Kansas had only three of forty state senators as it was. How would things be under consolidation?[81] What chance, wrote an editor in Ness City, "would we have divided into a few ranching counties against the political representation of the east?"[82] Some warned that a vote for the People's Party was a vote for consolidation and a vote for consolidation was a vote for diminishing the influence of the western region to an even lower point.[83]

The annoyance over disorganization and consolidation reminded regional representatives of their other grievances and led to calls for secession and division of Kansas into two states. Editors in the region often capitalized the "Western" in their regional designation, thus reflecting their sense that it had an identity of its own—Western Kansas, rather than just western Kansas. A Scott County paper thought it was more than "barely possible" that "the owners of the railroads, and the eastern land syndicates and investors who do not live in western Kansas with their families" were behind the county consolidation movement. Their children went to good schools, why should they worry about the education of the westerners? If "our part of the state has become a disgrace and burden to the east half of Kansas . . . why not let it step out and form a new state to govern over its own domestic affairs in a way applicable to its climatic and other conditions."[84]

There had been some talk of secession in the so-called Murdock rebellion of the late 1880s, when booming Wichita suggested that if it could not be the capital of Kansas as presently constituted, it might be the capital of a new western state.[85] There was enthusiasm in Western Kansas in 1892 for Murdock for governor, not on the grounds that he would promote secession, but that at least there would be a man in the governor's office who understood the needs of the western region. J. K. Barnd, editor of the *Ness County News*, wrote Murdock in 1892: "I have become heartily sick of the methods of the *political autocrats*, and would hail with delight anything that might tend to weaken or destroy their power. The 'rebellion,' of which the *Eagle* was chief, gave me renewed hope that the [Republican] party would return to the control of the yeoman of the land, the rank and file of the voters, who gave it strength." The Republican Party, Barnd thought, "had better die than continue as it has existed for a number of years."[86] A Dodge City man thought, "The great Southwest will give you practically unanimous support."[87] More attention to the western section would build up the trade towns of the central region and break the monopoly of the "river towns" on the eastern border of Kansas. Murdock, it was said, was the "broadest gauged man on the track."[88]

Murdock, however, was never very interested in promoting his own candidacy and did not make a serious bid for the office. That led straight back to the idea of withdrawing from rather than trying to change the state of Kansas. The *Globe-Republican* in Dodge City claimed late in 1892 that there was not a single newspaper west of the center of Kansas that was not in favor of division. There was no reason, it said, to think of Wichita as the capital. It should be Dodge City or even Ness City—some town centrally located in the new polity.[89] That state, it was thought, would definitely be Republican, since the region had returned a 5,000-Republican majority even in the Populist election year of 1892.

W. R. Hopkins, a legislator from Finney County, was a leader in the movement, as was S. G. Norris, editor of the *Garden City Herald*. Part of their motivation was their anti-Populism. Part of it was that they felt that the High Plains region was discriminated against in taxation. Norris wrote: "It was the eastern part of the Seventh district that saddled Jerry Simpson on us, and we want the new state line to cut those counties out. . . . The east has always dominated in politics; it has framed our laws, forced railroad legislation upon us that is averse to our interests and now, to add insult to injury, has forced us to swallow a noxious dose of calamity." The interests of the sections were widely different, Norris wrote, and the western region had paid its taxes for years and gotten few state institutions and less than its share of state spending. "The state is large enough to divide and our people are armed for the fray and do not propose to stop." Newspapers in the east said that Western Kansas was an "incubus" on the central and eastern part and an embarrassment to Kansas. Hopkins argued before a large crowd in Dodge City that it was the other way around. Maybe the new state could incorporate part of the Indian Territory to the south and some of eastern Colorado as well.[90]

Wrote Barnd from Ness City in 1895:

> If Western Kansas ever receives recognition other than being allowed to whoop it up for the ticket, or in paying its proportion of the taxes, it will only be by securing an absolute separation from the powers that now control the state. . . . There is certainly no community of interest between this part of the State and that which gobbles all the loaves and fishes, and the sooner some method of changing the plan of proceedings is devised the better it will be for western settlers.[91]

The next year he was pushing the same theme: "If this part of the state is solely adapted to cowboys and cow punching, the sooner it is turned over to the class of people that is personally interested in its development, with full power to make laws for the regulation of its affairs, the better it will be."[92] And the next year also: "So long as our senators and representatives go to Topeka as the fag end of the appropriations absorbing contingent adjacent to the Big Muddy, that long will western Kansas be the laughing stock of the world."[93]

Norris, at Garden City, added his spin. He wrote in 1895 that

> we are not part of Kansas, except in name. If there has been any dead load to carry[,] western Kansas has had to carry it for the benefit of the east end. Eastern Kansas has been a detriment to our development and prosperity. It has lied about and traduced the country and the people. It has willfully trampled upon the rights and privileges of our citizens and the yoke is growing intolerable. Just let us have the chance and see how quickly we bid farewell to eastern Kansas, her chinch bugs, chiggers, and gangs of blood-sucking politicians.[94]

We pay our own bills, he wrote in 1896, and even support the "penal, idiotic and imbecile institutions, all of which are established in the eastern part of the state from whose enlightened population they are being constantly recruited." But there would never be a right relation between the west and the east parts of Kansas, and Western Kansas should go its own way and be "given an opportunity to develop its own destiny without being hampered and retarded as it now is and has always been, by a prejudiced press and people ever ready to claim for eastern Kansas all the state's virtues and generously attribute to western Kansas all the vices and ills that afflict our commonwealth."[95] As Kansas was to the nation, it seemed Western Kansas was to the rest of Kansas—a whipping boy and a scapegoat, the wild and primitive relative who was only technically part of the family.

Western Kansas did not secede, though the 1890s was not the last time that that measure was suggested. But it would indeed have to "develop its own destiny" and struggle for economic recovery and for political recognition. People in Western Kansas had suffered a serious shock and had survived. They had worked through the quick fixes as they came and went. They had learned, as Harry Kitchen pointed out in his commencement oration at Garden City High School in 1895, that success was "the result of gradual development." There was a vast difference between potential and realization, young Kitchen emphasized, and stability came not through the magic schemes of the moment, but through self-denial, hard-won knowledge, and maturity gained over many seasons of suffering. The oak tree did not come to its strength suddenly, "but through the heat and cold, rain and sunshine of a hundred years."[96] Now, as the shadows lifted a little and the new century approached, it was time for the region's "stickers" to think, to adjust, and to adapt in a thoroughgoing way and for the long haul.

3

The Edge of the World

A writer for a Salina paper, looking west from his town in 1896, saw grim prospects for Western Kansas. He concluded that early observers who had called the region a desert "were not very far from the exact truth. The desolation of that region is appalling." Along the Santa Fe railroad west of Dodge City,

> the prairies, every acre of which once constituted a portion of a claim, are almost entirely depopulated. An inhabited "shack" can scarcely be seen in the whole sweep of the horizon. Occasionally weak attempts at farming are perceived; a patch of corn tasselling out with stalks fifteen or twenty inches in height, or a few acres of wheat, the harvested product of which would not make a wagon load. Irrigating ditches may be seen all along the route, but they are as dry as the streets of Salina, and have the appearance of having been abandoned. Deserted and tumble down dugouts and shanties, once the abode of bright promise, are to be seen everywhere, and usually one or more cottonwood trees have withstood the ravages of prairie fires and wave their green foliage in defiance of the drouth and heat.

The only signs of promise were the towns.

> The little villages stand solitary and alone in the midst of the great prairies. They are painfully small and the buildings are unpainted and unkempt. In several instances quite imposing court houses stand well back from the main

street, the belief evidently prevailing when they were constructed that the towns would grow up to them.

One town had only one building standing, imprinted with the name Union Printing Office. It must at one time have been the home of a newspaper.[1]

Such was the challenge. What remained and would remain and what was illusion? What was gone for good and what would return? What were lessons and what were cruel jokes? Those were the questions for Western Kansans who had made the transition through the worst of times and for those who were starting out in the country for the first time. A writer in the *Aurora* magazine in 1894 had repeated the joke about a railroad passenger who, when asked why the Almighty had created such places as Western Kansas, said that he did not know unless it was to hold the earth together.[2] William Allen White speculated in 1897 that "the whole land is a place of mirages—of false hopes, splendid dreams, strange visions, that have vanished, leaving only the dry husks of things to shuffle mockingly in the wind."[3]

It is a truism that good planning begins with a realistic assessment of the situation as it exists and that such an assessment must have in it a strong element of recent history. Perry Miller, historian of New England Puritanism, spoke of one generation's trying to warn another, in the manner of the prophet Jeremiah, of the dangers facing them and to transmit to their children what they had learned.

In Western Kansas, for twenty years after the 1890 crash, the prophetic theme turned upon the lessons of the 1880s boom. One editor noted that to write a complete history of his county "some erudite scholar" might think it necessary to go back to antediluvian times, but as far as his readers were concerned the most relevant history was recent.[4] The boom was gone and they did not want it back. "The story of the boom in Kansas was the story of a crime."[5] The very word "boom," wrote W. Y. Morgan from Hutchinson, "makes a Kansas man shy like a colt from a flying piece of paper in the road."[6] It was "an excited, unnatural and unreasonable condition," not the "throbbing of a healthy pulse, but the feverish frothing of delirium."[7]

It was unwise to look for a scapegoat. It was not all the fault of eastern corporations, or of the stars, that Western Kansans were underlings. Local people had "made fools of themselves by the wholesale" in the 1880s, and they needed to admit it before health would return. The editor of the *Ness County News* wrote in 1890:

> The fountainhead of the morality or depravity of the nation is with
> the people themselves, and to influence them for the general good
> of the whole it is the province of the local paper to do its work at

home. . . . If the people of a small community like Ness County cannot be won over to their own interests in matters of public polity, there is little use in turning the "muzzle of our bazoo" toward greater embattlements.[8]

The editor at Dighton, looking around him in 1897, saw the ruins of false hopes. Yet, he thought, "from out the wreck of busted booms has come a community of sturdy pioneers, self-reliant and strong of purpose."[9]

The towns resented lawsuits that were filed in the early twentieth century by interests trying to take advantage of the new prosperity to pay debts from the boom. In spring 1900, for instance there was a suit against Garden City for its default on the payment of interest on $32,000 in waterworks bonds issued during the 1880s and paid upon until the middle of the 1890s. The newspaper thought that the waterworks might be run more efficiently and that a sinking fund could be created for that debt, but admitted that the old financing was a burden to a more reasonable age.[10] John Stevens and C. J. "Buffalo" Jones of Garden City filed suits in 1906 to recover title to property they had once owned in the town and which was becoming valuable again. "It don't look right," wrote an editor, "for those people who abandoned Garden City to its fate twenty years ago, who have not paid a cent of taxes in those years, who have not contributed a dollar for the benefit of the town, should come in this late day and set up all sorts of claims to property that they now think is valuable." The people who had remained "and fought the long, hard battle, should be the ones who should have what benefit is derived from better times."[11]

There should be attention paid to the lessons of experience in the region. In the past, people had not understood the country, analysts said, "and have never, until recently, paused to study its climatic conditions, its varied resources, or what crops were best suited to the land." Instead, "the one desire and aim of the many was to raise six-foot Illinois corn, to boom the towns, sell 'city lots,' secure as large a loan as possible on their property, and if they failed (and they always did), to curse the country and skip it."[12] Now the "very basis of things" was changed.[13] Martin Mohler of the Kansas Board of Agriculture, in a speech at the Chicago World's Fair in 1893, said, "Having made the round on the agricultural Ferris wheel, we are again on solid land, wiser and richer by far in experience, if not in purse."[14]

The new caution could be seen in the attitude toward railroads. The enormous increase in railroad mileage that had fueled the speculation of the 1880s all but ceased in the 1890s, as did the advertising of the region by railroads with lands to sell.[15] There were some branch lines and connections built in Western Kansas in the early twentieth century. But counties and towns, which were trying to negotiate down the payments on the bonds they had issued in the past, debated carefully any proposal to create new debt on behalf of new railroad projects. People laughed at the railroad enthusiasm that had once so gripped them. Some boys at Sharon Springs in Wallace County found a wire contraption along the railroad tracks in 1907 and carried it to the newspaper office. Ed Ward, who, a fellow editor said, "has been talking in his sleep for the past few weeks about division stations," decided that it must be one of the instruments used by the civil engineers to lay out plans for a roundhouse. He wrote a couple of columns about it and set them in type, but then his wife came in and asked him where he got that lady's bustle. The *Times* was late appearing that week.[16]

It was considered better to concentrate on improving the rail facilities already in place than to dream of Gulf connections. The *Ness County News* went on a crusade about the inadequacies of the Atchison, Topeka & Santa Fe (ATSF) branch that served Ness City. The "old coffee pot arrangements that pass for engines" were always out of repair, the arrival time of the mail was a subject for betting, and there was a time in 1901 when the combined freight and passenger train took nearly three hours to make the eleven miles from Bazine to Ness City.[17] "It is questionable," wrote the press, "if the town would not be better off without any railroad communication than the abortion that runs through here and poses as a real railroad."[18]

The ATSF depot at Ness was unimpressive. Men and women mixed in the single waiting room there, "and some of the male humans have never been taught that smoking, whisky-laden breath and uncouth language is not pleasing to the nostrils and ears of real ladies." The depot was lit for the early morning train by a "dingy coal oil lamp," and there was no light at all on the platform of cinders and dirt where "passengers seeking a train must take their chances of barking their shins on trucks and miscellaneous articles that may be in the way." The local editor thought it was nice that he was invited to Topeka for a complimentary lunch put on by Fred Harvey and the ATSF officials but thought his readers would appreciate a little more attention paid to incremental improvements in the local service.[19]

Such disappointment was common. C. W. Cline of the Kansas Town & Land Company, the land development branch of the Chicago, Rock Island & Pacific Railroad (CRI&P) Company, found that at the turn of the century his company's assets were not in demand. He tried to collect small lease payments from tenants on railroad land, but they were often in arrears. "The weather is horrible," wrote a real estate man at Norton in 1899, "dusty and windy."[20]

Cline exchanged a series of letters at the turn of the century with E. T. Guymon, proprietor of the Star Grocery in Liberal, "buyers and shippers of Hides, Wools and Broomcorn, Wire and Queensware, Groceries Provisions, Flour and Feed," on the subject of a building, once the headquarters of the Rock Island land division in Liberal but now occupied by the Star Grocery and in poor condition. A windstorm in the spring of 1899 damaged it severely. Guymon asked the company to repair it or forgive a month's rent—$5. Cline refused, and Guymon improvised by putting up strips of tin and holding them down with two tons of corn in sacks.[21] A year later, the land company offered to sell the building to the grocery for $300. Guymon responded that that was ridiculous, as they could build a new building for that. "It has no paint on it, and the sills are rotting and you must remember that it has been standing there for 12 years. . . . We have everything moved in one side, for when it rains we cannot keep the water out."[22] Some days later, another wind blew the roof entirely off. Guymon reluctantly offered $250 but complained it would cost him $500 more to fix it and that he was getting the poor end of the deal.[23]

Things were no better at other points along the CRI&P. An agent at Goodland in 1900 sent along a plat of the railroad property there. He said that the town was "slowly and gradually moving South nearer the Railroad and the Shops" and that there might be more demand in the future but that for now sales were slow.[24] The only inquiry for the company's property at Minneola in 1901 was from a man who wanted to buy land at $1.50 an acre.[25]

The ATSF did build a $35,000 brick and stone depot at Dodge City in 1897–98.[26] The *Topeka Journal* reporter, commenting on the "imposing and attractive" building with its $2,000-worth of copper trim, steam heat, porcelain bathtubs, and electric light furnished by the Dodge City Water and Light Company, thought it introduced a new era for what had been "a narrow town of low frame buildings" with a "motley crowd" of cowboys on the street.[27] But it really did not. The depot was an outgrowth of transcontinental traffic and the Fred Harvey system more than any local prosperity. The *Kansas City Star* headlined a 1902 article on Dodge City as "A Town That Didn't Grow."[28] The best that could usually be hoped for by Western Kansas towns was to be designated a division point, as Liberal became when the Rock Island extended its El Paso division in 1906, and to get perhaps a twelve-stall roundhouse and some extra employees in the bargain.[29]

The 1890s was a nadir for railroads. In 1904, the total railroad mileage in the state of Kansas was only 5 miles more than it had been in 1890. By 1916, Kansas as a whole had added only about 600 miles to the 8,800-mile rail system it had had in 1890 when the boom busted.[30]

Atchison, Topeka & Santa Fe railroad depot at Dodge City, 1899 (courtesy of Kansas State Historical Society)

In the entire decade of the 1890s, only the construction of the Hutchinson & Southern, built in 1890 for the 85 miles from Hutchinson to Kingman at the east edge of the Western Kansas area, seemed at all impressive. Another tiny leftover was the Dodge City, Montezuma & Trinidad. It was a project of Asa Soule, the patent medicine magnate, as part of his magnificent entrée into the Western Kansas irrigation and town-building business during the boom.[31] The Dodge City, Montezuma & Trinidad was wise enough or poor enough not to expand in the 1890s. It reported earnings on its 26 miles of line of only a little over $4,000 in 1890 and was running a deficit of nearly $10,000.[32]

Most of the lines with names or routes that sounded or looked as though they were Western Kansas projects—Salina & Southwestern; Kansas Midland; Solomon Railroad Company; Rooks County Railroad; Ft. Scott, Wichita & Western; Topeka, Salina & Western; Wichita & Southwestern; Kansas Southwestern; Kanopolis & Central Kansas; Wichita & Western—were subsidiaries of larger companies. They survived only by the parent company making revenues elsewhere.

An example of the process in this era of scooping up a passel of incorporated hopes and shoveling them into a larger industrial box was the Kansas & Colorado Pacific Railway Company, a subsidiary of the Missouri Pacific. The K&CP was organized in 1890 by a consolidation of twelve boom companies.[33] Some of these had once had an independent existence. The Denver, Memphis & Atlantic (DM&A, or "Darling Mary Ann"), for example, was at its founding, in 1883, a narrow-gauge railroad that had the goal of connecting the Rockies with the South.[34] Others were just exotic names on incorporation papers. Even that apparent exception to every rule, Arthur Stillwell's Kansas City, Mexico & Orient, which did build hundreds of miles of track in the first years of the century from Wichita south into Texas and toward its planned Mexican west coast window on Asia, failed and was absorbed by the ubiquitous Santa Fe.[35] The gaggle of mass meetings and the intermittent "strong talk" to solicit aid for such companies as the Nebraska, Kansas & Southern; Nickel Plate; Great Bend & Gulf; and Gulf & Northwestern put no track on the map. The railroad map of Kansas, with company lines marked in different colors, tended toward monochrome as the years passed.

It did not quite amount to nothing at all. There was a line constructed in 1905 between Kiowa and Springvale by way of Medicine Lodge with the ambitious title of Denver, Kansas & Gulf. But only a few miles were constructed before the company was quickly absorbed into the Santa Fe, which realigned it slightly.[36] There was also the case that concerned some railroad work done west of the tiny town of Jetmore, Hodgeman County, where the Santa Fe branch, extended during the boom southwest along Pawnee Creek toward Dodge City and Garden City, had ground to a halt. In 1909, a lone man, Rudoph Myers, with a team of mules and a scraper, bought right-of-way and began grading along the old survey in the direction of Garden City. Four years later he was still at it. One observer thought Myers "probably the most eccentric Caucasian that ever wore shoe leather" and called his railroad a "bughouse project." What would the ATSF want with such a railroad even if it had it? "There is about the same crying demand for a railroad in that special territory that there is for municipal wharfs in Jetmore." That pitiful scenario was typical of the first years of the new century in Kansas High Plains railroading.[37]

Railroads represented an older technology, nonresident control, a discredited category of dream. It was no longer true that the sudden appearance of a new railroad was likely to be the making of a Western Kansas town or that farmers and town promoters in the region could have any serious impact on the strategy of the gargantuan concerns that provided their elevators and loading docks with cars.

There was more excitement about things that had not been seriously tried before, that were based on recent developments in science and technology and for which capital, at least in the developmental stages, might be drawn from the newly active state and/or federal governments. There was hope for improving regional economic prospects and for softening the asperities of living there. Among the initiatives seriously pursued in the former category before 1910 were dryland farming, alternative crops, pest extermination, forestation, irrigation, creameries, sugar beet farming, and power farming. In the latter category came regional higher education, the automobile, good roads, municipal utilities (water, electric, and telephone), and local cultural amenities.

The most basic of the new tendencies was an affinity for education. The bust was a humbling experience but also a learning experience. Western Kansans learned that avoiding harsh experience through the application of right knowledge was desirable. Anti-intellectual, antitechnological, or antigovernment attitudes no longer seemed appropriate. The *Kansas Farmer* in 1893 offered a set of the twenty-volume revised ninth edition of the *Encyclopedia Britannica* for $10. Payments were monthly, and the *Farmer* would send along a dime savings bank in which the farmer seeking to take advantage of "one of the grandest monuments of scholarly research . . . in the whole realm of literature" could deposit his savings.[38]

In many ways, the whole changed package in regard to learning was well represented by a single event that occurred right at the turn of the century—namely the transfer of the buildings and 7,500-acre land reserve of old Ft. Hays to the State of Kansas for use as a college, an agricultural experiment station, and a city park. The modification and modernization of this single resource, with all its associations with the primitive frontier regional past, fittingly introduced an era of mental application to local and applied problems. It also heralded a transformation of the cultural and social life of regional communities to suit the contemporary idea, advanced to the nation at the time by William Allen White of Emporia, that small towns, properly organized and motivated, were the best of all tools for ensuring that the utopian dreams of the reformers would be implemented with a modicum of common sense.[39]

The transition from "bivouac to campus," as the college's historian James Forsythe put it, began when Senator Preston Plumb, encouraged by P. W. Smith, a county commissioner in Ellis County, introduced a bill providing that part of the Ft. Hays land be used for an agricultural experiment station.[40] The mantle later passed to Hays pioneer and Kansas naturalist Martin Allen. Allen, while serving in the legislature in the 1880s, combined his interest in horticulture with the idea that science could best be applied to Western Kansas agriculture by creating a college and experiment station on the Ft.

Hays grounds. He advocated vast artificial forests in Western Kansas and thought that a college could show the way both to that and to better crops.

An 1884 congressional act provided for dispersal of the land, but there was considerable delay and frustration. Dodge City in 1890 got the Kansas Soldiers' Home that was proposed for a time by some Hays Civil War veterans as an alternative to Allen's experiment station and college idea. Several times during the 1890s, the Hays land was opened and then closed for homestead entry. Bills to use the land for the college and experiment station failed in 1895, 1896, and 1897, and the legislation that was passed late in 1899 was not accepted by the state until 1901. Even then, it was not all that locals had hoped for. The school was a branch of jealous State Normal at Emporia, which was "not about to let the branch grow." Its head was called a "principal," it covered only the equivalent of the last two years of high school, was limited to students wishing to get a teaching certificate (thirty-four at the opening), was sparsely funded, and had to make do at first with the buildings of the old fort, which had been abandoned and deteriorating in the hot winds for over a decade.[41]

It was, however, a start. In the secession movement, Western Kansans had complained that they did not have their share of state institutions. Now the Soldiers' Home was in the region, there was talk of putting an insane asylum there, and there was a college and an experiment station.[42] None of the original donations of federal property were, it could be argued, great prizes. The board of managers of the Soldiers' Home meeting at Dodge City in 1889 found the fort buildings "in bad condition; plastering off, roofs leaky, floors broken, doors, mantels, blinds, locks &c. stolen and everything in a dilapidated condition generally."[43] But Dodge City and Hays people were nevertheless determined to use their chances in regard to the federal government for all they were worth.

Martin Allen died in 1898.[44] But his idea had incorporated itself firmly into the fabric of his town and county. There was a mass meeting at Hays in 1899. Residents of the county came to town with their buggies and their families, joined the procession to the reservation, and then attended a speech by Congressman W. A. Reeder, who showed "that this is not a deal in the interest of a few real estate dealers."[45] However, there was cynicism too. The Hays *Republican* late in 1899 predicted that Reeder, like other politicians before him, would try and fail to get the reservation for a college and then would come back and ask to be reelected to try again. "This biennial story is getting to be a chestnut," the editor concluded. Perhaps it would be better to open the reservation to private entry. "Eight thousand acres of wheat each year will beat any building or appropriation that will be given by the state to any institution in Western Kansas."[46]

The promoters of a government reserve persevered and succeeded. The Hays project was not the first institution of higher learning in the region. The cities on the border had had them in the boom. There were Garfield and Fairmount colleges in Wichita, both abandoned for a time during the 1890s. It was joked that College Hill in Wichita was neither a hill nor the location of a college, but more than one college had been seriously proposed for that site.[47] In 1891, Salina had three educational institutions outside the public schools: Salina Normal University, Kansas Wesleyan, and St. John's Military Academy.[48] Further west, Dodge City had Soule College, constructed by the man who had promoted the Eureka Canal and other regional improvements. But, like so many products of the boom, the partly completed college building became a municipal liability in the 1890s. The National Bichloride of Gold Company of Chicago, which marketed a system of cure for drunkenness and the opium habit, looked at the Dodge City college properties in 1892 with the idea of using them as a sanitarium.[49] Dodge City citizens tried in 1895 to get land around the college used for an irrigation experiment station.[50] The ladies' clubs of Dodge established a library of 500 volumes in a large unplastered room at Soule College in 1894, and the school opened for a time then with eight faculty members and eighty-one students.[51] However, the next year it was reported to be tied up in lawsuits between the Presbyterians and the Methodists, neither of which particularly wanted the moribund institution.[52] The Hays education project was more stable.

The opening of the Western Branch of the Kansas State Normal School in June 1902 was a major event. Stores in Hays closed, and the Hays military band led a procession of teachers and students from the assembly room to the flagstaff. The appropriation had not been sufficient to build a new building, but college promoters repaired fort buildings and converted the 40-by-100-foot stone guardhouse into a gym. The minister of the local Lutheran church gave the address, reminiscing about the early times in the town and concluding: "We have, however, come to a better mood—a new history for the town of Hays, and the western part of the state." As far as he was concerned, he said, the school was better than a manufacturing plant. He had found in his travels that "it is not best for the people where smoke is emitted but where schools are located."[53]

Overshadowed at first by Normal School but equally important in the long run was the agricultural experiment station. Through this, not only did Western Kansas obtain facilities for doing real soil and crop science, but the region

Hays Experiment Station, 1904 (courtesy of Kansas State Historical Society)

also tied its interests to one of the state's major educational institutions, the Kansas State Agricultural College (predecessor of Kansas State University). KSAC was restricted in its experiments at its home location in the Flint Hills by lack of farm property sufficient in extent or quality for its work. Also, the experiments that it carried out there applied only to the eastern region of Kansas. The Hatch Act of 1887 provided federal money for experiment stations, and that is exactly what the Manhattan institution needed. George Clothier, a botanist at KSAC, waxed enthusiastic about the idea of a western experiment station in an 1899 article in the *Kansas Farmer*. The military reserve at Hays, he said, was "as fine agricultural land as can be found on the face of the globe." It would be a "bonanza" for his school, where it could test wheat varieties and then distribute them all over the western part of the state.[54]

Also, KSAC was interested in outreach. As early as 1868 when organizing Farmers' Institutes, the college newspaper had stated, "It is incumbent on the regents not only to provide for the well-being of the College by selecting learned and practical teachers for the several chairs, but also to extend the benefits of the institution to the people of the state at large."[55] The scope of this increased over the years, until by 1907 the college, which at that time had 2,000 students on its Manhattan campus, reached 80,000 farmers through institutes and distributed 20,000 bulletins each year.[56] The college was innovative in delivering higher education to nontraditional audiences and in new forms, ranging from what we might now call "workshops," to Farmers' Institutes, to special trains rolling through the region loaded with exhibits and professors.[57] It established the Kansas Extension Service in 1905, and by 1909 employed seven specialists to aid in county extension programs.[58] The college at Manhattan had felt itself to be a sort of "stepchild" to the University of Kansas at Lawrence and saw this democratization of

Plowing at the Hays Experiment Station (courtesy of Kansas State Historical Society)

agricultural education as a niche through which it could grow. It was a fortunate association for Hays.

The start was slow but promising. Secretary F. D. Coburn of the Kansas State Board of Agriculture visited the site in December 1901 with Hon. S. J. Stewart and Professor H. M. Cottrell of KSAC and pronounced it superior. At Hays there could be 20 or more farms of 160 acres each, and 40- to 80-acre experimental plots could be planted "instead of little plats of ground the size of a town lot."[59] They found the people of "most generous and kindly character," and everything purchased by the station at Hays was sold to it at cost.[60] The *Kansas Farmer* thought that "book farming" had good promise. It mentioned Coburn's enthusiasm for "having on a large and decisive scale an experiment station in the western half of the State, right at the naval of the continent as it were" and noted that he thought "a failure to make it in time the foremost example of its kind in existence would be an inexcusable and short-sighted folly."[61]

President Ernest Nichols of KSAC and two of his professors visited the site early in 1902 to select tracts. Nichols promised, "The College expects to go to work with energy and perseverance as soon as the frost is out of the ground." He confessed, however, that funding was short. To put the 3,400 acres assigned to the station under "high grade culture" and to provide barns, sheds, roads, and water would cost $50,000 to $100,000. But the biennial appropriation was only $6,000.[62] Still, the first superintendent, J. G. Haney, who had a degree from KSAC, worked 15 teams in the spring of 1902 to break 500 acres, clear a prairie dog town of 400 acres, move 4 buildings from the old fort, plant several crops and 30 kinds of native grasses, and put

Harvesting the 1919 wheat crop, Colby Experiment Station (courtesy of Kansas State University Special Collections)

down wells.[63] The historian of the station noted that its establishment was greeted in some quarters with "skepticism and even resentment" by those who did not believe that the High Plains area would ever support profitable agriculture, and that the 1890s depression should have taught that lesson. Also, "the idea of using a scientific approach to solving agricultural problems was foreign to most people." Fortunately, he concluded, officials at Manhattan ignored that skepticism.[64]

Originally the scientists thought this single western experiment station would suffice.[65] It turned out it was just the first of a whole series of western stations designed to test the different microclimates of Western Kansas. The experiment station at Garden City of 320 acres was founded in 1907.[66] The station at Tribune began operations in 1912 on a quarter section of land in a location "as near the central part of extreme Western Kansas as it is possible to locate it."[67] The Colby Experiment Station, one-half section in the far northwest, sharing grounds with the high school, commenced in 1914.[68]

These stations applied science in a major way to economic agriculture in Western Kansas. The annual reports of the superintendents gave detailed information on the regional climate in individual crop years; tested many crops, including new hybrids developed by the college; tried new methods of farming; tried new methods of feeding animals with careful attention to profitability; put in, operated, and did cost accounting on irrigation plants; held educational days for area farmers and homemakers; and even commissioned photographs of land, crops, and various sorts of damage at different times of year. The data went into bulletins published by KSAC and made available to farmers who might wish to apply lessons learned. It was no quick fix, but it did have an authentic and long-lasting impact. "It takes continued work for a long term of years to give results that are authentic," wrote the superintendent at Garden City in 1914, "as climatic conditions vary so much from year to year."[69]

Alternative modes of farming and crops were a fundamental focus of the experiment stations and of Western Kansas twentieth-century thinking. Dryland farming, with its techniques of leaving some of the land fallow in alternate years, plowing deep, keeping the soil fine and loose on the surface with a packed subsoil to hold water, holding the water where it fell, and cultivating to take maximum advantage of scarce rainfall, had been around since the 1880s.[70] However, it had been more popular to discuss it at conferences than to apply it in the field. Like so much of the new science, it took extra effort and planning and required a certain amount of study. New crops required study too. A farmer might well have to adapt to different markets or obtain certified seed—or both.

The innovator in the dryland farming method was H. W. Campbell. Kansas at the turn of the century was well advanced both in holding congresses about the method and in using it. J. P. Pomeroy of Boston, the largest landowner in the state in 1900 (80,000 acres), made a contract with Campbell that year to operate a model farm near Hill City to demonstrate that Western Kansas "can be made to produce crops every year, by a system of cultivation Mr. Campbell has invented."[71] By 1905, Campbell had supervised several model farms in Western Kansas, claiming that an "ordinary farmer" with 25 percent more work could get yields on wheat of 40 to 50 bushels per acre.[72] The estimate was that 7 inches of rainfall would produce a crop if it were all preserved. In 1909, a dry year, it was reported that 35 bushels to the acre for wheat crops was not unusual using dryland farming methods.[73] Dryland farming was once ridiculed, wrote the editor of the *Hill City Republican* in 1911, but the thinking had turned to less acreage and more culture. The traditional farming methods, he concluded, did "not give the country a square deal. Under such farming the farmer expects climatic conditions to make good for his failure of duty." By contrast, "the proper culture of the soil and the conservation of moisture will supplement the ordinary run of climatic conditions instead of asking nature to overcome the effects of bad farming."[74] The International Dry Farming Congress for 1914 held in Wichita testified to the interest and application in the region.[75]

There were variations on this dryfarming/water conservation theme. One of the best advertised was the "Dam the Draws and Summer Fallow" program that J. C. Hopper of Ness City pursued with an unparalleled zeal and knack for publicity for forty years. Hopper was a banker, farmer, and stockman who had come to Kansas in 1886 and who had been advocating his idea of using the local topography to catch water ever since.[76] His campaign reached a peak in 1908 when he took over much of the front page of the *Ness County News* for months in writing a series of articles on his ideas. His methods had the advantage of being inexpensive and working with Nature. Publicity, he thought, was important to creating regional unity. "Where many people push for a common end, even the elements can be harnessed and made to assist in the good work."[77]

Hopper was a vivid and personal writer who remembered the trials of his parents in trying to establish a home in Osborne County in 1871 and 1872 against the hot winds and dry weather. "It seemed as though it would never rain, and when it did it was in local showers that would be licked up by the wind the following day, or it would come in a gully washer and all run off through the draws."[78] He was determined to find a better way and was "absolutely certain of the results" of his methods.[79]

The key was organization. One dam on each of the 4,320 quarters in Ness County would hold 29,825 gallons per dam, and the whole system would impound 2.5 million barrels of water, or the equivalent of a river 36 miles long, 2 feet deep, and 45 feet wide. Ness County had 1,080 square miles of surface, and one 2-inch rain a growing season would be enough to fill these reservoirs. If every quarter had 100 trees planted 1 rod apart, there would be 2,700 acres of forest. "How simple it looks when you analyze it, and how complex some would have it look." People were so skeptical, Hopper said, "that we must be knocked down with the truth before we will begin to believe. . . . It is a wonder we won't doubt our own existence."

There was none of that unhealthy self-consciousness for him. "We are none the worse off if we believe and fail, than we are to try half hearted and sure to fail. Organization is what we want. Let us organize."[80] By 1909, Hopper had created an improvement society in Ness County with his damming project as a key element, and he had a program to introduce it in the schools. "A good idea continually pounded into the people's heads is almost sure to work some good," noted the editor at Scott City, observing with some wonder the dynamo that was J. C. Hopper.[81]

Mr. Hopper received some attention from the state of Kansas about 1915 when the office of J. W. Lough, state irrigation commissioner, investigated his ideas with the view of perhaps building a state reservoir at Ness City.[82]

The problem was where to find water even for small reservoirs. "The idea is all right," Lough wrote, "if we could find the place where we could get the water." He had seen Hopper's ideas, "& I can't do him any good—The people have great ideas along this line they think should do many things that don't look good to us. . . . I don't want to spend the money & get nothing out of it."[83] Hopper's plans remained mostly talk.

Some areas went further than simply adopting hybrids or alternatives to traditional crops and went into businesses that had never been thought of there before. An interesting example was the watermelon seed business developed in Seward County. With brands such as Rattlesnake and Kekley Sweets, the watermelon seed industry began there in 1888 and in the early years of the twentieth century produced more income for that county than all the county's cereal crops.[84] The watermelons themselves were often eaten by coyotes but were sometimes marketed at Liberal for 10 cents each. The seed, packaged in 125-pound sacks and shipped east, was where the profit came. An acre would yield 200 pounds of seed worth $20. A 300-acre watermelon farm would gross $6,000 and return a tidy profit.[85] About 1910, the area turned away from melons and toward broomcorn—always, however, innovating away from the standard answer that wheat was the crop to grow.[86]

Science applied in areas less directly related to crops also. For example, there was a strong desire to apply technology and organization to rid the region of two leftovers of its primeval past, fire and pests. The prairie fire was no longer only a colorful phenomenon from which one could hide in a sod house, but a real menace to wooden towns. Fireguards and waterworks were needed. And pests seemed eternal, but perhaps science was now in a position to deal with them.

Fires, like floods, were an inconvenience to nomadic people but a disaster for the fixed assets of an urban/agricultural civilization. Willis George Emerson, the son of a nephew of American philosopher Ralph Waldo Emerson, witnessed a prairie fire at Meade in 1887, which he later described in his novel *Buell Hampton*. Residents discovered "a thin glow of fire cutting the dark belt near the earth, like a blood-red sickle." Country folks and animals rushed into the village for shelter. Cattle gored wolves in a weird pandemonium that could have been taken right out of Ovid's description of the destruction of the world. "Flocks of prairie hens, quails, meadow larks, and thrushes, all blinded, singed and frightened, began flying against the buildings, many of them falling to the earth either crippled or dead. The entire town echoed with fluttering wings."[87]

It was an activity of the "fire demon" that no one wished repeated. Towns burned regularly enough from internal causes (I. M. Yost lost his flour mill at Hays three times before 1907) without some external flame sweeping down on them, originating perhaps from a locomotive spark or a lightning strike a hundred miles away.[88] In 1893, a fire started fifteen miles north of Russell, "driven by a terrible gale." It burned the Rooks County town of Palco so completely that only an elevator remained, and it jumped the Saline River easily.[89] Loss of life could be substantial and horrible. At Wilson in 1893, William Barley died "after suffering untold agony" in being "burned to a crisp." Two others who were with him fighting a prairie fire died shortly, one with his "hands burned to cinders."[90] These graphic stories made residents determined to prevent fires. The editor at Ness City wrote that he did not want to advocate extreme measures, "but, knowing the efficacy of hemp as a strengthening cordial to the memory in case of carelessness with fire in the West, we deem it our duty to warn those afflicted with this malady."[91]

The primary public action taken was a law passed by the state legislature in 1895 authorizing township boards in counties west of the ninety-ninth meridian to require the plowing of fireguards financed by a local tax.[92] The ATSF and Union Pacific railroads paid the tax connected with this legislation under protest and sued on the grounds that the fire law was unconstitutional.[93] They eventually prevailed.[94] There was a second prairie fire law passed in 1897 providing stiff fines and prison sentences for anyone willfully setting fires or negligently letting fires on the public domain burn unattended.[95]

Most Western Kansas editors approved of these measures. Some towns created fireguards around their city limits in lieu of establishing a fire department or a waterworks.[96] It was not enough. Residents of Plains, Meade County, including women with wet sacks, turned out in force to stop a prairie fire threatening their town in 1897.[97] Ness Citians the next year observed a fire 12 miles wide and 30 miles long that was stopped only by the railroad line.[98]

The fire problem was intensified by the invasion of the Russian thistle, which caused numerous other difficulties all on its own. Like everything else in Western Kansas, the eastern Kansas press exaggerated stories about it. In 1909, the *Kansas City Star* reported that at Sharon Springs a great wall of thistles struck the new courthouse and "the building was crushed beneath the weight." For 500 miles, reporters said, buildings, fences, and farmhouses fell under "the avalanche of thistles. The roundhouse at Syracuse was so full of thistles that it required snowplows to clear the stalls. Balls of thistles as high as the Washington monument went skipping over the prairies of Ness and Rooks counties, imprisoning steers. Heavy teams reportedly crossed the north fork of the Republican River on thistles "the same as on concrete bridges."[99]

But the truth was dire enough. The thistle was "a tumble-weed of the worst kind," which could spread fires but not be destroyed by fire. Instead it had to be "smitten hip and thigh by a sharp hoe in the hands of an active $1.25 a day man" to take it out by the roots.[100] "This pest has gotten a foothold here," reported a Thomas County paper, "and we cannot afford to let it get deep rooted."[101] Thistles propagated quickly and could overrun a county in no time. Secretary Coburn in a Board of Agriculture bulletin on them noted that a single plant could have 200,000 seeds, could interfere with both plowing and harvesting, and could carry prairie fires across fire breaks. Their spines "irritate and worry both horses and men" and caused sores on horses' legs.[102] "The few moments which it will take to stop a buggy or automobile," the *Tiller and Toiler* at Larned advised in 1908, "and get out and pull up one of these weeds might easily result in the saving of thousands of dollars in ruined crops besides untold days of labor necessary to destroy the progeny of this one weed."[103] It was discouraging for people in Garden City to see, instead of the wide-flowing Arkansas River that had once filled their irrigation ditches, a riverbed bone-dry and so full of thistles that they feared any water coming down would carry away their bridge.[104]

Pests, like fire, were ancient natives that did not fit into the new commercial world. Some of the scientific responses to them, such as the well-publicized program of Chancellor Francis Snow of the University of Kansas to exterminate chinch bugs by introducing diseased individuals purposefully back onto farms to infect their fellows, were sophisticated.[105] Others, such as strychnine bait, were crude and dangerous. But all represented a considered strategy to attack and eliminate threats to agriculture through the application of science and technology.

The big three in the pest category were the jackrabbit, the prairie dog, and the grasshopper. Rabbits reproduced as fast as the thistle, and there were many frightening estimates about how much forage they took for support. The primary early weapon against them was the county bounty. But even at a modest 3 to 5 cents for a pair of ears, some counties in the early 1890s spent $15,000 a year rewarding farmers for the huge number of rabbits they could easily kill.[106] At the first meeting of the county commission in sparsely populated Wichita County after it passed a law in 1893 offering a bounty, 13,000 rabbit and coyote scalps were presented for payment.[107] Greeley County paid out over $6,000 at a single meeting the same year.[108] It was perhaps fun watching blooded greyhounds chase rabbits across the open prairie, but this was hardly a means to reduce the numbers.[109]

Mass-organized hunts became common, but these were often not effective either. The 6,383 pounds of rabbits, 1,205 individuals, that a hunt at Garden City in January 1895 yielded hardly made a dent in the population.[110] A hunt in Hodgeman County in 1911 eliminated 700 examples of "Mr. John Rabbit," but it took 2,200 shells to do it. This made the cost of ammunition exceed that of the bounty and led to the suggestion, later widely adopted, that the rabbits should be driven into enclosures and clubbed to death.[111] There was a suggestion of setting up a jackrabbit cannery in Western Kansas, but it was hard to develop a taste for the critters.[112] Even so, Scott City on a single day in 1911 shipped out 30,000 rabbits by rail for fur and consumption markets in the East.[113]

Prairie dogs did not go over well for dinner either, and the pet market for them had not developed, though the idea was suggested.[114] The dogs were spreading at the turn of the century, and unless they were checked, local people thought, "there won't be enough grass left to feed a grasshopper."[115] There were patent devices that "faithfully failed to perform the work," and the main hope was in poisons provided by the Kansas State College of Agriculture experimenters.[116] M. C. Buffington commented in 1900 that prairie dogs had "practically ruined thousands of acres of our best grazing and agricultural land by their pernicious habit of gnawing the grass out by the roots, and mowing down as clean and close as a lawn mower anything that obstructs their view."[117] Buffington chaired a meeting at the Ness City opera house on the problem. The group decided to request a bounty from the county commission and to order supplies of bisulphate of carbon, which seemed to be effective when poured into holes. Grain baited with strychnine also worked. Using ferrets to flush them out was discussed, but no one seemed to know where to buy a large supply of ferrets.[118] In 1901, Kansas appropriated $5,000 and instructed that the college at Manhattan hire people to visit the western counties and advise on prairie dog extermination.[119] In 1902, the prairie dog population of Kansas was about 67,200,000, down by 17,000,000 from the year before.[120] In 1903, a bill, championed by the Trego County representative and passed, provided that township trustees should estimate the amount needed to exterminate prairie dogs in their districts and then report to the county commissioners who were authorized to levy a tax to accomplish this.[121] "At gatherings in the extreme western portion of Kansas now," wrote a *Topeka Capital* reporter in 1901, "while the women are in the house exchanging recipes for putting up fruit and making cake the men gather out in the yard and swap recipes for mixtures that will kill prairie dogs. The prairie dog will have to move on. He is occupying land that has become too valuable for prairie dog towns."[122]

The great and coordinated attack on the grasshopper was of a slightly later period and awaited the establishment of the experiment stations with their entomologists. However, at the turn of the century, people recognized that not only were cyclic attacks by migrating insects, such as the great invasion of 1874, dangerous, but the hoppers committed big depredations on crop-lands every single year. Eating them was the first suggestion, or at least feeding them to hogs. But since one could catch 6 bushels of grasshoppers per acre, this was not a feasible solution.[123] The most common approach was poison—the most popular mixture, called "Criddle" after its inventor, being one part Paris green, two parts salt, and forty parts horse dung mixed with water until soft but not sloppy and then spread on infested areas.[124] The University of Kansas in 1897 suggested biological agents, such as the introduction of a fly that was the natural enemy of grasshoppers. But in the short term, a kerosene pan attached to a clever machine called a "hopperdozer" to drown the critters was perhaps the most effective defense.[125] Some added that one could use strong electric lights to attract the insects to shallow troughs containing oil or kerosene.[126] Scientists should study "the habits, hopes, and ambitions of the ever present grasshopper."[127] And the state should help. Let something be done, wrote one editor, "to encourage the farmer in overcoming his enemies and subduing the earth."[128]

The tendency was toward the application of science and technology to modify the environment. But there was a countercurrent, involving using Nature itself for leverage and showing a healthy respect for the dangers of too-rapid environmental modification. This showed up in some of the work of the entomologists with predator balance. It was certainly there in the suggestions of the dryland farming theorists and with those proposing damming draws. And in regard to the grasshopper, it showed up in the suggestions that, just as jackrabbits and prairie dogs were proliferating partly because their predators, such as the coyote, were being exterminated, so the wholesale hunting of birds in Western Kansas—not only game birds but songbirds and not only by men but by boys—might have something to do with the size of the insect hordes.[129]

In Garden City, the city marshal in 1901 notified local boys that they should stop shooting songbirds. This was justified on the grounds that city people liked bird song and that it was unwise to cultivate an "instinct of cruelty" in children.[130] However, it was clear from other comments on the same topic that the move to protect songbirds and to establish hunting seasons on game birds was also a matter of self-protection. In 1897, a state game law passed protecting grouse, prairie chickens, quails, pheasants, robins, blue jays, and others, with the exception that the owner of an orchard might shoot blue jays, orioles, or yellow hammers at any time.[131] The *Osborne Farmer* in 1900 specifically made the link between more grasshoppers and fewer birds and blamed the "town sports." Town councils, the editor thought, should prohibit killing any bird except chicken hawks for five years. "The gardens in town suffer considerably from worms, and yet every little boy has his pop gun and shoots our best insect destroyers, such as robins, blue jays, gold finches, orioles, etc."[132] Ness County the same year thought it was time to introduce some ecology in schools. Classes could talk about watersheds and drainages and could go into the woods to observe trees and plants. Would this not open "great possibilities?"[133] Garden City officials thought it was too civilized for bird slaughter. The city council resolved in 1903: "Whereas, Garden City has outgrown that stage of development in which men and women decorated themselves with the scalps, teeth, hair, or bones of their human victims. Whereas, a portion of the people have reached the stage at which they are pained to see the remains of birds and animals used for decorations for head and other gear," therefore residents should stop killing birds for decoration or for sport.[134] "We can't afford to lose anything that is useful in Western Kansas."[135]

There were two changes in the treatment of the land that were pursued by the experiment stations but that extended well beyond their purview: forestry and irrigation. Both seemed at first strangely out of place on the Kansas High Plains and indeed proceeded against some cultural and political headwinds. Both developed in stages.

Forestry had the larger impact early. There were two parts to the forestry initiative. First, it continued the trend in place since the railroad tree-growing experiments in Western Kansas in the nineteenth century to test the hardiness of different tree species on the High Plains. In the 1890s this was done through a state program—the railroads having gotten out of that part of the promotional business. Trees grown on state farms were distributed to individuals hoping to improve their homesteads. The second feature of forestry was more surprising. There was a political move to create a forest in the sand hills area along the Arkansas River west of Garden City. This eventually resulted in the temporary establishment of a national forest in Western Kansas—a surprising find on a historical map of Kansas.

The Commissioner of Forestry office in the state bureaucracy originated in 1887. In 1897, this officer became the commissioner of forestry and irrigation. In 1905, the legislature eliminated the office for forestry and irrigation, stopped the free distribution of trees for a time, and transferred control to the Kansas State Agricultural College. In 1907, the functions divided and there was a separate commissioner of forestry. That lasted until 1909. Kansas created two forestry experiment stations in 1887, one near Dodge City and one near Ogallah in Trego County. Ogallah ceased operation in 1913 and Dodge City in 1917 when it became evident that state-controlled activity in forestry (as also turned out to be the case with similar state irrigation experiment stations) was far less successful than the agricultural experiment stations.[136]

Martin Allen of Hays was the second commissioner of forestry, taking office in 1889, and was an effective publicist and organizer. He had attended meetings of the American Forestry Congress in the 1880s, and in 1890 began sending out packets of 500 trees each to over 4,000 applicants from across the state.[137] He recommended black locust and box elder trees for planting in Western Kansas and thought planting castor beans around the trees would keep gophers from the roots.[138] Allen noted that Kansas forestry was a different kind of operation than in most places. In other parts of the country, the "leading idea" was the preservation of declining forests. "We in the prairie states have to plant tiny trees with the hope of their growing into forests; or at least making forest trees sometime in the future."[139]

The forestry stations were a noble experiment, and partly successful, if measured by the large number of trees they sent out to farmers. Western Kansans appreciated that they represented a state institution in their region. However, they were poorly funded and supervised.[140] The state asked for land donations from railroads and individuals and sited the stations wherever the gifts were forthcoming. The only advantage was that if trees would grow on these poor sites, they would probably grow anywhere. The Dodge City station was located on the highest and driest point of land in Ford County and exposed to constant winds.[141]

In the spring of 1890 the state forestry department distributed 100,000 trees. It passed out 320,000 in 1892, 1,750,000 in 1893, and 3 million in 1895. These trees cost about 40 cents a hundred. But, one man commented, "as years go on these trees will develop a value to the community, the increasing ration which is beyond human conception."[142] A Dodge City man wrote in 1892 that trees were then seldom out of sight, whereas, when he had first moved to town, "the only groves visible were the illusory forests" consisting "of a clump of sunflowers or a few straggling cottonwoods which skirted the streams."[143]

The Populist interlude was not healthy for the state forestry program. Bartlett considered the Populist forestry commissioner, E. D. Wheeler, to be "as ignorant of tree culture as a hog is of the day of the week." Wheeler allowed both forestry stations to deteriorate, and when George Bartlett took the state office in 1895, he said that the property at Dodge City had deteriorated "to such an extent that its condition became a matter of public gossip." Ogallah suffered more, but Bartlett restored it. "It is very encouraging," he wrote in 1896, "to know that while the population of this Western part of the State is diminishing the demand for timber becomes greater every year."[144]

In 1903, agitation began for a federal forest on nearly 95,000 acres of sand hill land in Finney, Kearny, Grant, and Haskell counties. President Theodore Roosevelt, speaking at Russell, Kansas, said he hoped to see it established.[145] So did Western Kansans, if for no other reason than the big federal money involved and the prospect of a timber-cutting industry some time in the future. But the federal forest would be a long time coming and when it came would thrive only briefly.

Irrigation was a panacea of the boom, but irrigation meant ditch irrigation.[146] Although many of the ditches, abandoned by their original promoters, were, in the 1890s, cleaned out and reopened by companies with local farmers as investors, the Arkansas River had not carried much water since Colorado irrigators had begun diverting it. Therefore, the fundamental approach to irrigation in twentieth-century Western Kansas had to be modified.

The problems were obvious. Kansas, wrote William Sutton of Russell, "like ancient Gaul, is divided into three parts." The western part was dry enough that "general farming of staple crops . . . is in the majority of years unprofitable, and years of abundance are too far apart to bridge over the failure."[147] Nationwide, there was concern that population was too concentrated in the eastern part of the United States and that, if a way were not found to distribute it to the open lands of the West, class warfare and revolution might result. William Ellsworth Smythe's 1900 book *Conquest of Arid America* only collected thinking that had been publicized through the dry 1890s.[148]

Kansas began in 1901 to sue Colorado over water rights. But while awaiting a decision, there needed to be another irrigation strategy.[149] Perhaps the upland would have to be abandoned for crops, but the valleys would support a dense population, provided the "underflow," the moving aquifer beneath the river valleys, could be tapped. This would require pumps and something to power the pumps—first windmills and later gasoline, diesel, and electric motors.[150] What was needed was a test, preferably financed by government, to determine the underground water potential and the economics of tapping into it.

T. J. Dyke's irrigation plant and earthen reservoir, Garden City, Finney County
(courtesy of Kansas State Historical Society)

The Western Kansas press in the 1890s was packed with irrigation news, irrigation speeches, and irrigation debates. An irrigation commission from the Kansas state senate toured Western Kansas in 1889 taking testimony.[151] There was a mass meeting at Great Bend in 1890 to consider the topic.[152] Richard Hinton, a special agent for the U.S. Department of Agriculture, stopped at several Western Kansas towns in 1891 in the course of traveling 13,000 miles by buggy and by horseback in search of irrigation solutions.[153] The Interstate Irrigation Commission, representing North Dakota, South Dakota, Wyoming, Nebraska, Colorado, Kansas, Oklahoma, Texas, and New Mexico, met in 1893 in Salina, where J. W. Bristow published the *Irrigation Farmer*.[154] Kansas sent delegates to national irrigation congresses elsewhere throughout the decade to get a better sense of "a movement, which must be pregnant with results of incalculable moment to the United States as a nation."[155]

Various companies proposed to go into the irrigation business. The Burlington & Missouri River railroad claimed in 1891 that it would invest $100,000 in a system of irrigation in Cheyenne County in northwest Kansas. It organized the South Fork Irrigation and Improvement Company to do so and did surveys of 120 miles of ditches and laterals in that area.[156] The same year, the Western Kansas Waterworks Irrigation and Land Company, based in Dodge City, filed for a charter. The directors included E. E. Soule, the son of Asa Soule, the patent medicine maven who had backed the ditch irrigation boom in the 1880s. Some land agents for the Santa Fe railroad were also involved. The company had a capital stock of $1 million and proposed to establish town sites, build dams and canals, and erect electric light plants.[157] In 1892, the Arkansas Valley Land and Irrigation Company brought families from elsewhere in the United States and from abroad to settle on its vast land holdings, which irrigation was to make useful and valuable. The company sold the land to settlers on credit, furnished seed and implements, and took half the harvest at the market price until full payment was made for land and supplies. Most of the backers were from Topeka, but George Watson of Larned was the southwestern superintendent and field agent for the corporation.[158] An irrigation company started at Tribune in 1894, proposing to pump water from 100 feet down and to irrigate a quarter section.[159] The Hoisington Irrigation Company appeared in Great Bend in 1896 with a capital of $300,000.[160] The feeling was, however, that these companies would accomplish little without further government-sponsored study. The *Kansas City Times* in 1893 concluded: "If the governor will do something towards making one-sixth of Kansas' fair and fertile domain absolutely certain, he would accomplish more for the state than if he would build a railroad from Topeka to Timbuctoo by way of the Bering Strait."[161]

In 1895, Kansas created a Board of Irrigation, Experiment, and Survey. This had a budget of $30,000 and consisted of a geologist from the University of Kansas at Lawrence, the president of Kansas State Agricultural College, and three members from the public.[162] The three public members were all from Western Kansas—Judge D. M. Frost of Garden City, Judge W. B. Sutton of Russell, and Hon. M. B. Tomblin from Goodland.[163]

Many were skeptical. Even one of the official reports of the commission, reprinting the authorizing act of 1895, commented, "The student of this act will be bewildered by its ample commands, and meager appropriations for the purposes intended."[164] Wrote one man, "Quit talking irrigation through your hats. If you are going to wait for the government to irrigate your 160 acres for you, the sooner you go east to live with your wife's folks the better off the country will be. This thing of talking about the government experiment grows woefully tiresome."[165] The superintendent of water service for the Chicago, Rock Island & Pacific railroad, writing to Governor Edmund Morrill in pencil from a moving train bound for Goodland, observed that an article he had read in the *Kansas City Star* about the state's plans for irrigation was "the greatest exposure of ignorance on the subject that has come to light in some time." The only people who would benefit were the state employees of the irrigation board and windmill sales people. "People may talk of irrigation in Kansas until their tongues get forked, and pass bills innumerable, but it can never be done profitably." Water could not be pumped up from 50 to 100 feet, where it lay in much of the Western Kansas upland, and used to raise 50-cent wheat and 25-cent corn. The vegetable truck farming idea was no better. "How can western Kansas people," the railroad expert wrote, " expect to pump water and depend on a *truck patch* and compete with eastern Kansas & Missouri where rains are abundant to produce crops close to market."[166]

Professor Erasmus Haworth of the University of Kansas, however, was no dilettante, and he was a believer. He was director of the university geological survey and was to become a pioneer in forming the geological basis for several industries in Kansas, most prominently the oil and gas business. Haworth traveled through Western Kansas in 1895 and carefully mapped the potential water-bearing strata.

Haworth suggested that the state establish thirteen irrigation plants in various sections of Kansas along the Arkansas and Smoky Hill River Valleys.[167] Some actually appeared. A pumping station at Goodland, established in 1895, involved a 180-foot well operated by a 10-horsepower engine.[168] One at Plainville filled a large reservoir using a 60-foot well powered by a windmill with a 14-foot wheel atop a 40-foot tower.[169] A year later, there was news of new state irrigation stations being constructed at WaKeeney and at Liberal. Since the Liberal plant was called No. 18, one might assume that the state was active in this business for some time.[170]

There was a state irrigation plant at Garden City, also. However, Garden Citians, sophisticated as they were on their own at studying irrigation and forming companies to build plants and supply equipment, were not impressed by the state effort. In January 1896, the editor of the *Garden City Herald* noted that the state plant in his town was being discontinued. It had been, he wrote, "a very unprofitable experiment to the state, and utterly worthless to the farmers of this county." The station managers adopted ideas that had been discarded by everyone else in the area years before and "the people are not a whit the wiser than if the station had never been in operation." Bureaucrats studying wind velocity learned only that "the wind did blow in western Kansas," but the only "actual and real thing about the station was the salaries and expenses."[171] The editor at Dodge City agreed and wrote in 1897, when the separate irrigation board was abolished, that no one in Western Kansas was sad to see it go.[172] An editor at Hays reporting that year on the sale of the state irrigation plant at Plainville commented, "Nothing could

The first steam plow at Garden City, c. 1892 (courtesy of Kansas State Historical Society)

be more absurd than the manner in which these irrigation experiments have been handled by the state."[173]

In addition to the fundamental and scientific changes in approach to farming, there was another that was simpler and had more to do with applied technology than with basic science. Trends toward larger holdings and labor-saving "power farming" were strong in the region, as they were in the nation.

Through the 1890s in the local press, one reads of the successes of the large farmers, of the corporate owners, and of the exploits of what was locally called the "steam plow." The steam plow, which appeared in the region early in the 1890s, was a traction engine pulling ganged plows or harrows. It could also serve as a stationery engine to run a threshing machine. "If they are adaptable to any country," wrote an observer there, "they will certainly prove a success on these smooth prairies." He awaited "the advent of the big double-barreled plow and the iron horse."[174] A traction engine pulled nine plows in a public demonstration at Garden City in the spring of 1892.[175] In the same month, Mr. A. R. Colt's steam plow dug up 20 acres a day in Cheyenne County. "It has been the talk for years," wrote the editor at Bird City, "that this country would never be what it should be until the land is all in cultivation[,] and now since plowing can be done by steam at such a rapid rate, it will not be long before this vast plain will be a vast field."[176] A Dodge City man felt good about the "wonderful steam plow," as he observed in 1892 its "triple cylindrical action" and the manufacture of electric light on board for night work.[177] In 1903, the editor at Ness City counted twenty-five "steam threshers" at work in his county, "and the smoke from them rises in every direction."[178]

Using machinery did require a sober operator and a knowledgeable one. There were numerous reports of boiler explosions, caused by letting the water level on the engine fall too low or, more often, by running too much steam pressure. Older engines would not sustain 120 pounds per square inch of pressure as when new, a Western Kansas engineer reminded users in 1900, and would not work reliably "in the hands of every Tom, Dick, and Harry who know only enough to shovel coal and pull the throttle." He recommended state licensing of the machines and their operators.[179] But the requirements could be learned, and the machines were worth the effort.

James N. Fike of Colby was a large farmer fond of technology. Thomas County was flat and just the place for big machines. In the summer of 1906, Fike headed an excursion to his farm six miles from town to observe steam plows. He had a big engine pulling four-disk plows that cut a swatch of sixteen feet. Behind these plows came two heavily weighted harrows pulverizing the ground. It took a crew of five to do the work of forty horses and eight men by ordinary methods. "When you look at this monster rig with its caravan of plows, etc. marching majestically across the field you wonder if the time has not come for big undertakings in farming in this country."[180]

The plow was not the only attachment for the traction engine. A reporter was in "something more than awe" in 1897 as he watched a steam traction engine at work running a threshing machine with a self-feeder and a pneumatic straw-stacker. "It is that benumbing absorption," he concluded, "with which the untutored savage regards the railway train." What a marvel for one who had threshed with a flail on the oak floor of a barn only a few years ago! "What monster is that, stretching along the horizon in the distance, over hills and through hollows, stalking on the levels with the heedless march of a juggernaut or the appalling sweep of a cyclone? . . . Has puny man then harnessed the wild tornado and tamed it to its use? . . . This is the steam thresher."[181]

The farms were monsters also. Fike and his partner I. W. Haynes bought a 32-horsepower Reeves engine in 1907 and seeded 5,000 acres from which they harvested 40,000 bushels of wheat. They claimed that by plowing and seeding quickly and at the right time, which machinery allowed one to do on large acreages, "the farmers of Thomas County can do away with wheat failures." The next year, Fike and Haynes seeded over 11,000 acres and said they would earn profit as much as $50,000. Fike ran into some dry years shortly and consequently experienced financial reverses before he died in 1914. But the good years made an attractive model of his methods.[182]

Through the 1890s, the small homesteaders who lost their farms to the mortgage companies were bought out by larger concerns, which consolidated the family farm holdings into larger acreages. These were operated by partnerships or corporations that could raise the capital needed to use big machinery and take advantage of the cost savings of not having to build a home, dig a well, or plant a garden on every little plot. In 1891, Eldridge Beach & Company, operating a ranch near Hays with 8,000 acres under fence, decided to plow 2,000 acres of grass to add to the 1,700 acres of wheat land it already had.[183] That same year, the Burlington & Missouri River railroad organized the South Fork Irrigation & Improvement Company, with capital of $100,000, to consolidate 100,000 acres of company lands in Cheyenne County and install a system of ditch irrigation.[184] Henry Cleveland of Brooklyn, Connecticut, visited Western Kansas in 1891, concluded that wheat was a safe crop there, and put in 6,000 acres of it that fall.[185] A colony of Germans from Russia bought 100 quarters at one time in Graham County in 1892 from J. P. Pomeroy of Boston, who, it has been mentioned, ran a large acreage himself.[186] The Arkansas Valley Land and Irrigation Company, owned by capitalists in Topeka, operated on a huge scale, developing their lands by recruiting families to live on them.[187] By 1894, the company cultivated 15,000 acres along the ATSF railroad from Barton County to the Colorado line.[188] The Chicago Land and Improvement Company bought 2,280 acres, 12 miles southwest of Wichita, in 1894 for $68,000, intending to subdivide it into 8-acre farms.[189] The Alfalfa and Irrigation Land Company of Kinsley harvested 1,000 tons of alfalfa from 1,500 acres in 1897. It built a reservoir 1,000 feet in circumference, with banks 8 feet high and 30 feet thick, and fed 5,000 hogs.[190] That same year, Ike Crumley, the county clerk of Thomas County, farmed what was said to be the largest wheat field in the country, at 2,000 acres.[191] The Syndicate Land & Cattle Company had an agent in Colby in 1899 and advertised there that it had 100,000 acres of railroad land for sale for $3 to $7 an acre on 10-year terms.[192] In 1901, Stephor Kanski, formerly the head of the czar's poultry farm in Russia, was running his own large wheat farm and poultry experiment operation near Hill City.[193] In 1905, in the same area, a real estate dealer showed a potential land investor sixteen tracts. After supper, the visitor called on the tired agent and asked him if that was all the land he had for sale. The man then bought it all, and the agent had to close his office for lack of land to sell.[194]

These were not quite the 15,000- to 30,000-acre farms found in the Bonanza farming areas of the Dakotas, but the *Kansas Farmer* thought the Sunflower State would share in the trend because it was sound economics. Farms from 1,000 to 6,000 acres were not uncommon in Kansas. "They represent the modern feudal estate, without the feudalism of baronial times." Big fortunes were to be made in big wheat grown and harvested with big machines. "Wheat-growing," said the *Farmer*, "is a legitimate business subject to the usual conditions of success, viz., market values, supply and demand, labor and all its appendages, the competition of the American farmer, the exhaustion of the land, supply of moisture and other conditions of the season, together with others too numerous to mention."[195] It was time, the journal editors thought, to concentrate on farming as a business, even as an industry, and to de-emphasize the casual, romantic, unscientific, and primitive mode of farming as a traditional lifeway. People agreed that the combination of modified or alternative crops, maybe some irrigation, large acreages, and power farming would suit the landscape well.

The great strength still, however, was in the regional culture, replete, as it was, with a hard-bitten, humor-laden optimism that had grown out of the ups and downs, the hardships, and the satisfactions. During a dry period in 1899, morale was low in Logan, Phillips County, Kansas. "Down deep in the hearts of all," one resident remembered over a half century later, "was the thought that civilization in western Kansas was doomed to failure. There was absolutely nothing to do but sit and watch the sun course its way through a sky of brass." But a small boy entered a store and asked if the proprietor would make him a very large kite, the largest that could be made to fly. The boy raised the money in town to pay for it, $3.45. That produced a kite 5 feet by 8 feet, constructed by "Professor" George Bridges of Logan. It flew well. There was another fundraiser and another kite appeared, this one 11 feet by 16 feet. That flew too, and optimism knew no bounds. Finally Bridges built a never-to-be-forgotten kite, 16 feet across the shoulders, 25 feet long, and 150 feet from the peak to the tip of its red, white, and blue bunting tail. "It was not only colossal in its dimensions but it was very beautiful. The cordage on it resembled those of a balloon such as we see at country fairs. It was covered with very gaudy widths of Holland shading in colors of red, yellow, and green." The end of the tail was in the form of a fish tail and was 7 feet across the forks. On the main body of the kite was painted an American eagle. Six men hauled this kite down Main Street hitched to quarter-inch rope. It flew attached to a windlass and demonstrated its strength by easily pulling along a new Studebaker wagon loaded with twenty-nine men. It delighted everyone present. It seemed that anything was possible and that even the wearing Western Kansas wind could be put to productive use if one just thought about it enough.[196]

The new approaches to making a living in Western Kansas were not magic. They would not change the environmental challenges that faced farmers, town builders, and industrialists on the High Plains. And, for a change, no one was suggesting that they would. Kansans, wrote Hutchinson editor W. Y. Morgan in 1896, had been too much occupied with systems when they should have been digging ditches. "We have expended our wind when we should have been setting up windmills." Now it was time to get down to business.[197] The latest suggestions for Western Kansas recovery and prosperity were things that worked. The only question was how well they would work and for how long.

4

Deus Ex Machina

In 1902, a traveling salesman arrived in Ness County marketing a patented contrivance for killing prairie dogs. It consisted of a bellows attached to a furnace, which blew the fumes of heated chemicals through a rubber hose into the prairie dog holes to asphyxiate the animals. The engineer demonstrated by placing a live cat in a closed box and then pumping in the gas. This "did not seem to be congenial to the feline, as it soon gave up the ghost." The local press noted that "everybody admitted that the cat" was dead, but Western Kansas skepticism in the face of large claims was alive and well. Prairie dogs would not stay in a box to be executed, the local editor noted, and no one should invest until the machinery actually cleaned out a dog town.[1]

Sometimes the effects of machines as they became awkwardly integrated with the landscape were less benign or amusing. A typically violent drought-breaking storm at Larned in August 1898 had more spectacular effects than the usual sound of breaking trees and the killing of some cows and pigs. This storm burned out the large armature at the town's electric light plant. For a time, "a ball of fire as large as a stove pipe hat danced around the dynamos." The house lights returned just as people were getting out the oil lamps they kept in reserve. But the city was without streetlights for a week.[2] Many graphic accounts documented how quickly and horribly a locomotive wheel could slice through the human body and how imperfectly the movement of these weighty behemoths was coordinated with the comings and goings of their tiny human "masters."[3] A Dodge City resident, unfamiliar with modern machines and with imperfect vision, visited the Copeland Hotel in Topeka in 1906.

Inside, he walked through an open elevator door, not realizing that there was no car there, and fell to his death through a dark shaft to the basement stories below.[4] Even the horse with machinery attached could be more dangerous than before. William Horton, fifteen years old, died in Ford County in June 1906. Searchers found his six-horse team standing still, with the boy pinned underneath a harrow, steel tines driven through his body and leg. He had gotten off the seat, perhaps to avoid the dust, and was walking between the harrow and the team when he lost his footing and the machine rolled on. A reporter noted, "A glance told the story of terrible suffering and struggle." The boy dug a hole with his hands trying to escape but was unsuccessful.[5]

The typical mode in describing machinery, however, was a paean filled with hyperbole. In 1898, the Boyd & Getty implement yard in Larned exhibited the "celebrated" Jones steel header and binder, manufactured by the Piano Manufacturing Company of Chicago. "It is easily adjusted, light running, strong and can be operated by a ten-year old boy with perfect ease. . . . Every piece is made for its place after scientific calculation."[6] The *Liberal News* editorialized in 1907:

> Western Kansas is about the only place where this power method can be a great success. Out here the plows may run along with no obstruction, save the roots of the Buffalo grass and the occasional soap weed plant. There are no steep grades to climb, no trees, nor stumps, nor rocks. The surface is smooth and if the engine is sufficiently large it will pull a gang plow, a disc, and a harrow and do all the work at one pull through the field. It does not take long for a farmer to plow all the ground that he wishes to put to crop and he will then have plenty of time to come to town and loaf around for a while.[7]

That the human being was in control of the machines, directing them to progressive ends, was in no doubt among the denizens of the redeemed desert of Western Kansas.

But it was not only farm machines that fascinated. Who could resist the movies? These were instituted at Larned in 1900 when the women at the Presbyterian church showed a "moving picture" at the opera house using Thomas Edison's latest Kinescope. "The pictures are large and clear, and do not vibrate or flicker."[8] Just as compelling was the automobile, a machine that influenced the world in ways that only a little earlier would have been unimaginable. And there was a host of other amazing machines, coming one after another in rapid succession. A generation ago, wrote a Garden City man in 1897,

Windmills on display, Finney County Fair, 1894 (courtesy of Kansas State Historical Society)

there were no sewing machines; no steam machinery; no motor cars; no Lucifer matches; no pneumatic cycles; no phonograph; no typewriting machines; no pneumatic tired vehicles; no electric lights; no Pullman cars[;] . . . no 20 knot torpedo boats; no free education; no breech loading guns[;] . . . no lady cyclists[;] . . . no triple expansion engines; no refrigerators; no free libraries; no telephones; no telegraph; no perfecting presses.[9]

What marvels would the next generation bring?

At the Finney County fairs held at Garden City in the mid-1890s, there was a clear indication of some of the changes science and technology would bring to the High Plains. In October 1894, at the second annual fair, there was a merry-go-round and an exhibition of irrigation machines. "It does not take much of a stretch of the imagination," wrote a visitor, "to imagine himself at the World's Fair viewing the City of Windmills." The Aermotor Company of Chicago had three of its windmills on the grounds. A two-and-a-half-inch Shulman & Dickinson "Wonder" pump on display could raise 125 gallons of water a minute, 27 feet above the ground. An Ideal Windmill with a 12-foot diameter wheel ran an 8-inch Frizell pump, designed and built by E. E. Frizell, one of the most successful politicians and entrepreneurs in Larned. Frizell had turned old Ft. Larned into a ranch, and there he employed for irrigating alfalfa the kind of technology he was selling to others. Fairbanks, Morse & Co. of Kansas City had a large exhibit of pumps, gas engines, tanks, scales, and windmills. Their No. 3 Centrifugal pump, run by a three-and-a-half horsepower engine, cost 45 cents a day to operate and could pump 650 gallons per minute. There were two 8-inch suction pumps, one run by a gasoline engine and the other by a 10-foot Eclipse windmill.[10] The next year, crowds were larger and so were the exhibits. The Kansas City Hay Press Company had three centrifugal pumps working that year, operated by a Weber 12-horsepower gas engine and throwing 2,000 gallons a minute from a pond. The Perkins Windmill Company of Mishawaka, Indiana, was there, with Mr. Perkins himself present to explain things. A Crane mill operated a pump at a complete miniature farm. The Worthington steam pump handled 1,200 gallons a minute and had been extensively tested in pumping water from the holds of ocean vessels. A Wichita firm exhibited a windmill called the "Governor." The United States Water and Steam Supply Company had numerous examples of its work.[11] The report was that at these events the machinery exhibits drew a larger crowd than the race track, "a thing doubtless before unheard of at an agricultural fair."[12] The photos of the scene show a city of windmills along the banks of the diminished Arkansas River. It appeared that all the powers of American civilization were assembled in one place to address the challenges of the land.

The irrigation convention held in concert with the 1895 fall fair and concentrating on science and economics more than on technology must have seemed almost beside the point compared to this riot of machinery. However, F. D. Coburn, the secretary of the Kansas State Board of Agriculture, made some prescient points at the meeting. He emphasized that the ultimate solutions, whether they employed irrigation technology or any of the other gifts of the modern world, had to be controlled, applied, and largely financed in the region itself, and mostly by private, for-profit enterprise, initiated by business people in Western Kansas communities. Western Kansans should not rely on Washington or Topeka nor be "subject to the whims of managers, nor defaults of corporations nor watercourses." They must not wait on utopian plans "to divert the Missouri river a thousand miles out of its course and make it climb twelve hundred feet in the air in order that it may irrigate their farms in western Kansas."

A key to this local strategy would be the strength of individual cities and towns in the region, combined with their ability to cooperate when intraregional coordination over large spaces was indicated. Garden City, Coburn said, was an excellent example of a community that had made the best of its resources, environmental and mental, and by focus and specialization had made itself a giant in influence. In the matter of practical irrigation, Coburn considered Garden City "the Mecca of all who would learn it as applicable to a prairie country."[13]

Actually, the pattern he noted was temporary. The first years of the twentieth century may have been the last time that there was a real opportunity for small-town entrepreneurs in irrigation. Mr. Frizell was able to manufacture and sell pumps successfully in the region in 1895. But by 1910, when Colby put in a waterworks, the contractors were English Iron Works, Kansas City; English Tool and Supply Company, Kansas City; United Iron Works, Iola; B. R. Electric Company, Kansas City; H. H. Alvis, Dallas; T. C. Brooks and Son, Jackson, Michigan—not a Western Kansas firm among them.[14] There was not much question that Kansas City itself was passing on technology developed in still larger and more easterly or westerly cities.

The latter-day role of Western Kansas towns was to import rather to invent—to adapt and adopt machinery and techniques that largely came from elsewhere. The sod house disappeared. In its place came fireproof brick blocks and paved streets, waterworks, electric plants, opera houses, libraries, and excellent schools. It all happened as the towns instituted new strategies and money flowed.

As time would prove, much of the positive change was simply another swing of the climatic cycle, upward this time, though with the usual fits and starts, which the deus ex machina intensified. *Webster's Third International Dictionary* defines that Latin phrase (literally "a god from the machine") as "a person or thing that appears . . . suddenly and unexpectedly and provides an artificial or contrived solution to an apparently insoluble difficulty." Indeed, this time the god was surrounded by machinery—literally. That the intervention was spectacular and beneficent was obvious. That it was "artificial" or "contrived" was not at first clear. And, as always, that it was temporary in a world that remained mutable in the extreme was the hardest lesson of all to absorb. When the engines on the new flour mill at Hays began to move in December 1908, the manager, swelled with pride, challenged heaven itself. He bragged, "While the celebrated mill of the gods ground exceedingly fine, it hadn't a 'look in' in competition with the new Hays mill, because the modern structure would turn out 1000 barrels of the finest flour on earth, while the old gods were fixing up a ten cent grist."[15]

J. R. Connelly, the owner and editor of the *Colby Free Press*, made the point about endemic cycles in 1915 while serving in Congress from the 6th District. "The Kansas farmer is right now in the saddle," he wrote, "but he should not lose his proper perspective in the maze of flattery that is coming his way. He has lived here long enough to know that the tide of prosperity is to no one an even-flowing stream." Connelly thought it his duty to point out that farmers in Western Kansas had "in the past twenty years drunk deeply many times of the dregs of adversity" and doubtless would again. It should therefore be a habit with them to make investments in such a way that "it will help them over the rough places in the road that are sure to come somewhere and may be just around the bend."[16]

Those were words by the wise and for the wise, and there is evidence that more were listening than once had. Still, the stimulus of a major positive trend was too much for the self-control of many who understandably thought that the latest wave was the one that would finally carry them over all shallows present or future. A 1901 ad for the Aermotor windmill had a fine lithographic illustration and boasted that the machine had fifty-five patents: "We make a windmill that regulates itself; that calls for no attention, save oiling. In a zephyr or a gale the Aermotor pump maintains the same speed. A simple attachment stops it automatically when tank is full and starts it when the water lowers. And it lasts. Durability is of enormous importance in a wheel that may revolve 200,000 times daily." Many sent for the Aermotor booklet from Chicago.[17] Connelly was against voting bonds for the Colby waterworks and electric plant when they passed in 1910 on the grounds that they were a needless luxury, but once the plant went in he was one of the first to install electric lights.[18] City services grew, isolation diminished, culture thrived, and progress was material and obvious to all. There was little room for a naysayer or a "kicker" when it looked as though, upon the backs of the regular, durable machines, boom times had returned.

The statistics told a story, this time as positive as the 1890s data was sad. By 1910, Western Kansas recovered its peak boom population: 630,389, compared with 629,982 in 1888. In assessed valuation there was no comparison. That number had been only about $150,000,000 in 1888 for the region and less than $130,000,000 in 1898. In 1910, it was $1,252,206,309—a remarkable gain. Sedgwick County alone in 1910 had a valuation of almost $110,000,000, about 85 percent of the value for all Western Kansas in 1898.[19] Watching the details of how it happened was stimulating.

There was an expression in prosperous times that the world was on wheels. It seemed in the first decade of the twentieth century that that was literally coming to pass. Farmers were "early adapters" of technology that eased their work or speeded their lives. To Western Kansans, perhaps the most revolutionary of these, in their widespread and deep effect, economic and social, were the rolling kind—the automobile, the gasoline tractor, and the combine. The gasoline tractor did not, however, arrive in the region until about 1908, and for a long time was an awkward hybrid, sharing more with the steam tractors of an earlier era than with more maneuverable machines of the 1920s. The combination harvester-thresher, or combine, which was

John Erickson and his pride and joy, Russell County (courtesy of Kansas State Historical Society, Halbe Collection)

to have such an impact on the length and labor requirements of harvest, did not appear in numbers until 1918.[20] By that time the automobile was nearly standard equipment.

When Ira Thompson's one-cylinder Oldsmobile arrived at the Rexford depot in far northwest Kansas in 1903 it was a sensation. Everyone in town was there and wanting a ride in the two-passenger car. Extras often rode backward behind the seat with their feet hanging down, though on the grade this extra load would nearly stall the engine. The car tipped over at least once, but the enthusiastic townspeople just set the light thing back on its tires, and it journeyed on.[21]

Time and familiarity hardly diminished the magic. "We washed the dishes," wrote Alpha Hansen about a family evening in Logan in 1907, "and spent the rest of the evening singing, playing, and talking 'automobiles.' That is the boys did."[22] A year later, she recorded that her father, who was an incorporator of the Logan Electric Light & Power Company, studied electricity day and night "and says we'll wash, iron, sew, and fan with electricity." Her brother Dane, meanwhile, spent a great deal of time with *Motor Age* magazine "and talks about cylinders, hoods, etc."[23] Autos were tremendously popular, making a mockery of the 1900 claim that the horse was in Kansas to stay.[24] It was said in Thomas County in 1916 that the county could fit its entire population of 4,000 into the 613 cars owned by local people.[25] Automobile mass excursions around the region became as great a feature as the Sunday drive. In May 1916, 87 cars carrying 400 people from the area around Quinter in Gove County took off for a tour of their region. The Quinter brass band went along, and all were treated wherever they stopped to a municipal tour and a dinner with elaborate speechmaking.[26] That fall, Rooks County people came en masse to the Ellis County fair in a "monster parade" of 350 cars. Trego County joined them with 50 cars, and other counties came with caravans. Wrote the amazed editor at Hays: "The scene of a thousand automobiles parked in one enclosure is something one can't easily forget, and speaks eloquently for the resources and prosperity of the people who can bring the cars."[27] Such tours were promotional tricks, and they were excuses to drive.

The teething pains of applying this machine to daily life were taken with good humor. The *Hugoton Hermes* reported in 1902 that its experiment with automobile mail delivery between Hugoton and Hartland was not working well. "This was expected," the editor at Liberal commented. "There is too much sand in that part of the country for such a delicate machine."[28] Two doctors heading overland from Garden City to Syracuse in their car in 1904 had "a series of mishaps and trials that those who go about in devil wagons have every reason to expect." After pushing their machine through sandy places, lifting it over ditches, and pushing it up hills, they abandoned their car and took the train.[29]

Reliability and functionality, however, improved rapidly. In 1907, Larned organized an automobile club, having among its goals to "encourage prudence and care in the driving of automobiles[,] . . . to promote good roads," and to prevent "illegal, reckless, or careless driving."[30] In Thomas County that year, cars were popular with real estate dealers. They could take a buyer out twenty miles, show him land, and have him back in three hours. With a team of horses that was an all day project.[31] Ness City heralded the arrival of the "real thing" in automobiles. Prior to 1907, it had been "content with a couple of wheezy, uncertain machines that either went or stopped, as the spell might happen to be upon them, but now it looks a little as if the fever might take hold in earnest."[32] Garden City bragged in 1908 that autos were looked upon there "as playthings, and many wealthy parents buy them for their children as toys." They were "so thick here that often the streets are blockaded, and if nearly everybody was not riding in one there would be serious danger of people getting run over."[33] When a Topeka reporter visited Liberal in 1910, he reported seventy-five cars, including a big Winton six. "Everyone here is a chauffer. Everyone talks the language of the clutch and sparker." That was only appropriate, he thought: "This is a country of distances and level roads and the auto is as much of a necessity now as the horse used to be in pioneer days."[34]

Not that auto driving ceased right away to be an adventure. Three brothers—Eb, Clyde, and Harry Tow—took their wives on an outing in a Rambler near Larned in the summer of 1908. They were heading for Stafford County, but at the county line, Eb, who was driving, wanted to slow down, but "by mistake he put his foot into the reverse thingumbob instead of the slow-up doo-dad. The result was that he 'pied' the internal workings of the machine in a hopeless manner." The men worked for an hour on repairs and then left a road "strewn with enough parts of automobile to make a couple of new machines" and walked back to town.[35] By contrast, E. E. Frizell, taking Senator Chester Long to his ranch on the Pawnee that same month, was making a steady 35 miles an hour over dirt roads, until the senator advised that 20 would be a great plenty.[36] But whether flying or "pieing," the automobile was a must.

Charles Harger, of Abilene, Kansas, writing in the *Saturday Evening Post* in 1908, claimed, "A new buyer has entered the automobile field, the well-to-do farmer." Instead of coming to town once a year to pay his taxes and newspaper subscription, the farmer with a car came into the county seat once a week, patronizing the merchants and the culture there. He went through stages with his car, Harger said. At first he was nervous and could not control the machine, sometimes running through a barn door or into a barbed-wire fence. Then he was curious, wanting to take the thing apart and find out how it worked. This stage could be frustrating for car dealers and repair people. Finally, the farmer was satisfied to leave the car repair to the experts and enjoy it as an appliance. He satisfied himself, too, that time was money and that the car was more than a toy for pleasure. At that point he was happy with it and with himself.[37]

Automobiles, however, were not the only application for the gasoline engine and modern machinery that thrilled regional residents. More to the point of using technology to create the wealth that would allow them to "mess about" in cars was the use of windmill and engine-driven pumps to operate irrigation plants. The automobile was a universal desideratum, a world phenomenon into which the Kansas High Plains were swept. Irrigation, by contrast, seemed directed specifically at the problems of arid regions, a group that it was long past time Western Kansas should join in its thinking.

P. I. Lancaster, speaking to a Sherman County Farmers' Institute in 1895, put the case vividly:

Irrigation is our quickest way out, our surest way out, our only way out. [The regional developers were] late listening to reason. We have wasted eight years of our lives. . . . We have wasted one-fourth of our manhood chasing an *ignis fatuus*—a chimera—living under the delusion that Sherman county was not in arid America; that corn and wheat and oats and barley would return us from year to year bountiful harvests of golden grain; that all we needed was land, more land. [People in Western Kansas had farmed] as if we were yet in Illinois or Missouri. . . . Extensive farming it is called. Expensive and crazy farming I call it. Oh, yes, sow your 200 or 400 acres in wheat every spring and reap a harvest of aid flour every winter!

Irrigation on the new model, tapping and pumping the sheet water in the underflow, would not "make George Gould envy us our Sherman county farms," but it would work.[38]

Observers thought Western Kansas should have learned from the boom and bust that it was semiarid. This fact, a Larned editor noted, had long been known to "stockmen and Indians, but denied by greedy land agents, and discredited by eager and hopeful settlers." When aridity reasserted itself, the superstructure of the regional economy collapsed: "All the nebulous industrial, educational, and railroad projects suddenly descended from the sublime to the ridiculous."[39]

There was no question that there were some long shots in the irrigation realm, too good perhaps to be true. Most of these involved exploiting the easiest sources of water by the least expensive means, i.e., river water or the shallow underflow, by means of simple gravity or wind power.

Cheyenne Bottoms in Barton County, for example, was much publicized in the late 1890s as a natural "hole" in the shortgrass that could be easily turned into a combination reservoir and game preserve by diverting the waters of the Arkansas River. The low place was 12 miles long and 6 miles wide, a natural basin covering about 40,000 acres. Since the land under it was described as a "dreadful gumbo," not much good farmland would be lost.[40] An observer enthused, "It looks as though the original intention of the Creator had been to make a lake there, but, finding he had neglected to furnish the country with water, changed his mind and left it as it was, just a common, ordinary hole in the ground."

A Wichita reporter was skeptical, though he said it was a "great scheme." He thought that "when the tide of the Arkansas is turned into that hole, the water will disappear like a candidate's money on election day."[41] Modern environmental historians have shown that he was right. There were significant problems in the implementation, both environmental and economic. Cheyenne Bottoms eventually became a migratory bird refuge, but even that part of the mission was not so straightforward as originally imagined. The Kroen ditch project, 24 feet wide and 13 miles long, which did bring water from the Arkansas to the Bottoms in 1900, was remembered, wrote historian Douglas Harvey, "as a failure at best and to some as a full-blown scam."[42] It was certainly not, as promised, just the beginning of a series of projects that could create a 30-foot-deep lake and irrigate nearly a half million acres of land.[43]

Not the least of the problems for Cheyenne Bottoms and other "natural flow" ditch projects was the unpredictable flow of the Arkansas itself. In 1904, a Garden City man commented that the more Colorado irrigated, the more bleak simple-ditch irrigation looked for Kansas. Without some legal remedy in the future, "the Arkansas River in western Kansas will be perpetually dry, the winds will fill the bed of the river from bank to bank with sand." And who knew how long a legal remedy might require.

Kansas was the last state in the union (in 1945) to abandon the common law doctrine of riparian rights in favor of that of prior appropriation. Prior appropriation meant, as the activity of Colorado demonstrated, that the first user had an absolute right to as much water as it could use, instead of respecting the old doctrine that it had no right permanently to interrupt the flow to downstream users.[44] "It will require the wisdom of Solomon," the Garden City man noted, "to adjudicate the case without injury to any interests, unless the judges can discover more water."[45] Kansas wanted riparian rights doctrine applied to Colorado and prior appropriation to apply when it became its turn to draw water from the river. The decision in 1907 by the U.S. Supreme Court in the case *Kansas v. Colorado* upheld neither doctrine but came up with a theory of equity that evaluated damages and let the courts determine fairness of distribution. Therefore, for Kansas, the legal issue of water rights to the Arkansas River was ongoing as the river and the regional economy changed.[46]

Despite this water problem, it was tempting to pursue the "easy" possibility of reopening the Arkansas River lateral ditches that had been expensively built during the 1880s. There was a major project in 1909 to clear and reopen the Eureka Canal in the area of Dodge City. The Eureka, nearly 90 miles long, had been constructed with capital from Asa Soule. It had been owned for a time by an English syndicate and then purchased by the Arkansas Valley Irrigation Company for a redevelopment, rumored to be costing as much as $1 million.[47]

A Dodge City newspaper called the Eureka dredging project "One of the Big Undertakings of the Present Age" but admitted there were difficulties: "The Arkansas valley, the Arkansas River and the Arkansas underflow is a perplexing affair altogether." The company reopening the Eureka knew better than to depend on the flow of the river altogether, but it was still eager to tap some sort of flow to save the expense of extensive pumping. It proposed, therefore, to create a sump 100 feet wide and 5 miles long, which would take advantage of the natural elevation drop in Western Kansas of about 7 feet per mile toward the east to tap the underflow. The sump would be almost 60 feet deep on the west end and only 16 feet at the east. The engineers counted on the extensive underground water in the underflow to run into the sump, just as a river would run into a ditch. Then they would, with minimal pumping, transfer water from this sump reservoir into the Eureka ditch for distribution to area farmers. The engineer on the project, John Traylor, had studied irrigation projects all over North and Central America and thought this method was the most feasible for this region. The estimate was that the project would take three years to complete.[48] Its modest degree of success is indicated by the fact that 50 miles of improved Eureka Canal was sold by the Arkansas Valley Irrigation Company in 1916 to a Great Bend man for only $150,000.[49]

The more study and experiment there was, the more it became clear that the seemingly simple solutions to using the slope of the land and the flow of the water to irrigate areas downstream or downgrade were impractical. A man from Lane County wrote Secretary Coburn of the Kansas State Board of Agriculture in 1907 asking why the natural slope of the land there could not be employed to use underground water. The water in Lane County was about 65 feet deep, and potential irrigators there thought that pumping it would be too expensive. Why not, therefore, dig a well 15 miles west of the area to be irrigated and connect it with a pipe 2 feet in diameter to the lower area to the east into which water would flow by gravity? Coburn, a considerable scientist and technician, sent a detailed reply through the columns of the *Kansas Farmer*. Surely, he wrote, the correspondent was not thinking of opening a ditch in which to lay such a pipe. "Without making figures it is readily conceded that the cost of such an undertaking would be so much like that of the Panama Canal as to be prohibitive." Even using some sort of siphon, the pipe would have to be buried 45 feet deep for a considerable distance, as there was a limit to how high water could be raised by the siphon method. Then there was the cost of the pipe. A suitable 24-inch pipe would weigh 200 pounds per foot or 7,920 tons for the 79,200 feet needed. The cost for the pipe alone, not counting joints and labor, would be over $200,000. Such a project might irrigate 1,000 acres for ordinary crops, but the income from selling the water would not even pay the interest on such an investment.[50]

Some sort of gravity flow continued, however, to be attractive. There were artesian wells, particularly in Meade County, that brought water to the surface through natural geological processes. These were developed successfully for small alfalfa operations in the early twentieth century but were not extensive enough to have very much impact on agriculture in the region.[51] There was a suggestion at Garden City in 1903 that an artesian effect might be created by placing a galvanized iron dam across the Arkansas River, extending to bedrock and forcing the entire underflow to the surface. But no one seemed to understand the costs or geology of this well enough to proceed.[52] Large reservoirs were considered. Lake McKinnie in Finney County was the largest artificial lake in Kansas in 1908. It was 6 miles long and half a mile wide and cost $350,000.[53]

If natural flow alone would not do, perhaps there was some renewable cheap source of energy for pumps. Wind power was the obvious application, but in 1904 something more exotic reached the planning stage. An article in *Scientific American* that year described an "automatic engine running by the heat of the sun," which the Solar Motor Company proposed testing at Tempe, Arizona, and in Western Kansas. The engine used a disk of reflecting glass more than 30 feet in diameter, consisting of nearly 2,000 small mirrors arranged to concentrate the sun at a central point. At that point was suspended a boiler, 13 feet long and holding 100 gallons of water. The solar concentrator melted copper in a short time, and a pole of wood thrust into the "magic circle" flamed like a match. From the boiler, steam went to the engine through flexible bronze tubes. "Everything about the motor is automatic," a Dodge City reporter said, "even to the oiling, and it is made to run all day without the intervention of man." The reporter thought one of these engines would be running irrigation pumps in Western Kansas before very long and that the "continual sunshine" there would create a perfect application.[54] There is no evidence a field test was ever conducted.

Windmills seemed more practical, particularly when used where the underflow was shallow to fill reservoirs. Windmill use in Kansas is found in the 1850s, and factory-made steel windmills were common around Dodge City by the late 1870s. The 1890s windmill experiments around Garden City, however, were innovative in the sense that they applied the mills not just to filling stock tanks but also to raising considerable quantities of water to fill reservoirs and to irrigate crops.

As noted, the Finney County fairs of the period were full of windmill and pumping equipment, partly of local manufacture. Historian T. Lindsay

Baker documents sixty-five Kansas windmill manufacturers, fifty-eight of them active before 1930 and twenty-one of those located in Western Kansas.[55] L. L. Doty, Israel L. Diesem, S. Schulman, and Dr. Walter Carter of Garden City had been active in experiments with attaching centrifugal pumps to windmills since the early 1890s. All were, at best, inspired amateurs. Diesem was the Garden City postmaster and a local coal and ice dealer; Carter was the fire chief; and Schulman, who marketed his windmill plunger pump design to the Dempster Manufacturing Company of Beatrice, Nebraska, was born in Russia, a tailor's son.[56] They did, however, have considerable success within the modest range such efforts could produce. In 1893, there were 55 irrigation wells in Western Kansas. There were 1,241 in 1895—96 percent wind powered. Admittedly, the wind pumps could only recover relatively shallow water, drilling technology of the time would only work well in sandy soils, and the earth reservoirs were subject to leakage and rapid evaporation. But it was a start. The claim was that a farmer in the 1890s in Kansas could produce as much profit on one acre of irrigated land as on the remaining 159 acres of his quarter section.[57] By 1904, a visiting writer researching an article for *Review of Reviews* reported that Garden City presented a "sylvan scene," with windmill-driven wells reaching the underflow at 16 to 20 feet and costing not more than $200 each. The attached reservoirs could be used for raising German carp as well as holding irrigation water.[58]

Diesem was an active publicist and lobbyist. He was a member of the Kansas State Board of Agriculture from 1892 to 1918 and president from 1911 to 1913. For seventeen years, he was president of the Finney County Agricultural Society. Starting with the irrigation of Stevens Park in Garden City in 1890 by windmills and pumps, he and his cohorts branched out.[59] Diesem was a perennial representative from Kansas to national meetings on irrigation and as a speaker on the subject was in demand across the state. He addressed a two-day convention of the Western Kansas Irrigation Association in December 1903. There he argued that private initiative needed government help, preferably federal financial help, to test the proposition that the underflow could be tapped economically for irrigation. Earlier that year, Finney County had defeated a proposed bond issue for irrigation on the grounds that there were too many unanswered questions about it. It was not likely that private capital in general could be attracted without more information. Millions had been paid into the U.S. Treasury for the land in Western Kansas, Diesem said, and it was "certainly but fair to ask that some of it be returned to this section of Kansas through the irrigation fund."[60]

Public study and investment and private development in Western Kansas took nearly parallel courses, both peaking about 1906. The federal initiative arose from the national political focus on irrigation to "reclaim" western arid land following the passage of the Newlands Reclamation Act in 1902.[61] The private development centered around the potential for the cultivation of sugar beets as a high-profit, extensive, irrigated crop that required both new technology and modified farming methods. Both employed Finney County as a test focus.

Late in 1901, as the Newlands Act made its way through Congress, Western Kansans began making suggestions about possible uses for federal money to irrigate their region. The *Globe-Republican* in Dodge City printed part of Theodore Roosevelt's speech on federal reservoirs.[62] The superintendent of the Ft. Hays Experiment Station advised the Kansas governor in 1903 that it would be a good idea to entertain delegates and reporters traveling through Kansas on their way to the National Irrigation Congress at Ogden, Utah, as there was federal money to be had.[63] Kansas supported several delegates to that conference. F. Dumont Smith, a Kinsley attorney, wrote the governor that there were two reasons for him to go: "First to get a share of the Govt. money for Kansas work and second to block any effort Colorado may make to pass a resolution against our case."[64]

Victor Murdock, congressman from the Eighth District of Kansas, thought that local interests must be clear and united if Kansas were to attract federal money. He noted that the departments in Washington were not much interested in Kansas irrigation. This was due, he thought, to unusual rainfall there during the settlement period and a consequent lateness in waking up to the fact that it was part of the subhumid West.[65] Murdock sent a letter to the Ogden conference pointing out that eastern and Western Kansas were linked in one commonwealth and that irrigation was possible in Western Kansas. "The true pioneer," he wrote, "never played a craven before a hard problem."[66] Murdock wrote the next year that people now knew the Plains and could "distinguish what is practical, and are studying actual conditions. . . . The leading spirits of Western Kansas are deeply in earnest and with governmental assistance will win."[67]

Early feedback from Washington was negative. W. G. Russell, a hydrographer for the U.S. Geological Survey, visited the southwest part of Kansas early in 1904. He concluded that this was not a good section in which to build a large federal reservoir. There were no topographic sites in the region for a dam, and both the Arkansas and Cimarron rivers had sandy beds, erratic water supplies, and broad bottomlands on both sides.[68] Congressman Murdock referred several letters from Western Kansas to the Geological Survey, notably ones from E. R. Thorpe of Lakin and from George W. Watson ("Colonel Underflow") of Kinsley, suggesting once again the idea of using dams constructed on a low grade to draw out waters percolating to the surface and thus avoiding pumping.[69] These were filed with no comment. The *Garden City Herald* concluded that there was little hope for federal aid and that the region "must work out its own salvation in its own way. The prospect is not encouraging, but why should the people of western Kansas care a rap. The problem confronting us is not insurmountable."[70] Attention in the national media directed to Kansas agriculture seemed to turn to traditional crops on dry land. "The man who goes to western Kansas to build a home," said a writer for the *Saturday Evening Post* in 1904, "need not expect a fortune in a day, nor that he will escape hard work."[71]

But shortly there were better signs on the federal front. In the spring came news that A. E. Wright would come to Western Kansas from Washington to collect data and to study pumps already working there.[72] In September, engineer Charles Schlichter of the new U.S. Reclamation Service conducted an investigation of the Western Kansas underflow and reported that the quantity of groundwater was greater than he had expected. "The underground drainage in these regions is so enormous," he wrote, "and the freedom of passage of water through the gravels so great that there is no surplus water left to form surface streams or to form a perennial supply for the Arkansas River."[73] Schlichter rejected the idea of using the slope to extract water, but thought federal funding might go into an experiment with larger pumping stations than had ever been tried.[74] There was no truth to the rumor, local papers emphasized, that Colorado was about to annex Western Kansas as a way to settle the inter-state water suit.[75]

I. L. Diesem continued to emphasize to the Western Kansas Irrigation Association, of which he was president, that pressure from the National Irrigation Congress over the past fourteen years had resulted in the Newlands Act and that it would be the activity of local organizations that would bring the money to their regions. "To this end," he said, "let us be a unit. We have the soil, we have the climate, and we have the water underneath—all we ask is for the United States government to show us how to get it on top of the soil in large quantities." Association members, including local real estate magnate George Finnup, took guests to the best irrigating plants in the region.

The *Garden City Herald* printed Schlichter's report in full in spring 1905 describing a government irrigation plant to be located just east of the Deerfield station on the ATSF railroad at the head of one of the revitalized 1880s ditches, now called the Farmers' Canal. The cost was first estimated at $250,000, or about $25 per acre irrigated. The federal investment was a loan, to be repaid by farmers in ten annual installments without interest. At the

Smoky Hill crossing, 1910 (courtesy of Kansas State Historical Society)

end of the ten years, the irrigation plant was to be turned over to the association that owned the ditch "free of cost and in first-class condition." No person could obtain rights in excess of 160 acres, as it was said that the reclamation act intended that "the small owner shall profit from government works and not speculators or corporations."

The specifications were impressive. There were a series of pumping stations—twenty-five were planned—each including ten bored wells operated by centrifugal pumps. There would be one 300-foot-deep well. The others would be about 40 feet deep. The pumps were connected by suction pipes to a No. 9 vertical shaft and powered by 25-horsepower vertical DC electric motors. The motors in turn were driven from a central power plant with three 250-horsepower gasoline engines. Pumping for 150 days during the irrigating season, the complex could provide 30,000 acre-feet for crops. The station employed a mechanic at $1,200 a year, two assistant engineers for five months each year, and three operators each paid $1.75 a day. The annual operating expense was estimated at $18,000, or about $2 per year per acre served.[76] At a total annual cost to the farmer of $5 per acre and the potential to grow higher-yielding, better-paying crops, it seemed a potentially profitable proposition. This plant, constructed by the federal government in 1905 and operated under later private ownership until 1940, has been called "the first instance of large-scale irrigation in the High Plains."[77]

Most regarded the government plant as a "Western Kansas victory." The *Liberal News* editor, however, commented that it did not take a genius to figure out how to irrigate when the water was only a few feet beneath the surface. It would take something more than that to make a change in agriculture in the majority of the region, which was upland.[78] And there was no question that Kansas was a sideshow in the considerable spending being done by the Reclamation Service.

Still, the technology of it all was thrilling. So was the methodology. A Wichita reporter wrote:

> A comparison should mentally be formed in the reader's mind between the government project and the old hap-hazard way of doing business. The government project, with its rigid restrictions, wise regulations, and constant and even supply of water, is infinitely superior to the old way, whereby there might be an abundance of water one season; none the next. Again there was always bickering between users; and the danger that one user would be careless and take more water than he needed, to the detriment of the man next below him.[79]

The experiment station at Ft. Hays put in its own small version of the government plant, using a 12-horsepower traction engine to power a 4-inch vertical centrifugal pump.[80] It appeared that the future for irrigation was with large machinery—with diesel and electric power—and not with gravity or the breezes.

Simultaneous with the federal initiative, and perhaps stimulated partly by it, was an escalation in private corporate activity, which not only promised large-scale irrigation, but also imaginative new uses of electric power, new railroad lines, a new crop, a new means of farm management, a new source and technique of using farm labor, and a Western Kansas manufacturing industry of considerable scale. All of it was predicated on the old dream of creating a sugar industry in the region and upon the new possibility that sugar beet cultivation and the production of table sugar from those beets could succeed where sorghum sugar growing and extraction had failed in the 1880s.[81]

There was talk of establishing a beet sugar refinery in Kansas as early as 1892.[82] George Swink from Rocky Ford, Colorado, visited Garden City in the late 1890s, urging local farmers to try sugar beets to take advantage of markets and federal subsidies.[83] In the late 1890s, the chemical department of the Kansas State Experiment Station at Manhattan began analyzing beets and providing seed to farmers furnished through the U.S. Department of Agriculture. In 1899, however, only forty-seven Kansas farmers requested the seed. The *Kansas Farmer* concluded that states in higher latitudes were better suited for the crop. Kansas beets tested had a sugar content of about 10 percent, as compared with 17 to 22 percent for the Colorado product and about 17 percent for those grown in California. Sorghum sugar had about 10 percent sugar content, which was a reason it failed to compete. The *Kansas Farmer* warned against "hasty and ill-considered efforts" to establish sugar beet factories in the state. The history of the sorghum sugar imbroglio was not "so far into the past that its value as an object lesson is entirely lost."[84]

True to form, however, the movers at Garden City agitated for something more. In December 1900, there was a meeting there chaired by John Ballinger, who had toured a factory run by the American Beet Sugar Company at Rocky Ford, Colorado, and was impressed that the success there could be replicated in Finney County.[85] "Can we afford to neglect an opportunity that will bring several thousands of people to the county," wrote a local editor, "and which will distribute thousands of dollars annually among the farmers?"[86]

The state joined the movement in 1901 when the legislature passed a payment of $1 a ton on all Kansas sugar beets containing over 12 percent sugar.[87]

That year, 75 Western Kansas farmers collected on 1,800 tons of product.[88] Average profit per acre was over $17.00.[89] Here, some regional papers began to think, was a use for the irrigation canals and the new pump technology more promising than alfalfa or cantaloupes.[90] One editor wrote:

> A tenant farmer in the east who pays cash rent for his farm can take the same money, come to western Kansas, buy his land, erect an irrigation plant, and have a home of his own. The poultry, butter, eggs, and garden stuff, small berries and fruit that he can produce will keep his family, then by cultivating a few acres to sugar beets he can lay aside each year a sum that will soon place him in the company of the nabobs of Kansas.[91]

Secretary Coburn of the State Board of Agriculture claimed in 1902, "The sugar beet has come to stay in Kansas and in a few years it will be grown in all the counties of the southwest, where the water can be turned on."[92]

There were, however, obstacles. The American Beet Sugar Company of Rocky Ford would buy beets from Kansas, and it appeared that beets with decent sugar content could be raised. But Congressman Murdock learned when he went to Washington in 1903, having promised the farmers "out on the edge of things" that he would do something for them in the field of irrigation, that it was not so easily accomplished. When he mentioned irrigation for the region in Washington, he found government officials "as cold as a dog's nose." The objection he heard constantly was that Kansans were not "temperamentally irrigators" and that there was just enough water "to make them lean heavily on the mercy of God and shy at the approach of the water tax collector."[93]

Agricultural writers agreed that "Western Kansas farmers have much to learn about beet raising." They tended to cultivate too many acres, and they were not used to the hand labor required to thin and weed the crop and to harvest it quickly before it deteriorated.[94] The Kansas farmer had been "spoiled" for handwork, one observer wrote. "He wants to sit on a gang plow, a riding cultivator, a self binder, and have a piece of machinery do his work."[95] Farmers in Western Kansas did not take kindly, it was said, to "sown-on-hands-and-knees work" such as the "peasants do in European countries where the sugar beet grows."[96] "It would be hard to find a more unpromising crew for beet hands," wrote Mrs. Henry Block of Syracuse, Kansas, in 1904, "than the average cattle ranch affords. When it comes to getting down on 'bended knee' and thinning beets the average cowboy will not 'stay hitched' to his job. It is not his idea of dignified employment."[97] Then of course there was the necessity for irrigation, the complications and capital intensity of its technology, and the current paucity of irrigation infrastructure.

The year 1904, however, was good for beets. The crop was nine times as large as the poor crop of 1903 and exceeded the 4,250-ton crop of 1902.[98] The Kansas State Board of Agriculture ran special articles on the "infant industry" of sugar beets in its 1903–1904 and 1905–1906 biennial reports. However, no statistics for the crop were included in the regular definitive listings of that organization until the 1907–1908 report, when perhaps the organization recognized sugar beets as a crop that would stay around for a time. Before that it was a curiosity in the Kansas commercial crop mix, on a par with the potato.

Early in 1905, there was a talk in Garden City by Professor Lloyd of the American Beet Sugar Company of Rocky Ford and a tour of D. C. Holcomb's impressive irrigation plant west of Garden City. Holcomb's operation had a Corliss steam engine of 60 horsepower. It could deliver 6,000 gallons a minute into a ditch but was limited by the 4,000-gallon-an-hour capacity of the well that fed it. Holcomb owned a thousand acres, which he expected to irrigate. The plant cost $7,000, but Holcomb and the visitors thought it was well worth it.[99] There was serious study of Diesem's windmills and reservoirs and his record of crops raised and evaporation suffered. An engineer from Hungary published an article there on Diesem's innovations.[100]

In the summer of 1905, as the federal plant began construction at Deerfield, there came the announcement that a string of sugar beet factories were to be built with "Colorado money" in Kansas and Colorado, and that the first one would be at Garden City. Officials of the United States Sugar and Land Company had visited Western Kansas, examined the 1,600 acres then under beet cultivation, and made arrangements for future cultivation of 16,000 acres. They promised considerable investment in the improvement of ditches and pumping stations. It was an understatement for the *Garden City Herald* to note that this corporate move, along with the Reclamation Service project, would "make things lively" in the region. It recommended that farmers get behind the move, looking for their profits to successful irrigation and beet culture and not from any short-term speculative gains from sale of land at an unreasonably high price to the sugar company.[101]

Rumors abounded. The Missouri Pacific railroad might extend to Garden City from Scott City. The Santa Fe could build from Jetmore to Garden City and erect a depot in that town to be used also by the Missouri Pacific; Rock Island; Chicago Great Western; and Denver, Enid & Gulf. A Colorado syndicate had supposedly let a contract for an electric trolley line from Garden City to Lakin and would built a railroad itself to Leoti. Sugar company men supposedly had bought all the vacant residence and business lots in Garden City. The town presumably would have 5,000 new people by the spring of 1906, "and Main Street is to be built up solid clear to the hill on the north." Six million sheep, said the rumors, were to be fed on beet pulp and alfalfa in Finney County. "It is confidentially whispered in the barber shops that Garden City is sure of two new railroads, and when the informant was asked why they are coming here, he said, 'God knows, but it is a good place to light.'" The editor was skeptical. He hoped all the information was correct "and that all these things may come true, but this is the greatest country in the world to stir up air bubbles."[102]

Certainly not all the rumors were true, but it was no bubble either. In November, men set stakes south of St. John Street for the Garden City sugar beet factory, now estimated to cost $1 million. The architect's plans showed structures covering about three city blocks in length. There was a sewer survey from the factory site to the river through which the plant would draw the 6 million gallons a day for washing the beets.[103] Wrote Miss Gertrude Coburn, daughter of the secretary of the State Board of Agriculture:

> There are no busier nor more enthusiastic Kansans just now than the farmers in the Arkansas Valley beet region. Real-estate agents can scarcely find vehicles sufficient to accommodate the landseekers who arrive by every train, and the high prices offered for the cultivated land would seem tempting even to the most contented of the older settlers. . . . Beet profits have paid off mortgages, bought gasoline engines, sunk wells, built reservoirs, and paid for strong teams and larger wagons, improved machinery, and better housing.

Finney County, in 1905, harvested 500 acres of beets; Kearny County harvested 600 acres. The crop was around 10,000 tons.[104]

Speakers were hard-pressed for phrases to describe developments on the government and private fronts, which came so suddenly after so many years of talk. Diesem, in December 1905, held forth on the topic of irrigation and civilization: "The people will awaken to the realization of this transformation much sooner than the most sanguine expected." There would be irrigation plants not only in the Arkansas River Valley, but in the Pawnee, White Woman, and Smoky Hill Valleys. "You can travel through the Arkansas Valley," he noticed, "and see the stirring enterprise in whatever direction you may cast your eyes. New head gates, new ditches, new laterals, and old ones enlarged and cleaned."[105] Newspaper editors and college professors alike were commenting upon the phenomenon. W. Y. Morgan, editor of the *Hutchinson News*, wrote that this was no false boom but the real article.[106]

United States Sugar and Land Company beet processing plant, Garden City (courtesy of Kansas State Historical Society)

The year 1906 was a banner one in Finney County. Plans and specifications for the federal project appeared in March, with bidding at Chicago late in May.[107] A Garden City man wondered in April if the theologians had not made a mistake in locating the Garden of Eden in Asia rather than in the Arkansas River Valley. Land could still be purchased for $25 to $100 an acre, and farmers were making $100- to $300-an-acre profit yearly raising beets, cantaloupes, onions, fruits, and alfalfa. "There is," he claimed, "any amount of water."[108] Four canals—the Garden City Ditch, the Finney County Farmers' Canal, the Kearny County Farmers' Canal, and the Great Eastern Canal—were in operation in June. The sugar beet factory was under construction, as was the Reclamation Service pumping station.

The activity of the United States Sugar and Land Company was remarkable from any perspective. Garden City gave the company a bonus of $30,000 in bonds to build a factory that would take in 800 tons of beets a day and produce 8 tons of sugar. The main factory was 6 stories high and 273 feet long; the warehouse was 255 feet, and there were sheds 700 feet by 120 feet. Over 350 people worked construction at a wage of $2.25 a day. The company by June 1906 had contracted with farmers for 7,000 acres of beets at $5 a ton and furnished them with seeds from Germany at cost. The company did the drilling for irrigation if desired and took its pay as a share of the crop. In addition, the corporation bought massive amounts of land—over 30,000 acres by the fall of 1906. There was talk already of additional plants and of dividing the company acreage into tracts of 160 acres with improvements, which would then be leased to farmers on a percentage basis. An electric belt railroad line was to circulate around the company lands. Electric lines to the farms to run irrigation pumps were also part of the promises. The company pledged to operate for a 100-day season beginning in October, and during that time to make 20 million pounds of sugar packed into 200,000 bags. Said R. P. Davie, the general manager: "We have come to the Arkansas Valley to share the field with our neighbors."

The company talked about increasing the 8,000-ton annual regional beet production to 800,000 tons. "The sugar beet," Davie said, "is going to make the Arkansas Valley team [sic] with population."[109] Garden City gained 1,000 in population numbers in the year 1906. This was the largest percentage gain of any town in the state and was half of the total population figure for the town at the depth of the depression in 1895.

Early in September, the plant in test mode produced 73,000 bags in a week. It took 2,000 tons of steel to build the factory, 3 million bricks, 18,000 barrels of cement, and 15,000 yards of sand. The machinery weighed 3,000 tons, and the steam power was 2,900 horsepower.[110] "By the side of the Garden City mill," a Hutchinson man commented, "the biggest salt plant in the world (the Morton at Hutchinson) would look like a switchman's shanty. The Capitol at Topeka could be stored away inside the main building. There is no structure of such size and appearance in Eastern Kansas, and none where between the raw material and the finished product connection is so closely, quickly, and profitably made."[111]

An auto trip through company lands revealed "a garden green with beets and alfalfa, or brown or russet with Kafir or sorghum all the way." Interspersed were four-room cottages of wood or cement. The company had built forty of these, each with a windmill and barn. It had planted 5,000 shade trees. Such development of irrigated tracts would result, wrote one wag, in a situation in which every man "would be his own thunderstorm."

Surely the production of sugar in commercial quantities in Kansas, said an editor, "after all the ridicule, doubts, and misgivings of the skeptics, will be an event in the history of Kansas worthy of commemoration."[112] And celebrate they certainly did. When the plant went into full production in November, the Industrial Club of Garden City served a banquet at the Wiley Hotel with $200 worth of cut flowers on the tables ordered by telegraph from Kansas City. The estimate was that 2,000 people were there from out of town. F. D. Coburn, one of the speakers, said: "The change that has taken place at Garden City is one of the most wonderful things I ever saw . . . almost beyond belief." The sugar plant was, he said, "epoch-making," not only for Garden City, but also for all southwest Kansas. R. P. Davie of the sugar company predicted that, in time, beet sugar would crowd cane sugar off the market and that it represented "one of the greatest possibilities of our American agricultural future." W. Y. Morgan chimed in: "It is no longer proper to speak of these things as 'coming.' They have arrived."[113]

Coburn warned that any business "must be conducted with sense and sanity or disaster and humiliation will follow."[114] But the newspaper could not be blamed for laying it on thick in a special edition on the "Western Gateway to the Great Arkansas Valley." Garden City would become the capital of the southwest, situated on the shores of the "Great Inland Sea" that the sugar company was building for a reservoir. "The gigantic prestige that will come amounts to a transformation more glittering and marvelous than anything found in the 'Arabian Nights,' classed as fables." The plant made "Finney and Kearny counties one of the most substantial practical business propositions in America today."[115]

The unalloyed statistics were impressive. The number of beet growers went from 132 to 245 in a single year, and production in 1906 was over 70,000 tons, more than 200 percent above the tonnage produced during the whole prior history of sugar beet growing in Kansas. The corporation alone had raised over 11,000 tons.[116] In 1907, production of sugar beets in Kansas was nearly 90,000 tons, although it dropped back to 53,000 in 1908.[117] There was a campaign in 1911 to produce 100,000 tons.[118] By 1916, production had stabilized at about 50,000 tons for the four major beet-growing counties in Western Kansas.[119] Garden City's population grew to 3,171 in 1910, to 6,121 in 1930, and to 10,905 in 1950, thanks partly to the sugar company, which was operating 47,000 acres by the 1920s.[120]

One clear reason for this growth, too, was fundamental change in the ethnic demography of the region. A good proportion of the new residents attracted to booming Finney County were Hispanic, with a smattering of Asians and Native Americans. These immigrants solved the problem of the local culture's being inappropriate to the intense cultivation needed by sugar beets. They also changed the previously homogeneous local culture in many ways. It has been often noted that the ethnic mix in Western Kansas and particularly in Garden City and Dodge City changed dramatically in the late twentieth century with the rise of the feedlot and packing plant business.

But both the industrialization of farming and the importation of different ethnic groups as labor had its roots far earlier.

Hispanic people were present before 1906 as railroad workers, but the sugar plant and the increases in irrigated sugar beet land increased that population.[121] Take the Santa Fe's "California Limited," a local publicist advised, and observe the beet-raising farmers. "After you have watched for a while the dusky Mexicans and the sprightly Japs down on their knees wielding the heavy topping knives, resembling decidedly the deadly machete, you may get to talking with the farmer himself, who is there busily overseeing the rush of work."[122]

At first this was transient labor. The Garden City directory of 1907 listed only three Mexicans, occupation listed as "sugar-makers," living in Garden City proper. The 1915 state census listed 134 Mexicans in Finney County, 84 living in Garden City, most railroad employees. The sugar plant itself employed Mexicans, paying them 35 cents an hour by 1920, but there is newspaper evidence that most worked in the fields.[123] In 1920, one hundred Native Americans came from New Mexico and Arizona to work in the beet fields. "The Indians are more dependable than the Mexicans who are brought here from Old Mexico," a reporter wrote. "They apparently are more interested in shooting Presidents than in shooting trouble in the beet fields."[124] But Mexican labor continued to be vital. The year the Indians came, 18,000 of 40,000 acres owned by the Garden City Sugar and Land Company (successor to the United States Sugar and Land Company) were farmed by the company directly using Mexican labor. This was day labor that paid 35 cents an hour, with a bonus of 5 cents an hour extra if the worker kept on the job until Christmas. "This is rather fair pay for Mexican peons who have been accustomed to working for next to nothing and having a larger debt hanging over them all the time."[125] By the 1920s, there was a Mexican mission in Garden City, a Mexican orchestra, a Mexican opera house, and celebration of Mexican Independence Day with Mexican flags flying. This suggests a fair-sized year-round Hispanic population.[126] There was a Mexican reunion in Garden City in 1928, which drew over 400 people from Dodge City, Syracuse, Scott City, and other Western Kansas towns. The crowd came together under the leadership of Jesus Ayala, president of the Benito Juarez Mutual Society, and enjoyed speeches, a banquet, and boxing events.[127] Often, however, newspapers of Western Kansas would advertise their populations "not counting the Mexicans," and it is sure the census-taker missed a number too.[128]

Reflecting the passions of the period, much more was said about the machinery than about the people, whether the latter were tenant farmers or

J. W. Lough's irrigation well, Scott County, Kansas (courtesy of Kansas State Historical Society)

wage-earning Mexicans. And on the mechanical front there continued to be headlines in Western Kansas involving new technology for the next several years. It seemed that corporations and machines would finally overcome any natural barriers, as had been so long dreamed.

Even the decision by the U.S. Supreme Court in *Kansas v. Colorado* in 1907, not granting Kansas the immediate relief it sought, did not seem to discourage Western Kansans very much. Wrote the editor of the *Garden City Herald*:

> This decision leaves Colorado in the happy possession of the river, to can it up, confine it in reservoirs, fondle it and bathe in its muddy waters, and Kansas can only stand on the border and suck her thumbs, and get dust out of her mouth by a C.O.D. package. Colorado is the owner of the river in fee simple, with all its catfish, quicksands, and appurtenances and there is nothing now to prevent her damming the entire river. . . . It is all right, Kansas has survived the hot winds, grasshoppers, the border ruffians of Missouri and she can survive the damage wrought by the border hogs of Colorado.[129]

It was even averred that government help was not required. A case in point was the career of J. W. Lough, erstwhile commissioner of irrigation for Kansas, but also a successful private irrigation experimenter on his own land near Scott City. In 1910, Lough completed what was called "the greatest irrigation well in the West." A 24-horsepower engine threw 1,500 gallons of water a minute from a well that penetrated from upland to water at a depth of about 60 feet and was 130 feet deep total.[130] Lough's plant irrigated nearly 200 acres of alfalfa and other crops, an enormous size for an irrigated farm at the time. The secretary of the Kansas State Board of Agriculture, visiting Lough's operation, admitted that its success far exceeded anything the state had been able to accomplish in the field.[131] Haworth commented that it proved that "Western Kansas has more water than will ever be used."[132]

Garden City thought it could go it alone also. The town, said its major newspaper, had been "quite successful in laying its perplexities, not on the Lord but on the National Government." But that could not be depended upon forever. "It takes enterprise, money and brains to build up a city and county. . . . The Lord and the government will help those who try to help themselves."[133]

However, to speak of automobiles and irrigation pumps and sugar factories in the first years of the twentieth century only in their direct application to the business they engendered in the region is to tell only half the story. The same technological talent that could create a tractor or a combine could provide electric lights in the parlor or a telephone in the kitchen. It could result in a gristmill or an oil depot in the smallest town as easily as it could generate a six-story factory. And indirectly the economic prosperity the machine brought to Western Kansas towns could put books in the library, create a music festival at the college, or even bring about a visit by an airplane to the county fair.

Professor Frank Blackmar of the University of Kansas, speaking on the "Economics of Irrigation," at the opening of the Garden City sugar plant, said that the new industry and technology was more than part of an economic engine. It was a "public blessing." People "engaged in producing wealth on legitimate lines are adding to civilization." Irrigation was taking the chance out of the science of agriculture and making the farmer "a manufacturer of crops instead of a raiser of crops." It attracted intelligent people with civic consciousness, who no longer had to be or chose to be isolated in a wilderness. "It improves our social life over that of the dense population of the city and the sparsely settled country. It brings people closer together, causes them to cooperate, exercise self-restraint, and enjoy life in a higher measure. It brings better education, more religion, greater culture, increased material comforts."[134] That more satisfying brand of life the application of machine technology started in the region, a Dodge City writer claimed, "has branched into many enterprises of town building," creating "a new order of things."[135]

5

"Hustle or Rot"

From the beginning of the application of machinery to the
challenges of living and making a living in Western Kansas, many
recognized that the impact of the new technology would be cultural as well as economic. It would impact the towns of the region
as well as its farms and change forever the relationship between the
farmer and the nearest town to him, and, through that town, his
connection to the larger nation and world. It was no accident that
the so-called Country Life movement, spearheaded by Professor
L. H. Bailey, head of the Rural Life Commission during the Theodore
Roosevelt administration, arose coincident with the widespread use
of the new technology, prominently the automobile. The "modernization" of farm life and the reduction of isolation had always
been desirable; now they were possible. Bailey, said, Teddy Roosevelt, was named as head "for the purpose not of making any inquiry into technical farming but to consider the general social, economic, sanitary, and educational questions of the open country."
Bailey noted, "I think it is fair to say that the intelligent farm boy
can secure the essential advantages of a new piece of land only if
he goes at the old place with the new intelligence of the time."[1]

There was some early resistance in rural areas to modernization, but perhaps less so in Kansas than in most places. Western
Kansas had learned caution but had not lost optimism or enthusiasm for worthwhile change. Kansans were early and enthusiastic
users of the four great "urbanizing" technologies adopted in rural
America in the early twentieth century—automobiles, telephones,
electricity, and radios. There was little "devil wagon" talk there even
about the crudest early automobiles, the tendency being to curse

the roads rather than the machines. There was resistance to the idea that distant mail order houses and manufacturing and marketing concerns would reap the prime financial benefit from these changes, but hardly the strong defense found in some places of "traditional" agrarianism against the acids of modernity.[2]

Their experience fits well Hal Barron's thesis that the "Great Transformation" of rural society in the early twentieth century was not a clear-cut battle between a Jeffersonian cooperative commonwealth and new corporate influence, but rather a "nuanced" situation in which "following finer threads of analysis" meant discovering that any Populist type dichotomies quickly broke down. Almost seamlessly in Kansas, where to be modern was a kind of imperative, rural ways of life changed. And despite obvious drawbacks and the ups and downs of adaptation, most not only accepted the changes but welcomed them, delighting in their more frequent visits in automobiles to livelier towns filled with things to buy. "Consumer and popular culture," wrote Barron, "arrive in rural America during these years . . . first through the mail in the form of a catalogue, and then by car or radio, which transported country folk to the nearest movie theaters and the worlds beyond."[3]

That people in Western Kansas so quickly and so thoroughly adopted modern consumer culture was among the reasons that the cash crop wheat became so prominent. There was a desire, driven by advertising from the outside and by boredom from the inside, for what was to be bought with money sales of farm products, not for what could be consumed directly from the farm by the farm family. What was wanted was not so much independence as joy—not so much self-reliance as fulfillment. The emerging American culture of consumption, growing from 1910 to 1930 by what it fed on, changed the older boundaries of community and shifted the social ethos—by wile, not by force.[4]

The *Kansas Farmer* editorialized in 1910 that the "great field" for the future operation of the automobile would be among farmers and among the 45 million Americans who lived in communities of fewer than 4,000. The farmer was a "natural mechanic" and "out here in Kansas you see him operating the alfalfa stacker, the stirring plow or the disk harrow by aid of his automobile. He can pull the road drag with it, operate the corn cutter and the dairy machinery." More than that, it got him to town, and it made the amenities of the town more important and more accessible than ever. On the simplest level, the farmer could drive a car to town to get a repair part without interrupting the work of his harvest crew. But more profoundly, the family could visit town more often. "In all American history the curse of farm life has been its isolation. Its workers were set apart and a visit to a library, a church, an entertainment was an event for which preparation must be made and not a matter of regular occurrence such as should be true of any wide-awake and up-to-date Americans." The *Farmer* noted that the "dreary monotony" of traditional farm life explained why insanity was a special problem for women living on farms.[5] There had been a lack of intellectual life in rural areas generally, and in Western Kansas particularly, "to stimulate the mental powers of an intelligent person." But that could change. "The typical American farmer of today," wrote the *Kansas Farmer* reporter, "is no longer the bewhiskered, hay-stem chewing individual of the comic papers, who reads nothing but the almanac. Today, he is a modern, well-informed man, often a high school graduate, with a wife, usually his superior in education. There is no necessity of the mind stagnating on the farm."[6]

A change in image should fit the changing reality. The *Kansas Farmer* complained about a geography textbook on Kansas published in 1910 by Charles Scribner's. It talked about cowboys carrying large revolvers, but there was no word of the Kansas wheat crop. "What idea of the value of geography," commented the editor, "can be gained by a Kansas boy or girl who is surrounded with every comfort that can be purchased by the bountiful crops of his father's farm when he reads such stuff as this and is given to understand that it applies to the country where he lives." There were three or four pictures of a cowboy in the book and one of an Indian "neither of whom was ever seen by the average Kansas boy." If such a textbook taught him "such rot about the country where he lives what idea can he gain about the rest of the world when he reads the same geography?"[7]

It required active promotion to counter stereotypes. Students from Western Kansas studying at the University of Kansas formed a "shortgrass" club there in 1912 to cement their identity and to brag about their region.[8] Promoters at Garden City and Larned tried without success in 1911 to get Governor Walter Stubbs to endorse their Kansas Development Organization and its promotion project, Kansas Postcard Day. The governor seemed to think such puffery was beneath the dignity of his office, but the Western Kansas men thought there were few more useful things a governor could do than push a new image for his state. Wrote R. H. Faxon of Garden City:

> I am one of those, perhaps strange, persons who believe that we have had perhaps a little too much politics in Kansas and that there ought to be a little more improvement and boost. I believe that good roads and the public health, the farm life, the products of the state, its soil, its schools, its streams, its towns and possibilities, all

Dodge City, c. 1915 (courtesy of Kansas State Historical Society)

need more attention from now on from every citizen, whether in public or private life, than politics.[9]

Mr. Bailey could have said it no better.

F. D. Coburn of the Kansas State Board of Agriculture was a treasure in the image department, combining as he did a firm grasp of the statistics of the farm economy of Kansas with an articulate and engaging writing and speaking style. In 1907, he toured the state with a speech called "A Protest against the Fake." The theme was a familiar one—the negative image of Kansas in the press—but, unlike in recent years when the Kansas realist had to admit there was some truth at least to the claim that Kansas had grasshoppers ("not just a few little, insignificant fellows, but big, husky brutes that ate the bark off the trees"), the early twentieth century was a genuinely good time for Kansas and for Western Kansas. Noah did experience a flood once, Coburn reminded, but it did not mean everyone had to talk about it year after year. He told the Kansas editorial association that even they had been taken in by "legend and fiction" about Kansas, and they were rocking the boat in which they too had to ride. "A patch of earth the size of this state, that can in two decades, as Kansas has in the past two, produce 3,017,743,073 bushels of corn and 1,027,483,401 bushels of wheat worth in the aggregate

$1,488,629,194 . . . is not the habitat of droughts." Western Kansas was supposed to be "wracked by unceasing winds," but the fact was that windmills and air motors had all but disappeared there because of the "absence and unreliability of breezes sufficient for their turning," replaced by gasoline motors. Most who had lived in Kansas all their lives had never experienced either a blizzard or a tornado, those things that were supposed to be so ubiquitous there.[10]

Boosterism in towns was not new to the region. There was hope, however, that the twentieth-century version would incorporate more substance and less wind. Towns were as competitive with each other as ever and felt a responsibility to adapt to the changes and seize opportunities in a timely way. Townspeople could not be ciphers, lest they be forced to "hire an engineer and have the town re-platted and turned into a cemetery."[11] The smaller town looked to the bigger town, the bigger town to the city, Wichita or beyond, and none any longer could escape the wider world—or wanted to. The elements were there. "Everything favors us," wrote an editor at Dodge City, "but the thing will not do itself." There was no time for dreaming. A town must either go backward or go forward, and the key was organization. "It's up to the town. It is hustle or rot."[12]

The masterly recent account by James Shortridge of the growth strategies of Kansas towns, entitled *Cities on the Plains: The Evolution of Urban Kansas*, illustrates the variety of approaches and the universality of fierce regional competition. Whatever the individual spin, however, the materials shaped were ones all had in common. Therefore what emerges from the welter of local detail are some regional parameters concerning the look of the "new order," born as it was from money and machines, from a social, political, and cultural perspective.

The look of towns changed in the first decade of the new century, as did fundamental aspects of the way towns functioned. Prominent among the changes were the introduction of electricity, waterworks, telephones, and street paving, all of which moved quickly from novelties to necessities for any town that proposed to be competitive.

The largest towns in the region, those on the "borders" to the east— Wichita, Hutchinson, Salina—had built the basic modern infrastructure in the 1880s. Medium-sized regional towns—Garden City, Dodge City, Hays— often had the basics in the boom period but lost them later. In the early twentieth century, they recovered these.[13] When Garden City organized a new electric light company in 1898, the *Hutchinson News* commented, "Good old times are getting back."[14]

Laying water pipe, Oakley (courtesy of Kansas State Historical Society)

However, when the townspeople of the medium towns reintroduced the infrastructure, it was with some trepidation, modifications, and caveats and was based on their experiences and changed priorities. Garden City was proud to be electrified by a new company formed in 1898, and proud that the Windsor Hotel had its own waterworks and was connected by telephone with the bank and the depot, but it was not so completely carried away by modernity alone at the expense of everything else as it had once been.[15] There was a strong desire that the new growth be sustainable and respectable.

There was concern, for instance, about the destruction of shade trees. The Garden City council demanded that the electric company put its poles in the center of the street to prevent destruction of the trees the town had gotten established.[16] The city had a judgment against it of about $30,000 for failing to protect its rights in a contract made during the boom period with contractors to plant trees and to ensure they were a certain size by a certain time. Many of them were never planted and many that were had died during the 1890s. Now, there was concern that with the new dispensation the total package, beautification along with electrification, be implemented.[17] In 1911, the city of Garden City, which operated the waterworks, took over the electric light plant, partly on the grounds of economy and partly for the purpose of control in the interest of the community.[18]

Financing, too, was more conservative. Garden City had defaulted on interest on $32,000 in bonds issued during the 1880s for waterworks. In 1900, the town worried about the resultant poor publicity. The newspaper advised reform in the waterworks operation and better collections in order that the city might meet its obligations.[19] In 1903, water meters went in to stop "the water thieves . . . having their own sweet way."[20] At Springfield, in Seward County, where only cellars remained of a once-booming town, there could still be seen amid overgrown weeds the fire plugs of what had once been a complete waterworks system. Awareness was high that such a failure could happen again, but must not.[21]

Smaller towns faced the issue of modern infrastructure and its consequent expense for the first time. In these, the difficulty was that without some minimal moves in that direction, the entire town enterprise might be doomed either to extinction or to a place further out than ever on the periphery of things. Ness City, a town of 600 souls in 1900, when not complaining of the "measly mixed train" on its branch railroad line, or hunting wolves that were still destroying livestock near town, was trying to attract industry and afford city infrastructure and amenities.[22]

It had organized an Old Settlers Reunion, which was to occur every five years to celebrate the powerful pioneer heritage of the region, but that hardly seemed enough.[23] An effort to form a commercial club failed in 1901, as did a proposal for a telephone exchange and a new courthouse. "There is something out of kilter in Ness City these days," wrote editor J. K. Barnd. "In fact the town seems almost too dead to skin. There is no effort to better conditions, and everybody seems content to allow things to go to the demnition bow-wows without an effort to call a halt." Ness City had a good flour mill, but there was little local patronage or encouragement for it. Barnd feared Ness City would fall behind the "awake" towns in Kansas. "There was a time," he wrote, "when Ness City was no second-hand corpse, and people here knew how to get on a first-class hustle."[24] However, at some point it had "stubbed its toe."[25] Why was Ness City so dull? Barnd thought it was because

> everybody depends upon some one else to be public spirited and full of push. Everybody wants to look after his private business and permit some one else to look after the interest of the general public. That is the reason nothing is done, and we have taken on the semblance of dry rot of aggravated character. . . . Ness City should do something, if for no other reason than to convince the world that she is not dead.[26]

In 1904, there was some progress on the town's infrastructure. The Ness City Electric Light Company made arrangements that year with the Ness City Milling Company for the installation of a lighting plant at the mill, using the mill engine to operate a dynamo. There had been a thought to locate a waterworks plant with it, since there had long been a fear that without something better than the windmill-driven city well, one of the prairie fires that still regularly swept through Ness County could burn down the town. However, that was too big an undertaking. It was even impossible for the city to plan for many streetlights, as its treasury was slim. However, boomers said, "a few lamps should be so placed as to make it possible to travel the streets in the principal parts of town with ease and comfort after nightfall. It is now very inconvenient to get to the business part of town dark evenings, and the churches are almost hopelessly lost when the moon does not shine or the weather is cloudy."[27] Harold Miner, who had built a house at Ness City for his bride-to-be coming from the East, was impressed that when he installed the electric lights they turned the house into a "crackerjack" and made it "show up scrumptious at night."[28] But other townspeople complained that the company might make a profit. Editor Barnd felt they should not find that so remarkable, since there were real risks. Townspeople should "put your shoulder to the wheel, and help push the old car of progress along."[29]

There was satisfaction at the "brilliant" event of lighting the Ness City downtown and opera house with electricity in May 1904.[30] But difficulties continued, with only marginal operation. In July, the lights "blew up," due to strain on the dynamo, and people "got a taste of old time conditions on a dark and rainy night."[31] In November, the independent electric company sold out to the milling company.[32] In 1906, the mill engine gave out. It could not be run on rainy days because it was outdoors and the belt got wet. Lights could only be operated for three or four hours in the evening.[33] In 1907, with the mill itself in bankruptcy, there was a threat of a court order to close the electric plant.[34] The mill and electric plant sold for $6,600 that year.[35] In 1908, a 150-horsepower engine went in, and the "hitherto dilapidated and woe-begone" mill structures began to look decent—at least not any longer "as if they had passed through a serious siege."[36] There was no waterworks, but an ice plant was built.[37] However, in January 1909, the big shaft carrying the drive pulley of the dynamo broke. Since the operation was still losing money, there was fear that the "old-time and ill-smelling kerosene lamp will be back."[38] And what if there were a fire? The few tanks on the street often contained no water, and not many in town knew where to get buckets.[39] Engineers patched the dynamo, but the marginality as a private business of what was considered an essential public enterprise continued.

There was plenty of rhetoric. "If your neighbor has electric lights and you have not," went a company ad in 1910, "just step into his house some evening after dark and compare his lights with your own. Study each point of convenience, cleanliness and beauty carefully, and then figure out for yourself if it would not pay you well to have your house wired for electric lights at once."[40] But hoping did not make it so for Ness City. Marginal enterprises cannot withstand the slightest accident, and the accident happened in July 1911 when fire destroyed the plant of the Ness City Mill Light & Ice Company. It was, a reporter noted, "the heaviest blow ever struck against Ness City's welfare." Finances meant that the operating crew was minimal. Lack of waterworks and fire department meant that the response to the blaze was minimal too. There was not even enough money in the company to tear down the charred walls; the townspeople volunteered to do it. The $50,000 loss was covered by only $10,000 in insurance. The *News* editor thought there would not be another flouring mill in Ness for "a double decade if ever," and the chances that there would be another electric plant soon were slim.[41] The fire "demon," wrote J. C. Hopper, "put our beautiful city in darkness; stopped the making of that cold article we like so much to have about the house these sultry days, and forever put a stop to the manufacture of that staff of life so necessary in our homes; bid defiance to stone and steel; without a thought of its value, left it a smoldering mass, repulsive to the eye of man."[42] The city leaders met about establishing a municipal electric plant but moved slowly. Meanwhile individuals and businesses started putting in their own lighting plants.[43] The newspaper was running its linotype on an individual dynamo when it reported that, despite the disaster, a fire department in a town the size of Ness City was not practical. It just could not afford one.[44]

Probably the experience of Ness City was more typical than the infrastructure achievements that commercial club editions of local newspapers usually advertised. Small towns, like small farmers, had difficulty affording the new machinery—and even more difficulty changing the expectations, fueled by national propaganda, that every person and every community had to have the full gamut of these things—the sooner the better. Ness City's imposing limestone Merrill Trust building, constructed in the 1880s and often called the "skyscraper of the Plains," was a symbol of mixed meaning to the town for the next century. It showed to what it aspired but reminded also that it had peaked early and suffered long.

Each town had a pattern to itself, but all faced the same necessities. Colby was able to vote $50,000 in bonds in 1905 for an elegant courthouse. Yes, there would be a tax, but the *Free Press* thought it would be well worth it, as the improvement was local. "The tax we are opposed to is that levied on us by the trusts and monopolies to build up an aristocracy of . . . dudes."[45] But in the place that was to advertise itself in the 1930s as the "taxless town," due to the success of its municipal utility, there was much caution in starting an electric plant. There was doubt as late as 1908 that electric lights were practical in a town the size of Colby (1,539 residents). The detractors argued that most small-town plants operated only from sundown to midnight anyway, which would involve retaining oil lamps, "as most of us are too poor to lay in bed until sunrise."[46] A combined waterworks and light plant did not go in there until 1910.[47] Even then the local editor wrote, "Away down deep in our own judgment we are not very enthusiastic for the bonds." The town was out of debt and perhaps needed a couple of good crops before undertaking such improvements.[48]

Larned, on the other hand (with a 1908 population of 2,914), had enjoyed electric lights since the early 1890s and was accustomed to making the most of electricity and everything else modern.[49] For visitors' week, in October 1908, A. A. Doerr placed a big display platform on lots north of his hardware store on which he had machinery and pumps in operation and a tent filled with buggies and vehicles. C. W. Smith Electric and Ice Company had an electric display, which consisted of lights spaced 3 feet apart on both sides of Broadway from Fourth to Seventh Streets and a big "Welcome" sign of electric lights mounted on a flagpole. On South Broadway, Gabel & Sons had an electric sign advertising Keystone Flour. Local merchants were so impressed by the special event that they considered creating a "White Way" of intensive electric lighting downtown such as in Wichita.[50]

Hays, in 1901, with a population of 1,550, had a private electric plant run by local entrepreneur Justus Bissing with no city or county bond aid.[51] In 1904, the city, experiencing a jump to 2,500 population, installed a waterworks, which allowed toilets in the basement of the new building at the college, equipped also with steam heat and electric lights. "With city water for flushing, these conveniences are possible," a reporter enthused.[52] The Hays City Milling Company, which had constructed a 40-by-78-foot building to replace one recently burned, was in 1904 illuminated with over 200 electric bulbs.[53] In 1907, the Hays City Electric Light Plant put in all-night service. The paper wrote, "There are so many uses that electricity can be put to, such as electric irons, heaters, fans, attachments for running sewing machines and other power appliances."[54]

Liberal (with a population in 1908 of 1,500) was more like Ness City than Larned in its infrastructure. The editor of the *Liberal News* commented in 1905 that it would be nice to have a complete electric light plant so that the local stage could be illuminated and first-class touring shows could be

Road work on Hackberry Creek with horse-drawn graders, Logan County, early twentieth century (courtesy of Kansas State Historical Society)

attracted.[55] A light plant did come about in 1906 but did not, as predicted, automatically make Liberal "one of the important points of the entire West."[56] Septic tanks were still considered the best solution for waste, the lay of the land and the finances of the town not being right for a sewer.[57]

Facilities varied in quality as well as in quantity. Dodge Citians complained in 1903 that the town's electric lights went out at critical moments, and "when they do burn they are little better than tallow dips"—and when there was a fire, the water mains burst.[58] Certainly, however, there was no town in Western Kansas that was not acutely aware that delaying too long in installing these expensive amenities would be fatal to its aspirations.

Waterworks were more than just a convenience. It is remarkable how frequently serious fires occurred in these towns. Salina, by 1892, had a waterworks, a population of 10,000, six weekly newspapers, a sewer system, an electric light and power company, a Gamewell Electric Fire Alarm system, double-nozzle fire hydrants on most corners of its 8 miles of streets, and a well-organized hose company.[59] Yet in January 1895 it had a disastrous fire destroying several fair buildings at Oak Dale Park.[60] Two months later, another large fire caused a $150,000 loss over nearly a block. "Structures which were an adornment to a city of fine buildings, are now in smoldering ruins, and bare, blackened walls tremble in the tempestuous north wind, tottering reminders of the 'glory which has passed away,' in smoke."[61]

At the less-well-protected towns, the fire danger was worse. WaKeeney burned in 1895, taking out completely the plants of its two major newspapers.[62] The same year, Hays had such a big fire that some claimed it was ruined for all time.[63] Of twenty-five buildings in one block on North Main, only seven survived, and most of the city's historic cattle town buildings disappeared that day.[64] Liberal, still lacking a city waterworks in 1908, had only "a limited supply of water and a few garden hoses with which to fight fire." The water pressure from the steel tank or the railroad facility was not enough to throw water to a second-story building.[65] It was a regular and sad recreation for the Hansen family at Logan to watch fires. When the schoolhouse burned in 1904, family members felt helpless: "We just had to stand and see it go as we are without any thing with which to fight fire. It was the saddest thing I ever saw." Children stood and wept, as did teachers and townspeople.[66] A downtown fire at Hays in December 1903, beginning at the large I. M. Yost mill, caused a $108,000 loss, with only $34,000 insured. Heat from the fire set wooden buildings across the street on fire. The "chemical engine" and the bucket brigade that responded were inadequate to the crisis.[67] The company rebuilt the mill, only to see it burn again in September 1907.[68] Garden City lost a similar-sized flour mill to fire in 1897.[69] In 1898, it lost half a block, the whole east side of Main.[70]

Such losses could not be tolerated. It was no accident that Hays citizens immediately began agitating for a better waterworks and issued bonds for one in 1908.[71] Garden City asked its $30-a-month fire chief in 1909 for a plan, and he recommended an automobile fire wagon of 60 horsepower to carry 12 to 15 men, 1,200 feet of hose, scaling ladders, and 50 gallons of chemicals.[72] Garden City had a $20,000 waterworks, built with bond funding in 1907, which it bragged was one of the best in the state.[73]

There was increasing awareness of fire hazards and of the responsibility of city government to do something about the danger. In 1905, Garden City residents petitioned to remove the Standard Oil tanks from the center of town. The editor of the *Herald* was against that on the grounds that the city could not afford to offend a major employer. And why pick on this company when so much else about the town was dangerous or unsatisfactory? "We would just as soon be blow up by gasoline as to be smothered with sewer gas, or drown on a street crossing."[74]

Garden City avoided that particular type of disaster, but Hays did not. In the fall of 1919, 9 people died and 150 were injured in Hays when Standard Oil tank No. 3 there blew up.[75] The exploded tank flew north just above the ground, crushing sheds and houses in its way. The flames were visible for 40 miles, and "the scream of escaping gas could be heard piercing above the

A. A. Doerr of Larned (courtesy of Kansas State Historical Society)

roar of the fire sounding like an intensified exhaust of a dozen locomotives." City leader and newspaper owner John S. Bird sustained injuries trying to rescue women and children at one house. The point about civic responsibility was not lost on him or on other eyewitnesses.[76]

Regional business, of course, grew apace, supported by the recovery of the farm economy. Population increased, and stores in Western Kansas towns looked finer than ever. What could compare with A. A. Doerr's hardware store in Larned? His letterhead advertised that he ran "The Square Deal Store Hardware, Furniture, Vehicles, Implements, Harness, Saddles, etc. Everything for Farm, Field and Home."[77] And his store became more than a local institution, emerging as a nationally known success story. A. B. McDonald, editor of the *Country Gentleman*, visited Larned in 1920 to write about the Doerr store in his series "Big Country Merchants." By then Doerr had three floors and a basement filled with merchandise, the largest retail store of its kind in Kansas.

While McDonald was there, farmer George Couchman came in to buy a car. Couchman had three cars already, plus a truck and fifty-six horses. He wanted a big open car to carry harrows and plows and cordwood. "A fellow gets in a hurry, you know, in harvest, or when the coal runs shy, and he just chucks any old thing into the car. It's handy." Couchman had lived in a sod house when he came to Pawnee County in 1876 and now resided in a fourteen-room home. Doerr had had somewhat the same experience. They agreed that many had lived "a long time in the early days without any comforts; and now we're all prosperous and able to have them, and we're getting them. . . . Why shouldn't a farmer live as well as anybody—better for that matter? Doerr had done $700,000 in business in the year 1919 and expected soon to gross a million a year.

It was all based on sales of labor-saving machinery to eliminate the hired labor that was increasingly hard to get and the backbreaking work that would have driven the next generation off the farm. Doerr sold his first gasoline tractor in 1910 and his first combine harvester in 1918. Both became popular because they worked and because Doerr knew how to explain them. That brought him a long way from the time he had founded his business in 1898 with $3,000 in merchandise.[78]

Doerr was indeed a visionary about new technology and a pragmatist at making it work. He decided in 1903 that the disc plow had come to stay and "put a quietus on the regular kickers. We have yet the first report to hear where the fields plowed by the disc did not yield up to fields tilled by any other method."[79] Doerr made an arrangement to sell the Emerson disc harrow, manufactured in Rockford, Illinois, in quantities unprecedented for his region. He introduced the whole methodology as well as the brand. From his extensive store and warehouse complex, established in 1901 at the corner of Broadway and Sixth, he pioneered the selling in the area of not only Emerson farm implements, but also of Superior drills, Anchor buggies, Bain wagons, Majestic ranges, Round Oak heaters, and Samson windmills. He sold furniture, had tinsmith and plumbing departments, and was a carpet buyer and undertaker. "The history of the development of the business itself," wrote a Larned reporter, "reads like a chapter of fiction."

And he made money doing it. By 1909, Doerr had sales of nearly $7,000 a month and sold 400 Emerson implements, 100 farm wagons, and 100 buggies that year. By 1910, when he incorporated, there was paid-up capital of $100,000.[80] When it was time to gravel the roads, Doerr was in on it, providing the gravel for city contracts shipped from a Chicago supplier.[81] He owned a newspaper.[82] He served in the statehouse and senate and was for a time Kansas state business manager. He was active in national hardware trade associations.[83] He was, wrote W. G. Clugston in *American Magazine,* "a storekeeper who studies farmers' wants."[84] The store motto was "We Always Try to Please."[85]

An example of a storekeeper on a smaller scale was William D. Miner of Miner's Cash Store at Ness City (with a population of 750 in 1910). Miner, who had arrived in town in 1884 from Iowa, had been a loan agent, an attorney, a judge, and mayor of Ness City before establishing his store in 1895.[86] Like Doerr, he was a serious patron of the local newspaper, taking out flashy ads even in the depths of the depression. "THAT TIRED FEELING," a typographically diverse ad from 1895 went, "may easily be overcome and life again seem worth living if you buy your goods where your honest judgment must tell you is the only best place in Ness City. . . . Those who are not credit-bound and who are disposed to be fair minded must certainly admit that it pays to trade at Miner's cash store."[87] During the hard times, Miner took farm goods as payment ("Butter and Eggs as Good as Money," "Bring in Your Chickens") and offered premiums such as "artistic" pictures for the home.[88] In 1897, with the return of prosperity, Miner expanded his store and stocked the biggest line of shoes in Ness County, direct from the factory of C. M. Henderson & Company in Chicago, for which he was the sole regional agent.[89] He emphasized that he sold "standard" goods and that these could be obtained more cheaply from him than from city catalog houses or "tramp peddlers."[90] Miner's wife played the piano at local gatherings, his children participated in quartets and drama groups, and he served both as director of local companies with potential, such as the Ness City Oil and Gas Company formed in 1904, and as toastmaster at community gatherings, "presiding with ease and grace."[91] In 1911, Miner's son Harold (Hal) served on the Ness City council.[92] Hal wrote once that he did not care much for some of the civic activities in which he was involved, "but a fellow has to join everything that comes along in order to be a 'good fellow.'"[93]

Merchants congratulated their communities and emphasized that good times were "opportunities for buying high grade goods at Low-Down Prices."[94] L. N. Wilson, Miner's father-in-law and a former journalist, wrote a piece in the local paper in 1903 praising the new prosperity and rejoicing that people like his relative "who weathered the storm are now independent and the tide has its flow again. . . . The amount of business is amazing and everything is up-to-date."[95] The technique was sharp trading. In 1902, for instance, Miner, through his real estate partnership of Miner & Eibert, received a consignment of carriages, buggies, and implements, which he

Doerr hardware store, Larned (courtesy of Wichita State University Special Collections)

then offered at rock-bottom prices.[96] By 1903, Miner had a branch store in a nearby town run by one of his sons, two floors of merchandise, and a warehouse filled with sugar, flour, and salt bought in carload quantities.[97] His firm Miner Brothers, formed in 1910 as a vehicle for his children, sold insurance and did abstracting.[98]

When Hal married in 1907, his bride's parents in western New York state worried about her going to Kansas. But Hal had built her a snug house in Ness City. He loved the trips he took into the country with his "dandy little team" to make land sales, and he reported to his fiancée that there was only an occasional hot, windy, and dusty day to remind the progressive denizens of the place where they were.[99] You say the roads are almost impassable there, Hal wrote on February 17, assuming a publicist role even in his most private correspondence: "How different from that here. They are just fine and smooth as can be. In three consecutive days I drove the same team 150 miles and never hurt them a bit. No sir, I wouldn't like to live there at all. This country may have its draw backs, but I'd rather live here than anywhere else. There's more of liberty and freedom, the air is purer, opportunities better and everybody is up and doing."[100] A little later he added, "All crops are growing scandalous and the farmers (and land sharks) feel pretty good."[101] One week in March he sold 1,500 acres of land for $22,000.[102] His father was still around the business, and Hal commented: "Pa and I are still having a fine time and it's pretty hard to tell which of us enjoys the other's company

Miner Brothers office, Ness City, c. 1917: William D., right, and Harold, left, both standing in doorway (courtesy of Miner Brothers, Ness City)

the most. Papa helps us considerably around here and seems to like it the same as he used to in his methodical way."[103] Indeed, method seemed to be the key against odds and over generations. "It is not 'busy' in a sense like a clerk in a store would be," Hal wrote, "but rather it is simply to keep our mind on our business with several strings in hand and to be ready to pull the right one at the right time. It is a little trying on a fellow but there is something fascinating about it too."[104] Above his desk was a bright red card reading "Do It Now."[105]

Albert Doerr and the Miners are only examples of a type. The type was legion in these years, and their brick edifices with plate glass display windows hummed with activity. And since they so hummed, the tax revenue was generated to fund the modern infrastructure and government and culture at a level of sophistication for which it would not be necessary to apologize.

There was no longer any pride in being "wild" western places, if there ever had been. The message was one of unity, and local people needed to be inured to the "habit of success." Wrote an editor at Dodge City: "In town if the businessmen will all pull together on any proposition that comes up they may

Boy and chickens, Sherman County, c. 1912 (courtesy of High Plains Museum, Goodland)

after a while have a large business and be riding in automobiles. But if they try to get up by pushing someone else down, no one will get very high."[106]

Town political reform seemed to fall under the heads of order and quality of life. Order came first. There was near-universal concern that prosperity loosened the bonds of discipline, not only perhaps bringing "riff-raff" to the region expecting an easy life, but softening the pioneers, and especially their sometimes-delinquent children, into thinking that they had it made.

The call was strong to rein in the young people, through a curfew or simply stricter enforcement of the laws. "Garden City is harboring as nice a set of young gallow-birds as ever went unhung," was the conclusion of one man in 1898. Parents should control these boys. "Let them take a club to them, and if that don't do take a gun, for such boys are better out of the way."[107] Garden City boys were shooting songbirds, indicating that their parents were allowing them "to cultivate an instinct of cruelty."[108] Schools were disorderly. "Is a teacher required to sit back," said a local commentator, "and let a few young bloods run things and then brag on it?"[109] The women in town responded that maybe there should be a curfew on husbands as well as boys. "They are in the habit of going down the street after supper on a little business and then are dragged into a high five game, or a little whirl at draw, and that settles it until it is time for the cocks to crow in the morning."[110] There was a mass meeting in Garden City in August 1898 concerning the moral condition of the town—and coming up with the means to deal with "debauchery and crime." Volunteers divided into squads to control wild boys and to notify "a colored family . . . to behave themselves." Shortly, thinking better of the vigilante method, townspeople investigated legal means.[111] There had been too few criminal convictions in Western Kansas in the Populist Era and that needed to change.[112] Garden City passed a curfew ordinance in 1898, requiring all under the age of sixteen to be home at nine P.M., with a fine of $25 assessed on the parents if they were not.[113]

Other towns also experienced problems with juveniles. At Hays, young "town sports" were killing all the prairie chickens and quails, leading to an increase in grasshoppers.[114] At Dodge City in 1902, some teenaged boys loaded a gas pipe with blasting powder as a Fourth of July celebration experiment. They tried more powder until the pipe blew up and took the head off Uriah Hanna, eighteen, son of the president of the Jones & Hanna grocery firm.[115] At Colby in 1901, a group of boys got drunk and celebrated, it was said, "in the same manner as a lot of Comanche Indians would have done." The editor of the *Free Press* threatened to send to the governor for militia "if our improvised shade over our office window is again disturbed."[116] In 1907, a gang of boys upset a meeting at the Colby armory by throwing stones on the roof while the lecturer was speaking. Some boys in town were playing poker two or three times a week "and forming a habit that will cast a shadow over their lives as long as they live."[117] People at Liberal commented in the early years of the new century about smoking in the schools and complained about a young peoples' element who made "a special effort decorating sidewalks with obscene and profane literature."[118] If a man has a $50 dog, wrote editor Abe Stoufer there, he does not let him run around at night. It was apparently not the same with boys and girls.[119]

The law and order, moral-reform syndrome was hardly limited to juvenile behavior. There could be a discussion of the pool hall question, or the tramp question, the sidewalk-spitting question, or the peddler/gypsy question as it played out in the towns. And there was the debate on the behavior of modern women. Why did women kiss each other, wrote a man at La Crosse in 1900? "They can't enjoy it. Like hens pecking at corn. Should be discontinued."[120]

Some scandals of a type hardly spoken of earlier, much less experienced, rocked towns. A disturbing one at Garden City was headlined "A Victim of Illicit Love" and concerned an abortion performed in 1901 in a Chicago hotel room on Miss Irma Brown by Dr. Robert E. Gray. Both had gone to the big city for that purpose from their homes in Garden City. Brown died of complications. The body of the child turned up under the Randolph Street viaduct. Gray was arrested, charged with murder, and locked up at the Maxwell Street police station in Chicago.[121] It was a lesson, the Garden City newspaper said, "not to be forgotten by the young men of Garden City."[122] A court acquitted Gray, and, after being divorced by his wife and having his medical license revoked on grounds of "gross immorality," he returned to Garden City. This met with a mixed local reaction.[123] His ad in the local paper in 1909 read: "Physician and Surgeon. Scientific Therapeutist. Diseases of Women and Children. Nervous and Functional Diseases. Office Practice a Specialty."[124]

Governmental attention in the new era, however, was directed at more than the criminal basics. For example, the question of beauty began to join that of practicality in discussions of what made a good town. Aesthetic considerations were tied to health and sanitation, an issue brought to the fore partly by the action of Dr. Samuel Crumbine, once of Dodge City, in his new role as head of the Kansas State Board of Health.[125]

"To speak in plain terms," wrote a Garden City citizen in 1906, "the city is filthy—disgustingly, criminally filthy—foul smelling sewers and privy vaults, dirty hog pens and table yards, alleys reeking with filth, and stagnant ponds. It is a wonder some epidemic has not swept the town."[126] A Ness City resident commented in 1905 that the appearance of the sidewalks there was "something awful." The one that led from the depot was "an abomination in the sight of the good people," consisting of "a few measly rotten boards resting on mother earth and miscalled a sidewalk." The sidewalks and even the streets were cluttered with hitching posts and with "new fangled machines" exhibited by implement dealers. "It is a shame that we should be compelled to drive over hay rakes, windmills, mowing machines, wagons, corn planters and all kinds of machines" every time one ventured into town. Then there were the dogs. It was not uncommon to see twenty on one block. "I never come to town," wrote a farmer, "but what I see ladies threading their way through a mess of snarling, worthless curs on the sidewalk."[127] A woman in Garden City, complaining in 1903 about a deep mud hole in the street there, commented that

> it isn't very pleasant to live near this mud hole and have to listen to the curses of men and see them whip their horses through such a place. . . . The Christian realizes the need of a deeper work of grace

in the heart, a higher standard of Christian living to enable us to withstand temptation and have more patience with others, be kinder to dumb animals and make everybody happy, and the world brighter and better.

If the city council did not do something about the mud hole, the complainer said, the women of the town would organize to do it themselves.[128]

Proposals for beautification were many. In a number of towns along the Santa Fe railroad, the company beautified its depots about the turn of the century with landscaping, with strong approval from local people.[129] Churches, particularly the Catholic churches of Ellis County, funded by prosperous Russian farmers, were extraordinary architectural statements. The "Cathedral of the Plains" at Victoria, dedicated in 1911, remains a landmark in the twenty-first century, and it had many peers.[130] The Liebenthal church, finished in 1905, was 148 feet long and 56 feet wide, with an interior ceiling 42 feet high and a 150-foot steeple. Local people constructed it of local stone, with the interior millwork handled by Justus Bissing of Hays and only the $2,000 stained glass imported from Germany. It was, said the Hays paper, "extra fine" throughout.[131]

Towns pointed to their beauty with pride. A trip to Dodge City, wrote the editor of the *Kinsley Mercury* in 1902, "shows the beauties of our own little town . . . with its many trees and homes and gardens." By contrast, Dodge City was "barren," built "on a hill with nothing to soften the bleak outline of prairie or sky."[132] Dodge City disagreed with that sentiment. An editor there in 1895 noted that "the esthetic" was not a possession just of Oscar Wilde, but of the people, and it was practical. "As civilization advances," he noted, "decoration keeps pace. In the architectural makeup of Dodge estheticism is manifest." There were some lapses, such as "the accumulation of rubbish in hallways recesses, cellar ways, etc., much to the advantage of the incendiary." But neatness would follow prosperity, and pride was already asserting itself. Dogs and hogs were being restricted from the streets and derby hats and buttonhole bouquets were in evidence among the population.[133] Trees became a feature of the streets by 1910, and by that time in most Western Kansas towns there were street addresses and free mail delivery. "At last," a local paper said, "Dodge City people know where they live—It is now even possible to impart information to others."[134]

These improvements created some complaint from overburdened taxpayers. When Garden City officials proposed a concrete bridge over the Arkansas River in 1909, a resident thought that in the new spirit of aesthetics it should have an allegorical design. It might show "the pioneers and taxpayers stripped of nearly everything and staggering under a burden of bonds of every description that a fertile brain could think of voting on them."[135]

Aesthetics and the trappings of culture, however, did not presage much increase in human sympathy. Western Kansas newspapers continued to run surprisingly racist comments. The word "nigger" appeared in print, not only with reference to African American visitors and residents of the region, but even referring to enemy combatants in the Philippines.[136] Ness County, the *News* editor reported in 1901, had, according to the secretary of the State Board of Agriculture, "no sheep, no wool, and no niggers."[137] Liberal averred in 1907 that it was not a "nigger town" and that there was not a "colored soul" resident there.[138] Dane Hansen of Logan described his teacher in 1899 as someone with "lips like a nigger."[139] The *Kinsley Graphic* reported in 1901 that a "darky" had been arrested for stealing drugs from the local doctor. He and a "white nigger" who played craps with him were shortly arrested.[140] About the same time, referring to the burning of a Negro man near Limon, Colorado, the editor wrote: "We have no special reasons to be harsh on the colored race and there are no doubt many worthy people who are in no way to blame for the color of their skin, but we believe that the Negroes have no right to settle among the whites and the white people are equally out of place when they settle in a Negro settlement."[141] In 1908, there was a sign posted in a store at Hugoton, Stevens County: "Positively no niggers allowed in this store." When a black man tried to enter, the owner came after him with a gun.[142] That same year, night riders in Stevens County threatened Major Stokes, an elderly African American, on his claim. Masked and armed with whips, ropes, and guns, they broke into his house, destroyed his furniture, and burned $450 worth of broomcorn. A grand jury indicted the perpetrators, but not before the man abandoned his claim for a time in fear.[143] When an ATSF crew on the Kinsley branch discovered a black man hitching a ride on the train, the brakeman gave the interloper a "vigorous pounding upon the bum's trouser seat" with a stick he carried. Other members of the crew ran up to see the sport. However, the man landed on his feet, took the stick away, and attacked the onlookers. "He was the most active coon alive," a Hutchinson reporter wrote, "and was ready to meet any ten train crews on the system."[144] In 1902, Dodge Citians attended a musical comedy called "The Hottest Coon in Dixie," presented by "the only recognized high-class colored organization in the United States."[145]

Mexicans, Indians, and Russians did not escape the stereotyping, the slanted reporting, and the crude jokes. A Kansas City paper claimed in 1901 that the Russian population of Ellis County, amounting to 4,000 people, drank whiskey straight, had not assimilated well, and "shut their eyes and vote[d] the Democrat ticket."[146] The average Russian town, a visiting reporter from Topeka wrote, was "distinguished for the meanness and filthiness of its residences." The homes there were ones "at which the average dog would sniff, if it were offered him for a kennel."[147] When diggers found an Indian skeleton at a mound a few miles east of Ford, Kansas, complete with burial array, the excavator said he was "going to have the big Indian skeleton mounted, get some one to manufacture history for it and sell it to some eastern institution for a fabulous sum."[148]

When there was a favorable story about a member of a minority group told without slang, it seemed almost an exception to a general rule. A black man named George McCue, who had once been tried in town for assault on a white woman and threatened with lynching, won a Carnegie medal for heroism when he saved a young Garden City girl from an onrushing train at the risk of his own life in 1909. The press had to report that without prejudice.[149]

Still, notwithstanding the backsliding and bad habits, and by whatever means cultural amenities were advanced, culture emerged as a central goal and concern in regional towns of all sizes. It was regarded as a part of what town life should and must be for men as well as women, rather than as a kind of "window dressing" to be enjoyed only when business was slack.

An obvious and defining example of the cultural change was the prominent place of music in the life of Western Kansas towns. There had been town bands and touring musical entertainment. But the early twentieth-century regional ambitions and achievements in music went far beyond anything that preceding decades had suggested.

Lindsborg, due to some of the special circumstances of its Swedish founding, Bethany College, and thriving art community, had long been a regional enclave of special cultural achievement. The performance of Handel's *Messiah* every Easter had been a regional tradition since 1882. Ling Auditorium at Bethany College, constructed in 1895, was filled at the performances given by a 500-person chorus of mostly local people with a few guest soloists. Emory Lindquist, the historian of the college, noted that the yearlong preparation for the event represented nothing less than "a great laboratory of community living."[150]

The start at Hays was smaller but significant. N. A. Krantz, a graduate of the Royal Conservatory of Music in Stockholm and a teacher for twelve years at Bethany College, established a conservatory of music in Hays in 1900. The subjects were voice culture, piano, organ, mandolin, guitar, harmony, and composition, and the lessons were on the second floor of William

Ft. Hays Normal School chorus, July 23, 1914 (courtesy of Kansas State Historical Society)

Ryan's clothing store for $9 a term.[151] In 1904, the Bissing Conservatory of Music, operated by Petrowitsch Bissing, a concert violinist trained in Bohemia, put on an operetta and offered sheet music for sale.[152] Bissing joined the mechanical age by patenting an "orchestra machine," which simulated thirty-nine violins and twelve cellos by playing on a keyboard and activating bowing with a revolving wheel.[153]

Music awareness and performances of music and drama became ubiquitous regardless of the size of the town. Alpha Hansen was a schoolteacher at Logan, Phillips County. She yearned to attend the University of Kansas but meanwhile tried to offer good lessons to her charges and keep her sister in Japan informed on her busy life—Alpha was planning to go to the Halloween flower carnival put on by the women's club and to a touring performance of *Romeo and Juliet*. The latter she thought would likely be put on by a "bum" outfit, but she, as a purveyor of local culture, felt obliged to attend.[154] A friend of hers at Goodland taught Roman history, bookkeeping, literature, physiology, and orthography but, unlike Alpha, was not responsible for the music.[155]

This regimen tired Alpha, but she loved the challenge. And her letters illustrated how thoroughgoing were the attempts in small towns to inculcate culture. When she attended a lecture in 1907, she found it "fair" but wrote that she would prefer musical numbers. The same was true of the literary.

"It was the funniest thing. Those great boys and girls got up and went lickety cut in a sing-song until they forgot. Then they'd blush and stutter and begin over again." She was a judge in the debate that followed on whether city life was preferable to country life.[156]

In 1907, Logan, population 762, not to be outdone by Lindsborg, staged a cantata. It used a chorus of 125 people, and Alpha was in charge of organizing it. "It is going very well," she reported, "but it takes *so* much time and thought. I have practice at every hour or minute I have to spare." It was a challenge to get "all those boys like Willis D. (Willie) Smith, Leo Templeton, Ward C and all the rest to *sing*." She said she did not realize the boys were so big, but that if she could make them work, the cantata would be "the finest thing we've ever had."[157] It was not easy. "I have drilled on those boys voices to get them to harmonize but they don't sound just right yet." The girls were working on costumes and the women of the town were preparing a dinner.[158] Shortly she admitted, "I was so worried about the cantata that I was almost crazy. . . . Really I'm becoming quite fierce."[159] But she thought it would be worthwhile. After all, Logan was a fairly dull place. "We had a *train* this afternoon and it was the funniest thing. You would think we never had seen one before. When it whistled there were carriages, autos, bicycles and people coming on the run from all directions as if their very life depended upon their getting there."[160] It was better than watching a fire, but it was hardly real culture. "I'm bound to do something," Alpha commented, "and I don't know what. . . . It makes me feel so foolish to see all these youngsters going to college."[161] The cantata came off, and in 1910, Alpha registered in the Fine Arts School at the University of Kansas.[162]

The same quotidian cultural thread is evident in the daily life of Harold Miner at Ness City. He reported to his fiancée on a "dandy literary" in February 1907. "These Saturday night meetings are quite a success and the city hall is filled at every meeting. The programs are varied with music, recitations, impromptus, etc. and a good live debate."[163] The Memorial Day program at the opera house that year was doubtless typical for the time and place. There was music by the Ness City Concert Band, music at the opera house, music by a quartette, a patriotic address, a reading of Lincoln's Gettysburg Address, and a closing rendition of "America" by the crowd. The drum corps then led everyone to the cemetery for further ceremony.[164]

Ness City was a bit of a special case but not wildly unusual. Its advantage in culture was that the editor of the *Ness County News*, J. K. Barnd, was a former thespian.[165] He helped organize the Ness City thespians, who went on tour in 1903 with their play "The Chimney Corner." He remodeled the Ness

City opera house, which he began renting out in 1903 at the cost of turning on the utilities.[166] He raised money in 1904 to buy a piano for the place and to put in the chemical fire extinguishers required by the state.[167]

There was a real effort to make culture in Ness City commercially viable. In 1905, the Ness County Musical Society appeared, which held its first concert at the opera house in December and received $70 for its effort at putting on an oratorio. It was good, but, Barnd wrote, "there must be a little in the line of ballads and rag times, as well as the classic, to make a concert acceptable."[168] The society presented an oratorio called "Christ and His Soldiers" at Ransom early the next year. The gate there was only $22, partly because Ransom was out of coal oil. But the thirty-four singers did get a free dinner at the Commercial Hotel.[169] The second concert of the musical society at Ness City in spring 1906 was not "as pretentious" as the first but was even less appreciated. The weather was poor, "and the people do not care a great deal for classical music, no matter what may be the fad in other places." More "snappy, catchy popular selections," with more "attention to the enunciation of the words," would help at the box office. "It requires considerable patience to sit an hour or two to hear people whom you know to be able to 'talk United States' straining themselves to their utmost to make their language as unintelligible as possible."[170]

The art gallery at the Lion Block struggled also, but at least there was an art gallery in Ness City, run by a photographer.[171] He unfortunately turned out to be a drug addict and had to be institutionalized.[172] When Shakespeare's *Julius Caesar* played at Garden City in 1906, the audience was rude. The press noted, "The play of Julius Caesar does not appeal to the masses, but that is no reason why those who do like Shakespeare and wished to hear, should be annoyed by a lot of hoodlums in the gallery."[173] The Ness City Concert Band did better, partly because members bought their instruments themselves, performed for free, and combined their concerts with cakewalks and box suppers.[174]

That tiny Ness City had these amenities indicates their importance to any town aspiring to respectability in the era. Dodge City in 1898 had a lecture on the Shakespeare-Bacon controversy and a performance of the nurse scene from *Romeo and Juliet*, all organized by the women of the St. Cornelius Guild. It was, said a reporter, "one of those social events for which our city is becoming noted."[175] Larned had an orchestra playing for dances by 1907.[176] The town hosted a touring company of *As You Like It* at the opera house the next year, although the audience was small. The press commented, "Most of the actors and actresses spoke as though they had their mouths full of hot mush."[177] Liberal staged the chariot race from *Ben Hur* at a church in

1901.[178] In 1908, the press there reported that there were 200 pianos in town, about as many organs, and some violins. There was a cornet band orchestra, a male quartet, and many church choirs. There were also lots of phonographs "rasping out stuff by the rod, which some people call music."[179] When the men of Ashland (population 910) fell to arguing over what pieces to play, the town substituted an all-female cornet band.[180] The Ladies Study Club there in 1912 staged the play *Union Depot* ("Catchy Music, Noted Characters and Lots of Fun") for the benefit of public school drinking fountains.[181] The town had an orchestra by that time, or what it called an orchestra.[182] Hays residents watched *The American Girl* put on by the Sterling Stock Company in 1904. Between acts were a number of "new and novel specialties . . . embracing the latest single and double songs, dances, sketches, musical eccentricities, etc. which together with the pretty costumes and unsurpassed scenic equipment, have helped to earn for the widely popular company the merited reputation it now enjoys."[183] On a more elevated level, there was a performance of *Hamlet* in 1908 at the Normal gym with a local professor in the title role.[184] Remarkably, the town of Kinsley in 1912 began a series of outdoor community drama productions of Shakespeare that lasted several years. Under the headline "Fairies in the Short Grass," the *Kansas City Star* covered a production of *Midsummer Night's Dream* involving a good deal of the population of Edwards County. Over one hundred people took part in the production, and hundreds sat in buggies and motorcars on chilly evenings to watch it during its three-night run. Proceeds went to the Kinsley public library.[185]

Another cultural initiative prominent in town news in the first decade of the century was the creation of libraries. And invariably these libraries, whether public or private, were the creations of women's groups, often as the initial project of a woman's club that was part of that quintessential regional progressive organization, the Kansas Federation of Women's Clubs.

Reading was popular, and there were indications that, as with music, the taste of the population could be slowly elevated. True, sports were more popular than reading. At Larned in 1902, people thought it was keen that J. T. Whitney had installed a "wall exercising machine" in his bowling alley, which for a penny recorded the force of blows directed at it by would-be pugilists.[186] A rally and box supper for the high school football and basketball teams at Larned drew a big crowd, which was entertained by yells and "bazoos" from the "Spook Club."[187] The new "Air Dome" movie house at Hays drew a crowd of over 600 on its opening night, drawn there by a "colored light" advertisement across the street.[188] Perhaps the sports, bowling alley, movie, and pool hall enthusiasts would be difficult to raise to their usual pitch on behalf of libraries, but cultural activists of many towns hoped not.

In Dodge City, in 1902, there was a survey, "What Western Kansas Reads," consisting of interviews with citizens. A. B. Reeves liked Macauley's essays and the poetry of James Whitcomb Riley. H. A. Cord, the principal of the second ward school in Dodge City, read magazines, the novels of Richard Carvel, and the Bible. Fred Gardner sampled the material in the railroad reading room. All felt positive about reading. Reading, the reporter commented, placed Western Kansans in contact "with the best society in every period of history" and provided models for emulation.[189] "Of course we knew," the reporter added, "that Dodge City had emerged from its Pliocene age when no one read anything but the Police Gazette and the Live Stock Indicator, but we were not prepared for the simple and Arcadian, not to say archaic tastes of its citizens. . . . It has gotten beyond the Dare Devil Dick stage."[190]

Women, many emphasized, read with discrimination. Did they choose wisely, wrote a woman in Larned, or just pick books as they would their garments, from the latest fashion? That depended upon the woman, she said, but women who thought for themselves, who picked a biography or some essays or a history instead of the latest novel, "have the advantage of a large training and a larger culture" over their "sensational" sisters. Those latter, however, were no worse than men who read only the newspaper, a large class.[191]

To create libraries to house these books was a central project for women's clubs, and these clubs were a prominent feature of regional life in the early twentieth century. "The woman's club," wrote Mrs. Mary Wade, speaking as mayor of Hays in 1896, "is a living, breathing, influencing institution in Kansas and should be an inspiration to every woman to lift her outside of herself and lead her into the green pastures of thought and beside the still waters of hope. Better days have dawned for Kansas."[192]

Hays women formed the Saturday Afternoon Club in 1895. Its yearbook of 1899 listed as study topics the following: current events, mythology, French history, science, and debate. That year it organized the Saturday Afternoon Library Association, to which each member contributed $1 a year. In October 1900, thanks to their efforts, the Hays library opened. The club met in the library and sponsored successful book talks, mostly by professors at the Normal, on currently popular volumes. The library became a city institution in 1904 thanks to a matching grant from the Carnegie Foundation, for which the Saturday Afternoon Club officers applied. A new building came in 1910, constructed with tax money.[193]

This was a standard pattern. Salina women held a large public rally in 1896, including entertainment from the Presbyterian and Lutheran church choirs and addresses by W. W. Watson, "The Library from a Business Point of View," and by Mrs. T. L. Bond, "The Library as an Auxiliary to the Schools." Salina had just turned down a request for funds for a public library, but the women persevered in their efforts to get one.[194] The Phenix Club at Dodge City held a library social in 1904, asking every person attending to bring a book to donate to a public library.[195] The women there contacted the Carnegie Foundation, got a $7,500 matching grant, and brought the library issue to a successful vote in town in 1905.[196] At WaKeeney the women formed the Tourist Club in 1903 to study history and travel, "so that they might keep up their education and interest in cultural matters after their school days were over." They bought a set of John L. Stoddard's Lectures around which they organized their study, but shortly collected more books. By 1906, the Tourist Club opened a library with 300 books. The members hired a librarian at their own expense, raising the money through holding ice cream socials. That library was run privately until the city took it over in 1916.[197]

At Garden City, the Lady's Library Association ran the library, located in the Buffalo Block, beginning in 1899.[198] The association charged $1.25 a month for a reading ticket in 1905 and opened the 1,100-book collection on Wednesday and Saturday afternoons.[199] There was a fierce debate at Garden City in 1909 about the desirability of establishing a free Carnegie library using tax funds, partly because the women had been doing such a good job with the private library.[200] However, the vote in town that year for the library proposition was favorable.[201] In 1915, Garden City got a Carnegie library, thanks to a matching fund campaign organized by George Finnup.[202] The Liberal Women's Club organized a successful campaign for a Carnegie library in 1907. The tax per person, they said, would not be more than the price of one or two good books. "These dollars can not be carried into the grave. All shrouds are pocketless."[203]

It was the same at Belleville, where the Star History Club, consisting of women, pushed the library campaign. "The choice of good home reading for the boys and girls of our city," they advertised, "should be a more important subject to every mother and father in the community. There would be less demand for cheap novels and yellow back journals if there was a public reading room provided where only the best literature was to be found."[204] The *Kansas Farmer* agreed on the practical value of reading. "I am sure," wrote the editor in 1912, "Kansas farmers are reading more and better today than ever before. There is the same reason for the farmer reading and keeping himself posted on the best practice in his line as there is for the doctor, lawyer, or dentist knowing what is going on in his line."[205]

A succinct statement of what women's clubs were about was given in 1902 by the retiring president of the Portia Club, which had formed at Larned in 1894 for the purpose of studying literature, art, science, and "mutual improvement." The club, according to the statement, was "a school in which the busy housewife may learn of art and literature and in this school she may open her eyes upon a more expansive view of the great, grand world." The clubs in Western Kansas established libraries, reading rooms, and rest rooms; cared for the destitute and suffering; raised money from local businesses for art exhibits; sold photographic prints of art masterpieces with the proceeds going to the schools; staged mock conversations between famous historical figures; marked the Santa Fe trail sites; and visited poorhouses to make "the surroundings more cheerful and homelike for its aged ones." The members hoped to create an interest in sanitary conditions and transform "the unsightly places about depots and other public places into attractive parks." They moved to decorate schools and introduce industrial education into the curriculum.

Some clubs admitted men to their meetings, although none allowed them to vote. To educate a man, it was said, was to educate an individual; to educate a woman was to educate a family. How much better it would be if "in place of the silly chit-chat and gossip, we could talk intelligently on any subject." That was vital to the progress of society in the region. "The time has passed," said the Portia Club president, "for any right-minded person to sneer at the woman's club."[206]

At a regional reception held by the Portia Club in 1903, women from all over the region converged on Larned for a reception and a program. The program opened with favorite quotations, followed by a duet based on an arrangement of a Mozart symphony, a synopsis of the club's work for the year, a paper on Scotch poets, and, finally, poetry by the county superintendent of public instruction, Grace Norton. Norton, attendees said, "gave ample evidence of woman's fitness in a new sphere."[207] The women of the Hays Civic League ran a baby-sitting stand in 1913 to "enable mothers to leave their babies in the care of a competent woman and enjoy the Chautauqua." It also provided a drinking fountain near the tent and later in the year sponsored an exhibit of art reproductions at the high school assembly room.[208]

There were exceptions to the rule about the dominance of women's organizations in the advance of culture and bookishness. As with J. K. Barnd in Ness, sometimes a small town had an individual "angel" who had money to spend, made culture a priority, and single-handedly created a kind of oasis. Such was the case with Howard Barnard of La Crosse, Rush County. Barnard had come to Western Kansas in the late 1870s from New York City, where his uncle had founded Barnard College. After working for some years as a cowhand, he bought a 10-acre plot of ground and in 1906 founded the Entre Nous School with inherited money. He ran it for eight years and spent $40,000 on it before his money ran out. He had a passion for books and collected one of the finest libraries in the region. When the mortgage company closed his school, the residents of the county took up a collection to make him librarian of the La Crosse city library, an institution which became as a result one of the finest small-town libraries in Kansas. Barnard at his death in 1948 left his personal collection of 15,000 books to the children of Rush County.[209]

Not unlike Barnard was George Finnup of Garden City, sometimes called the "Western Kansas Carnegie." By 1915, Finnup had a foundation active in helping country schools and churches in six Western Kansas counties by providing them with buildings and books. "No 'yellow backs' or coarse books are permitted," was Finnup's rule, and he supported culture and religion generally, although he was not a churchgoer himself. Culture and religion were part of the development of the region, he thought, and that was important to him. The region had "enabled me to prosper and I am no ingrate."[210]

Many rose early in the spring of 1910 to watch the return of Halley's comet in the eastern sky. None were immune to the strange beauty of the comet, or to the mystery of its comings and goings. It reminded any sensitive person of the passage of time and of the deep rolling of destiny for individuals, societies, and regions.

A Ness City man, observing Halley's at 4:30 A.M., found it an impressive sight: "It extended from the horizon north of east, obliquely to the southwest along the ecliptic to a distance of nearly eighty degrees." Were it better placed, one could get an even more spectacular view of "this historic monster."[211] It was not up to advance notices, said another, but it "furnished sufficient excuse for the ordinary individual to do the rather unusual stunt of star-gazing."[212] It must have seemed to residents that they had the best of both worlds, being able to arise from their warm beds, switch on an electric light, maybe call a friend on the telephone, and then step out onto the dark and quiet brooding prairie to see Nature in its grandeur on the farthest horizon.

Something else came from the sky at this time, and got much closer to home—the airplane. In 1910, in the shortgrass country, the airplane definitely was in the category of exotica. But it got people's attention and it promised

First biplane exhibition and flight made in Kansas, Larned, November 2, 1910 (courtesy of Wichita State University Special Collections)

a new round of transforming technology that might make the electric pump and even the automobile seem primitive. The Larned Fair Association and the Pawnee Country Agricultural Association arranged with Captain William Evans to exhibit his flying machine at Edwards Park in the fall of 1910. He promised a cross-country flight from Larned to some adjoining town, the first airplane flight ever attempted between Topeka and Denver.[213] The result was "a dismal and disappointing failure."

The weather was perfect. There was a crowd of 2,000 to 3,000 from as many as 100 miles away. But the wind wrecked the plane almost as soon as it got off the ground. The crowd "talked politics and killed time."[214] Evans returned to Larned in December to prove that he could fly "and that he has the machine to do it with." On that occasion he made a "beautiful and thrilling flight" of 5 miles and was in the air 11 minutes, at an altitude of 500 feet. The motor gave out after that and the pilot had to jump out of his craft a few moments before it struck the ground, suffering bruises and a bloody nose. The airplane set down on a plowed field upright on its wheels but pitched forward and was damaged. The crowd of 3,000 was ecstatic. People rushed forward and tore the airplane apart to take home parts of it as souvenirs.[215] They had seen this "monster," too, and they were much more enthused by it than by the motionless, noiseless celestial one.

This rickety machine did presage something—a future of progress when time and distance would be conquered, just as weather and darkness seemed now to be. Hays was a good town, an editor there had written in 1903. It had two newspapers, "clean, well written, carefully printed; fit to be sent anywhere and compared with any papers." There were three pretty churches, an up-to-date dentist, a good flouring mill, "and a wealth of brainy, bright lawyers."[216] By 1910, it had electric lights, a public library, and a musical establishment. Optimism had never disappeared among the resilient residents of Western Kansas, but now there seemed real grounds for high hope. It appeared that here at last was the beginning of a substantial and well-founded period of prosperity, irreversible by the caprices of Fortune.

As usual, people were wrong about the irreversible part. But indeed, after some early sputtering, the next decade in the region did seem the fulfillment of dreams. It was to be a time looked back upon from the dust of the 1930s with almost as much wonder as it was looked forward to by the crowds of farmers driving their stylish automobiles to the airplane demonstration at Larned in 1910.

6

The Golden Age

The best years for Western Kansas often followed hard on some of the worst. This was almost archetypically true of the second decade of the 1900s, beginning as it did in dust and ending in glory. The period of World War I was, due to a remarkable convergence of national and regional trends, a time of unparalleled prosperity for the towns and farms of the Kansas High Plains. In the grim years immediately proceeding 1914, however, there were few who could have glimpsed the light in the distance, and then only with eyes of faith.

The superintendent at the Garden City Experiment Station, established in 1907, submitted his first annual report in 1908. He had 320 acres at an altitude of 2,940 feet. There were 40 plowed acres, and the rest of the property was in native buffalo grass. On the farmed section were 148 one-tenth-acre plots devoted to experimental work in dryland agriculture in cooperation with the U.S. Department of Agriculture and Kansas State Agricultural College. In 1908, moisture was 8.18 inches during the growing season from April to September. The superintendent said he needed more horses, a barn, and a gasoline engine.[1] By 1914, the station had an irrigation division.[2]

The Tribune station submitted its first report in 1913. That year it presented an exhibit at the International Dry Farming Congress to show what could be done in a region where the annual rainfall was only about 15 inches, which "does not come at the right time or in the right manner in order to mature profitable crops." The director noted that the altitude at Tribune (3,616 feet), combined with the weather conditions, was "often quite discouraging to the average farmer of this district."[3] Greeley County was not a population center, consistently ranking near the bottom among Kansas counties in this category, and Tribune, the county seat, had fewer than 200 people when the station started there. However, it represented a definite climatic zone, and that was what was important to science.

Colby first reported in 1914. "This station," the director said, "will attempt to show by example that it is worth while through all this section of the country to make a farm home attractive and comfortable rather than simply a place to exist."[4]

The mildly defensive tone was attributable to a recent history that had been ragged on the agricultural front. The Colby station superintendent spent some time talking about the "blow" area in Thomas County and what was to be done about it. A reporter from Kansas City, visiting the area in 1913, mentioned that a tract of land about 15 miles square "lies brown and naked, stark and choked with dust, and scarcely a shoot of green is in that tract. Houses stand knee-deep in a pile of siftings of the field and the wind, after the lawless manner it has pursued since the first breeze wafted through Eden, blows where it listeth, with utter disregard for wheat crop needs."[5]

Thomas County people did not like the exaggerated publicity, although they admitted that the truth was bad enough. Several eastern papers, a local paper wrote, "have put the matter in such a light that a stranger to this part of the country would naturally think that we were in the midst of a desert something similar to the great Sahara."[6] J. N. Fike, Colby's largest farmer, took the Kansas City reporter on a tour and was full of optimism for the future. But the writer noticed, "They are a little sensitive about the desert out in Thomas County, and they much prefer to refer to it as 'the blow district.'" What Fike called a "dust flurry" seemed to the reporter to be a "smoking cloud," and he failed to be convinced that the dust storms that had come in the spring of 1912 and blown out so much land would not return. He was encouraged, however, by the appearance and attitude of the town. "There are bathtubs in Colby, and fifteen minutes intimate communion with one helps wonderfully to restore some hope to life, and bring back sight and hearing and power of speech. Best of all is to talk with these fellows who are campaigning against the wind." W. D. Ferguson, the leading Colby banker, was upbeat. He said he regarded the blown district as a good investment, with lands selling at $10 to $14 an acre. Six inches of topsoil had blown away, but this revealed a richer soil underneath. Such a blow had happened before in the 1890s, and the district had recovered. The soil was good; it was not a real desert. And "if the desert can come back for a little while, why so can Colby, and no small matter of a few month's wind is going to be allowed to count."[7] The citizens make the country, said a local editor, and "one would have to travel a long way to find a place where they will fight as hard for their country as the people here do."[8]

The area did come back. The businessmen of Colby joined together, and each took a quarter or half section of the damaged district to farm and to rescue. "It is their purpose," wrote a reporter, "to farm every bit of the ground just the same as if they were living there and if they do this the dust problem will doubtless be solved forever." The Foster Lumber Company of Colby purchased several sections of the blow district and rented twenty quarters in addition. The company had fifty teams plowing and listing in the spring of 1914 for a spring crop.[9] H. M. Cottrell, the agricultural commissioner for the Rock Island railroad, spent twenty-five days in Thomas County in the summer of 1915 fighting drifting soil. The Rock Island gave $4,000 for the enterprise, the Union Pacific pitched in $1,000, and the wholesalers and jobbers of Salina and Topeka gave $1,000 and $1,500, respectively. Cottrell's crews plowed deep trenches with listers, planted kafir, and tried to hold the remaining soil.[10] The blow district grew a crop of wheat in 1914, as war in Europe increased the price of that commodity. J. M. Carpenter had a 2,500-acre wheat field that year, and speculators from Kansas City, who had bought a good deal of the land at a low price, paid off their debts with a single harvest.[11]

The experiment station worked hard on the problem of the blow district. The superintendent there, supported financially by the county commissioners, took charge of a half section in the region and farmed it in such a way that it would not blow again. He listed the land in alternate rows and planted native corn and dwarf kafir. These produced a heavy and profitable crop of forage and increased the confidence of local farmers that science could be of use in the deepest crisis.[12]

In the statistical details coming out of the experiment stations was contained a dramatic story of challenge and response. At Tribune, on March 23, 1913, there was a strong westerly wind, which was "very destructive, blowing out soil and doing damage to buildings in general. A severe electrical storm accompanied this wind, which injured the wheat crop beyond recovery." April and May had little rain and "a great many hot, dry winds." Between July 18 and September 16, no rain fell in Tribune, temperatures were often near 100 degrees, and the winds were "hot and high," causing substantial evaporation. Grasshoppers descended on what remained, destroying the entire corn crop.[13] In 1914, temperatures at Tribune were over 100 degrees for several days as early as June. The superintendent took a nice photograph of growing wheat on June 10—"four days before it was totally destroyed by hail."

The drought and wind created "electric storms," which Superintendent Charles Cassell described vividly: "During such storms, which in no way resemble the ordinary type of thunderstorm, objects, especially of a metallic nature, become highly electrified and discharges of electricity take place between them and also between them and the body of a person approaching them too closely." Windmills and wire fences retained a charge and shocked people who touched them. The leaves of trees blackened and discolored almost as badly as if affected by a heavy frost. Windmills made a snapping sound. Prairie fires broke out. It was awesome and unusual—but not uplifting. "The air usually has a depressing effect on people in general which is partially due to the intense dust in the air." People riding in buggies often got a tropical tan although the sun was completely obscured by dust and clouds.[14]

Garden City reported that 1914 was the driest season on record. There were 9.70 inches of rain that year at the station, compared with an average in the period 1897–1914 of 20.3 inches. The report contained a frightening photograph of an approaching dust storm and an account of a hard hail in July, which injured the trees badly and wiped out the winter wheat crop. The irrigated section of the farm depended on a well that was over 170 feet deep, which was expensive to operate. The well alone, using a 75-horsepower engine, cost nearly $3,000 and used 6,000 gallons of fuel that year. It was questionable whether the average farmer could profit from such a plant. Wheat yields at the station were zero for one reason or another from 1909 to 1913. In 1914, although rainfall was less than 10 inches, the station harvested a crop of 12.5 bushels per acre. In 1915, the yield was 21.3 bushels. In any case, the staff was not there only for the short term. Its lease with the Board of County Commissioners of Finney County ran until the year 2006.[15] Equally sanguine was the staff at Hays, which by 1913 had 2,000 acres under cultivation, owned sixty horses and mules, and had electric power and telephone service.[16]

However, the negative aspects of things in the region could not be ignored. In 1912 was the advent of legions of green "stink" bugs. They were as big as a thumbnail and had a terrible odor when smashed. One night in Dodge City all business had to be suspended and the electric lights turned out. When trains came into the depot there, the passengers went into the Harvey House in the dark until they were safely inside with the doors shut. At a point where an electric light was suspended over the track, the bugs on the ground were so thick that a train stalled and had to back up to get a running start. Insects ruined the fair at Larned and people went home early. A cold autumn rain

Avery steam engine and plow, Sherman County, c. 1912 (courtesy of High Plains Museum, Goodland)

numbed the invaders, but the streets in several towns were strewn with them the next day and the sides of buildings and light poles were covered with them.[17]

A man from Scott City, who was a crop reporter for the U.S. Department of Agriculture and an entomologist, complained to Governor George Hodges in 1913 that the recent combination of circumstances in the region had been disastrous. There was a drought in 1911, a horse plague in 1912, and a grasshopper invasion in 1913. "The hoppers kept 90% of the plants eaten to the ground as fast as they came up. It is a condition that nobody but a 'crop-killer' would dare to describe and we must not let it get into print. It is a combination of adverse conditions that 'won't happen again in a thousand years' but it *did* happen and it hurts—hurts awfully!"[18] These were reminders that Nature was not yet controlled. "Kansas," a Larned reporter said, "is no country for a nervous man. Unless a man is equipped with nerves of chilled steel imbedded in ice, he should go to live in Iowa or Nebraska, or some state where nothing ever happens."[19]

A Goodland farmer thought the drought might be a good thing if it could open the eyes of Western Kansas farmers "to the necessities of better ideas in farming." However, the editor of the *Kansas Farmer* thought big changes away from wheat culture were unlikely. He wrote: "The western section of

Kansas has so long worshipped at the shrine of wheat, that when wheat fails their god is gone, and they do not know to what they should resort."[20] There were creameries in Western Kansas, just as there were beet factories, but farmers did not like the extra hand labor of cultivating beets and they did not like the work and responsibilities of diversified farming. Farmers disliked milking cows, wrote one from Western Kansas in 1913, "and thought an easier way to acquire prosperity was through the growing of wheat."[21] Fifteen years later, little had changed. Charles Scott, a newspaper editor from Iola, observed in traveling through Western Kansas in 1928 that wheat only became more ubiquitous as the years passed. "A man who is likely to make $25,000 to $50,000 a year riding wheat growing machinery," Scott observed, "is not about to develop much of a taste for milking cows two or three times a day, and he does not get much of a kick out of gathering eggs one at a time."[22]

The machine remained a magic element. There were giants in the old days, an editorialist wrote in 1914, and there are giants in these days too, namely gasoline tractors:

> This modern giant will not only do the work of several men but of several horses as well. He will run your separator, turn your churn, saw your wood, pump your water, cut your fodder, grind your corn, plow your land and many other things. The ancient giants were troublesome, hard to manage, and great eaters. The modern giant is tractable, always handy, always ready and willing to work, never gets tired, never runs away when you want him most. He is kept at very little expense. A drink of gasoline, or kerosene, when he is thirsty, and a little oil is all he needs, and that only while he works.[23]

If the Western Kansas farmer kept "to the front" in the latest machine methods and kept careful accounts of cost, many thought he could prosper in wheat. "The wheat grower on a large scale," was the advice, "can no longer afford to plow his land with a two-horse walking plow; neither can he afford to harrow it with a two-section, two-horse harrow; neither can he afford to harvest it with the old side drop reaper." But then hardly anyone did. In the summer of 1914, when there was good wheat selling at a decent price, grown on low-cost land with efficient machinery, real estate agents in Western Kansas reported vigorous demand for wheat lands. "We have no doubt," wrote the *Kansas Farmer*, "that thousands upon thousands of acres of land in Western Kansas will this year be bought by people who think they see a chance to grow wheat in profitable yields with sufficient frequency to make their investment in land profitable."[24]

There were projects from Washington, Manhattan, and Topeka—and from the experiment stations—that gave encouragement in gloomy years. Most visible among federal initiatives other than the irrigation projects was the Kansas National Forest, which showed up on maps between 1906 and 1915.

The forest did not fall into the region's lap accidentally. The idea originated in 1902, when A. W. Stubbs and C. J. "Buffalo" Jones called on Gifford Pinchot, the chief of the forestry division of the Department of Agriculture. They suggested that a reserve along the western reaches of the Arkansas River in Kansas be used for testing the growth of pine timber. Pinchot was surprised that there would be any suitable land for this in Kansas but agreed to study the proposition. There had been reserves of this type established in Nebraska, and some thought that it could result in a "veritable park" to enhance the beauty of the region as well as eventually in a cash crop of saleable timber.[25]

Details began showing up in the Garden City newspapers in 1903. Since the sand hills along the banks of the Arkansas River from Garden City to the western border of Kansas were not suitable for agriculture, the U.S. Department of Agriculture proposed to set aside from private ownership about 95,000 acres of land in Finney, Kearny, Grant, and Haskell counties to be planted in pine trees. President Theodore Roosevelt, who visited Western Kansas that year, made mention of the forest a highlight of his addresses there.[26] It was to be the largest tract of forest grown from nursery trees in the world (some estimated five million eventually).[27]

Pinchot's Bureau of Forestry published a pamphlet in 1904 entitled "Forest Planting in Western Kansas." Royal Kellogg, the forest agent who wrote the piece, made the creation of Kansas forests, as well as shelterbelts and homestead groves, sound plausible. Trees would not change the climate, but they would moderate winds, slow evaporation, and beautify farmsteads. Former efforts to promote tree planting had failed, but it was too early to conclude that a treeless prairie was inevitable. Care was required. Success with trees at the Pomeroy Model Farm near Hill City or on the grounds of various courthouses was not so easily duplicated over miles of isolated landscape. But Kellogg thought that large stands could be grown without irrigation.[28]

The act authorizing selections of land to be withdrawn for a Kansas forest passed Congress in 1905.[29] In 1906, planting began on eighty sections. "To the uninitiated," a local editor wrote, "this may seem uninteresting and of little practical value or utility; but to those who know of the possibilities of growing forest trees in the moist, sandy loam of the vicinity, set apart for the purpose, the establishment of this Forest Reservation is a source of great satisfaction." The forest, combined with the "great inland sea" that the reclamation project might create, would amount, the press said, "to a transformation more glittering and marvelous than anything found in the 'Arabian Nights,' classed as fables."[30]

It also resulted in too much dependency to suit some. The region was happy with the federal spending and was glad that the state of Kansas in 1911 settled on Larned as the site for an insane asylum.[31] But Larned had to bid against other towns for the state institution and offer almost 1,500 acres of land.[32] There was fear that the forest and irrigation expenditures by government might not be such a gift to the area as advertised either. The *Cimarron Jacksonian* editorialized, "It makes one tired to see the 'pieces' written for metropolitan newspapers by misguided advertisers of western Kansas by telling of the 'reclamation' of this section. . . . What is needed here is not 'reclamation' by costly ditches and pumping plants, but careful farming by the moisture-conserving Campbell system."[33] The government presence did, however, create an opportunity for regional advertising and instruction: "Strangers coming here can learn the best methods of irrigation to follow; they can see the crops and plants being grown that flourish in the semi-arid regions; they can see how the government is growing trees in the forest reserve; they can see the great government irrigation pumping plant in operation."[34]

The forest reserve, backed by the entire Kansas congressional delegation, was extended in 1908 to encompass 200,000 acres.[35] In 1909, the press admitted that it was "still in the experimental stages." A nursery west of Garden City grew cottonwoods, pines, mulberries, and red cedar for possible inclusion, but things did not advance rapidly.[36] H. B. D'Allemand, head of the project, held examinations for the forest service at the Finney County courthouse in the fall of 1909, hoping to create a staff.[37] The U.S. government authorized a $60,000 federal building in 1910 to be constructed at Garden City and to house the forestry service, reclamation service, and experiment station employees. "Quite a nice little plum," one man said.[38]

But, of course, the forest did not work as expected. In 1910, things there began to run in reverse. The Commercial Club at Syracuse expressed anger that the government was considering eliminating several ranges in their area from the forest reserve. But Garden Citians thought there was not much to worry about one way or the other. "Every member of the Syracuse Commercial Club and all the rest of us will be picking harps on the other side long before there are trees big enough on the forest reserve to shade a grasshopper."[39] By 1915, most were willing to admit that the forest had been a failure. It had not produced timber for fuel, poles, and fence posts as planned, and consecutive dry seasons had killed most of the trees. Slowly the area of the Kansas National Forest was restored to settlement and entry or leased for grazing.[40] The reserve had grown to 138,000 acres, thought to be worth about $4 to $5 an acre as grazing land. All that remained eventually of its special purpose was a five-section game preserve, which sheltered bison and antelope.[41]

More promising was new railroad development. Although it had nothing like the scope and importance of the major regional rail expansion of the 1880s, rail construction between 1909 and the outbreak of World War I in Europe opened new farming territory and provided a balance to the employment and investment that would be required for a prosperous and stable economy. And it was especially encouraging after such a long period of mere placeholding and survival in the field of Western Kansas railroading.

The first promise came from the Garden City, Gulf & Northern railroad company, organized in 1908, with the strategy to tap the sugar beet and irrigated farming districts served by the beet factory in Garden City. Its goal of building a line from Garden City to Scott City, a distance of about 40 miles, and providing electric power for irrigators along the route seemed feasible.[42] Another project, the Nebraska, Kansas & Southern, which was backed by the Burlington railroad, projected a line south from Superior, Nebraska, to Garden City, connecting with the Garden City, Gulf & Northern or its proposed northern extension, the Scott City Northern.[43] When the bonds for the Garden City, Gulf & Northern passed, the paper reported that "the Garden City spirit manifested itself in bonfires, screeching whistles, ringing bells, and the hurrahing of hundreds that gathered on the streets. Strangers entering the city on the night trains must have thought that pandemonium had broken loose, but the people had a reason for their enthusiasm."[44]

In 1908, there were rumors also of a "gigantic" enterprise in the region involving electricity. A. B. Hult, a representative of the Northern Electrical Company of Madison, Wisconsin, addressed a large crowd at the Garden City Industrial Club on the topic of joining with the sugar company to build a power plant at Canon City, Colorado, near a cheap source of coal, and building an electric railway and electric transmission line down the Arkansas Valley as far as Dodge City. The estimated cost of the project was $15 million. Hult said it could furnish power at 3 cents a kilowatt and could raise water much more cheaply than by any other method.[45] It was proposed that over 700,000 acres of arid land could be reclaimed by the project.[46] Four hundred delegates attended an electric power convention at La Junta, Colorado, in May to discuss the idea.[47] The new company, the Kansas-Colorado Power & Railroad Company, had backing from the General Electric Corporation.[48]

The new electric railroad company (with capital of $5 million) asked Finney County for aid. The *Herald* editorialized, "The small amount of aid asked is a drop in the bucket. . . . The man who opposes the bonds stands in the way of the greatest enterprise that can ever come to the valley."[49] An editor at Dodge City felt equally enthusiastic. "Nothing so stupendous, in this age of electricity, has before been attempted." The company would provide "power for lighting towns, raising the underflow, running mills and all kinds of machinery, and many other things besides operating a great railroad system; to make the valley a network of electric veins that will give it life in agriculture and commerce above any known country."[50] Bonds passed easily in several towns—by a nine-to-one margin in Garden City.[51]

In 1909, there were rumors that the Wichita-based Arkansas Valley Interurban, building toward Newton and Hutchinson, would be only the beginning of an extensive electric traction system that would not only vitalize the Western Kansas economy but would also enhance immeasurably its social and political connections.[52] The reopening of the Eureka Canal with its proposed enormous sump for natural flow occurred in that same year. The beet crop in 1909 was good. Beet farmers netted $30-an-acre profit. There had been no trouble getting Russian and Mexican labor under a single contract to work the fields, but the experiment stations were working on hybrid seeds to reduce the need for such labor. "Plans are being laid now to make the whole shallow water district of the Arkansas valley from Dodge City to the mountains just one big beet and alfalfa field."[53]

That summer, thousands of ties and stacks of switches and spikes piled up at the sugar factory ready to push the Garden City, Gulf & Northern railroad toward Scott City on a flat survey that would allow 40 mile-per-hour speeds.[54] That line opened in December with an excursion of seventy-five persons from Garden City. The train left the Tenth Street depot "and in a graceful curve swept around the south and west parts of the city, past the great sugar factory, that teaming hive of industry, past the machine shops of the road, over the many irrigating ditches and out into the country, past comfortable farm houses and large cattle ranches, past the little white school houses, through a country rich in soil, pregnant with the possibilities of the future, and so level that sky and land doth meet." Half the Scott City population met the excursionists and escorted them to the Central Hotel, where they had a meal of cream of oyster soup, roast turkey, sirloin steak, apple fritters, and spiced beets, followed by coffee and cigars. B. M. McCue received accolades for building the railroad, after such a long period of "hot air" projects in the region, "at last fulfilling the hopes of the people for a quarter of a century."[55] Perhaps the chance of the great regional electric grid was a long shot, but the steam railroad could still be magic. An editorialist for the *News-Chronicle* (Scott City) wrote that the new railroad would soon extend from the Gulf to Canada, and that "geographically and commercially fate has fixed the destiny of this city," so long as it continued to push and to keep "the wheels . . . rolling constantly."[56]

Actually the line never made it even to Nebraska. In 1915, it was purchased at a sheriff's sale by the sugar company, with only about 12 miles of its northern extension from Scott City ever having been constructed.[57] By 1916, the road was in the hands of the Atchison, Topeka, and Santa Fe. It became a good regional feeder, coordinated and backed by a major system, but hardly the redeemer of the desert or the regional powerhouse that had once been imagined.[58]

The electric line from the Canon City dynamos did not materialize either. There was gentle kidding by rival towns about Great Bend's claim to be an objective of the great Winnipeg, Yankton & Gulf railroad, or about Garden City's pretensions. "Garden City springs a new railroad every week," a Larned reporter commented, "notwithstanding the fact that the Santa Fe is still the only road which really goes through the town."[59] A Ness City man spoke tongue-in-cheek in saying that the name Nebraska, Kansas & Southern was "not sufficiently comprehensive—that it does not take in enough of the world in this day and age of gigantic enterprise. . . . There should be some far-away terminals attached to it like San Diego, California, and Panama Route or Isthmus Canal Route, or something of that kind to attract the attention of the world."[60] Most saw the joke. The smaller projects worked, and that was enough. People recognized that each little piece contributed to the whole and that a railroad represented more than track and cars. "Better towns will give you better schools, better business establishments, better amusements, better everything, and make you feel less like wanting to live some place else where there is something doing."[61]

A second ganglion of small Western Kansas railroads originating in that second decade of the century that experienced some success and remained in local hands longer were the so-called Byers roads. The Anthony & Northern (A&N), incorporated in 1912 and headed by Otto P. Byers, was the first of these. Byers had an investment in a flour mill at Pratt and wanted to move wheat to this mill from points further west. Construction began at Iuka in 1913 and the railroad angled toward Pratt. There followed a western extension to Kinsley (reached in 1916) and a northern extension through Larned and to a terminus in the middle of nowhere somewhat north of there (reached in 1917). The system took the name Wichita Northwestern in 1919, though there was little chance by then that it would ever connect to Wichita.[62] There was, however, always hope and faith in the not-yet-seen. When the railroad in 1915 asked Larned for $20,000 in bonds, the editor of the *Tiller and Toiler* was all for it: "No price is too great to pay for such a railroad as the Anthony & Northern gives promise of becoming."[63] In 1917, the corporate headquarters of the A&N moved from Hutchinson to Larned, adding an estimated 200 people and 100 jobs to the town."[64]

Increments of building were small, progress was slow, and financing was tentative. In 1914, the A&N constructed a total of 6 miles of track. It had freight revenue of $5,533 and passenger revenue of $85.02. Net operating revenue was $2.81. By contrast, the ATSF in Kansas made over $17 million in freight revenue and $7 million in passenger revenue that year.[65] Two years later, the A&N operated 25 miles of line and had operating revenues of $30,000.[66] In 1918, it had 80 miles of line and a profit of $18,000, though it had over $132,000 in current liabilities and was burdened with over $2 million in long-term corporate debt.[67] By 1915, it had a motor car with an auto engine carrying a few passengers.[68] Although it never reached Nebraska or Oklahoma as promised, it was responsible for the towns of Hopewell and Trousdale.[69] It survived, and it was real.

More important, surely, than these local projects, were extensions of the major railroads. A significant one in the era immediately before the war was the ATSF line running from Dodge City to the new railroad town of Elkhart in the southwest corner of the state. Elkhart was the last significant town founded in Kansas, and its establishment in 1912 marks in some ways the far limit of the settlement and development period of the region.

The first inklings of such a line came in 1902, when the story circulated that the Santa Fe might build from Dodge City to a connection with the Rock Island at Liberal.[70] The Rock Island had built an extension from Liberal to El Paso, Texas, so the connection, called at first the "Santa Fe cut off," seemed especially desirable.[71] Wrote an editor at Liberal: "It looks like Liberal is to have another chance to be great."[72] The southwest branch would shorten the times of California passenger trains by six hours, as it created a 100-mile shorter route on level ground where the locomotives could be run at maximum speed.[73] It would open an "empty sector" of five entire counties with sparse population and no railroads, but where the potential for wheat growing was good. Congressman J. R. Burton said that the land west of Dodge City was good only for grazing, the *Wichita Eagle* reported, "but humanity is going to tackle it again."[74]

The Dodge Booster Club, organized in 1905, argued that businesspeople must "drill together for battle in the interests of Dodge City, keep their pickets out and keep posted upon coming events in Western Kansas. . . . The old time feeling that things are going to bump along just as they have been doing in the past must give way. Because a dozen railroads have been built on paper, and never elsewhere, is not necessarily an argument that this will be so in the future."[75] Dodge City had a population of 3,500 people in 1906, up 700 in one year, thanks in no small part to railroad talk.[76] A Dodge publicist wrote, "The opening of such a road would be the beginning of our history as a jobbing point. Branch wholesale houses would be natural, and certainly follow and the importance of this place would be doubled instantly."[77]

Things, however, developed slowly. There was a charter taken out late in 1906 under the name Wichita, Dodge City & Western. Dodge City was the headquarters, but there was nothing yet to crow about. However, the Commercial Club was behind it, and it was a fine project for a town competing with Garden City, which had just gotten a big sugar plant. "Home people have hooted at the idea of Dodge City making a big place, when the idea has been advanced by visitors. We want to get the fact of our possibilities appreciated by ourselves, and go to work to make these possibilities over into realities."[78] It was a Kansas craft to develop towns, and Dodge did not want to lose the knack through inattention or lack of practice.

By 1909, it seemed inevitable that big things were about to happen on the Kansas rail front. Seventeen railroad companies took charters in the first few months of the year. These included the Farmers & Stockgrowers' railroad, headquartered in Plains and planning to go from Pratt to the Colorado line; the Nebraska, Kansas & Southern line #2, headquartered in Stockton, to go from Ness City to the southern boundary of the state; the Wichita, Kinsley, Scott City & Denver Airline, headquartered in Kinsley, to be built from Wichita to the western boundary of the state; the Gulf & Northwestern, headquartered in Goodland, to build two lines of 250 miles each across Western Kansas; the Kiowa, Hardtner & Pacific, headquartered in Hardtner, to build 350 miles through Barber, Comanche, Clark, Mead, Seward, Stevens, and Morton counties; the Kansas Northwestern & Great Bend, headquartered in Great Bend, to build 300 miles from Wichita to the west and south boundaries of the state; the Garden City, Gulf & Northern, headquartered in Garden City, promising at that point to build north from Garden City to Hill City, and also northwest from Garden City to St. Francis, Cheyenne County, with a third branch from Garden City to Liberal and thence northeast to Hays—400 miles total; the Hutchinson, Huntsville & Western, headquartered in Hutchinson, to build from Hutchinson to Huntsville in Stafford County; the Dakota, Kansas & Gulf, headquartered in Beloit, to build through Mitchell, Jewell, and <u>Smith counties</u> to the Nebraska line.[79] Most of this was, of course, in hindsight, mere dreaming.

The Farmers & Stockgrowers' company had a connection to the proposed Santa Fe cutoff. It would build from Dodge City through Santa Fe, Ulysses, and Johnson City to the Colorado line. G. C. Brown of Plains headed it, and the plan was that it would be financed by farmers along the line, who hoped thus to increase the value of their lands.[80] Doubtless the threat of this was a factor in diverting the ATSF from its purpose of building to Liberal and turning its attention toward a line along the Cimarron River Valley and through the above-named tiny places. Garden City kidded Liberal in 1910 that if half the paper projects worked, Liberal would not have room for its railroad terminals and shops.[81] Two years later, as the ATSF bypassed Liberal and started its own competing towns, the people of Liberal were crushed. Five years before, there had been predictions of 5,000 in population and streetcars. In 1912, the actual population was 2,000, and "the only cars are the autos, baby buggies, and farm wagons, and they are sufficiently metropolitan for a while at least."[82]

The manuscript records of the ATSF, now at the Kansas State Historical Society, throw interesting light on the railroad's strategy in the southwest Kansas expansion projects of 1912 and immediately after. The rail corporation intended to benefit from the new line exactly as the farmers promoting the Farmers & Stockgrowers' line intended—directly through an immediate increase in the value of lands and independent of perhaps slow returns on rail traffic. E. P. Ripley, the president of the ATSF, wrote to W. D. Hines, the chairman of the board, in 1909: "Almost every year since I have been connected with the road efforts have been made by landholders and promoters to afford transportation facilities to that large area of territory lying west of Dodge City and south of our main line." The soil was good, he noted, and there was abundant water at shallow depths. Although rainfall was "rather scant," it was equal to the territory through which the ATSF ran west of Amarillo, Texas. Farming was successful there and provided the road with good local earnings. "This territory is now so remote from transportation that it is used almost wholly for grazing purposes and has but a scant population, but the building of a railroad would result in its immediate sale and colonization." If the company were to build 100 miles of track west of Dodge City, the price of lands would immediately double or triple. They should at least go from the current $10 an acre for grazing lands to $20 for potential wheat lands.

Ripley went on to make a remarkably straightforward statement of how such an extension might be made worthwhile to the company in the short as well as the long run. The company should buy large amounts of this land before announcing its plans, and then profit from a resale almost in the way the land grants had worked to reward rail regional development in the nineteenth century. "Why should we not furnish an auxiliary company with the funds necessary to buy say 200,000 acres of land, and thus recoup ourselves doubly for the cost of the road?" In the three years after completion of the line, Ripley thought, the company could sell enough of it to get back all the construction costs and would have good first mortgages on much of the rest. Absent this, the new line might earn its operating costs at first, but it would be several years before it would earn even the interest on the capital investment required.

Ripley pointed to the example of the Garden City, Gulf & Northern. It had been built from Garden City to a connection with the ATSF at Scott City "through a country no better than what we are now considering, and [they] have their eye on a proposition to continue south from Garden City." The Santa Fe should not allow that territory in Gray, Haskell, Grant, Stanton, Morton, and Stevens counties to be penetrated by a rival company, especially when there was such a simple way to finance its own occupation. "I really see no good reason why all the benefits should accrue to the present landholders since we should create with our own money all the additional values. This cannot fairly be called real estate speculation—there is nothing of speculation in it at all. We can sell the land with our own existing colonization machinery and at small cost."[83]

Hines was not certain of the wisdom of this, citing legal concerns. He was not sure, he wrote, of the "propriety" of the Santa Fe's organizing an auxiliary to deal in land along the proposed southwest Kansas route. "It may be true that there would be no element of speculation in such a step, but I feel it is perfectly clear that it is a matter wholly outside the purposes for which the Atchison Company was formed." This was a pure money-making scheme, and the reasons justifying it seemed to Hines "far fetched." Would it not put the company in a "vulnerable" position, making it subject to "hostility and attack" and to charges of conflict of interest?[84]

The executives got a legal opinion. The attorney said perhaps the formation of a subsidiary was questionable, but the Santa Fe Corporation did have the power under a 1905 Kansas statute to "take and hold . . . real estate" for the purpose of "aiding in construction maintenance and accommodation of its railway." The lawyer agreed, however, that were the company to do this, it might "create great hostility" on the part of other landowners in the area.[85] With that opening, the executive committee decided to leave it to Ripley whether to purchase 200,000 acres of land before announcing the route, and Ripley of course did it, using a California subsidiary corporation, the Santa Fe Land Improvement Company, for the purpose.[86]

Plans became definite in 1910. The land buying would be further insulated from the Santa Fe proper by having it done in the name of A. C. Jobes, a vice president of the First National Bank of Kansas City and a Santa Fe director, with whom the Santa Fe Land Improvement Company would have an arrangement.[87] An agricultural agent sent to southwest Kansas reported that the land there was suited for wheat culture.[88] In the summer of 1910 the Santa Fe authorized an expenditure of $1.2 million for land in the area and made contracts for 1,665 quarters, or 256,000 acres, at an average cost of $6.60 per acre.[89]

The combined operation of railroad building and land buying in a territory new to wheat monoculture was most successful. "A man will have to work hard to learn to handle the soil differently from the eastern farmer," wrote a railroad agent in 1915, "but it is done and will be done in that country."[90] Land did not shoot up quite as rapidly as predicted, but some sold for $15 an acre as early as 1915.[91] This represented a tidy profit on the $6.60 the Santa Fe had paid. Among the buyers was the Standard Oil Company.[92]

Town development worked well also. Even the two towns for which the ATSF had chosen names of older boom towns that had come and gone—Ensign and Montezuma—were actually wholly new towns at new locations, and the lot sale business started all over again.[93]

A second round of buying in 1916 in the area that the projected Satanta branch would open cost the company less than $6 an acre. It purchased 26,600 acres in Grant and Stanton counties immediately and kept buying. "My impression," wrote their agent in the field, "is that if we do not build this year we are likely to get them somewhat cheaper. It seems to me there is no objection to our saying frankly to everyone who inquires in that country as to our intentions that we do not propose to build this year and we do not know when we will undertake the work. This ought to reduce the price of land and enable us to pick up a good sized acreage."[94]

In March 1916, there was an accounting of the activity thus far. The Dodge City & Cimarron Valley line, as the southwest extension was called, had been built. The company had sold a little over 100,000 acres, less than half of what it held along that line, for an average of $13 an acre, or about twice what it paid. And it was still holding 150,000 acres for a further rise. The Satanta branch would add a 60-mile line from Satanta (a town founded in 1912 when the Cimarron line was built) to the west line of Kansas. There was no hurry about the branch, Ripley said, and it was not undertaken until 1922. The strategy that worked so well with the Dodge City extension would work just as well again whenever the railroad wished to employ it.[95] Seldom has rail development strategy in the early twentieth century been better documented. The railroad profited and profited big, while taking little immediate risk. And it opened up that part of the Western Kansas country for the type of enterprises that would result in profits to many more.

The transformation the latter-day railroad brought was thoroughgoing, extending to politics as well as economics. O. H. Bentley of Wichita remembered in 1906 how he used to take the ATSF line to Syracuse and then ride 60 miles by mail carrier's rig to Richfield, the county seat of Morton County. The party stopped on the way at Johnson City, where they ate dinner in the stone basement of a dugout. Richfield, population sixty, was in 1906 said to be the smallest county seat in the world.[96]

Richfield had a $75,000 courthouse and was determined in its ambitions, but few saw how it could survive, much less retain its political status, after the new Santa Fe line bypassed it.[97] It is a tribute to local resilience in the face of seeming inevitability that Richfield won five county seat contests with Elkhart, and that the county seat of Morton County changed only in 1950. This was partly due to another in a series of elections and court cases that year and partly due to a fire that destroyed the courthouse at Richfield, but mostly, according to every savvy observer, due to the death in 1950 of Edward Marion Dean, one of the most remarkable Kansas politicians ever.

When the railroad came, and with it increased prosperity, Dean was ready. He knew every tract of land in the county and controlled the county records. The railroad company made Dean its agent in Morton County and authorized him to buy land at a slight commission in a very large volume. He did not prevail in getting the railroad to build through Richfield nor in his program of keeping ranches in grass, but he parlayed his influence into collecting the votes to keep Richfield the county seat.[98] In the 1920s, he manipulated the oil and gas boom as effectively as he had the railroad boom in 1912, and all to the benefit of Ed Dean and his little town.[99]

Other little towns of the old era declined more quickly. Santa Fe, which in 1887 had won a bitter fight with the town of Ivanhoe to become county seat of Haskell County, went the way of its former rival to oblivion when the Santa Fe extension missed it by 8 miles. In 1920, and not without a lawsuit going all the way to the Supreme Court of Kansas, Sublette became the county seat, and the town of Santa Fe disappeared.[100]

Johnson City, a town fewer than 20 miles from the Colorado line, did a little better. It had beaten out Eli in the 1888 county seat fight for Stanton County and managed to remain the largest town in the county (its 1976 population was 1,200) into the late twentieth century. It survived—even though, as an observer of small town America wrote in 1978, it "has been a borderline case often in its life." Partly, this was due to the fact that, unlike Richfield, which was far distant from the new railroad, Johnson City was on the Satanta branch. The ATSF tried to develop its own competing town, Mentor, which sprang up from the prairie in 1923, but it could not overcome the momentum of Johnson City. In fact, Johnson City revived from near dead due to the railroad, and in 1923 elected its first set of city officials since 1893.[101] The 1922 extension ended in the middle of a farm field with not a house in site, but the towns on it benefited from a train every other day.

The regional railroad revival in all its variety did suggest great things for the future. Some made the point that it was only a new kind of pioneering and that "the pioneers have not yet passed Kansas or passed in Kansas," but the older type of pioneer certainly had passed into the realm of nostalgia.[102] The Satanta-Mentor branch of the ATSF connected the last truly isolated piece of Western Kansas with the world of commerce and civilization that a modern railroad system represented.

Elmer Peterson gave an address connected with the dedication of Pawnee Rock, entitled "Only One Kansas. " It had a tone that would have been nearly unimaginable a decade earlier: "I want to be known as a Kansan, without prefix or suffix or affix, interlude or aftermath." He thought the "Western" should be left out of the designation of his region, and when used should not be capitalized. "The deadline is a myth, an absurdity. You can no more have a deadline dividing Kansas into two parts than you can make a clear dividing line between evening and night or between loud and very loud." Why did eastern editors continue to talk "of people going to western Kansas as if they were about to cross an ocean, or perhaps the river Styx itself, instead of perhaps moving over a county or two?"[103]

When the war broke out in Europe in 1914, creating demand for wheat and upping the price, while at the same time a wetter, more gentle period of climate ensued for farmers who were increasingly good at getting maximum production through mechanization and science, it ushered in an age that was golden for agriculture throughout the nation, but was particularly so in many ways for Western Kansas.

The basis was wheat, and it was in wheat culture that Western Kansas had learned its most profitable lessons. Yes, Finney County could continue to ex-

Harvest trucks at Colby, awaiting their turns to unload, 1919 (courtesy of Kansas State University Special Collections)

periment with sugar beets and irrigated alfalfa. Yes, the experiment stations grew a wide range of crops and the professors at Manhattan urged diversified farming as a hedge against the ups and downs of the market. Yes, the market was volatile and the cooperative marketing associations that formed could not do much to influence the speculations at the commodities exchange in Chicago. But hard red winter wheat was ideally suited to Western Kansas.

Increasingly, the region was seen not for what it lacked but for what it had—fertile soil and rainfall and heat that came at the right times to mature certain types of wheat. It was arid and cold in Western Kansas in the winter, but the wheat was dormant then. It did not rain much sometimes, but rain came in the spring when the crop needed it. And the June and July dry heat was ideal to get machines into the field to harvest and to ripen the heads. Kansas was flat, which meant little erosion and a wonderful environment for the gasoline tractor and the combine. The weather stressed the wheat just enough to bring out its fine milling qualities and give it high protein content.[104] New varieties of wheat became available in the early twentieth century, along with new methods of farming and new ways to spend the money that only a commercial, specialized farmer might hope to accumulate.

It became increasingly clear that the "wheat belt" was expanding and that Western Kansas was becoming the "breadbasket"—of Kansas and of the nation. "Western Kansas," wrote the *Medicine Lodge Cresset* in 1905, "is going to be the great wheat field of the world. Lands that have been thought only fit for short grass are proving it can also produce wheat, and the western counties are attracting immigration from all over the country."[105] That year, when the state raised 75,576,876 bushels of wheat on 5,854,047 acres, the top producer was Barton County with 3,552,858 bushels. All the other top counties, those raising over 2 million bushels, were in Western Kansas—McPherson, Reno, Pawnee, Rice, and Sumner. Since 1900, the state had regularly produced close to 100 million bushels of wheat a year.[106] Acreage increased also. In fact, the early twentieth century in the western region of the state was the time of the great plow-up. The acreages in wheat by 1930 remained steady through the rest of the twentieth century, although yields continued to increase.[107] Ford County in 1907 planted 122,000 acres in wheat, compared with 33,829 only six years earlier. Clark County went in the same period from 3,000 to 25,000 acres of wheat and Finney County from 1,600 to 12,000. The trend was everywhere, even in the far west. Lane County expected to raise a million bushels of wheat from 80,000 acres in 1907, and Cheyenne County planted 22,000 acres. Seven shortgrass counties, which two years earlier had raised a million bushels combined, raised three million in 1907.[108] As early as 1904, three-quarters of the Kansas wheat crop grew west of the center of the state in the true High Plains.[109] And the traditionally largest wheat-growing counties, Sumner, Reno, Sedgwick, and sometimes Barton, left out of that statistic, were still part of Western Kansas as defined by most Kansans. It was clear that as Kansas became "the wheat state," what was really meant was Western Kansas.

The "Wheat Kings" of the region did not stop there. In 1906, the average price per bushel of wheat was 58 cents. In 1911, it was 86 cents. In 1916, it was $1.44; in 1917, it was $2.12; and in 1919, it was $2.14. Never before or again did the American farmer enjoy so favorable a position in purchasing power relative to the rest of the economy. Acres harvested reached new highs; 1907 was a record year with 6,880,000 acres cut. In 1914, Kansans harvested 8,650,000 acres, and, in 1919, 11,524,000 acres. In 1914, there was a 100-million bushel crop, and by 1931, it was 200 million bushels.[110]

And there were the new varieties of wheat. The most famous early genetic improvement of wheat in Kansas, a variety called Kanred, grew originally in 1906 in the lab of H. F. Roberts, a member of the Department of Botany at Kansas State Agricultural College. He selected from a bulk lot of Crimean wheat, looking for leaf and stem resistance. This variety went into general use in 1917. A second variety, Blackhull, was the invention of Earl Clark and was based on selection from his father's fields near Newton. Clark later also developed Chiefkan, Red Chief, and Blue Jacket.[111]

Western Kansas families in the country, c. 1909–1916 (courtesy of High Plains Museum, Goodland)

These varieties were the culmination of experiments that had gone on for some time. The Hays Experiment Station harvested 380 varieties of wheat in 1905.[112] In 1912, it sold over 6,000 bushels of "pure-bred Kharkhof" seed wheat to farmers in Western Kansas to improve their strains.[113] Mark Carleton, who moved to Kansas in 1876 and graduated from Kansas State Agricultural College in 1887, did important work in this area. He obtained an M.S. in Botany and Horticulture and in 1894 became the assistant pathologist in the Division of Vegetable Physiology and Pathology of the U.S. Department of Agriculture. Carlton did field work all over the Great Plains on plant diseases and hardy varieties, publishing a major pamphlet on the latter subject in 1900 entitled *The Basis for Improvement of American Wheats*. He thought demand would drive large expansion of wheat acreage on the Plains and felt that genetic experiment would make production more efficient. He traveled extensively in Russia, and published a pamphlet in 1900 entitled *Russian Cereals Adapted for Cultivation in the United States*. He was chairman of the jurors of cereal exhibits at the St. Louis Exposition in 1904. Although a personal scandal interfered with his effectiveness later, Carleton made contributions to wheat science right up to his death in 1925. His biographer wrote that he "loved exploring the Steppes and loved likewise ranging the Plains, talking with farmers about their problems and aspirations."[114]

Of course, so-called Turkey wheat from the Crimea had been an example of better production through selection of an area-hardy variety that had established the crop adaptation pattern for Western Kansas in the 1870s. Just as settlers there learned that wheat worked better more often than corn and increasingly turned to it, so did they select the crops they grew in their fields as carefully as they did the flowers they grew in their gardens or the trees that surrounded their homesteads.[115] If farmers in Western Kansas were going to "persist in growing wheat," wrote the editor at Ashland in 1913, "then they should learn how to grow it every time they try. . . . Lands are becoming too valuable to be wasted and the way most wheat is planted is a waste of the land."[116] A man from Hays wrote the governor in 1914 that farmers were averaging 24 bushels to the acre, "a wheat crop such as the world never saw." His only complaint was the price of 60 cents, which he thought the state government should do something to increase.[117] A Colby man in 1915 thought there were no longer any limits in wheat production and marketing:

> The fine crop last year and the magnificent price has almost erased from the memory of our people the lean years, the blown strip and the other adversities of recent years. . . . The fellow who is on the breakers this year and has worn calluses on the end of his nose rubbing it against the wire wicker at the bank in his efforts to get his note renewed, may next year be one of the heaviest depositors in that same institution. . . . There are no set lines in the west that will always remain set lines and it is this eternal and ever present hope that the tide of good fortune will throw upon the sands at our feet the salvage from the ship of plenty that makes men cling to the west as they do.[118]

The experiment stations and the colleges played an ever-increasing role. They were, said C. W. Burkett, director of experimental stations at Kansas State Agricultural College, "towers of strength to farming."[119] The college sent educational trains all over the region. In 1907 it answered 100 letters a day on farm problems.[120] Hays Normal hosted a Western Kansas farmers' conference in 1910, with 1,500 in attendance. "Here," reported the press that day, "are to be solved the problems which still confront the farmer by the cooperation of the individual, the state, and the nation."[121] Josiah Main at Hays Normal was a national leader in agricultural pedagogy, who advocated that nature study in the school garden, practical agriculture, and agricultural science be taught in the Kansas public schools. In 1912, the college dedicated a new agricultural building, and it did not confine its activity to those walls. There were adult education courses of three weeks for "farmers and bookkeepers," given the first time late in 1912 by faculty from both Hays and Man-

J. W. Lough's irrigated alfalfa crop, harvested May 30, 1916, Scott County (courtesy of Kansas State Historical Society)

hattan. In December 1914, the course enrolled 2,000 people, 200 of these over sixty-five years old.[122] In 1912, lobbyists from Manhattan managed to get the U.S. Department of Agriculture to fund a field advisor in dryland farming for twenty-five counties in Western Kansas. The idea was to bring about a general application of the principles that had succeeded piecemeal locally, and to do it over a long period, ignoring cyclic ups and downs. "Opposition to the various plans for agricultural development cannot help but result in the farmers and business people standing in their own light. It is to be hoped, therefore, that there will be no opposition until it is found that the plans are not practical."[123]

There were some influential dissenters. When a bill arose in the state legislature in 1913 for two new experiment stations in the west, I. D. Graham, editor of the *Kansas Farmer*, noted, "Every time a legislator has a desire to do something for his farmer constituents he proposes establishing an experiment station; then he forgets that it needs money for its support and the station amounts to nothing." The Dodge City and Garden City stations, as well as those at Hays and Ogallah, he thought, were too close together and should be moved rather than starting anew. And did there need to be more varieties of wheat, when, according to Graham, the "wheat fever" had already advanced in Western Kansas "to the point that everything has been lost sight of except wheat farming?"[124] Graham emphasized the possibility that such commercial wheat farming might not be sustainable or permanent, and that it might damage the soil and be an irresponsible use of the environment. "The power of environment," he wrote in 1912, "is a fundamental law of life. . . . Landscape makes humanity more human and divinity more divine; giving to the one its proper environment and to the other its material expression. . . . Each home is a part of the landscape and should be a part of its beauty."[125]

Another prophet of doom for wheat monoculture was Professor J. H. Miller of Kansas State Agricultural College, head of the experiment station there. He sent out a circular in 1912 despairing of the trend toward big and exclusive commercial wheat farming in far western Kansas by farmers not using the summer fallow method but planting border to border year after year. It only exaggerated the cycles that were part of reality in the region anyway, he wrote: "Every exaggerated report of a big yield costs the real wheat farmer a few cents on every bushel of wheat and it tends to encourage shiftless farmers to increase their acreage, and this always means poorer farming." Usually, the next year the winds came, and the "Kings" moved out. Fifteen Kansas counties had less population than a year earlier. "Too much wheat. Too little forage. Too little livestock. . . . Of what avail is it to gain thousands of people in one 'fat' period if we lose them in the first 'lean' period?"[126]

Politicians and corporate officials sometimes chimed in. Grant Harrington, private secretary for Governor George Hodges, made some comments about wheat growing after traversing Western Kansas on a Union Pacific demonstration train in 1913. The western counties where the wheat failed so often, he wrote, ought not to be regarded as wheat counties. The tillable land should be put into forage crops:

> Traveling over that country one is impressed with the fact that the great majority of the people regard it only as a stopping place. There is no more greenery or attempt at improvement around the houses than in the middle of one of the fields. People do not live. They merely "stay" on one of these places. . . . The problem of the shortgrass is one of patient use of the advantages Nature has given it.[127]

This was not an uncommon academic stance. However, most of the population saw science and education as a way not so much to modify the trends in agriculture as to enhance farming efficiency in producing whatever crop paid best. There was more pride in human ingenuity than humility before Nature. Also, many did not accept the thesis that without irrigation wheat would not thrive on the High Plains and that it would therefore have to become a grazing country. Events since the 1890s had proved to the satisfaction of businesspeople that this was not the case.

Robert Wright, who had been at Dodge City through all its changes and had especially observed the transition from cattle to wheat, believed that wheat culture there was permanent, sustainable, and desirable. At the end of his 1913 reminiscence, *Dodge City: The Cowboy Capital and the Great Southwest*, Wright averred that the 1912 wheat crop was an important achievement. "She was at the very foot of the ladder," Wright wrote, "and she was bound to climb." Dodge City, with 5,000 people in 1913, had found the "happy medium." It was "all push and energy" and "founded on the broader firmer foundation of the development of territory and the natural pressure of modern civilization" so that it had no longer anything "mushroom like in its nature."[128] M. G. Blackman of Hoxie, tracing his experience in his region since 1895, concluded that the "matter of the most importance . . . is the fact that the conditions necessary to a profitable crop are so fully under man's control."[129]

Boosters in the towns loved wheat stories, and these were all about bigness. The 90-million-bushel crop Kansas produced in 1912 would fill 45,000 freight cars, making a solid wheat train 55 miles long. It would produce 6,400,000,000 one-pound loaves of bread and would feed 1,754,402 people every day for a year.[130] The residents of Dodge City and other wheat belt towns were proud of that.

President William Lewis in his inaugural address at the Hays Normal in 1914 said that Western Kansas had many things to solve

> of an elemental nature. . . . It is theirs to use the knowledge of the scientist and work it into an art applicable to a climate, soil, and season whose counterpart can be found nowhere else in the United States. . . . Our treeless plains, swept by the biting blasts of winter and scorched by the sun and drying winds of the summer, present a task of mastery fit for the brain of the greatest student of soils and plants and offer an opportunity to try the skill of the craftiest farmer who ever tilled the soil.[131]

Lewis added, in 1915, in an interview with the *Kansas City Journal*, that the mission of his school was "to teach teachers how to teach farmers how to farm. . . . Our central purpose is agricultural. . . . An institution which is to give valuable service to western Kansas cannot be the same in construction as a school in Illinois, Iowa, Missouri, or even eastern Kansas." In 1917, the *Country Gentleman* wrote up the Hays program for a national audience.[132]

Of course, big gains in wheat could mean big losses as people began to speculate. Perry White, thirty-six, owner of the White Fox Grain Company, left Larned early in 1916 with $29,500 in liabilities and less than $10,000 in assets. He held 38,000 bushels of wheat when the price slumped in the spring of

1915, and he lost $13,000. There were rumors that he had abandoned his family, even that he had committed suicide. White had strayed from doing a "straight grain business" into speculation because conditions tempted him to do so.[133]

People still looked for disaster stories from Kansas, but they became fewer in number. F. D. Coburn of the Kansas State Board of Agriculture continued collecting agricultural statistics and including them in cogent stories, which he fed to the media around the country. "When I started work as an information getter and news disseminator for the Kansas farmer [in 1894]," Coburn wrote, "the state was the most maligned and most misunderstood of all the states in the Union group." It was "plastered with labels," which "stuck like barnacles and they blistered like red hot sores." If the wind blew over a Ford County chicken coop, "some Chicago or New York paper would run a column story of a tornado that had carried five thousand Kansas hens, two hundred head of hogs, fifty beef critters, the county court with the judge, jury and tipstaves over the Oklahoma border." Coburn knew that people rummaged through his reports "in the hope of reading of some of our abnormal Kansas Kalamities." What they got instead was Coburn's measured and well-documented account of "plenty and progress."[134]

Ed Howe of Atchison wrote it up that way too. In a long article that he penned in 1917 about Western Kansas, he told of the impact of $1.74 wheat on everything and everyone there. William Kuhrt, a German living near Goodland, had a fine farm with a water plant and electric lights and was worth $100,000. Twenty-five years earlier he had worked on the railroad section for a dollar a day while his wife stuck to the homestead. There was a merchant in Goodland said to be worth a million dollars.[135] Rags-to-riches tales of this kind from Western Kansas became common, circulated nationally, and drew attention and people into the new boom.

In quoting the criticisms of Western Kansas both from the outside and from sometimes over-honest Kansans themselves, it is easy to miss the tremendous tone of optimism that was present in the early twentieth century and that reached a crescendo in the World War I era. "Father was dedicated to progress," wrote Harry Mason about his childhood near WaKeeney, "his own and that of the community as a by-product." Harry was interested in machinery and got every encouragement to become a mechanic. One summer about 1916,

> Father and I sat, almost every evening, on the concrete wings at the
> end of our cyclone cellar while daylight lingered then faded. He told
> me how a steam engine cylinder turned the expansion of steam into

Bountiful harvest on the Mangus farm, c. 1915, Sherman County (courtesy of High Plains Museum, Goodland)

powered rotation of a belt pulley. He described the double-acting piston, the slide valve, the eccentric mechanism, the crankpin and the pulley itself, the boiler, the steam dome, the flyball governor, the firebox and flues and the Penberthy injector which magically forced water into the boiler against its 150-pound pressure. I remember listening with rapt attention.[136]

And it is easy also to neglect the substance behind that optimism. Perhaps it was early to say so in 1905, but a Kansas City paper that year noted that there were

never such times in Kansas as they are having now and as they are going to have. [Farming in Kansas was] not only a safe venture—it has become one of the pleasantest of occupations. The sting of isolation and drudgery has been extracted from the farmer's life. The free rural delivery brings him his daily paper, the telephone keeps him in touch with his neighbors, and his automobile makes the distances beautifully less. Compressed air in his windmill tank supplies him with water, hot and cold, on the top floor of his house. Agricultural colleges have taught his boys scientific farming, and a complete crop failure is now hardly possible.[137]

By 1915, there was no hyperbole in such claims. So wealthy were area farmers that they had to guard against "the horde of jitney grafters" who took advantage. For months, a Larned editor wrote, these opportunists had been "alighting from every train, and ride the brake beams, and they come in automobiles and Zeppelins and taxicabs and submarines and motor boats."[138] In 1916, 1,000 cars showed up for auto day in Larned, with 7,000 people accompanying them. The town hired a movie crew to record the event.[139]

Wichita was wondrous, fed as it was by its western trade territory. It was, one man thought, "resurrected." Douglas Avenue was "a thoroughfare of unrivaled brilliancy," made so by "civic pride and private enterprise." People on the streets there were "not meandering along with Western carelessness but pushing their way ahead with purpose and intent."[140] What would one do without the telephone, a Hays man wrote. One could not "call the grocer or other business house, could not set down and talk to your friends, even way off in the distant city when sickness or death called you." As it was, a Hays merchant could talk with the Kansas state building at the San Francisco exhibition and hear as plainly as though the people there were right next door.[141]

The "purpose and intent" was evident in every aspect of life on the High Plains. The cultural gains that had been obvious before 1910 became impressive, even spectacular, in the decade. True, some of it was adaptation to popular taste. The Dodge City Cowboy Band put on a concert in 1915 featuring the latest pop tunes, including "Aeroplane Dip" and "I Love You California."[142] Doubtless this represented no great elevation of the public taste. But in other venues there was much earnest effort and some serious success.

One great promoter in the musical field was Professor Henry Edward Malloy of the college at Hays. Malloy was a Lindsborg alum and former leader of the *Messiah* chorus there. Hays Normal hired him in 1914, and President William Lewis told him to "sing Western Kansas into harmony and cooperation."

It fit Lewis's idea of "culture or art for the community's sake."[143] Lewis once said that there must be in the college curriculum at Hays "enriching materials which give expression in wholesome social joys and serviceable citizenship." There must be languages, literature, music, and history "to make people warm blooded, sympathetic, and patriotic." The college might seem especially materialistic, but, Lewis protested, "we put little reliance in the judgment of the man who has only contempt for the fine, joyous things of life as we do in the judgment of the man who confesses that to use his hands he is helpless, and wears this helplessness as a badge of honor. We simply assume that both of these types represent a species of mutation."[144]

The school purchased a large refracting telescope and a $20,000 organ, both among the largest of their kind in Kansas. Because of its "consecration to community ideals," people said, "the school has become famous. . . . This Normal school is not a mere bit of architecture filled with mental machinery to fashion and train teachers for the classroom only. The faculty realizes that every community is thirsting for ideals toward which to work. The school is doing that for its immediate territory and sending out instructors whose platform of service is as broad, unhampered and natural as the fountain head from which they draw their inspiration."[145] In 1915, a Beethoven piano sonata was performed, with Chopin and Liszt on the same program.[146] In 1917, 3,000 attended *Il Trovatore* at Sheridan Coliseum. The opera used a large local chorus and several imported professionals.[147]

Regional newspapers were ecstatic about the first annual Music Festival at Ft. Hays Normal in 1919, a week-long event, featuring Margaret Matzenauer of the Metropolitan Opera in New York City and Toscha Seidel, the young Russian violin virtuoso, among other guests.[148] An editor enthused, "The musical critics of New York, Chicago and Kansas City watched the rise of a new musical center in the Middle West, that of Hays." The $200,000 Sheridan Coliseum, the paper claimed, was "the Convention Hall of Western Kansas," seating 3,500 in comfortable opera chairs. Nearly 6,000 people requested souvenir booklets for the festival and heard Professor Mallory's talk on Handel. "It is our ambition," Mallory said, "at this state institution to have people go out from Hays into all parts of the empire of Western Kansas and there [begin] their own community choruses. . . . The sublime tragedy of Christ illustrated through the genius of Handel is to become a great part of the spiritual development of the Great Plains country." The evening performance of the *Messiah* at Hays rivaled the one at Lindsborg. Malloy directed a 50-piece orchestra and a chorus of 650 voices. Four professional soloists received $2,500 each for their week of services.[149]

Western Kansans had become so sophisticated that there were even some threats to traditional values there from the new scientific humanism. There was a group of atheists at Great Bend in 1915 protesting against religious instruction in the public schools. The leader of the Church of Humanity there said it was a tragedy that textbooks taught children "religious superstition for truths." He thought the motto of all should be: "There is no real God; Man has no soul; Life ends forever at death."[150]

So much became so modern. Western Kansas towns organized city commission and city manager forms of government. The citizens put in sewers and municipal light and power plants. They formed oil and gas companies, though production in the region did not establish itself until the time of the Carrie Oswald #1 well at Russell in 1923. They paved streets and highways.

They passed auto noise ordinances and speed limits. Dodge City (with a 1915 population of about 4,000) launched a daily paper in 1912, marking a start of a revival of dailies west of the eastern border cities and on the true High Plains. It was done, as the editor of the *Dodge City Daily Globe* put it, "in the belief that the town had reached a point of development where a circulation of the news more rapid than the weekly was necessary to the continued advancement of the town, and accurate review of the happenings as opposed to the old word of mouth gossip." People in Western Kansas towns acquired soft water. They used parcel post and rural free delivery. They published city directories. They offered college correspondence courses. They purchased personal airplanes. They built new courthouses. They organized historical societies. They built and operated public hospitals. They elected women to office. They even collected things. John Baughman of Liberal, a successful land salesman, acquired a valuable collection of western maps in 1913 and also collected stamps.[151] At Liberal in 1917, 180 stacks of the Montgomery Ward catalog arrived at the railroad station, with 25 catalogs apiece. Local merchants complained, but there was little to stop the trend.[152] Airplanes regularly flew over Liberal in those days. "Just get the habit of looking upward," a reporter said; "you who scoff may see many strange and beautiful things."[153]

Perhaps as surprising as any of these developments was the health of the Kansas Shortgrass Motorcycle Club and Dodge City's successful sponsorship of a nationally recognized motorcycle race. The Shortgrass Club held a tour from Hutchinson to Denver in 1913, which attracted 200 riders and had a moving picture camera along to record its activities.[154] The two-mile dirt track at Dodge City, built by the local Commercial Club in 1913, was the most impressive of several tracks in the region and hosted its first big races in 1914. Factory teams from Harley-Davidson, Indian, Merkel, Thor, Pope, and Excelsior brought highly modified machines to the 300-mile race, with riders that were earning as much as $20,000 a year. The crowd that year was 10,000. The race was an "international" event, and Dodge City became the "Indianapolis of Motorcycling." National and international racing journals covered the race. In 1915, the crowd was 15,000 and the winning cyclist averaged 76 miles per hour. In 1916, there were 20,000 spectators. Dodge City became one of ten sites chosen for the annual national championship motorcycle races and had the prime date of July 4. With some hiatus during the war, the national championship races in Dodge continued until 1922, a phenomenon of high times in a small town.[155]

The whole nation became interested in what was going on in the Western Kansas wheat belt. In the fall of 1917, the Kansas Council of Defense produced a film on the "romance" of the Kansas wheat fields. It was shown at the International Wheat Show and Food Conservation Congress at Wichita that October. "The people who take part," a western editor wrote, "are the people who know what they are doing, unlike the grotesque caricatures posing as 'farmers' in the typical 'old homestead' stuff put on at Los Angeles or New York studios with cardboard scenery in the background and the air full of whiskers."[156]

The editor of the *Troy Chief* in eastern Kansas visited Colby in 1918 and commented on the wonders of prosperity. Charley Murray took him around in a big car to see miles and miles of wheat fields worked and harvested by machines. "Skimming along in an automobile, a man can cover an immense lot of ground in a day, for there are no bad roads and you can duck out of the road anywhere and cut across a wheat field if you want and never slack speed." Murray and the editor interviewed Claude Schnellbacher, who had 800 acres of wheat that year and a thoroughly mechanized operation, including a "combine"(the emphasis then was on the second syllable) that cut and threshed the wheat at the same time. "We can't begin to describe it," the editor wrote, "but it takes two men to run it besides two men in the wagon to catch the grain as it comes from the spout of the machine." The combine cost $5,000, but that did not worry Schnellbacher: "5,000 don't amount to anything in this country." The eastern guest visited Jacob Lewellen also, who owned a combine and two or three cars. He had given up once and gone back east but then returned. "It is the man who stays with the game who makes the money—the quitter never does."[157]

Lewellen, of Thomas County, was the subject of an article in the national magazine *Country Gentleman* late in 1919, entitled "The Man from Thomas County." Lewellen told the reporter, "A fellow who has ever lived out in Western Kansas never gets it out of his blood." He had been borrowing money, harvesting wheat, and buying land since 1904, and it had paid off richly. His farmhouse had ten rooms and was complete with a billiard room, plumbing, hot water heating, and electric lights. He had weathered the drought of 1913 and kept buying, so that by 1919 he owned 2,640 acres clear of debt. That year he harvested 21,000 bushels of wheat on his farms and sold it at an average price of $2 a bushel, bringing him a gross income of $42,000. He had $9,000 worth of tractors and planned to keep using them:

> The farmers of Iowa and Illinois and eastern Kansas knock this country out here. They say it is all desert half the time, west of the 101st meridian. But I've got those fellows skinned a thousand miles. I'm so far ahead of them they'll never catch me. I have had only a few years out here when I don't make expenses. I've had several

years when I've made more clear money from one crop than they'll make in twenty years of what they call divers—What do you call that? Diversified farming?

He had at that moment $30,000 in the bank.[158]

High times engendered high rhetoric. Western Kansas had large and profitable farms, said a reporter in 1915, "which have no semblance to the failure story or hard luck whines." The statistics were impressive, "and the array of figures which the farmers compile every season on their electric adding machines no longer startle us in wondering why we didn't purchase a Kansas farm before the prosperity wave."[159] Farmers in eastern states were paying 1 to 3 percent on loans to buy $250-an-acre land, whereas in Western Kansas many farms paid off their purchase price in one year.[160] A group of employees of International Harvester Company in Chicago purchased a 3,440-acre ranch in Scott County in 1916 for $68,000 and named it Tractor Ranch. They hoped to break it out with the most modern machinery from their company and duplicate the $15- to $40-an-acre profits others were experiencing on wheat farms in the region.[161] J. W. Nelson, development superintendent for the Garden City Sugar and Land Company, managed 22,000 acres that year in several counties.[162] "A knocker can't live in Shallow Water," said an observer of the Scott County irrigated district. "Should one drift in here, he would hate himself to death within thirty days."[163]

Yet there were reminders that Western Kansas could be a dangerous place, and that a hailstorm could mow down in minutes that fine wheat crop. Garden City had such a storm in June 1917. People there noticed two

> black settling clouds that seemed to stretch from north to south as far as could be seen, and in between the two black streaks was a dense mass of greenish looking clouds. In less time than it takes to tell it the wind shifted from out of the west and the storm broke over the city. For a few moments the velocity of the wind was terrific and the hail driven before this wind stripped the leaves from the trees, wiped out every flower and vegetable garden in the city, crashed through window glass and beat everything into the ground.

The storm caught the train on the Garden City, Gulf & Northern railroad from Scott City near the Alfalfa station. All the glass on one side of it shattered "and the train was stalled by the masses of ice." Passengers and crew took refuge in the baggage car until the storm passed. Many people caught in the storm had bleeding faces and hands. Horses panicked and ran, and

Harvesting on the Tractor Ranch with International Harvester equipment, Scott County, 1919 (courtesy of Kansas State Historical Society)

many dead jackrabbits and destroyed bird nests littered the prairie afterwards.[164]

Tom McNeal, a Kansas journalist, expressed the state of mind of the area residents well in 1917:

> Farming in western Kansas is a gamble, a lottery in which nature turns the wheel. Sometimes the players draw prizes of astonishing value and sometimes they draw blanks. Perhaps for that reason the people have acquired the calm philosophical bearing of the gambler who takes his gains and losses without apparent elation or despondency, always filled with a hope that when fortune frowns it will follow the frown with a smile on another day. These western Kansas people have apparently acquired the nerve and hopefulness and stoicism of the gambler without his accompanying vices.[165]

Six planets aligned in a rare conjunction in December 1919.[166] There was no more real hint, for soothsayers, in that of the future than there had been in Halley's Comet in 1910. Still, it took no prophet to know that it was unlikely such high times as had been enjoyed by Western Kansas in this decade would continue long—or perhaps ever again return. The old-timers at the pioneer picnics enjoyed the glow, but their own experience was a warning.

7

A Storm of Readjustment

In the midst of the good times came the Great War—a thing that both impressed and terrified, enriched and appalled. The Civil War veterans, who had been middle-aged when the boys were sent off to Manila in 1898, were rickety senior citizens in 1917, but they waved the flag again.

Many saw in the war a mixed blessing. J. C. Hopper of Ness City ruminated on the distortions of human cleverness. He wrote in June 1917: "As the writer stood on the main street of Hutchinson, and viewed a freight train cross the street, more than a mile in length, every car closely packed with cannon, my mind could formulate but the one thought, of what a great pity, that man, endowed with such high ideals, with inventive brain, should be using his talent, his strength, planning destruction of fellow men." Better he thought to build a national canal from the Dakotas to the Red River, to reclaim the arid regions.[1] The defense movement was the "talk of the town; it's the talk of the farm; it's in the shop and pulpit," Hopper observed.[2] But war, he thought, was a diversion from the real business of "assisting nature," mankind's proper work.[3] Hopper had the problem right, but his cheery Industrial Club, amateur science solutions were simplistic. He probably knew it. He quit his "Dam the Draws" and Great National Canal articles in the *Ness County News* in 1918 and moved to Hutchinson.[4]

The war was a complex phenomenon, leading to high wheat prices, price subsidies, and a large expansion of wheat acreage farmed with machinery. It also led to federal regulations, labor shortages, and the dispatching of young people needed on farms to die in trenches in Europe. War seemed to promote unity and patriotism among Americans, but it also enhanced parochialism and intolerance—toward Germans, toward socialists and radicals of any kind, toward Mennonites, toward ethnic minorities, toward draft evaders, and toward anyone who might be considered a "slacker" during the national emergency.

There was a strong push for agricultural production. The Federal Farm Loan Act, passed in 1916, created Federal Land Banks, which were to be a boon to small farmers, "whose lack of touch with financial centers, or the modesty of whose demands, have hitherto prevented their securing loans."[5] Governor Arthur Capper thought rural credit was the way to keep "soldier boys" on the farm. "Next to the war, nothing tended more to sap the vitals of America than the movement of people from the farms to the cities."[6]

Local land sellers caught the spirit. John Baughman put an ad in a Liberal newspaper in May 1917:

> Here It Is—Almost June. And you have not done the big thing for your country. You have talked and thought but you have not put your thoughts into execution. Now don't let a good thought commit suicide. This is the year of all years to acquire land. Never were crops so utterly necessary as now. You can do yourself and your country a great service if you own and farm land. . . . The world looks to America and America looks to the Middle West for her food supply.[7]

Ray Hugh Garvey's land ads in Colby often were titled "Romances in Real Estate."[8]

The federal farm loan program, however, could give the national government power to set maximum prices for farm products as well as minimums, and that worried farmers in Western Kansas.[9] Despite high prices for farm products, government price guarantees were not as much an advantage as it might appear, since farmers were paying more than ever during the wartime inflation for machinery, labor, and consumer items. It cost farmers in Ford County, Kansas, $1.82 a bushel to produce wheat in the crop year of 1919.[10] That made the federal target price of $2.20 less than a windfall.[11] President Lewis of the college at Hays, a member of the Kansas Council of Defense, thought Kansas could raise 200 million bushels of wheat in 1918 "if the Government will meet it half way" with subsidies. "The farmers are entitled to this protection in order that their business may be stable and they are entitled to the further protection that the United States Government shall wipe out of existence money on gambling and margins and not on legitimate rate of profit through the handling of wheat."[12]

The problem was how to prevent a temporary emergency from resulting in a permanent change in control of the farm economy. There were complaints that state banks were not being allowed to invest in Federal Land Bank loan bonds.[13] There were complaints about federal grain inspections that rewarded big-city "line" or terminal elevators as opposed to local elevators and unfairly docked prices for moisture, shriveling, and foreign matter in wheat.[14] A Great Bend editor complained of how much "government junk" the war brought in his daily mail. Included were pamphlets such as "How to Prepare the Angle Worm for Fish Bait" and "Best Rope for Making a Swing."[15]

The general wartime regimentation and bureaucratization of life was symbolized by the juggernaut of the draft. It was frightening when former governor Walter Stubbs told a crowd of 2,500 at the Hays Experiment Station Field Day in 1918 that he would register every male between the ages of 17 and 70 and prohibit men from doing any labor other than that directly aiding war work.[16] Western Kansas ministers protested the moral conditions in military camps, which compromised the "innocency" of farm boys.[17] Parents trying to seek out their wounded sons in military hospitals met with obfuscation in getting information and found appalling conditions when they visited children. A man from Liberal who visited his dying son in a camp hospital wrote: "The nightshirt that he had on looked as if it might have been worn by some man that had just unloaded a car of soft coal." The government rule said the bedding was to be changed only once a week. The regulations would not allow the father to hire a private nurse for his son. He bought his boy some clean clothes "so his mother would not have to remember him like this." His son woke up long enough to say, "Hello Daddy." But by the time the father got permission to take care of the patient himself, the boy was dead.[18] This kind of story greatly offended the sensibilities of Western Kansas farmers.

The war pattern formed habits of several kinds. One of them was looking to Washington or Topeka for help. The Board of Health sent out a health car, filled with exhibits, staffed with public health nurses, and named "Warren" after Dr. Samuel Crumbine's deceased son. The health car imposed unwelcome standards even while trying to be helpful. The physicians and nurses on board offered to measure local babies and compare their development to an "ideal" chart.[19] The farming education trains cosponsored by the railroads and Kansas State Agricultural College, or the federal weather stations coordinating data from every region, or the federal labor offices setting up branches to control recruitment and wages of harvest hands—all were an outgrowth of the science, propaganda, and big government experiments of the war.

So was the expectation that helping to "adjust" the economy was a governmental responsibility. A farmer near Scott City wrote Governor Henry Allen that returning servicemen needed help in reintegrating into the economy.

I hope you will not ask our boys, when they come home, to put themselves down to the level of the common sexual prostitute by forcing them to hire their brain and brawn to the dictates and gratification of another's mind; but instead, create a method by which these world saving soldier boys may select, own, and operate a business of their own; even if the good old state of Kansas must adopt or pattern after detestable Kaiser Bill.[20]

Certainly, many returning veterans deserved the highest consideration, whether the market could provide it or not. Charles McDermott in 1919 became the newest employee of the Goodland garage. He was one of eighteen survivors, only eleven of whom "now retain their normal minds," among 1,800 men who had charged into a German gas release. McDermott was trapped beneath seven dead men for four days before being picked up barely alive. He spent nine months in a San Francisco hospital before taking his job as a mechanic in Western Kansas.[21] Were such returning veterans, wrote a Colby editor, "to become aimless wanderers, with the ultimate possibility of augmenting an army of menacing loafers?" Government needed to ensure that they did not and that the agricultural golden age continued even though the war that had brought it on was over.[22]

In addition to this dependency or feeling of entitlement, a second habit was a patriotism that could be cruel to any person or group perceived as alien or disloyal. There had been that tendency all along in Western Kansas, seen in the attitudes of some toward blacks and Mexicans. Now Germans became a target, and the other ethnic minorities got swept up in the xenophobic passion. Towns held "loyalty" days, with patriotic singing and speeches, many of them virulently anti-German.[23] "There is no Bolshevism in Barton County, " wrote a reporter after viewing the proceedings at "Americanization Day" in 1920, "if the loyal crowd in Great Bend today is to be considered as a criterion."[24] Wrote an editor at Liberal: "In these days and times, every American citizen's patriotism should be one hundred per cent perfect, but if there abides in this land of the free a single Hun sympathizer he should have his property confiscated and be either deported or given the penalty of a traitor."[25] A man from Ness County recommended stopping the printing of all foreign language newspapers in the United States. "If they can't read English, let them learn."[26] A group of a hundred Rock Island shop employees brought William Bode to the sheriff at Goodland on the grounds that he had refused to buy Liberty Bonds and "has been too Pro-German to suit them."[27] A minister, whose loyalty local people suspected, found himself escorted out of Colby in the spring of 1917 by a committee of patriotic citizens.[28] The same town refused to allow Kansas congressman Joseph Bristow to speak there on the grounds that he was anti-American.[29] Near Seldon, Sheridan County, in 1918, a prosperous farmer named Elery Wyant had his house, barn, and outbuildings painted yellow because he was worth $100,000 and had subscribed only $600 to the Liberty Loan. A local man thought this would set "a good example for all communities to follow."[30] A Bazine woman wondered "how can we go about to check the German talk. Four fifths of our customers persist in talking Germ. and as we have been in business more than twenty years I can understand them. But I am Scotch, Irish, English and *not* German and am tired of hearing it. . . . It makes me want to fight when they persist in using the German language exclusively."[31] At Hays there was agitation to remove draft exemptions for the children of prosperous farmers, who, it was said, were "lying and mooching" and therefore were pro-German.[32]

Other groups felt the sting. The Mexican consul wrote to Governor Capper in 1916, enclosing a petition from Mexicans living at Hutchinson who feared that there was a local movement to exterminate them by organizing bands of lynchers.[33] A group of Mexicans at Herington claimed that mobs had broken down the doors of their homes at night, and "the only crime with which we are charged is that of being Mexicans."[34] In 1915, people in the first ward in Salina, where a black man was running for city council, left notes at the doors of African Americans reading, "All Negroes must leave town by April 1, under penalty of death."[35] The techniques of intimidation had been well practiced on the wartime "slackers," and there was danger that it would spread under the broad cloak of "Americanism."

And then came influenza. The latest study of that epidemic, which caused more than twenty million deaths, concludes that the first incubation in the world was in Haskell County, Kansas. Recruits from there carried it, in February 1918, to Camp Funston, where Kansas troops trained.[36]

The disease spoiled the homecoming celebrations in Western Kansas. In the Goodland area, there were 200 cases in the fall of 1918. Church services ceased, there were no dances and movies, and officials dismissed school after 124 students were absent from illness.[37] There were fourteen deaths from flu in Goodland, a town of 2,200, by mid-October. Accounts of each citizen who died, including descriptions of the course of the disease, was front-page matter in the *Goodland Republic*.[38] Dodge City was planning a new auditorium, brick streets, a junior college, and a community playground when the quarantine hit. In December 1918, there was concern whether a public gathering in honor of the returning "Ammunition Train" truck company of Dodge

City men would be permitted. The country club, which had been closed for a year due to rationing from the U.S. Fuel Administration, reopened, only to close again because of the disease. The new Rotary Club could not have its luncheons regularly. The Phenix Industrial Club could not call a mass meeting to discuss a bond issue. Such a situation was not to be ignored. "It is time to quit monkeying around with this epidemic," wrote editor Jess Denious in November 1918. The job of the town, he said, was to "bottle it up."[39] But it was easier said than done.

In 1919, when the Red Scare was getting national headlines and the coal miners strike in southeast Kansas by the United Mine Workers was dominating the Kansas press, the attention of patriots in Western Kansas turned to the Industrial Workers of the World (IWW) and the Nonpartisan League. Both organizations had taken an antiwar stance and in the wake of the war were trying to organize farm workers. The best-publicized regional incident involving the agricultural organization efforts of the Nonpartisan League occurred in 1919 when members of the American Legion forced League speakers out of Ellinwood, Kansas, and put them on the train in Great Bend with a number of bruises. The *Great Bend Tribune* approved: "If the Nonpartisan League grows and prospers in Barton County, it will only be after the last member of the American Legion . . . [is] safely dead and buried." M. L. Amos, a member of the Nonpartisan League, was the editor of a newspaper at Ellsworth. However, he was described by the Great Bend paper as "more or less what is commonly known as a 'sap-head.'" J. O. Stevic of Salina, the paper said, "had all the earmarks of a foreign agitator," and Walter Mills seemed to be a "Bolshevik."[40] In June 1918, an IWW organizer at Ellsworth was given five minutes to fetch his luggage and then was marched out of town at the point of bayonets.[41] IWW, wrote a regional paper, stood for "I won't work."[42] In 1921, 600 American Legion representatives and an equal number of nonaligned citizens organized the National Defense League at Salina, whose sole purpose was to oppose the Nonpartisan League.[43] The Nonpartisan League was, an editor wrote in 1920, "a straight-out radical organization trying to make a 'nut' state out of Kansas."[44]

The "study" that the issue generated was peremptory and emerged from the atmosphere of shallow patriotism, which the homogeneous and morally earnest population of Western Kansas easily engendered. When a threshing machine exploded near Copeland in July 1916, the crew blamed a bomb, though there were no radicals around and it could have been just dust and heat.[45] The Wichita Rotary Club published a document in the spring of 1918 suggesting that the Nonpartisan League was not for the benefit of farmers but for "the few demagogues who are exploiting the farmer." Arthur Townley, head of the league, had gone bankrupt in farming, opposed the First Liberty Loan, and was now employed as a "socialist agitator." He had, the report said, "a long record as a stimulator of class hatred and inciter of industrial disturbance."[46]

Actually, the Nonpartisan League spoke to issues that were of concern to all farmers. The stands it made against low farm prices, middleman speculators, high freight rates, government interference, absentee owners, and corporate elevators were not unlike native regional rhetoric. Between 1915 and 1922, the League was a potent political force in North Dakota and Minnesota, and of lesser significance in Montana, Idaho, Wisconsin, and Colorado. Townley proposed an organization of farmers "not based on half-hearted adherence to general principles . . . but with each member having a definite stake in success and [he would] pledge to support a concrete program of reform with his votes." In North Dakota, the League organized an industrial commission, a state bank, a state-backed home-building association, and a mill and elevator association. Kansas, however, was a sideshow for the League. Organization began in Kansas in 1917 but was not very successful. In 1919, national membership in the League was over 200,000, but Kansas was combined with Iowa, Texas, and Oklahoma in a miscellaneous category, which contained in total 11,000 members.[47]

Some Kansas farmers tried to defend it. One in Ford County wondered "why the editor of a country paper in a strictly agricultural district should choose to antagonize the interests of 95 per cent of his readers and patrons" by attacking the League. It was "the first farmers' organization born with teeth."[48] The League, a Ness City paper commented, advanced a platform that "is skillfully drawn to appeal to the average voter from the standpoint of fine sounding phrases and easy reading."[49] An editor in Colby, reporting the organization of a cell there in 1918, wrote, "Whether it is a good thing or not we are not in any position to tell but the organization has been very successful in the Dakotas."[50] A Sterling farmer and graduate of Kansas State Agricultural College wrote Capper, "The league is a patriotic organization from cellar to garret. [The organization wanted to] see that the common people . . . are not preyed upon by a worse than useless class of middle men that serve no useful purpose, but extract a large toll from both producer and consumer of agricultural products."[51] M. L. Amos claimed that he had never taken a pro-German into the League and that patriotism was just a screen used by the organization's enemies to discredit it. The Farmers' Union, Amos thought, was jealous because the League was taking its members and was striking back politically.[52] Amos had run for Congress in the Kansas Seventh District in 1911 as a socialist. "I find serious conditions confronting the people," a broadside of his at that time read. "Great numbers of wage workers thrown out of employment. . . . Able bodied men and women begging for work . . . . The Democrat and Republican parties carried good principles in your father's days, but have since been captured by the Capitalist class. Stop! Think! Ask yourselves, shall I continue to vote starvation for wife and babies."[53]

That argument had only a slim chance in dusty Western Kansas in 1911 and a slimmer one in the prosperous wheat belt of 1919. Governor Capper, in March 1918, after receiving complaints that Nonpartisan League workers were "spreading, or trying to spread the wildest sort of anti-government propaganda" among farmers, called the League an agent of a "powerful and satanic enemy."[54] Critics said it consisted of "socialist farmers and well to do," who were "shadow Germans."[55] A Dodge City newspaper called 1918 "Agitator's Harvest Time": The war had disturbed economic conditions and extremists were taking advantage of the uncertainties. Ultimately, the editor thought, "these wartime schemes or isms will amount to two whoops in a rain barrel."[56] Phil Zimmerman, head of the Kansas Anti-Bolshevik League, said at the Hays Normal auditorium, "The government in time of peace welcomes every honest and sincere effort at political experimentation and social reform, but now when our enemies are doing their worst to sow discord and disloyalty in our ranks . . . we can't permit any one to monkey with the organizations of whose sincerity and loyalty there is any question."[57] At a meeting of the Kansas Wheat Growers' Association at Hutchinson in May 1920, cheers and applause greeted a resolution denouncing "the 'Red,' the organized and unorganized elements threatening our institutions and attempting the installment of the Russian Soviet regime."[58]

Nonpartisan League members were escorted out of Dodge City in 1920, "at the request of and with the assistance of American Legion members." Denious at the *Globe* did not object. People should not be fooled by the college degrees and neat appearance of the radicals, he said. Their education was only applied to sorting out the chemistry of bombs and in demanding "exorbitant wages" for harvest hands.[59] "It was natural," he wrote, that war veterans should be "standing at the gate when an organization of uncertain standards, with a leadership of questionable loyalty to their own country, seeks to enter their community."[60] That was patriotism. It was also parochialism.

The same tone was present in Great Bend. "Men coming to Kansas to work in the harvest fields this summer," wrote a reporter there in June 1920, "will be welcomed. Men coming for the purpose of spreading the teaching of radicalism in any form will be jailed."[61] The convention of the Kansas

State Peace Officers held in Great Bend included sessions on the "infernal machines" for terrorist attack found on IWW members and featured exhibits of homemade bombs. The thinking in Great Bend was that the answer was probably immigration restriction, since surely this kind of radicalism did not thrive on native ground. In the short term, it was up to the Legion "boys" to see that radicals were "pretty roughly handled."[62] The National Partisan League, went local reports, sent out books on free love to schoolgirls in North Dakota. "The NPL and the IWW were made to order for German interests," and local people were against anyone who "wants to change our flag and make it red."[63]

When Kansas ex-senator Joseph Burton drew crowds in Barton County in 1921 defending the Nonpartisan League, editors referred to the scandal that had forced his resignation from the U.S. Senate and characterized his current activity as more evidence of poor judgment.[64] In March 1921, when rumors went around that 500 to 600 League sympathizers would be holding a meeting in Barton County "just to show they could," local people attacked League organizers. J. O. Stevic received two black eyes, an injured backbone, a twisted thigh, and bruises. C. O. Parsons had enough injuries to be confined to his bed. Both had tar applied to their bodies while surrounded by cars in a remote country location. When several League members escaped from their tormentors and walked twenty miles to a farmhouse, they reported that the farmer "said he doubted if we were human beings." Senator Burton felt he narrowly avoided physical injury but did not avoid "humiliation."[65]

The former senator thought the intimidation directed against him did not "represent the spirit of the people of Kansas." That was not necessarily true, as he may have suspected. The American Legion lobby told Governor Allen that the League was pro-German during the war and contained many draft evaders: "We boys don't approve of that kind of citizens," said attorney Ted Kelley of Great Bend, who had served in the air service in France. "And we don't want their teachings grafted into our citizenship. We have tried to take enough men along always to preserve order, instead of just enough to start trouble. We don't want trouble. Neither do we want that kind of folks to spread their doctrines among our people."[66] Arthur Capper chimed in as U.S. senator in 1921: "No doubt many well-meaning men are in this movement in good faith," he wrote. "Their fight on profiteers and grain gamblers would have my sympathy if that was all there was to their movement, but I cannot endorse the socialistic state ownership program which the league has been advocating."[67] A local paper responded to Burton's complaints and the lawsuits in 1921 by noting, "Great Bend and Barton County are not for the league and it would save a lot of unpleasant gatherings and disturbances if the league organizers and sympathizers would stay out of the county."[68] Stevic sued the city of Great Bend and three local men for $160,000 for "nervous shock, permanently injuring his nervous system," and for "great mental and physical anguish" at having become the "subject of ridicule and derision."[69] The court dismissed his case.[70]

The extreme reaction was not universal among farm spokesmen. T. A. McNeal, editor of the *Kansas Farmer*, expressed shock in 1920 about the physical and verbal violence directed at the League. He wrote that he was surprised that Barton County people would even have to ask him what he thought of it. The speakers who were attacked at Ellinwood in 1919 had not even given their talks and "had done nothing which any American citizen has not a right to do." McNeal criticized the modern tendency to "act upon prejudice and passion."[71] He did not recommend joining the League, as he thought state ownership was not a good idea, but added, "I have, however, no patience with those who froth at the mouth every time the Nonpartisan League is mentioned and I have no excuses to offer for those who resort to mob law to drive Nonpartisan League speakers out of the state."[72] However, McNeal's paper, at the same time as it published these editorial observations, quoted Kansas farm leader Maurice McAuliffe, who told a crowd in Hutchinson: "The farmers of America have always stood true to the cause of their country in battle. But this new contest is not a contest of arms, but a contest of judgment against irrationalism; a contest of order against disorder." Farm organizations, McAuliffe said, would "fight radicalism in every form."[73]

However bogus the "straw man" of radical terrorism might have been as a postwar issue, the agricultural issues the IWW and Nonpartisan League addressed were real. The economic situation in the wheat belt in the early 1920s was no longer evoking "golden age" epithets. Historians argue that by 1923 American agriculture was in a genuine depression, of a severity the rest of the country would experience seven or eight years later.[74]

Even in 1919, with wheat selling at $2.00 a bushel and some newspapers charging farmers with "profiteering," the Kansas State Board of Agriculture was ready with statistics that showed that farm profits were minimal and that grocery costs went mostly to the middleman. The Board instructed the uninitiated that it took four-and-one-third bushels of wheat to make a 196-pound barrel of flour. That barrel, with $1.35 of byproducts added, could produce 294 one-pound loaves of bread at 10 cents each, or $29.40 worth at retail. Thus the shopper paid $7.14 a bushel for wheat that the farmer sold for $2.00.[75] That represented the high point in commodity prices. The farm situation, said Clifford Thorpe of the Council for the American Farm

Bureau, was worse in 1922 than it had been in any year in the current generation. "It is time for agriculture to organize as never before. It is time for agriculture to tell the people of this nation that it proposes to organize for self-protection, in business, in commerce, in society, and in government."[76]

Conditions in Western Kansas were as disastrous as they were anywhere. In 1921 wheat prices in Kansas dropped to less than $1 a bushel for the first time since 1916.[77] That was half the price of recent war boom years, and it was a hard transition to make for people in debt for the new machinery, higher wages, and larger acreages required in modern production. None could imagine that wheat would ever sell for 25 cents a bushel, as it would in 1932, and most could hardly envision that for the decade of the 1920s the price would remain at $1 or lower. But people realized that there was a crisis. The average price received by Kansas farmers went from $1.86 in 1920 to 97 cents in 1921.[78] In 1923, the average wheat price in Kansas was 77 cents.[79] There was a "gasoline war" in the region in 1923 that reduced retail prices at the pump to 16 cents a gallon, which helped, but otherwise the cost of living failed to parallel the farmers' economic distress.[80] Western Kansas, which raised 75 to 85 percent of the Kansas wheat crop, was in dire straits when that market suffered.[81] Dr. Henry Waters testified at a railroad rate case hearing in Kansas City in 1923 that the farmers of the region were "on the brink" and that "agriculture has weathered the storm of the last four years solely and simply by drawing on its reserves."[82]

Diversification remained a possibility. A Denver reporter visiting northwest Kansas in 1923 felt that "the only salvation of the farmers of western Kansas is to get back to the old times of farming, by this we mean raise more corn, more feed, milk more cows, raise more hogs, raise more chickens, have a bigger and better garden, work twelve months in the year instead of about one hundred twenty days. . . . Right in the heart of the cow country farmers flivver to town to buy their beef-stakes."[83]

Alfalfa was a more valuable crop than wheat, often yielding $50 per acre, and was seen as an alternative to wheat. But alfalfa required irrigation.[84] Despite years of experiments, irrigation had never established itself as a large factor in the whole region. Wheat areas and, in general, upland areas in Western Kansas did not irrigate. It was uneconomic and unnecessary. The Upper Arkansas River Valley accounted for 81,000 acres of irrigated land, or 85 percent of the 95,000 irrigated acres in Kansas in 1922. Compared with the eleven million acres of wheat, this was nothing. And 75,000 acres of this irrigated land was in two counties, Finney and Kearny, neither of which, not coincidentally, grew more than about one-fourth the wheat grown in any surrounding county. More than 65,000 acres of the irrigation was the old-style ditch irrigation, which was constantly threatened by drawing off of water by Colorado.[85]

Pests remained a problem, for monoculturalists especially, and there were suggestions that moving away from single crops and from chemical solutions would be helpful in combating them. Thomas Bragg, a prominent Ford County farmer, wrote a long article in 1923 despairing that broadcast poisoning methods, which had originated at the turn of the century to fight prairie dogs and had been extended during the 1913 drought to grasshoppers, were killing birds. Birds, he argued, were, in the long run, the farmers' best defense against insects: "Shall we give the birds a chance to again become our defense, or shall we continue as we now are to encourage indirectly the permanence of the grasshopper scourge."[86] Bragg's argument might almost have been made by a member of the sustainable agriculture school of the twenty-first century, criticizing the methods of commercial agriculture on environmental grounds but also, ultimately, on grounds of long-term economic health.

Academics and editors generally advocated diversified farming as a proper response to the wheat price. J. C. Mohler, of the Kansas State Board of Agriculture, estimated that wheat production costs nationwide in 1923 were about $1.36 a bushel and that consequently U.S. farmers had lost $472 million and Kansas farmers $95 million for their labor and investment in growing wheat in the 1922–23 winter wheat season. The Kansas State Agricultural College recommended that Kansas farmers feed their wheat to hogs. True, the region had been down before and had recovered. This could be seen by comparing 1893 with 1918. However, Mohler reasoned, "the situation is such that farmers simply will have to give up raising wheat in such large quantities. It is idle to expect legislation or any other factor to increase wheat prices while the world markets are being flooded."[87]

Jess Denious in Dodge City agreed: "The immediate future offers poor inducement for the growing of wheat." But he did not think the economic or cultural changes involved in moving away from it would be easy. "The farming equipment in this part of the state and our habits of procedure have been built up around the wheat growing industry." Western Kansas had "grown up with the wheat industry."[88] However, people would need to face market facts if farms were to survive. Young people would not be kept in Ford County by "bathtubs, and furnaces and flower beds and motor cars." Nor would the advice of the "self appointed guardians of rural life" necessarily save the rural economy.[89]

Such advice was common. L. L. Taylor, of Dodge City, a former employee of the Federal Land Bank, thought the situation of Western Kansas farmers in 1920 was "humiliating" and was upset that farmers were "on their knees . . . praying for a dole from the national treasury."[90] William Jardine, president of Kansas State Agricultural College, worried about farm tenancy. Renters in 1920 occupied 47 percent of Ford County farms, and Western Kansas led the rest of the state in percentage of tenant farmers.[91] Age of farmer upon acquiring ownership had been increasing since 1875. "Is this to continue until the farmer must spend his entire life as a tenant, and a land-owning class of farmers becomes a thing of the past?"[92] E. E. Frizell, a state senator from Larned, thought the bleak condition of farmers could not be cured by legislation alone, but it would take more cooperation to fix the "unwarranted transportation situation and the speculations of the grain gamblers." The farmer himself, he wrote, "is the only man who can bring order out of chaos and devise any satisfactory solution to these vexed riddles."[93]

Wheat growing, for all the talk, did not diminish. Instead, there were adjustments in the varieties grown and in the way it was farmed and marketed. Even with small annual returns, there remained the sustaining hope of land price appreciation. In 1920, Marion Taylor and his brother sold 36 quarters in Sherman County for $32.50 an acre, or $187,200 total. That represented appreciation of about $130,000 on the original cost of under $10 an acre, over a bit more than a decade, or over 15 percent annual return on investment, leaving out any farming profits.[94] Each such story drew headlines—"From a Soddy to a Twentieth Century Home and 3,200 Acres in Fifteen Years"—with the implication that it could, even probably would, happen again.[95]

Wheat growing using modern equipment seemed a concomitant of modernity. A *Kansas Farmer* editorialist wrote in 1919: "Airplanes shoot out into the blue space and reach Europe in less than 100 hours. . . . Civilization has taken a new stride, a new speed, and it cannot go backward. . . . The soldier has returned with new ideas, with new conceptions, and with a new vision. The streets of his home town look narrow and cramped."[96] There was a certain romance about it. "Men and women once loved horses," said a writer in 1925. "Now they love engines . . . eager, willing engines."[97]

There was some movement off farms. The population of Western Kansas in 1923 was a little over 670,000, up only slightly (about 6 percent) from 630,000 in 1910. But of that number, Sedgwick County had over 100,000 people and the metropolis of Wichita about 85,000 of those. Other Western Kansas towns saw gains also. By contrast, Sumner County, a big wheat grow-ing area but without a substantial town, lost 4 percent over the period, as did Harper County, which was configured similarly with many wheat farms and few substantial towns.[98]

Wheat prices during the decade of the 1920s were poor, and rainfall was sporadic. Yet wheat growing remained the industry of choice. Kansas wheat production was 93,008,441 bushels in 1918, 145,795,455 bushels in 1919, and 140,641,175 bushels in 1920. In 1923, the low price did correspond with a short crop, 76,082,906 bushels, and there were regional calls for a reduction of wheat acreage of one-third. But the pundits of diversity could not easily corral thousands of independent farmers. In 1924, with the wheat price only about $1.06, Kansans raised over 150 million bushels, the largest crop ever up to that date. In 1928 with the price at 94 cents, Kansas wheat production set another record at 177,383,509 bushels, over 80 percent of it grown west of Wichita. Even in 1930, with the market price at 62 cents, Kansas produced nearly 160 million bushels of wheat, about one-fourth of total U.S. production.[99]

In far western counties especially, the statistics for land broken for the first time and planted to wheat in the 1920s were remarkable. Wheat growers plowed more than 88,000 acres of virgin prairie land in Sherman County alone between 1924 and 1926. There were 316,748 acres in cultivation in that county in 1926, and 356,894 acres were sod. Some noted that only 1,000 of these acres were categorized as untillable; the rest should be plowed, they thought, and sown to wheat.[100]

The trend was broad. In 1930, only seven counties of the twenty-four in southwest Kansas fell below a million bushels of wheat production. Ford County that year produced seven times the wheat it had in 1905. Stevens, Grant, and Haskell counties in the same period each had gone from a production of under 10,000 bushels a year to more than a million.[101] "Wheat," wrote H. M. Bainer of the Southwestern Wheat Improvement Association in 1930, "is the natural crop of the Southwest. No other area is as well fitted for growing wheat as economically." His article was headlined, "Sticking to Wheat."[102] Another editor commented, "The business of the area . . . is raising wheat. . . . Being peculiarly adapted to wheat it is therefore not particularly adapted to anything else on a large scale. The area cannot diversify and prosper on the same [scale] as growing wheat." He suggested that the government force the eastern and midwestern states out of the business and let Kansas grow all the wheat for the U.S. domestic market.[103]

Climatic mutability led to a mix of hope and despair. In Colby, 1918 was a terrible year that killed the orchard at the experiment station.[104] But 1919 was extraordinarily good. Wheat averaged 15 bushels per acre throughout Thomas County, with several plots at the experimental station yielding 50 bushels per acre.[105] In 1921, the Colby station received nearly 20 inches of rain and in 1923, 26.54 inches. Then there were "freak" frost conditions in 1925, and in 1926 came the driest year ever for the station with just over 10 inches of precipitation and 4-bushel wheat. In 1927, the wheat plants were "friable and ashy," and there were frequent electric wind and dust storms.

The agent reported, "There were many heads in the winter wheat that were so badly shriveled that many kernels were merely chaff and in threshing many of the heads failed to thresh out."[106]

Other stations documented even more serious obstacles and even fewer gains. At Garden City, the agent wrote that jackrabbits had "pastured" the wheat close all winter in 1921–22 "and so weakened the plants that they were unable to continue growth."[107] In 1928, after wonderful rains (over 30 inches for the year) had produced a beautiful wheat crop, a storm lasting only a few minutes destroyed it. "Wheat that stood thirty-six to forty-two inches high was cut down as completely as if it had been mowed by machinery."[108] Tribune added to the account of the poor year in 1922 with several photos of dead chickens after a killing hail. The 1926 rainfall there was 8.78 inches, with only 5.35 inches coming in the first eight months of the year. The agent planted a grove of trees and a garden around his house as a palliative for the "pioneer blues." He said, "Practically any of the garden crops of Kansas can be grown here if they are watered a little and given a little attention." But he thought it unwise to hope for too much, too regularly from commercial small grains. "Nature," he wrote, "has herself written the program for this station."[109]

Still, the anecdotes about the rich years from farmers themselves appealed more strongly to a core of regional optimists than the more sober calculations of the crop scientists. An editor in Stockton, Rooks County, commented in 1917 that Uncle Sam wanted one billion bushels of wheat grown on three million acres to feed a hungry world. That would be a string of 50-bushel capacity wagons 16,923 miles long, and "every fifth driver will be from 'Bleeding Kansas.'"[110] If a farmer could raise 50-bushel wheat one year in one place, why not in all years in every place? And if the price had reached $2-a-bushel once, it could again. Costs could be lowered and lowered again. Yields could be raised and raised again. Marketing could be improved and improved again. It surely was a matter of correcting mistakes, changing the system, and backing programs with unified verve. The headline "One Crop Paid for His Farm" never disappeared from the local press, and that crop was always wheat.[111]

It is remarkable how quickly the resplendent optimism of Western Kansas reemerged after even slight improvements over the absolute lows. The *Dodge City Daily Globe* in 1924 heralded the return of prosperity after the "depression" of 1923. Good crops at "excellent prices" ($1.06 a bushel for wheat) made Kansas a leader in the nation down "prosperity road."[112] By 1925, the confidence was even stronger. The Chamber of Commerce of the Southwest, organized that year by towns in southwest Kansas and in the panhandles of Oklahoma and Texas, suggested a highway paralleling the Dodge City & Cimarron Valley Branch of the ATSF from Dodge City to Elkhart. Said C. C. Isely of Dodge: "All this southwest needs is more people. We have ten million acres of virgin land here awaiting the farmer, and offering the greatest opportunity in America for the man with small capital who wants to get a start." The headline at Dodge City was "Millions of Acres Wait Tractor in Great Southwest."[113] The dean of agriculture at the Kansas State Agricultural College, L. E. Call, reported in 1926 on the planting already done. He said that tractors, combines, adapted varieties of crops, favorable climatic conditions, and cheap land had made a difference. Wheat acres in Grant, Haskell, Morton, Seward, Stanton, and Stevens counties, since the building of the Dodge City & Cimarron Valley Branch railroad had opened the region to wheat marketing, had increased from 75,000 to 290,000 acres. There were no combines in the area in 1915; there were 140 in 1925. The number of tractors was up from 33 to 493.[114] At Hugoton, the estimate was that 100 new combines would be sold to area farmers in 1926, representing an investment of $200,000.[115] In Stevens County, formerly hardly wheat country, 1.5 million bushels of wheat had been marketed by July 1926, and it was estimated that half of the crop was still in the stack.[116] One man reported 50-bushel-per-acre wheat on 80 acres.[117] A wheat farmer from the Goodland area, speaking to an eastern audience in 1926, said:

> Some people call our country desolate, but it's the greatest wheat country in the world. Don't let anyone tell you the Kansas wheat farmer is hard up. Men who started on little more than a shoe string are today independent in a small way and they made it all in wheat. . . . Of course you may strike an off year or prices might drop a bit but take it as it comes and put away a bit for a rainy day and you can stand it.[118]

It was an old dream, it was fed by constant new material, and it died hard.

The debate in the 1920s for Western Kansas farmers was not about alternatives to wheat but about how to make wheat more profitable. Some suggestions were modest and obvious, such as using wheat pasture to feed stock in the fall.[119] Sheep feeding had become a profitable business in Pawnee County by 1923, with the most successful feeders using electrically lighted barns to make sure their animals not only grazed during the day but also ate all night.[120]

Some schemes were broad and nearly utopian. In 1920, the Francis McCarty Land Company, 220 State Street, Chicago, proposed using "all its great organized forces" to bring thousands of farmers to Finney County, Kansas to settle 100,000 acres of land. Growth would no longer be "spasmodic and slow," the company said, but would be founded on scientific advertising techniques used by "clean-cut salesmen." McCarty predicted that Garden City would be a place of 25,000 people within a year.[121] Reports came of a few McCarty excursions, and then the local press stopped talking about the great Chicago initiative.[122]

Tom McNeal, the much-quoted commentator for the *Topeka Mail and Breeze*, offered his own brand of farm utopianism that same year. It was what Jess Denious in Dodge City called "a socialistic scheme for the relief of all economic ills." McNeal proposed forming a great corporation, purchasing 64,000 acres, laying it out "to meet community needs," and having it run by a professional manager. There would be a "modern up-to-date little city" in the center of the tract. Each stockholder would do what he was best suited to do and receive a share of the profits. The operation would have a packing plant, creameries, a flour mill, and a canning factory. "It would be," McNeal thought, "a great co-operative community, a new productive Utopia, that would avoid trouble and solve the problem of human happiness."[123] Big corporate farming did indeed appear by the late 1920s—an idea whose time had come, or rather come again, for Western Kansas—but as instituted it did not contain the industrial/agricultural/community services nor the stockholder voluntarism of "each according to his ability" central to McNeal's dream.

Simon Fishman of Tribune was another broad-gauged thinker. Fishman farmed 35,000 acres, making him the largest farmer in Kansas in the early twenties. He suggested, in 1923, that he divide his acreage into 160-acre plots, build houses on them, put in 400-barrel cement tanks for watering gardens, and lease the plots to small, diversified farmers for a share of their profits. "The thing for the farmer to do," Fishman said, "is to manage his business scientifically. Crop rotation is the thing."[124] Fishman admitted that this had not seemed to work in the past, but claimed, "The only reason a lot of farmers out there can't grow anything but wheat is just because they never tried very hard."[125] But they had tried very hard, and Fishman's kind of thinking was more attractive in newspapers and agricultural reports than in the field.

Other modifications suggested were somewhere in the middle on practicality. These envisioned making serious, but not fundamental, changes in the way wheat farming and marketing was done. As in the past, that was the route to stepwise, but real, progress in adjusting to recurring crises.

The harvest hand "problem" was long-standing, going back to the much-ballyhooed "tramp" issue of the 1890s. It was partly a question of cost and

Pitchers at Eldridge, 1918 (courtesy of Wichita State University Special Collections)

supply. But there was a social element also. The harvest hand question was connected to class-consciousness and to the insularity of Western Kansas communities, which feared the yearly importation at harvest time of thousands of transient male workers of unknown background, character, and intention. The first response to the transient labor question was local and regional economic organization; the second was social organization in the towns; and the third was mechanization, to eliminate the human factor altogether.

During the years of World War I, harvest wages in Western Kansas went from about $2 a day to $7. Some laborers in 1920 commanded as much as $12 a day. By 1921, regional farmers were thinking they needed to reduce this to $3, even $2.50, a day to have any hope themselves of profit.[126] Still, wages of $5 a day were common in the region.[127] In 1923, regional wages were $4 a day for single hands, $5 for stackers, and $6 for a man and team.[128] In 1925, wages were still averaging $4 a day, and Ford County alone estimated it would need 1,000 workers.[129] In 1926, there was a claim that as many as 45,000 outside workers were needed to harvest the Kansas wheat crop.[130]

The erratic supply meant competition in wages by farmers desperate to get the wheat out of the fields. In July 1919, D. W. Stallard, H. D. Miner, and R. J. Price of Ness City went to Kansas City to compete with labor bureaus and representatives from other counties to round up workers. They put 300 men on a special train and carried them through to Ness County, despite offers along the way to the workers of as much as 90 cents an hour if they would disembark in some other county. When they got to Ness County, "they were loaded into automobiles and trucks like the soldiers were in France and distributed all over the county as rapidly as possible." The train cost $3,500 to charter, but the local press thought it was worth it. Two more similar trains ran from Kansas City to Ness County that summer.[131]

That stressful annual scenario, however, was not satisfactory. Therefore, local and regional employment bureaus became the rule. Farmer meetings set a target wage before harvest, tried to remain unified in enforcing it, and cleared transient workers through a central office.[132] In 1922, there was a central office in Kansas City operated by the Farm and Labor Bureau of the U.S. Employment Service. There were branches in larger cities in eastern Kansas and temporary harvest offices in the west.[133] These were cooperative ventures among the federal government, local Farm Bureau organizations, and the Kansas State Agricultural College.[134]

The tramp question had been debated by the high school literary society in Dodge City in 1896, when it was suggested that these transients thought the world owed them a living. "What is trampdom but the fungus growth of society," wrote the editor of the paper.[135] Those attitudes toward "seedy looking" individuals arriving in the community carried over to harvest hands.[136] The Rev. P. L. Mawdsley, who innovated at Larned in providing services for harvest hands and became in 1921 the state director of the Harvest Welfare Service, said that the idea that harvest hands were bums or tramps or maybe radicals was a function of the way they were treated. They were not hoboes, but "men who will rank with the average in any community." Town attitudes "forced them to live along the railroad track, in the jungles and like places, like bums, and then we think they are just because we force them to live similar."[137]

Mawdsley received much regional publicity for his efforts to allay fears by organizing the social life of the harvest hands. He started his program in Larned in 1920, when hands there were stuck in town waiting out a rain. Mawdsley, who had worked as a harvest hand in 1918 and 1919, knew that many were Christians, and that they would respond if farmers treated them "more like their own people." Mayor E. E. Frizzell and the Larned Businessmen's Association supported the minister morally and financially in establishing a "Harvest Welfare Room," at the county courthouse. There were four or five tables, a piano, a phonograph, a selection of newspapers, and stationery with pens and pencils to encourage the men to write home. The facility was not intended for sleeping, but cots appeared, and soon as many as 300 men a night stayed there. The city fed those who were broke, and Mawdsley conducted Sunday services and organized a series of lectures and entertainment.[138]

That model appealed to other towns. Preaching a text of "trust the harvest hand like a white man," Mawdsley traveled the state in 1921 distributing pamphlets printed by the Kansas State Agricultural College and organizing libraries and sleeping quarters for hands in various Western Kansas towns. A. B. McDonald wrote in *Country Gentleman* that

> once a year Kansas becomes hysterical about hands, and every town in the Wheat Belt is faced with the problem of this gang of strange men, roughly dressed, unshaven, without much money, loafing for a week or more around the depot and on street corners, hungry looking, a few willing to steal, but the great majority of them just in this hard luck of having to wait for work. . . . To the townspeople they are all I.W.W.s or Reds or hoboes. Kansas seldom thought of those strange harvest hands as real men with homes and wives and mothers and sisters.[139]

Mawdsley's program was detailed in a chapter entitled "Ministering to the Migrant in Larned, Kansas," contained in a book called *Churches of Distinction in Town and Country*, published by George H. Doran Company in 1923. The "shirt-sleeved" pastor in Kansas was credited with revolutionizing the reputation of "the modern Ishmael, the migrant laborer who is the backbone of the wheat harvest." In 1922, 418 Pawnee County farmers volunteered to drive harvesters to church. "It was one thing," the book noted, "to tell the farmer to treat his casual laborer humanely; it was another thing to explain just what this changed attitude entailed."[140]

However, regardless of this improved relationship, the economics and the logistics of bringing thousands of harvest hands into counties and distributing them to farmers on a "just in time" basis remained unattractive. It was almost as unattractive as caring for horses, which ate whether they were needed or not. And the solution to both difficulties was the same—mechanization. "My wife will not run a hotel for hired men," said one Plains farmer to an interviewer, "and I'll not run a livery stable on the farm."[141] "We work to live rather than live to work," said F. D. Farrell, president of Kansas State Agricultural College. "Like the Greek hero, we must . . . straightforward answer our own prayers."[142]

In 1915, there were 2,493 tractors in Kansas and, by 1919, 8,639—the latter figure a gain of 60 percent in a year.[143] Any man "of ordinary intelligence," the *Kansas Farmer* claimed, "can operate a tractor in an entirely satisfactory manner, provided he is willing to spend a little time in studying the principles of operation."[144] The Wichita Thresher and Tractor Club and the Wichita

Mule-drawn Deering combine (courtesy of Kansas State Historical Society)

Chamber of Commerce in 1920 held the nineteenth annual Midwest Tractor and Thresher show at Forum auditorium. There was no "freak" machinery on exhibit, promoters said, only stock items the farmer could use—$4 million worth of machines from 100 manufacturers. There was a parade on Lincoln's birthday, February 12, featuring the new combined harvester-thresher.[145]

The adoption of the combine escalated the replacement of the harvest hand and the horse. Historian Thomas Isern concluded, "The coming of the combined harvester, or combine, suspended prevailing traditions of the harvest."[146] J. C. Mohler, secretary of the Kansas State Board of Agriculture, wrote in 1926, "The combine has completely revolutionized farming, transportation, and banking methods so far as the wheat crop is concerned."[147] Will Townsley, writing in 1927 in the *Great Bend Daily Tribune*, observed, "Nothing illustrates more forcibly the transformation of farming from the manual labor era to the mechanical era than the dwindling of the stream of harvest hands into Kansas." In 1927, "three or four men with a combine, a tractor, and a truck can do the work which formerly required the labor of twenty or more."[148] Henry Allen of the *Wichita Beacon* wrote that year of the "wonder" of the combine, which eliminated the "breathing discontent" of the harvest hands. The bindlestiffs, he said, had "gone to join the buffalo hunters, the gamblers, the herds of wild horses, and the other elements which have helped this wide agricultural country at various periods of its development from its raw state to its present circumstance."[149] At Colby, at the end of the decade, the editor, in discussing the changes in the social landscape, wrote that

> combine farming is making it possible for the wheat farmer not only to stay in business but even to make a little money now and then. . . . Combines are doing what no legislation as yet has been able to do, bringing a little prosperity. . . . You need only look back many years and recall the crime wave that swept the state every time during and immediately following harvest. Robbery, holdups, highjacking, and murder were all too common when thousands upon thousands of the riff-raff of the cities poured into Kansas during June and July.[150]

An editor at Dodge City in 1927 noted that the harvest was "once the cause of great commotion," but no longer since combines replaced binders. Stores no longer laid in huge stocks of food in July. The harvest hand had followed the cowboy and the western sheriff into the realm of Kansas history. "The combine has taken the chance and speculation out of the life of the general storekeeper in Western Kansas. It has made his life humdrum too, for the harvest is no longer an adventure for everyone concerned, but merely business."[151] The motto in early 1920s combine ads was "One Man Does It All."[152] It was a plain fact, a Great Bend observer thought, "that the farmer is not going to do without the combine any more than he could do without an auto."[153]

The success of the tractor prepared the way for the coming of the combine. But it took specialized and specific marketing also. By July 1920, Doerr alone had sold thirty-two new combines in his trade area.[154] Doerr, like Henry Ford, sold a concept at first as much as a machine, reassuring his customers that combines were reliable and worth their considerable price. He addressed the Kansas State Board of Agriculture in 1920 on the new machine, emphasizing the "startling facts" about its use in his area. He claimed that, for equivalent 75-acre fields, harvesting the field the old way with header, stacking, and threshing, the harvest cost was $7.50 an acre, but harvesting with the combine cost 50 cents an acre. On that single field, therefore, the farmer saved $2,800 in cash in a single year, or enough to pay for his combine, with $1,000 in cash left over for his pocket. The farmer profited in many other ways, Doerr said, including getting about 2 bushels more per acre from the combine's efficiency and having his grain ready for market before others and when the price was often higher:

He got his money early, paid his bills, kept his credit good, his net profits were figured without the usual delay and guess work and he knew right where he stood for the year's work without worrying about winds, rain, or fire. . . . He was free from many annoyances, such as the uncertainty of getting labor, and the cooking for a large number of men. He was free from the bother of building stacks which might be burned or soaked or blow over. . . . He missed no tools stolen and the usual breakage of harness and wagon, and the wasting of hay and grain were all missing. He had no worry about I.W.W.s on the threshing crew to ruin the separator and to throw pitchforks and monkey wrenches into cylinders.[155]

Doerr's success during the decade seemed to confirm his expectations. By 1920, he did a large business selling the Deering Harvester-Thresher, at a price of $1,650. His ads contained testimonials about this "new method of harvesting, threshing, and saving money."[156] Ed Williams of Pawnee Rock wrote Doerr in 1927 that the 10-foot McCormick-Deering combine he had bought in Larned did wonders for him. It was light in draft, and, pulled by a Fordson tractor, cut 40 acres a day, bringing in around 1,000 bushels. For a man with only 400 acres, the small combine was all that was needed. He should "hand his wife the $1,200 he saved at first cost. She will appreciate it."[157]

Doerr became a national leader of the Western Implement and Hardware Dealers Association and at its meetings made the point that the local merchant had a great advantage in providing better service and information to farmers, whom he already knew, about a new technology. The manufacturer, dealer, and the farmer, he said, were a trio: "Harass one and the others will share in the distress." Local dealers were "mingling constantly with all the people in his community, and knowing from personal contact and observation the hearts and minds of the rural citizenry. . . . The hardware and implement dealer is in a position to disseminate practical ideas that will aid in the solution of many annoying problems. . . . Instinctively he creates, builds, and constructs."[158]

That was the theory at least, and, for a time, when combines were first being introduced in his region, it worked well. Doerr offered to take back any combine that a farmer did not like, and, since many farmers in the region had bought their automobiles from Doerr's business, there was already trust.[159] He sold two combines in 1918 and twenty-two the next year, the most of any dealer in Kansas. "You ask me why? Because we pushed these machines; we went out among the farmers and gave demonstrations. We created a demand." He thought the results of those experiments would

Combined harvester-thresher, Macksville, Stafford County, 1920s (courtesy of Kansas State Historical Society)

mean near automatic sales in the future. His other business included installing electric light and electric automatic water systems on farms and selling electric churns, washers, irons, and vacuum cleaners to go with them. "The days of pioneering are over out here in Western Kansas," he told the reporter. "The days of backbreaking, hard labor on the farm are gone." Looking after the little wants of people even if this did not result in a profit would bring a profit in time, Doerr said. "Hard Times? Boo! The only hard time I see ahead is to get hold of all the stuff I will be able to sell."[160]

Combines went up in capability and in value each year. First employed in Kansas about 1917, there were over 8,000 combines in Kansas in 1926, and farmers used them in cutting 30 percent of the wheat crop by then. In 1930, 27,000 of the 75,000 combines in the United States were in Kansas.[161] The *Hugoton Hermes* could advertise in 1925 that the Case combine cut a swath 12-feet wide and, "at two or three miles per hour, threshes and delivers the grain, cleaned and ready for market at the rate of 25 to 40 acres a day."[162] The operator sat on a large, roomy platform, out of the dust, and the machine was easy to operate. The farmer was "no chump," the *Liberal News* reported, in describing the Case machine, "and the buyer very largely gets what he pays for, whether he buys clothes, automobiles, or combines."[163] Implement dealers at Hugoton estimated that there would be 100 combines sold in Stevens County in 1926, representing an investment of about $200,000. Only the large ones were in demand. "No one cares to fool with the small machinery any more."[164] In Ellis County that year, 150 were sold before the harvest and it was estimated that these saved the labor of 600 harvest hands.[165] A trainload of Holt combines arrived at Liberal in 1928, direct from the factory at Stockton, California. Seventy machines were unloaded at Bert Allen & Company there from that train, averaging $2,400 in price. It was the second load for that business in a short time.[166] A visitor to the Dodge City implement show in 1931 thought the only thing lacking from the new model combines were radios.[167] And those would come soon enough.

The dream of mechanization, now some decades old in the region, reemerged with the success of the combine. Charles Scott, an editor from Iola, drove through Western Kansas in 1928 to find an answer to the question of why Kansas raised more wheat than "any other political unit on the planet." What he saw was "a distinct technique" for wheat growing, different from any other in the world, and the intense application of machinery. The preferred method for plowing was the one-way plow, invented by Charles Angell, a wheat farmer in Meade County, and manufactured and marketed by the Ohio Cultivator Company. It came in five sizes, left no ridges on the surface, and cut up the trash, using the old stubble to hold and fertilize the ground instead of its clogging the plow. At the other end of the growing cycle came the combine, "a huge machine that cuts and threshes the grain at one time in about two motions." Behind all was the tractor. "The tractor doesn't get tired and it is not a very wearing job to drive it, so two men can take care of 24 hours work between them every day very handily. It is really more of a manufacturing than an agricultural proposition." Horses "for farm purposes throughout that section are about as extinct as buffalo."[168]

By 1930, the phenomenon could be seen of a crowd of 600 attending a combine school in Ness County, watching a promotional film and observing a Baldwin Gleaner do its magic in a local field.[169] Editor Denious at Dodge City waxed eloquent about it that year:

> Power, cumulative and mounting power, marks this age of achievement. . . . What was an impossibility yesterday is child's play today. The uninterrupted march of power has transformed industry. It has captured most of the salients on the field of agriculture. [Western Kansas is] quickening to the advent of power farming. We have seen it transform the sodlands into granaries, translate fortitude into

wealth and daring into independence. All of this has been done in the last two decades.

The next step, the joining of chemistry with power in the transformation of Nature, would only enhance what the mechanical age had begun.[170]

There were testimonials galore to just this. R. I. Montgomery from Montezuma, Gray County, wrote in the fall of 1925 that he was able to bin wheat using power equipment for 5 cents a bushel or $2 an acre. "Farmers to the eastward cannot compete with us here even if we lose a crop occasionally." Business methods were the key:

> The farmer has the greatest opportunity of anybody. If he will only use his head, he need not envy the merchant, the banker, or any fellow with a city job. I speak from experience because I am a businessman as well as a farmer, and I know where my money comes from. I know that a well-managed, mechanically powered wheat farm in Gray County will give better returns and insure more satisfaction than any job or business, requiring the same effort, that a man can undertake in Western Kansas.[171]

There were parallels in the early 1920s to the technique of regional cooperation in establishing labor bureaus for harvest hands that addressed other problems of cost and profit in wheat production. Rotary Clubs sprang up, which got farmers and businessmen talking. The Farm Bureau movement took hold. And there was a more short-lived movement to create cooperative marketing associations among farmers to influence price through better control of the timing of sales of wheat and the circumstances of its storage and shipment.

Both the Rotary Club (and often subsequently Lions and Kiwanis clubs) and the Farm Bureau were combinations of information exchange and activism on a community and even regional level. But although the community service clubs were mostly interested in politics and culture, the Farm Bureau was primarily an organized approach to practical problems of farm economics.

The Farm Bureau movement was an outgrowth of the extension departments connected with land grant state colleges, which had for years sponsored farmers' institutes. The Smith-Lever Act, passed in May 1914, made federal funds available to expand a county agent system, which had originated in the south, to every agricultural county in the United States. Although the name "Farm Bureau" attached to this agent system was unfortunate, smacking as it did of government bureaucracy, the concept caught on. County organizations joined into state bodies, and then, in 1919, into a national federation.[172] One history notes that this organization was "strikingly different" from the Nonpartisan League and other previous attempts to organize cooperatives. It was created "along safe and sane lines and hence [was] more in keeping with American tradition."[173] Kansans agreed that it worked. "Perhaps," wrote the editor of the *Kansas Farmer* in 1920, "it is not out of place to link the ultimate public good behind the prohibition, the woman suffrage, the industrial courts, and the Farm Bureau movements, all of which have won in Kansas."[174]

In Kansas, a Farm Bureau bill went into effect in the spring of 1915. When 25 percent of the farmers in the county organized a county Farm Bureau and appointed an agent, Kansas State Agricultural College contributed between $800 and $1,600 to that agent's salary. The county Farm Bureaus, which had begun in Kansas in 1912 without state involvement, were and remained locally controlled. A 1915 pamphlet on the movement stated that its purpose was to make farming more profitable, farm life more enjoyable, and rural communities better places to live. The county agent's office became a clearinghouse for information.[175]

Farm Bureau units established themselves quickly in Western Kansas, taking on among their first issues the harvest hand question and the gathering of information about machinery purchases.[176] Larned had R. P. Schnacke, a former Pawnee County farmer and recent student at Kansas State Agricultural College, as a county agent in 1916. His office was in the Business Men's Association rooms downtown, and he promised to visit every farmer. Schnacke would work with the farmers, "while, at the same time cataloguing the results of each man's own experience and keeping it available for reference. Farming, like any other business, should be systematized."[177] In 1920, the Pawnee County Farm Bureau had 750 members and represented 90 percent of the farmers in the county.[178] In 1918, the Ford County Farm Bureau began, by which time it was able to consolidate fourteen already-existing township bureaus.[179] In Ellis County, where the Farm Bureau organized in 1920, there were arrangements made in 1921 to receive high-powered, wireless, telephone broadcasts from Kansas State Agricultural College of daily market reports.[180] In 1922, there was a mass meeting of the Farm Bureau at the Hoover Pavilion at Dodge City, complete with a free meal of baby beef, fresh country butter, and farm cream and milk, to hear an address by the dean of the extension department from Manhattan and from local dignitaries.[181] "The farmer who joins a so-called farm organization which is conducted by some long-haired reformer," the local paper commented a few

Field Day, Tribune Experiment Station, August 26, 1925 (courtesy of Kansas State University Special Collections)

years later, "is in about the same position as the fellow who gets into the gambling game at the rear of the circus tent. All he can do is to increase the winnings of the guy who fixed the game." The Farm Bureau was a different thing. It was "probably the cleanest of all the farm organizations operating in this part of the state." It was run by farmers and did what farm organizations should do, which was "to supply a clear field for the best minds among active farmers." And it seemed a sound alternative to government control of agriculture.[182]

That last sentiment, turning as it did on the traditional rural value of self-reliance, was vital. Fred Steward, a Sherman County rancher, addressed a Farm Bureau meeting in 1926 on the theme that farmers could not maintain their "self-respect" unless they challenged the disparity between their condition and that of other classes. "No system of subsidy will ever be popular in this country. It is a bad idea." Farmers, therefore, through the Farm Bureau, must "play the game, not sit on the sidelines."[183] Secretary Mohler noted, "Self-styled economists, professional friends of the farmer, and propagandists have seized upon the depression in agriculture as a means of access to press and platform," offering "an avalanche of panaceas." But the key, he thought, was "individual responsibility in improving conditions through matters under individual control."[184] The locally based Farm Bureau, with dues of $10 a year, was just the ticket.[185] Once farmers had thought that the Farm Bureau was "something being thrust upon them," said the *Ness County*

News in 1924, but after a "gratifying year," opinion was favorable. The 222 farmers belonging to the Ness County Farm Bureau wanted to work with the organization to "cause a gradual progressive growth and development of the rural home and rural life."[186]

On that score, there was constant daily activity. Most newspapers ran a Farm Bureau column filled with advice on everything from gopher control, to poultry house plans, to how to make an oil shampoo to rid hogs of lice.[187] "We feel," said the editor at Ness City, "that if these farm bureaus are to do any great amount of good their work must be reported in the local papers."[188] The Farm Bureau sponsored health fairs and baby clinics, often headed by specialists from Manhattan.[189] Women sent out from Manhattan taught "domestic science" and "scientific management" for the home. There were education programs in nutrition.[190] Boys' and girls' clubs organized by the Bureau were popular.[191] The small tax levy necessary to support it was considered worthwhile, especially since dues and federal funding added to the financing, and banks, businesses, and railroads paid most of the county tax. In Ness County in 1924, the county agent personally visited over 200 farmers each month, and "many times the introduction of a new variety of grain or a new practice of any kind amounts to many times the cost of the farm bureau in a single year." Like a school or church, the Ness County paper said, if the Bureau were not used, "it becomes a useless institution in our social structure," but if it was used it had a great effect. It was perhaps the prime adult educator, the editor thought, a more effective investment than paying a rural schoolteacher $80 a month to teach only three or four pupils.[192] The Bureau's "schools," such as the "wheat schools" it held throughout the High Plains, were practical.[193]

There was a statewide educational campaign in 1917, with a talk illustrated by lantern slides, called "What the County Agent Can Do for You." The answer was, much indeed. Mr. Schnacke in Pawnee County that year organized a canning club and hosted a man from Manhattan who spoke on a simple method for keeping farm accounts. There was a livestock meeting at Scott City concerning the use of registered stock. At Dodge City, the agent visited 38 schools and enrolled 136 in the Farm Bureau Boy's and Girl's Club.[194] The agents kept careful records, too, on weather and crops and explained the credit provisions of the Federal Farm Loan Act.[195] A film, "Winning with Wheat," showed in 150 towns, drawing a total audience of 30,000, during a push for Farm Bureau organizations in 1917. It advised using the new hybrid wheat seeds. There were Farm Bureau booths at the county fairs and at the Old Settlers picnics, and they drew a crowd.[196]

It worked. C. W. Mullen, county agent for Barton County, reported in 1918, "There were very few who knew anything about the purpose or intention of a Farm Bureau. For that reason a good deal of newspaper work was done for a couple of weeks in order to get the Bureau before the people in the right light." He enrolled his quota and started right out with a meeting on poultry production, attended by 130 farmers. Shortly after, 356 Barton County women attended a meeting on wheatless cooking during the war emergency. The county Farm Bureau had a bulletin board in nearly every bank in the county, which was always packed with information, and it published circulars on many subjects.[197] In the Barton County report for November 1919 to April 1920, the agent reported a membership increase from 250 to 750. The agent treated 6 animals for blackleg, assisted 50 farmers "in buying or selling," passed out 50 farm account books, made 81 farm visits, and consulted 594 times in his office. Over 6,000 people attended farmers' institutes held by the Bureau in the county, and over 3,500 copies of 9 circulars went out. The county agent's office cleared 30,000 farm laborers.[198]

A major project promoted by the Farm Bureau, as well as by the service clubs, between 1920 and about 1924 was cooperative marketing—or what was popularly known as the "wheat pool."[199] The power of the idea was evident when President Hoover turned back to the principles of cooperative marketing in the Agricultural Marketing Act of 1929.[200] There had been many efforts to improve the demand for wheat, including a scheme by the Kansas State Board of Agriculture in 1920 to produce motor fuels from wheat straw.[201] However, the most practical approach seemed the control of supply, or at least a marketing system that distributed the supply better over time. There was consideration of a wheat strike, but the majority felt that a marketing organization would be less controversial and more effective.[202] Cooperative buying organizations had been operating successfully for some years, and there were, in 1920, over 4,000 farmers' cooperative grain elevators in the nation, handling over a billion bushels of grain a year and purchasing $250 million in supplies.[203] Wrote one observer, "Unless he [the farmer] can learn wisdom from the experience of those who at present ride on his back he will continue to bend and grunt under his load."[204]

There was disagreement among Kansas farmers on how to go about forming a pool. One school of thought advocated the optional or voluntary pooling plan ratified by the American Farm Bureau Federation at its convention in Chicago in 1921. This was the "Committee of Seventeen" plan, developed by a national organization called U.S. Grain Growers, Inc. The

Farm Bureau doubted the legality of compulsory pooling, fearing that it would violate antitrust legislation, and wondered whether enough farmers would agree to such contracts. The optional or voluntary pooling plan provided for a five-year contract. At the time of each yearly harvest, the grower had several options, including cash sale and local and regional pooling. The farmer retained ownership of his wheat. Farm Bureau advocates argued that this plan recognized that the farmer had a brain and would act in his own best interest given the proper information. "The optional pool . . . will supplement the exercise of individual judgment and may be counted on to take care of the surplus."[205] Seven of eight Kansas delegates to the convention that ratified the voluntary Farm Bureau plan voted for it.[206]

But many in Kansas objected that this plan could not be effective and supported instead the compulsory pool of the rival National Wheat Growers' Association. According to this plan, the farmer contracted to turn all wheat over to the association for five years and could not sell on his own account. The farmer received money as the association sold wheat. "We cannot long continue to raise and sell wheat at a price of a dollar less than it costs to produce it," said a speaker at the organizational meeting of the Kansas division of the National Wheat Growers' Association in 1920.[207] A. C. Bailey of Kinsley wrote that year that "for a long time the wheat and meat growers have been the goats and have been ridden by speculators and grafters."[208]

In 1921, Western Kansans in considerable numbers signed up for a compulsory pool for the marketing of wheat. The convention of the National Wheat Growers' Association was at Hutchinson that year. The convention favored trying to gather 51 million bushels of Kansas wheat held by "iron clad contracts" with "enough mucilage . . . to make them stick."[209] W. H. McGreevey stated: "The old plan that has been in vogue for forty years will but thrive under the optional plan and the board of trade will but fatten at the expense of the farmers off the profits of voluntary consignment. Optional pooling is uncertain and confusing. The compulsory pooling of wheat, for a term of years, on a 100 percent basis, is the only feasible plan now before the growers."[210]

The philosophy behind all varieties of pooling was represented by newspaper ads with the slogan "Merchandise Your Wheat."[211] The Kansas State Board of Agriculture promoted the slogan, invented by Wichitan Woody Hockaday, "Kansas Grows the Best Wheat in the World." A Dodge City reporter argued, "Southwestern Kansas wheat could be made as famous as Sunkist oranges," if only there were an effective national education campaign and cooperation among producers.[212] "There are some good people," wrote Secretary of Agriculture Henry Wallace, "who seem to think that the

Main Street looking south from 10th Street, with flags flying in front of stores, Goodland, 1924 (courtesy of High Plains Museum, Goodland)

farmer should not concern himself with matters of marketing. They look upon him as a man whose sole business is to produce. . . . And they seem to think further, that having produced abundantly he should turn his crops and his livestock over to the nearest buyer and be thankful for whatever he may receive."[213] Pooling was a protest against that view.

There were dissenters from the whole idea from the first. A writer for the *Country Gentleman* in 1920 expressed the thought that the wheat pools would fail, as the extreme attempts of organized labor had, and was "aghast" at the "impulse that would withhold bread that was raised by the free gift of sun and rain."[214] C. C. Isely of Dodge City favored dumping surpluses on foreign markets as a way of raising domestic prices.[215] J. B. Brown of Larned noted, "A wheat pool . . . can never be effective until it is worldwide."[216] To say that a pool of 40 percent of the Kansas wheat crop or that of any other state "is going to revolutionize the wheat market is so absurd to us that it is foolish."[217]

As pools of all models failed to make a great difference in prices—and the compulsory organization began to sue farmers for reneging on their contracts—the method became unpopular.[218] People began to argue that the farmer who signs a pool contract "signs away his individual rights and becomes a chattel of the association."[219] Isom Wright, a large Barton County wheat grower and early backer of pooling, organized a group of over 1,000 dissenters in 1924 demanding more of a voice in the policies of the Kansas Wheat Growers' Association pool and complaining about its high overhead.[220] The organization controlled only about 3 million bushels, compared to the 51 million Isom thought was necessary.[221] The pool's November 1924 annual meeting at Wichita was "so tumultuous" that "no speaker could make himself heard." There were "oratorical outbursts, [and] hypothetical questions."[222]

An ad paid for by independent elevator operators and placed in the *Goodland Republic* in 1924 called pooling "A Costly Failure."[223] Pool members were gaining nothing, it was claimed, and "if anything could be done to take away the salaries of those promoters, the whole thing would die over night." J. B. Brown, president of the Farmers Co-Operative Grain Dealers Association of Kansas, wrote that neither pools nor government could change market realities. "If we do not furnish the wheat someone else will. As long as we create a surplus we come in direct contact with the world market and our surplus causes every bushel of wheat sold in this country to be influenced . . . by the world demand."[224] W. Y. Morgan of the *Hutchinson News* strongly agreed. "There is nothing," he wrote, "to be gained by denying or dodging the facts," about wheat raising costs and market prices.[225]

Despite the philosophical tilt toward private, business-management solutions, with disillusion about the pools came a shift in interest toward lobbying Congress through the "Farm Bloc" of western senators and representatives. Congressman J. N. Tincher expressed the views of many in his Western Kansas District when, in commenting on the Capper-Tincher farm bill in 1922, he said, "We don't propose to close the exchange, or to curb the market. But we do propose to make it just as unlawful to steal 20 percent of the wheat crop of a farmer as it is to steal his automobile or his team."[226]

There was a parallel emphasis on still more-cost-effective farming. E. E. Frizell, elected president of the new Southwest Wheat Producers at its first annual meeting in Wichita in 1923, discussed diversified farming, summer fallow, and increased quality seed, with "an orderly marketing cost for production."[227] "The farmer," wrote editor Townsley at Great Bend, "is looking at things more from the business man's standpoint and finding they have interests that are mutual. Safe, sane legislation and still more safe and sane management of private affairs is what is needed."[228]

Despite the frustrations, however, the region adjusted well to the 1920s commodity price decline and stayed in the wheat growing business. The look of the towns and the farms there showed that it had not been wholly overlooked by the prosperity of the 1920s.

8

Sitting on the Moon

As a combination of education, theater, and civic boosterism, nothing else could compare to the excitement of the trains
cosponsored by the agricultural college at Manhattan, the Farm Bureaus, and the railroad companies. And of those trains, which ran
regularly through Western Kansas in the first third of the twentieth
century, none had more impact than the Atchison, Topeka & Santa
Fe's "Opportunity Special" of 1925.[1]

The success was partly due to experience. Vada Watson, the
farmer's daughter who served as the "Wheat Girl" on the 1925 train,
drew far larger crowds than had the registered Durocs, Chester
Whites, and Poland China hogs designed to attract members of "pig
clubs" to the Cow, Sow, and Hen Special of 1922.[2] The new train's
theme, wheat growing, struck a note of optimism with those hoping
for profits and prosperity in a way the usual focus on diversified farming did not. There had been something dreary about the 1922 train's
slogan, "Not More Poultry, But Poultry of High Quality."[3] One of
the train's sponsors in 1925 was the Southwest Wheat Improvement
Association, with its message of better yields through science.[4] The
weather was fine in 1925, and the roads were dry. And the trip, orchestrated by the Santa Fe's publicist Frank Jarrell and running
through Western Kansas from July 21 to August 1, was a triumph.

The train, consisting of seven cars, stopped for a two-and-a-half-
hour program at a rate of about three towns a day, concentrating on
county seats.[5] Advance men visited the stops, distributing posters,
planting press articles, and making suggestions for events. "In our
wake," wrote one of them, "we are leaving a trail of publicity with
towns planning the biggest agricultural events in their history. . . .

Vada Watson (second from left) and Harper County wheat queen candidates, 1925
(courtesy of Kansas State Historical Society)

All the papers are puffing the thing for all they are worth."[6] The Chambers
of Commerce, along with local banks and farm organizations, organized attendance and presented the local wheat queens and their courts, along with
the county wheat king (the best grower), to Watson and her press entourage.
Electric lights had been a feature for some time, but in 1925 there were the
new innovations of motion picture and stereoptican machines operating on
the 32-volt train power supply, as well as a full 250-watt broadcasting set, accompanied by an announcer hired at a fee of $750 a week.[7]

Woody Hockaday, the Wichita car dealer and master promoter who had
marked Kansas roads and had organized the highly successful Wichita
booster trains, advised the railroad and the college on features needed to
please the crowd, and indeed they did please. Watson had gone to Washington to present President Coolidge with a bag of Kansas wheat, with the
slogan "Kansas Grows the Best Wheat in the World," and the attendant national publicity, carefully orchestrated by Hockaday, had generated the enthusiasm with which this new media star ("internationally known," it was
said) would be greeted on her travels.[8] Indeed Hockaday, before he drifted
into insanity and had to be committed to an institution, showed himself to
be a master planner and promoter, and nowhere more than with his wheat

Crowd at Dighton for the "Opportunity Special" demonstration train, Atchison, Topeka & Santa Fe railroad, 1925 (courtesy of Kansas State Historical Society)

and wheat train promotions.[9] He carried a "bouquet" of wheat with him wherever he traveled and used it to explain what wheat was and its importance. He distributed 25,000 bags of Kansas wheat in Atlantic City and got front-page publicity in the *New York Times* eleven times. Hockaday put Watson on the radio in New York City, and the next day she received 450 pieces of fan mail. He was just as careful with the small-town events in Kansas. At Ness City, on July 4, 1925, Watson appeared in front of Miner's Cash Store before a crowd of 2,000. The Kansas Wheat Girl, the local editor wrote, was a "short, unaffected little girl who had to mount a box so that she could be seen. . . . She is just a loyal Kansas girl, pretty (as they all are) and with a very pleasing personality. She was dressed simply and her face guiltless of any powder or paint; she doesn't need it, however, as she is pretty enough without, and her bobbed hair was cut quite long and free from waves and curls." Hockaday managed to transfer to the Ness Chamber of Commerce 5,000 of his bags to be filled with county-grown wheat and sold at five cents each.[10]

At one time the railroad had agonized over how to provide special sleeping accommodations on their promotional trains for the female members of the extension service, brought along to give bread-baking demonstrations. But by 1925, the value of a pretty girl was evident, and few thought that the reason Watson was present was primarily to give her talk on how her father handled wheat smut. "I love Kansas," she said, "and I love our wheat." That was sufficient. Miss Watson, the newspapers observed, was "as handsome as her picture in the papers indicate her to be."[11]

On Tuesday, July 21, the train visited Osborne, Lincoln, and Alma. It then proceeded west in a great loop, with rallies at McPherson, Geneseo, Holyrod, Little River, Lyons, Great Bend, Rush Center, Ness City, Dighton, Scott City, Garden City, Cimarron, Dodge City, Kinsley, Montezuma, Sublette, Hugoton, Elkhart, Ulysses, Mentor, Johnson, Larned, St. John, Stafford, Goddard, Kingman, Pratt, Ashland, Coldwater, Medicine Lodge, Kiowa, Anthony, Harper, and Wellington.[12]

The advance group predicted attendance of 100,000 for the forty-three meetings planned in forty western counties in Kansas.[13] Actual crowds totaled 115,000 plus, up from 13,000 recorded on a rainy 1923 "Safer Farming" Special tour of forty-six Kansas towns.[14] At Lincoln, over 5,000 people turned up.[15] There were 5,000 at McPherson and 2,000 and a brass band at Medicine Lodge.[16] There were 6,000 at Garden City and 2,500 at Rush Center.[17] Attendance was 6,000 at Great Bend, and 10,000 in Barton County cast a vote for the local wheat queen.[18] At Pratt, a crowd of 10,000 watched a "Bucking Ford," a picnic, an auto barrel race, and a contest among girls with red hair.[19] At Lyons, 1,500 greeted the train, and Hockaday and Watson went 1,100 feet down to visit a salt mine.[20] Even at tiny Ulysses, which had a rare rain that mired the roads, 500 appeared.[21] One participant, noting that the railroad would receive the largest file of clippings for this run ever assembled about a single event in any single state on the ATSF, added, "I have been on a good many demonstration trains in the last few years, but I never was on one that hit the nail on the head as this one did."[22]

Some were less enthusiastic. It bothered Ed Jones that the college and the Farm Bureau had moved away from their traditional emphasis on diversified farming in order to play to the crowd and push wheat. There should have been a car, he thought, devoted to fruits, vegetables, and flowers that could be grown next to a farm pond. "We can't expect the Lord to do much for us," he wrote Congressman Clifford Hope, "when we won't do what we can for ourselves. . . . We have got to save the water the Lord gives us or we'll go broke."[23] But doubters were scarce.

The Santa Fe "Wheat Festival Special" of 1926 was less successful, and some of the trains of the 1930s were lonely affairs.[24] However, the promotional tradition and the partnership among educators, farmers, and the Santa Fe and Rock Island railroads in Kansas continued. The optimism that it symbolized and the efficiency that the operation of the trains represented were a constant encouragement. Things were fine, wrote a reporter covering the 1926 tour, "and the combine and tractor did the job."[25] Dodge City constructed a wheat temple for the train's visit that year.[26] "No rocks or any-thing to bother the plow," a Stevens County man remembered of the 1920s, "and a new heaven was at hand. . . . We got money mad and motor crazy. It was wheat, wheat, wheat. Because it was easy to farm we forgot all else."[27] Western Kansans were, wrote a man at Goodland in 1925, "Sitting on the Moon," flying high, with just a vague memory of the curves illusion had thrown them in times past.[28]

The change, however, was not positive in all ways. Sometimes when insti-tutions or ways of life are threatened, the commitment to them becomes stronger. There are indications of that pattern in Western Kansas towns dur-ing the decade of the 1920s—the boosterism of hoary tradition was supple-mented by a defensiveness about the independence of small communities in the face of a statewide highway program, the consolidated school, merged newspapers getting their copy from wire services, extractive industries with their headquarters elsewhere, flyovers and bypasses in transportation, man-ufactured tastes for sports and recreation, the mail order and chain store phe-nomenon, imported culture, and even a commercial and artificial "re-created" local historical heritage. Sometimes this defensiveness was sinister, as with the appeal of the Ku Klux Klan. But usually it took the form of a weary struggle against powerful and seemingly inevitable trends of a kind that were strengthened with the centralization and dependence on the federal government that came with the economic and weather reverses of the 1930s.

The road fight was representative. The "Good Roads" movement in Kansas was strong from the early part of the century, culminating in the pas-sage of an amendment to the state constitution in 1928 providing for a state highway department and uniform standards of construction and routing. Such a move seemed only rational to many who laughed at the idea that 105 county commissions could create any sort of modern highway system. However, resistance to state control was strong in the western region, on the grounds that it would tax that district for the benefit of urban areas and tourists, that dirt roads were satisfactory in the arid uplands, and that a high-way department would be another victory for centralized control in Topeka. Tellingly, when the amendment did pass, it was due largely to pressure on the state from the federal government, which demanded that Kansas fall in line with other states on highway policy in order to continue receiving fed-eral highway matching funds.[29]

There was tension all along. "The time has come," wrote an editor in Scott City in 1922, "when the farmer must look deeper into the road prob-lem than he has in the past." No rural community could afford hard-surfaced

Grading roads, Thomas County, April 13, 1926 (courtesy of Kansas State Historical Society)

roads, he thought, and federal aid to highways should be repealed.[30] Why not have someone from southwest Kansas involved in the committee work on roads in Topeka, asked a Dodge City editor in 1917. "Instead of urging southwestern counties to line up behind an eastern Kansas road scheme, some one should be looking for a Moses who could head off the eastern chaps."[31]

Decent roads were needed, to be sure. There were 114,000 autos in Kansas in 1917. Seven thousand people attended a car show at Dodge City that February. The Santa Fe Trail road, later Highway 54, handled 500 cars a day in 1918.[32] Harry Mason, who ran a garage at WaKeeney, had to run a wrecker constantly in rainy times of the 1920s to rescue cars mired in mud. He recorded once riding in his Dodge when the "right front wheel had grown to the diameter of a wash tub, with sticky clay mud fouling the space between wheel and chassis until the car could not be steered and would not proceed in high gear." Mason had to dig with a spade and his hands in the mud until the wheels would roll and then do it again and again until he reached the paved streets of town.[33] "With civilization," wrote a Garden City booster, "naturally come good roads[,] and a fellow who objects to good roads because they cost something would buy a one horse buggy instead of an automobile because it was cheaper."[34]

The question was to whose design and at whose cost.[35] The situation was complex. There were highway planners, called "ungrateful pigs" by some editors in the West, drawing "black lines" on maps.[36] Then there were the railroads defending their interests against the new rights of way. The ATSF in the early 1920s sued western counties to stop the corporation's being taxed for subsidizing its auto and bus competitors by paying for road resurfacing.[37] Towns were at odds with each other over roads, even intraregionally. The federal standards for road construction, necessary to get federal aid, were daunting.[38] And farmers had their own viewpoint.

Typical of the western side of the debate was an October 1922 editorial by state legislator P. L. Jackson in the *Ness County News* on the topic of why Ness County taxpayers should oppose paved roads. Eastern Kansas might benefit from these, wrote Jackson, but soil and climatic conditions in the west made properly dragged dirt roads perfectly satisfactory. The Kansas Highway Commission, created in 1917, was an expensive bureaucracy. To build to its standards, counties would have to assess land adjacent to the highway as much as $7 an acre. "How many Ness county farmers would welcome a deal of this kind?" Counties were forced to cooperate with the plans lest they get no benefit from auto license fees residents were already paying to the state. Jackson thought the Highway Commission law should be repealed and full control returned to the counties. In a county like Ness, roads meeting the state engineer's requirements would cost $50,000 a mile. Over 100 miles were planned for that county, costing $5 million. The federal government contributed $15,000 a mile, but the rest must come from Kansans through bonds and benefit district land assessments. A good sand road could be built for $5,000 a mile or less and maintained for $500 a year. "It seems to me," Jackson concluded, "that a little retrenchment in road expenditures for a time would be better than too much boosting." He was, he wrote, for "good roads we can afford."[39]

Many others agreed. The editor at the *Hugoton Hermes* reported in 1925 that he got an "armful" of good roads literature every week, and implementing the ideas contained therein would mean "a big bond issue and a millstone about our neck. . . . Our opinion is that the people of Kansas better think twice before they get tied to a deal fostered by cement plants and job seekers."[40] Public debt in Kansas had gone from $370,000 in 1914 to $28,500,000 in 1925, mostly due to road building.[41] Would the state lose federal aid if it did not cooperate with the program? So be it. "We might as well make up our minds now," wrote the *Kansas Union Farmer*, "that we must get along without any dollars from Washington."[42] The editor at Colby objected to western counties being "clubbed into acceptance" of a State Highway Commission plan.[43] There were lots of touring experts, wrote a man at Dodge City in 1925, but "the people are a million miles from agreement over how roads should be built."[44]

In addition to the ancient issue of locus of control, the source of the Kansas sectional quarrel on the road issue was dirt versus concrete, with a gravel option thrown in. Some Western Kansas towns thought they should join the modern age. Gravel or sand would not stand the strain, said the *Ellis County News*. "Hays, with its state college and Catholic college and state experiment station will run the dire risk of being left very high and dry on the improved road proposition if it does not step right up and make its bid . . . for a paved surface for South 40."[45] However, at a Chamber of Commerce meeting in Hays that had taken place just two years earlier, almost all delegates had spoken against paving. Paved roads in Western Kansas, one man said, "buckle, 'blow up,' slip[,] tear and do various things that no well-behaved and orderly road . . . would think of doing."[46] The *Goodland News Republic* predicted a 50 percent increase in tax with no better roads. "It is in line with the general tendency of increased taxation, more public employees, and better working political machines. . . . We never believe much of that bunk about needing a new highway law to 'lift Kansas out of the mud' or to keep tourists from detouring around us."[47] The editor at Liberal would not believe "that the county commissioners or a few newspaper men who can't even put out a good paper let alone build a road" had the wisdom to oppose paving.[48] But a Pawnee County commissioner was reflecting the views of many of his compatriots in reacting vigorously against a 1927 article in the *Kansas City Star* pushing paved roads. Gravel roads were best, he argued. The newspapers were filled with articles about some "lawyer, or editor, or politician" traveling across the state and being delayed by a cloudburst, and of what a disgrace that was. "But I have never seen a single article about Bill Smithy, who lives thirteen miles northwest of town, starting to market with a truck load of wheat and getting stuck in the mud." Instead of spending the money for a few through paved roads, it ought to be spent for many gravel roads. "If these roads over which we ourselves can travel in the rain at thirty to fifty miles an hour with comfort and safety, are not good enough for [the tourist] he has our consent to go around through Nebraska or Dakota or Oklahoma or Texas or the Panama Canal or straight up, and if we have a rain and a good wheat crop we will still be a happy and prosperous people."[49]

Modernity, of course, came to Kansas roads over all objections, and western towns involved themselves in an "awful rumpus" over the spoils of the routing of the federal and state paved highways, fretting about decisions made somewhere else.[50] Just as the highway amendment passed, there was another flurry of talk about Western Kansas secession. One editor in the northwest corner of Kansas, however, noted that it was time for the section to "grow

Oakley consolidated school and buses (courtesy of Kansas State Historical Society)

up," accept the inevitable, and lobby for its fair share. "Some day Western Kansas may get alive to itself, and instead of making ludicrous suggestions about secession will organize to pull together, and make its power felt as well as heard. If the present [road] agitation brings that time nearer, it will have done some good."[51]

Another controversial importation was the consolidated school. The *Colby Free Press* in 1921 reprinted an editorial from the *Christian Science Monitor* about the popularity of the concept nationally. The eastern editor noted, "Farmers are becoming more interested in community progress, and are declaring themselves as having come to the conclusion that the giving of one's whole time and thought to raising a crop is a one-sided existence and making one's self a slave to the soil." Just as the hired man needed to be treated better and receive more wages on the modern farm, so good teachers, if they were to be attracted to rural areas, needed to live in modern houses in good-sized towns where they had "easy access to a good library, motion pictures, and all the rest that makes a normal person content." That suggested consolidated schools. Good roads traversed by autos and buses made them possible.[52]

Implementation of school consolidation in Western Kansas was rapid in the early 1920s. In September 1920, there was a "triumphal procession" of ten buses, built in Wichita and costing $19,000, carrying one hundred educators, state officials, and newspaper people from Wichita to the Holcomb consolidated school in Finney County to show off the benefits. A man with a movie camera filmed it, and Professor C. E. Rarick, professor of rural education at the college at Hays, lectured to the guests.[53] That same year, Gray

County replaced eighteen one-room schoolhouses with four well-equipped consolidated schools, served by sixteen buses. The *Kansas Farmer* thought the old schools were "standing empty and unmourned." A student interviewed said, "I have some fellows to play with here and I'm learning faster, too. I've been beating those town boys in my studies and it's fun."[54] Teachers liked it too. They made better salaries, had better equipment, and could earn 60 cents an hour in spending money by driving the buses themselves.[55]

But here, too, there were difficulties. In 1921, a scandal over sex education broke out in Atwood, when a male teacher instructed twenty-six high school girls, not according to the textbook, "but as he viewed sex from his personal point of view." He had to give his lecture and show his drawings to a group of local businessmen who were wondering whether modernization of education was all that had been promised.[56] A Colby lawyer complained to the governor in 1924 that the consolidated school was putting too much of a tax burden on farmers and ruining old-time education:

> More consolidation, more athletics, less study and more mischief seems to be the rule out this way. Upon the least provocation school is dismissed and the children loaded into motor busses and hauled to neighboring towns for some competitive game. [There was an] enervating influence [upon a child who was] babied around and hauled to and from school . . . from five years old until grown. No place left in the country for a social center—no more spelling schools, literaries, or debates, in fact no place for the country boys and girls to go for social amusement but to crank the car and go to town. With such an environment the "back to the farm" movement is but an idle dream and our boys and girls of the farm pine for the city with its bright lights and midnight frolics.[57]

Statistics, however, did not seem to support the passion of critics. Thomas County circulated a questionnaire in 1922 when it was reported that some were not satisfied with the consolidated schools. A few complained about loss of land values due to higher tax, and others griped about the time on buses or said the large schools were cold. But the overwhelming majority felt consolidation was a success.[58] The head of the state Good Roads Association, who toured the state promoting consolidated schools, said, "People are beginning to see everything on a broader scale."[59]

That broader scale included more institutions of higher education for Western Kansas, particularly the junior college or the specialized technical institution. To some extent, the college movement was an outgrowth of the consolidated school and the discovery by local Rotary Clubs and Chambers of Commerce that only about a third of the graduates of the modernized high schools were attending college.[60]

Individual success stories when college educations were closer at hand inspired towns to lobby for state-supported institutions of higher learning in the western region. For example, there was Jeannie Owen, who published a book in 1927 while working for Rolla Clymer at the *El Dorado Times*. Owen had started at the *Emporia Gazette* as a protégée of William Allen White after graduating from college at Hays. She was what in the modern age would be called a "nontraditional student." She entered the high school program at the Hays Normal in 1916, at age thirty-one, after sixteen years of housekeeping, and went straight through the high school and college program and on to a journalistic career.[61] Perhaps with more regional junior colleges and colleges more area residents could do something similar.

Four-year institutions were also considered desirable. It was time, wrote the editor at Dodge City in 1927, to show "fighting spirit" on that issue. "The people of the southwest want a state school. They have been appraising both the cultural and economic advantages which other parts of the state have been receiving from the state's educational system, while the southwest has been shifting for itself." Dodge City asked for a state school in 1921 and again in 1927. However, the bill for a Southwest Kansas State College was defeated by the state legislature.[62] Likewise defeated were bills for colleges at Kinsley and Garden City.[63] Congressman Clifford Hope certainly hoped for little when he proposed that Congress appropriate $18 million for the establishment of a U.S. Naval Academy at Garden City.[64] The Kansas House passed a bill in 1927 to establish a polytechnic school at Great Bend, but it failed to become law.[65] Dodge City tried again and lost again in 1929.[66]

Western towns took to sniping at each other in their common disappointment. "Great Bend," wrote the editor at Dodge City, "has its heart set upon a state school for the teaching of pyrotechnics, phrenology, permanent waving, witchcraft, palmistry, and magic. If its disappointment is so great of the loss of a thing like that, it ought to recognize how much deeper have been the disappointments of Dodge City after its many campaigns for the kind of a state school that would really amount to something." Great Bend laughed at Dodge's pretensions, too, in claiming to have twenty-seven daily trains running each way through the city.[67] But all fussed at the parsimony of the state toward them and the feeling that they were being treated as second-class citizens.

There was disagreement on what kind of an institution was appropriate. Dodge City had promoted a straight liberal arts institution. "The propaganda in Kansas," one wrote, "carried the inference that the young men and women of this part of the state are of too low an order to warrant any effort to give them a liberal education and that, therefore, something should be substituted which might help them to become self supporting."[68] But some at Hays, which admittedly already thought it had a lock on regional liberal arts, thought that other towns ought to go for a more vocational focus. Lots of boys and girls had "gone to our state colleges, frittered away their time and their parent's money and returned home worth less than a ventriloquist's dummy."[69] But there was agreement that somewhere on the continuum between technical institutes and four-year liberal arts institutions the region deserved more state institutions of higher learning. Western Kansas had paid over 50 percent of the taxes in Kansas and gotten little back.[70]

Perhaps the most annoying of the outside influences arising in the region in the 1920s was that of the mail order catalog and the chain store. Although it could be argued that the economy was improved and prices were lowered by such enterprises, the distribution of the profits was less local than before, and some felt strongly that the community was damaged, as "home merchants" with roots and affinities with their neighbors were absorbed or replaced by industries with headquarters elsewhere and only their market feelers located in Western Kansas. Related was the perception that tastes and technology were developed elsewhere. This was particularly obvious in the newspaper business, where the operations of local papers changed significantly in the 1920s, in the direction of homogenization with the outside world. These newspapers were, after all, not just businesses but also monitors and symbols of the community.

Early in the 1920s, a series of ads and articles appeared, placed by local Chambers of Commerce and service clubs, on the theme of patronizing the home merchant. A large ad signed by many Ness County merchants in March 1922 elaborated on that theme in typical fashion. "What is prosperity? It is made up of many things, but the big item is good business, more sales, quicker turnovers, and increased profits to the business man, and good crops and good prices for the farmer." But good times were "not just going to happen," and they would certainly not happen unless the farmers and the businesspeople in the towns recognized things they had in common in developing the local community and in uniting against outside forces. "Did you ever stop to think that the home merchant is the very heart—the very lifeblood of the town?" The merchant lived to serve the public, the ad writers averred. "If he didn't he wouldn't be here. He is not a fly-by-night concern. He advertises—he has his home here—his children in school. Yes, and every dollar spent with him stays here." The paper claimed that, in a recent competition between a mail order house and Kansas merchants in providing supplies to state institutions, the local people were low bidder on all but 2 of 175 items.[71]

The rhetoric became stronger as the problem became more serious. A Great Bend newspaper documented in 1925 that the parcel post ran at a loss because of the mail order lobby and that local merchants were being taxed to pay for delivery of mail order packages to their own communities. The cost of delivering a mail order package from Kansas City to a Great Bend customer was less than the cost to a local grocer to deliver a package across town. There were $5,000 a week in orders from Great Bend to mail order houses, or $250,000 a year, "enough to run one of the largest businesses in town." One company alone mailed 5,000 catalogues to Great Bend citizens.[72] Chain letters from mail order houses recruiting people to act as their salesmen were, said the *Tiller and Toiler* at Larned, "calculated to shackle the old home town."[73] In a 1926 campaign for "my hometown first," Ness County had a list of points in favor of the home merchant. "Not here today and gone tomorrow; Not rushing into town grabbing all business to be had and out again; Not by extravagant talk and over-statements forcing inferior merchandise on to you; Not dodging taxes, civic responsibilities and all duties of citizenship; Not a parasite; Not an insidious Home Town destructionist; Not a peddler." The future of the community, the writers exclaimed, "hinges absolutely on community loyalty from every one of its citizens."[74]

The erosion of local business initiative, however, was clear, and was well illustrated in the changing fortunes of the A. A. Doerr hardware store in Larned. Doerr wrote a fellow merchant in Oklahoma in 1921 that "conditions are very bad with us," and collections from farmers were uncertain.[75] His trade organization noted in 1924, "There have been times of late when we have quoted prices on our wares with a tremor in our voice and an apology in our manner."[76] That year Doerr had to resign as state business manager for Kansas because his mercantile business demanded his constant attention. "I must return to my community, to the people who by their constant patronage have aided me in building a business worthy of any man's efforts. I feel that my constant presence is demanded in order to render to them every service possible, so that nothing will be left undone that might aid our people to weather the financial depression by which they have been overwhelmed."[77]

Yet, by late in the decade, no fame, no attitude, no local loyalty to the pioneer in introducing combines to Kansas could change the fact that the implement manufacturers were bypassing local dealers and selling direct or through their own stores at discounted prices. "Many of the companies are showing no regard whatever to the established dealers," wrote Doerr in 1928, "and are contracting with farmers to handle their lines. It seems we are making no progress toward checking this habit of about all of the implement manufacturers who are in business at the present time. They want their lines represented in the various territories and care little who does it."[78]

Doerr's fellow small-town merchant in Oklahoma, Otho Mooney, noticed in 1929 that a Montgomery Ward store was coming to Larned. That, he said, would change much. Mooney thought that the "progressive" home merchant could survive. "I do not think there is any way that the individual merchant can be put off the map as long as he really serves his community as good or better than someone else can do." But he admitted that the chain stores had bested him in displays, marking down merchandise, and keeping track of their inventories. He was scrambling to adjust.[79]

Indeed Montgomery Ward did come to Larned. It leased the Frizzell building in the spring of 1929, spent $17,000 in alterations (including electric elevators to all three floors), and hired thirty employees. Local merchants surveyed seemed to accept that it was better that the store was in Larned than in some adjacent town, but they were dismayed that the giant firm, which had 250 stores in the United States, was reaching towns as small as Larned, population 5,000.[80] Doerr's friend Mooney that year sold his store in Oklahoma to Sears Roebuck Company.[81] Doerr sheepishly asked his friend for information about the mode of operation of Sears. "Perhaps all this may appear foolish to you, but I am groping about trying to strengthen my organization, and perhaps you by reason of your recent connection . . . can give me information of much value."[82]

Only months earlier Doerr had used Mooney's store as an example of local enterprise and the importance of personality and community loyalty in business success.

> Your customers must have confidence in and trust you and you must believe in them. There are men who trade at our store year in and year out. Their families trade there. In fact their children grow up and trade with us. Most of them call me by my given name, which shows that we have their good will and confidence, and have a fine spirit of relationship existing between our store and the people who patronize us.[83]

Apparently, however, such loyalty, the force of such personality, and community pride were hard-pressed to overcome a price break or a flashy ad.

Montgomery Ward at Larned advertised the Airline 8 radio in 1930 for $59.95, about a third the price of radio consoles offered by competing home merchants.[84] Doerr offered the forty-five tube Model 92 with "Majestic Power-Pack battery" for $167.50, minus tubes, in a time when a man's suit was $24 and boy's knickers were $5.[85] Perhaps the quality or service was different, but so was the price. The editor at Ness City wrote that patronizing mail order and chain stores was a contradiction. "Why boost in one direction, while committing community suicide in another?"[86]

Small-town newspapers would in time sometimes find themselves taken over by chains, but long before that came the impact of outside forces on the way they operated, as well as their content. Stereotyped plates containing whole pages composed by national firms and sent by express to be printed by local papers had been a feature of the newspaper business since the 1890s. The smallest-town reader expected the national serial story and the art work that came with this homogenized product, which often looked much more sophisticated graphically than the hand-set local page.

William Allen White, the dean of Kansas newspapermen and an exponent of the newspaper as a community institution, claimed in 1916 that it did not matter that "our little country papers seem drab and miserably provincial to strangers," because they played to the strong "country faith" of their readers. If the passenger on the California Limited, White wrote, could only "take the clay from your eyes and read the little paper as it is written, you would find all of God's beautiful, sorrowing, struggling, aspiring world in it, and what you saw would make you touch the little paper with reverent hands."[87] However, in the Jazz Age, such quaint sentiment no more sold newspapers than it sold hardware.

One force changing newspapers was technology. The Associated Press wire service began to offer subscription national news instantaneously to even smaller papers, giving them, according to one Western Kansas sheet that installed it in 1927, "a metropolitan newspaper appearance."[88] And, of course, local papers had also to compete with the immediacy and national focus of radio. Linotypes were a sine qua non for any newspaper by the 1920s. New high-speed newspaper presses were next—efficient, but expensive. Pressure to purchase a modern perfecting press from the Duplex Company of Battle Creek, Michigan, was there in most middle-sized Western Kansas towns in the 1920s. Affording such an admittedly impressive machine, capable of printing 5,000 newspapers in an hour, often meant consolidating formerly competing local papers that gave varied perspectives on local news, making weeklies into dailies, and working for regional circulation and more entertainment for the casual reader.[89] The operation of these big presses was automatic, their registration was perfect, their speed was impressive, but the editor/owner often felt he was being carried along by a tide not wholly controllable.

The *Liberal News*, which became a daily in 1929, touted that it would be "thoroughly metropolitan in appearance," dealing always "in the latest and the best."[90] At the same time, it ran a series of articles about the influence of newspapers in community welfare, harking back to an earlier ideal. "Large papers may cater to political or industrial factions at times, but small town newspapers play to the brick houses, and the green, yellow, and white cottages on 'main street.' It wins their friendship, places them on the stage of activity, and applauds them." The small-town paper, the Liberal editor argued, "isn't a machine. It is the heart of the community and all lives count time by it. . . . It moulds community thought, is revered as an oracle, enjoyed as a chronicler, consulted as a friend and a guide. People may laugh at its information, and call it a twice told tale, but they read it, search for their names and find them." It sold its own people on their town as well as impressed outsiders with it.[91] "All towns, no matter how small," wrote a winner in the home paper and community contest at Goodland in 1924, "must have loyalists, people who boost it and thus further its development and growth." The home paper, wrote another, "is a great power in the community. . . . From it we learn of the financial, educational, moral, and religious conditions of the community."[92] Perhaps. But the "acids of modernity" were eroding that picture and replacing it with a new model, much less adapted to the specific dreams of its local readers.

The development of an oil and gas industry was no more a native initiative in Western Kansas than had been the Good Roads movement or the consolidated school. The upshot was unmistakably economic development and a reduced dependence upon agriculture, but with these came outside control and distant markets. If high capital electric light plants, airports, and dry-milk plants appearing on the Western Kansas landscape in the 1920s appeared complex and nontraditional, the oil and gas rigs were an even greater surprise.[93]

There was experimental exploration activity in oil and gas in Western Kansas during World War I when the price of crude and the demand for gas by utilities were both especially high.[94] Soy #1 at the Cheyenne Bottoms marsh near Great Bend began drilling in 1917 but did not produce oil in commercial quantities until 1923.[95] A wildcat well operated by the Garden City Oil & Gas Company went down to 1,500 feet in 1919, and the local press reported that several oil and gas companies had leased 60,000 acres in the region.[96]

There was drilling for oil near Scott City beginning in 1921, reaching 4,000 feet the next year.[97] Some gas shows excited the people of Liberal when Boles #1 was put down by the American Fuel & Transportation Company in 1920.[98]

The two great defining moments, however, for the Western Kansas industry, were the drilling of Carrie Oswald #1 near Russell in November 1923 and the completion of Crawford #1 near Hugoton in December 1927. The former confirmed that Western Kansas could and would be a substantial producer of oil; and the latter, when it came in at 16 million cubic feet a day production, instituted continuous substantial development of one of the largest natural gas reserves in the world.[99]

The development of the Fairport field around the Oswald well had a local flavor, with stories of the sudden wealth of a local farmer and the spectacular discovery of the "Lucky Seven" group of Russell businessmen. However, by the time Nate Appleman brought back the Fairport field with his innovative acidizing technique in 1933, science had outrun stories about staking fields based on seeing a coyote.[100] The Hugoton field had a national and international flavor from the start, and although it filled the pockets of lease owners, it had far less impact on the growth of regional towns than had oil activity.

Oil doubled the populations of Lyons and Hays and tripled that of Great Bend. Great Bend went from 4,460 to 12,665 people between 1925 and 1950, unquestionably mostly due to its status as an oilfield supply center. Not so with natural gas. Hugoton and Liberal benefited but could hardly be called boom towns, as the offices there of regional pipeline companies were only local branches of large companies with headquarters elsewhere, and the wells were so large that there were few of them, only 200 wells in the entire field by 1938.[101] Stevens County population increased only from 4,060 to 5,351 between 1921 and 1931. Seward went from 6,265 to 6,637 in the same period.[102] With big gas wells coming in all around it in the late 1920s and pipeline companies forming to connect regional towns with the field, Hugoton was, an observer said, "keeping its senses." The newspaper got a new linotype, a spate of homes went up, a municipal water plant appeared, but the comment was, "Nobody said a thing about Hugoton becoming another Wichita or Tulsa." The president of the community club said: "We're not much excited. We had a good town before gas was found. . . . We are going right ahead with our farm program. This new wealth in sight is all right but we have a greater wealth in the man and woman power in Hugoton."[103]

However, there was no missing the drama and the potential in the new extractive industry. Victor Murdock, traveling west from Wichita in 1928, saw that around Hays the countryside by night was laced with "glittering derrick necklaces . . . and there are scouts in the hotel lobby long after midnight lounging about talking leases."[104] At Great Bend, there was admiration for the "undaunted men who made it possible—who strode boldly into virgin territory and staked their time and money and skill against a brief bit of geological data and Mother Earth's perversity in the belief that oil would be found." The oil story, the observer thought, contained "all the epic elements of the pioneer." There was not "a tinge of yellow in the whole gallant army."[105]

A gas franchise for the city of Liberal passed by a heavy vote in 1922 under the slogan "Make Liberal's Future Safe."[106] As the decade passed and the discoveries became larger, it was obvious that the supply was far too large for the immediate needs of towns in the region and that not enough brick and tile plants were likely to be built to utilize it. Therefore began a kind of colonization of the type that had led to protest by the "Kansas Gas for Kansans" organization in the eastern Kansas gas fields in 1905. This time there were no night riders and no protest marches, just resignation to the way things tended to go in the big and integrated modern economic world. By 1929, large outside corporations were active in the Hugoton field, both in drilling and in transportation. "Hydro-carbons in Southwest Kansas," a Hugoton editor wrote, "are turning the eyes of Eastern capitalists to this section and within a short time they may be developed to the point that natural gas for Chicago, Detroit, Cleveland, New York City and other eastern cities will be piped from the Hugoton field." Indeed they were. Regional gas pipeline systems developed in 1928 and 1929, constructed and operated mostly by the Argus Gas Company. There were 86 miles of 8-inch lines connecting southwest Kansas towns by 1930. Argus had headquarters in Dodge City but was a subsidiary of the Moody-Seagreaves Company, which was owned partly by Electric Bond and Share, a branch of General Electric, and partly by Standard Oil of New York.[107] Shortly, the big interstate pipelines began building. O. H. Bonner, president of the Central Oil and Gas Company of Chicago and vice president of the Atlantic National Bank of Boston, was one of a series of eastern capitalists visiting southwest Kansas late in the decade. He told a reporter in Elkhart: "You are burning the finest gas in the United States here. . . . We believe there are other gas areas out here with which to supplement the flow from the Hugoton field to help meet the enormous consumption of the giant cities of the east." There could be "extraordinary returns for eastern capital," he thought. Local residents heard him with interest, but they were more fascinated still with the Pierce-Arrow car in which Bonner and his son were traveling through Western Kansas.[108]

Before the Depression struck full force, the implications of the gas industry were clear, including the pattern that lease money to tide farmers over through the hard times would amount to a small part of the take involved in providing gas to major midwestern cities from Western Kansas. In 1930, a 900-mile pipeline from Hugoton to Omaha began taking natural gas from a 300,000-acre lease block in Stevens and Morton counties, operated by the Missouri Valley Gas Company and capable of delivering 100-million-cubic-feet per day to keep Nebraska toes warm in the winter.[109] This line was the largest in the world at the time, 24 inches in diameter.[110] Front-page stories in the *Hugoton Hermes* in 1930 predicted that the Missouri-Kansas company, which employed 5,000 men at a cost of $650,000 a month, would soon link a half million acres of gas land extending from Texas into Kansas with markets in the east, using 2,500 miles of pipeline.[111] The *New York Times* in the fall of 1930 marked the Hugoton, Kansas, area as one of the four principal natural gas areas in the United States.[112] As though to confirm this, a second major gas pipeline was announced late that year—to reach Minneapolis and St. Paul by way of Lincoln and Des Moines.[113]

Western Kansans appreciated the size of the enterprise. A Hugoton newspaperman wrote:

> We were setting out here on the prairie in a farming country a country raising wheat, maize and kaffir. We had no industries, no factories, nothing to depend upon but agriculture. . . . One day along came the gas men. . . . Hard times hit the country. All the rest of the country suffered from depression, was in dire straights. Crops failed, prices went to smash, bills came due, taxes came due, mortgage interest came [due] with nothing to fall back on. This community suffered some, it is true, but the lease money came in. It helped out materially.[114]

Economics allowed the adjustment; politics and culture made of the materials a regional life—changed, but vital enough. There remained in the 1920s a good deal of self-consciousness of Western Kansas as a region, but as a semi-oppressed region, not only colonized by outside corporations, but exploited by Topeka. The capital city was now seen as taking its bite of the oil and gas income as well as the farm returns drawn with such difficulty out of hard weather and low prices. When Sinclair Lewis published his satirical *Main Street*, there was reaction in Hutchinson and Dodge City and Great Bend, which saw themselves as much like the prototype small town that Lewis pilloried. Maybe big cities got boring also, maybe "the lure of the bright lights in time grows wearisome with its empty nothingness," with people "repeating the same old drivel and inane remarks." Yes, Lewis was right about American country towns being laid out on similar plans with "the same box-like houses and two story shops," but some of his criticism was not endemic small-town culture but the bland hysterias brought on by national advertising of the kind that led people to listen passively to mechanically reproduced music, to find their art in advertising, to talk of flivvers and safety razors and dollar watches rather than of love and courage. That "savorless people, gulping tasteless food," was imported to Western Kansas. Chester Leasure of the *Hutchinson Gazette* commented in 1921, about the Lewis book, that his cynical conclusion must not be accepted lest the six-cylinder engine become the national symbol. The "feverish restlessness" came from the "unreeling of salacious movies," not from those things most close at hand in Garden City or Goodland.[115] It was an intermediary reality that corrupted, not the actual native place.

Kansans could be guilty of stereotyping, too, about the western region. William Allen White in 1922 talked about Garden City as "a little sunburned pine board town." This led to an impassioned response from city leader I. L. Diesem, noting that as early as the 1880s Garden City had more substantial buildings than did Emporia. "All that Finney county and western Kansas ask is a square deal."[116]

Newspapers boosted, but with realism and irony of a type that had not been present in the regional boosterism of the 1880s. A Dodge City paper reported in 1920 that the Arkansas River was a strange stream, sometimes producing mud and sometimes dust. "Catfish in this river have to come up to the surface to sneeze. From the great wide sand bars along its course, great clouds of dust arise and inundate the towns and villages along its course and cause trains along the Santa Fe to collide at irregular intervals." But for all that it was a "nice old river," and when it rained in Colorado, the Arkansas was thin enough "that it can be poured from one vessel to another like an egg nog, but ordinarily it has to be stirred with a stick before it can be poured from anything." The river was not much to look upon, "but there is some of the grandest country in the valley on either side of it that the sun ever shown upon, and how such a river ever came to run through such a grand and glorious paradise is more than we can understand."[117] Old stories about mirages and ghost towns and jokes about how frogs lived in Western Kansas for four years before they learned to swim and how people there had to stop chewing tobacco because they could not produce saliva were now quoted from eastern papers with wry amusement by western sheets, confident as the region was that its statistics could quickly put a lie to the image.[118] There were coyotes still, but Western Kansans were roping them from cars at 45 miles per hour.[119]

Regional politicians were sophisticated, attuned to their constituents, and expert at speaking the Western Kansas language. Clifford Hope of Garden City became a state representative in 1922 and a member of Congress from the Kansas Seventh District in 1926.[120] A Hope supporter wrote him in 1926 that he "felt like singing the Doxology" at news of Hope's interest in the congressional seat. "I was wondering when some representative man or woman would come forward and rid us of the incubus of this drunken, blatant, demagogic, old political Frankenstein. The bunch of professional, pie-counter, thimble-riggers who have run Republican politics for a generation, on a mental and intellectual shoe-string, ought to be taught a lesson."[121] The former representative, J. N. Tincher, was from Medicine Lodge and had cosponsored the Capper-Tincher bill against speculating in grain but withdrew in the primaries, sensing a turn against him.[122] Hope was a western man and a young man (in his early thirties), with "a young man's dreams of public service and public honors."[123]

Hope heard from his constituents a great deal and was excellent at responding to them promptly and sensibly. In 1927, he got a long letter from a Great Bend "dirt farmer" on agricultural policy, illustrating considerable sophistication. The man complimented Hope on his "out for business" attitude about wheat marketing, hoping that Congress would use its powers over interstate commerce to prevent people from trading in what they did not own. In doing this, the trader was "only bluffing, and his bluff is interfering with my business in that it prevents me from getting a decent living price for what I have to sell." The Great Bend man was against loaning public money to farmers. "I don't want to borrow any more money; I've borrowed too much already. What I want is just a halfway decent chance to earn and pay back that which I already owe." It was best, he thought, to ask the farmers about farming. "What college professors, Department of Agriculture specialists and others can add is only incidental."[124]

There was a realm of politics, however, that was a long way from Hope's practicality, civility, and tolerance. Kansas in the 1920s supported a strong Ku Klux Klan, and that organization had its attraction in the west part of the state. The *Tiller and Toiler* at Larned reported that 107 new Klan members were initiated one week in August 1922. There was a 30-foot fiery cross on Bissel's point near Great Bend and 500 autos gathered along the road near the Charles Slentz pasture where 75 robed men patrolled.[125] A similar ceremony involving 500 persons occurred in Barber County the next month.[126] The editor at Liberal said it was hard to get definite information on the Klan but that it seemed to be well organized in Seward County. Despite unfavorable national publicity, it "seems to continue to grow like a mushroom in the night." The secrecy was offensive, but the defense of traditional values was attractive to a beleaguered region. The editor wrote, "If it succeeds in putting the fear of the Lord into the hearts of some who seem to have no respect for anything or anybody it will accomplish one useful purpose."[127] He did express the hope that control of the Klan locally "never gets out of the hands of the level headed class and into the radical element which possesses neither fear nor sense[,] for only God can then tell what hellishness it could perform."[128] By mid-September 1922, the Klan had 200 members in Seward County and it was the talk of the town in Liberal.[129] Goodland and Colby that same month reported functioning Klan units.[130] A newspaper in Sharon Springs was purchased in 1925 by Rev. D. P. Abbey, a Klan leader whose card read: "Be Klanish. Be 100% American." On the reverse side was the appeal: "Remember, every criminal, every gambler, every thug, every libertine, every girl runner, every home wrecker, every wife beater, every crooked politician, every dope peddler, every moonshiner, every shyster lawyer, every white slaver, every pagan papist priest . . . every brothel madam, every Rome controlled newspaper—is fighting the Klan. Think it over. Which side are you on?"[131] "Don't be Ku Kluxed into buying something you don't want," went a merchant's ad in the Dodge City newspaper.[132]

Of course the Klan was what modern slang might call "politically incorrect" from the start, and its defenders were shy about speaking publicly on its behalf. But there were intimations in the local press of the sources of its strength in regional politics and culture. The *Kansas Farmer* in the fall of 1922 received many letters from church members praising the Klan for its defense of morality. "When a man flirts with other men's wives," one wrote, "then the Ku Klux Klan takes one of these fellows out and spanks him and issues warning to others of like caliber while the law can only stand by and the flirt cannot be touched by said law if the flirt uses any brains at all."[133] Ness Citians heard a lecture, "Americanism and the Ku Klux Klan," delivered by a national lecturer in December 1923.[134] The talk got front-page coverage in the *Ness County News*, which reported that the lecturer "explained to everyone's satisfaction the creed, ideals and objectives of the Klan."[135]

Klan ads appeared in Western Kansas papers with the official sponsorship acknowledged. For example, a June 1923 piece paid for by Local Klan No. 23 of Liberal was put forward, "that the public may be fully advised on the aims of the Ku Klux Klan as an organization." The Klan made "no fight on races or religion," the ad said, and discriminated no more than the Masons or the Jews or the Knights of Columbus. Its primary purpose was to develop character, support law enforcement, and through those things to improve communities. It defended the "sacred relationship of the sexes" and supported better pay for teachers and church attendance. In short it was, along with churches and fraternal societies, the bulwark of traditional values against modernism. "What we need in every community in America is some coordinating medium that will bring together all these various organizations into one militant body, so we can present a solid front."[136] In the fall of 1924, during William Allen White's anti-Klan campaign for governor of Kansas, the Ku Klux Klan placed a full-page piece in the *Ness County News* with a similar message. Not one charge against it had been proved, it averred. "We claim to be the Negro's best friend" but were indeed "an organization for the betterment of Protestant, Gentile, American born citizens." It was the enemies of law and order that were out to destroy the Klan. "They talk much about the mask to frighten, but they only want information to be better enabled to destroy our power for good."[137]

The Klan was barred from Kansas by legal proceeding in 1925, and that was a watershed moment. Pawnee County turned down a Klan request to use the county courthouse for a lecture, "What a Jew Thinks of the Ku Klux Klan." The grounds were that a public building should not be employed for the "stirring up of racial prejudice."[138] The next year there was an investigation of the Klan's having funded, and to some extent taken over, the local Chautauqua program and of it having used Chautauqua equipment for disseminating its message. The manager of the Redpath-Horner programs was indignant when he learned of the charges but admitted that Chautauqua was a "commercial enterprise" and would take anyone's money. "And thus low," said the local editor, "has the Chautaqua with its alleged high purposes, its purported educational and inspirational aims fallen in Larned at least." The newspaper called Klan sponsorship of the Chautauqua for two years running "sinister."[139]

There had been all along some forceful objections by editors and citizens. A Catholic priest said in 1923 that he might have to go to Russia, "where they make no pretense of loving liberty," if the Klan's views of Catholics began to prevail in Ness County.[140] A man from Brownell, Ness County, thought the new Klan was merely a money-making operation and a "cheap political machine," using "hoodoo" to scare people.[141] A woman from Goodland argued in 1924, "It is a new thing for self-respecting men on errands of helpfulness or generosity to borrow this livery of criminals. It is a new thing for churches to allow their sacred precincts to be invaded by such mummery as sheeted figures and masked faces, and to submit to being patronized by the Lord only knows whom." But she knew "a lot of rabbits in this town, and I am guessing they are fairly flocking to the Ku Klux Klan."[142] Before the forceful legislative and editorial reversal, indeed they were.

Perhaps the Klan was reflective of some aspects of Western Kansas culture, but it was not the part of which the majority was most proud. That was reserved for their cantatas, their golf courses, their libraries, their town orchestras, their fairs and rodeos, their civic leagues, their women's clubs, and their fashion shows—the things they crafted locally to enhance the communities with which they identified. Theodore Dreiser wrote in 1923 that he thought there was no hope for Kansas. It was "simply a hopeless country for intellectuals and thinking people." But that was not to be unchallenged by Western Kansans of the 1920s. Instead, the editor at Dodge City said that Dreiser was hopeless, since he wrote only two kinds of books, one unfit to read and the other that did not sell. "Kansas, we believe, never will be a state that he can be proud of. It has the same tendency to pick its own books that it has to cling to marriage."[143] The weeklies and dailies in the shortgrass country were filled in the 1920s with far more than crop, rainfall, and real estate reports.

Music remained significant. One music house reported selling fifty-four pianos in southwest Kansas in 1916 and expecting to sell more than one hundred in 1917.[144] Liberal had a Jenkins Music Store by the early 1930s stocking Steinway pianos.[145] Syracuse put on an Easter cantata in 1920 to a capacity crowd at the Methodist church, employing the combined voices of the Presbyterian and Methodist choirs.[146] The tiny Ness County town of Bazine did the same five years later, recruiting 110 people for their chorus and even having an orchestra.[147] The new radio was, in the time before everyone had one, used to enrich public culture. There was a radio concert at the Barnd Opera House in Ness City in the fall of 1922 that used a Western Electric loudspeaker to entertain a crowd admitted free with a concert. "The prohibitive costs of the entire machine," the press commented, "is the only real drawback to 'radioing.'" After some problems with eliminating the static, the concert came in clearly. Ness received programs from as far away as Davenport, Iowa, and Talanta, Georgia.[148] The Wesley Choral Society did a program at Goodland in the summer of 1924 that featured Miss Agnes Warriner playing Mendelssohn and Miss Josephine Arensberg Liszt. "It was equal or even better than many musical programs put on by professional artists on the Chautauqua platform," the local reviewer thought.[149] Liberal, which like most towns had long had a town band, in 1925 discussed forming an orchestra. A local teacher had developed enough violinists that it was thought possible to start with some free concerts. A piano went into the band room for practice, and the newspaper hoped that the orchestra could get together with local choirs to put on a high-toned annual musical event.[150] The Garden City Night Hawks orchestra (a curious combination of violin, sax, drums, and piano) began touring the shortgrass area in 1925, after having entertained at local banquets and theaters.[151] The town also had a Mexican orchestra, consisting of a clarinet, three violins, a bass viol, and two guitars. Their leader was a graduate of the Conservatory of Mexico.[152] Dodge City put on the *Messiah* that same year, with fifty voices and performing ten choruses.[153] By then, it boasted a Little Theater and the Dodge City School of Music, complete with violin and speech departments.[154] On the popular side, there was a dance in Larned in April 1920 that featured the Deep River Jazz Orchestra of Oklahoma City.[155]

The serious musical activities at Lindsborg and Hays continued in enhanced form. Lindsborg offered much more than the *Messiah* performance. In April 1925, for instance, many drove there to hear Reinhald Werrenrath, the popular baritone. The accompanist on that day was Herbert Carrick, who also played Chopin's Waltz in C-sharp minor and Polonaise in A-flat. That same Sunday there was a performance by the Bethany Oratorical Society and violinist Albert Spalding.[156]

Hays people were even criticized for being too high-toned, morally as well as musically. It was said the college had "a cop in every bush" and that too many students were sent home "convicted of the heinous crime of spooning and going to the American Legion dances."[157] President W. A. Lewis of the college threatened in 1924 to refuse teaching certificates to any student who patronized the public dances in town. Local churches had circulated petitions against these.[158] Critics observed that at the "hops," girls hopped too high, "thereby disclosing to the view of onlookers and other dancers parts of the human anatomy that in bygone days were deemed sacred to the bath and the bather."[159] It was true that there had to be some defense against 1920s poplar culture, where movie ads in the local paper might contain such texts as "Her full round arms—encircling charms—appealing, compelling. The amazing bare-foot, silk-clad beauty in a romance of the Harem."[160] Hays residents thought it was better to attend the annual music festival and its attendant art show.[161] In 1928, Hays staged the opera *Aida*, by Verdi, at a cost of $2,000. There was a $500 loss, but the fact that the college had staged the first grand opera in Western Kansas was an achievement.[162] The spirit had spread to other towns. "There is appreciation of music in Dodge City," the newspaper there recorded. "Music is a symptom of the joy of living. Out here we take time for the finer things of life. We have pride in our schools, our families, our orchestras and our growth."[163]

Culture, however, was broader than the orchestras and the operas. It included athletics and other forms of recreation. The sports news took up ever-more-space in Western Kansas newspapers in the 1920s, and the fortunes of the high school football and baseball teams became a significant part of the way communities thought of themselves. When the Garden City Junior College football team played Panhandle A&M from Goodwell, Oklahoma, in October 1924, it was an occasion to close all the stores in town.[164] There were serious editorials on football.[165] At Goodland in 1926, the editor wrote that the argument about the football championship of northwest Kansas was "inane and useless" and that Goodland was simply a good team, one of thirty undefeated high school teams in Kansas, but he was in the minority. The town sent a booster train with the team wherever it went.[166] When the Goodland team of two years later was defeated by Atwood, the editor hated to see their rival "make our team look like a grade school playing a college" but was "mighty glad if we had to be beaten that bad it was by Atwood rather than Oberlin or Colby."[167]

There was much attention also in the era and in the region to swimming pools and golf clubs. Garden City set the standard in swimming pools when its sealike outdoor concrete "beach," claiming to be the largest in the world, opened in 1922.[168] The pool was 337 feet long and 218 feet wide. It could be used by 2,000 people at a time, with water changed every 10 days by an 8-inch pump.[169] In the winter, the Garden City municipal pool became a skating rink, lit by electric lights and patronized by people from many miles around.[170] Other towns built pools with great enthusiasm. Meade put one in at its park in 1922, arguing that it had voted sewer and railroad bonds and it was time to do something for "our boys and girls."[171] Liberal citizens, noticing that over 100 people swam in its primitive pool with a dry wind blowing in June 1924, thought the town needed a municipal campaign for a bigger one.[172] The town voted $12,000 in bonds for it in 1927. At the time, Liberal people were often driving 50 miles on a Sunday for a swim.[173] The dedication of the Larned pool in 1931, with its southwestern-style building, drew a crowd of 5,000. There was a free movie at the Electric Theater to celebrate and a performance by the Boy Scout drum and bugle corps, and ten local firms provided bathing suits for the beauty contest.[174] The only hint of doubt came concerning the dress standard at swimming pools. The Hugoton editor was worried about this but said that little modifications would cure the problems. Hugoton had a "clean" pool, the newspaper claimed, "conducted along lines that will keep it that way."[175]

Golf was equally compelling, and golf clubs, even an occasional tennis club, appeared all over the High Plains of Kansas. The greatest golf club, unquestionably, was on the east edge of Western Kansas, but set in an evocative High Plains landscape—Prairie Dunes at Hutchinson. Designed by Perry

Maxwell, one of the world's great golf course architects, and funded by the Carey family, whose fortune came from the local salt, the original nine opened in 1937. It remained a well-kept secret from many golf professionals for decades. Eventually, however, it became a site for major tournaments and is still admired for its special prairie beauty.[176] Other pioneering regional courses of the 1920s were hardly world-class, but the courses and the clubs that went with them were objects of pride to their communities.

Liberal claimed to have sponsored the first golf tournament in southwest Kansas, held in 1921. There were fifty-five players, representing seven clubs in Kansas and ten players from Oklahoma. First prize was a leather golf bag. On the last night of the tournament, the players met at the Hotel Modoc in Liberal and organized the Great Southwest Golf Association. A reporter wrote: "Golf is a new game in southwestern Kansas and most of the links have been laid out in the past year or two."[177] By 1926, Liberal was mounting a campaign for a $5,000 clubhouse.[178]

Larned laid out a course on Jenkin's Hill, one of the most scenic places in the region. "We've watched the coming of the radio," wrote a local poet. "The whir of man-made wings is in our ears/ Across the silversheet we've watched her go—the movie actress, drenched in glycerine tears; We've heard strange sounds from a disc of wax. On top of this, bobbed hair has knocked us still; But now we're flabbergasted in our tracks—There's golf on Jenkin's hill."[179] Hays created a country club at the old fort, concerned with preserving the remaining buildings but looking for some use for them.[180]

The move to preserve Ft. Hays illustrated perhaps the most striking of the Western Kansas cultural innovations of the 1920s. Not only was there new interest in the physical preservation of things like the 1867 Ft. Hays, now in a "sad state of dilapidation," but also there was a serious interest in the early history of the region, both as a route to community pride and as a way of building a tourist business. The Hays blockhouse had quartered Custer and Sheridan and was once Hancock's office. Should it now be the residence of the golf club caretaker? Should the old guardhouse be a chicken house on its way to becoming a "heap of stones?" People around the state began thinking not. C. M. Harger, a member of the Kansas Board of Regents and editor of the *Abilene Reflector*, wrote in 1927 that he wondered if Hays residents understood what a valuable "historic treasure" they had in the old fort buildings.

> Kansas is notably remiss in preserving its reminders of the early days. It has already lost much that was precious. . . . Hays is so rich in tradition and is becoming so prominent as a center of business

and educational interest for all Western Kansas that it should neglect nothing that will maintain the fame of its early days. . . . Were these buildings in some town in New England, they would be made into things of great community pride and would be tableted and treasured with great care.[181]

Libraries, parks, recreation and entertainment, historic preservation, and the very idea that business had something to do with beauty were all considered "sentimental babble," until the women's clubs began to demonstrate their impact. They now became essentials for balanced western towns. "Human requirements can not be fully met by material wealth alone," editor Denious wrote. "There is an increasing desire for the inspiring benefits of music, art, and literature. There is a search for a finer spiritual experience. There is a growing appreciation of the things and places that are distinguished for their beauty."[182]

Local history became a central part of this. Long reminiscences of the histories of the towns, written by old-timers from first-person reminiscence or by amateur local scholars, became in the 1920s a feature of Western Kansas newspapers to a degree they never had been before. However short the local history, it was fascinating. The main problem seemed to be in finding the material. Nearly every Chamber of Commerce promotion of history had been successful, wrote representatives of the Kansas Chamber of Commerce in 1927, but its "Story of Kansas" campaign was not doing well. "The story of Kansas has not yet been told," the promoters commented. "What is worse, nobody knows exactly what story Kansas has to tell." There was confidence, however, that when the facts emerged, they would "surprise the residents of the state as much as those who live in other states."[183]

There were many indications of the practical promise of history. There was a crowd of 8,000 at the unveiling of the Pawnee Rock monument to Santa Fe Trail pioneers in 1912. There was a Ferris wheel there, a balloon ascension, a band from Pratt dressed like Indians, and 700 automobiles. Governor E. W. Hoch, in his address that day, said that the men of Kansas should "feel ashamed that they had allowed the women of the state to accomplish something in the way of preserving the rock which should have been done before it had been despoiled of a great deal of its beauty and historic features."[184] Old Settlers' reunions and picnics became ubiquitous and popular.[185] Materials collected at some of these gatherings metamorphosed into "pageants" of local history, and these became civic events of the first order. One put on by Dodge City in October 1921 was for "visualizing the city's history" and brought 20,000 people onto the streets. Over 3,000 participated directly in the pageantry, in a parade over a mile and a half in length. There were mounted buffalo from the Hays Normal School; the stage coach in which Horace Greeley had ridden; floats with themes, such as the one showing "a Prairie Home," entered by the Dodge City Council of Women's Clubs, and ones that were industrial ads, such as the float of the Great Southwest Goat Club.[186] In 1923, the Kansas State Teacher's College began to take intermediate grade pupils to historic spots in Kansas and to encourage them to get firsthand information from the aging pioneers themselves."[187] There was a recognition that the chance to obtain authentic information from the lips of those who had lived during the pioneering period of the region would not come again. Small markers began to appear, and historical societies regularly formed. True, these did not usually have scientific acquisition methods. The Pawnee County Historical Society in 1925 had among its treasures an old ox yoke, the bell used at an early race track, a Civil War cartridge box, a buffalo skull that had hung in the Pawnee County land office, and a Sharp's buffalo rifle. But this hodgepodge was a start and represented genuine local interest in collecting objects representative of the regional past.[188] "The struggle for bare existence during that time was so fierce," wrote one would-be historian of the local frontier past, "as to leave no leisure for careful writing of history."[189] Modern residents had no such excuse.

The strengths and the weaknesses of this sort of systematic mining of the past for nuggets capable of a reinterpretation that would be useful to the modern towns was well illustrated by the new acceptance and promotion by Dodge City of its colorful early history as the "Cowboy Capital."

The key to Dodge's historical reinvigoration was Boot Hill, the burying place of many an outlaw or simple unfortunate in the early days. The bodies had long ago been moved and the Third Ward School built on the site. However, in the mid-1920s, the school stood abandoned and the town needed to find another use for the hill. There was, in 1925, a "spirited campaign" by an organization of Dodge City citizens to encourage the city to purchase Boot Hill so that it might become a historic site. That plan did not come to fruition, and the hill was sold to the Protestant Hospital Association. That group promised to remodel the school, but in two years did nothing. In 1927, the site came up for sale again, and again there was agitation to make it a historic attraction.[190] This time there was a bond election that created a $12,000 fund, and the city purchased Boot Hill with the intention of building a city hall in southwestern style on it and the vague plan of making it some sort of tourist attraction.[191]

It was some time before much was done in the way of interpretation on Boot Hill. And when it did happen, the focus veered away from the scholarly and toward the commercial, even toward "hucksterism." In 1929, a concrete statue of a cowboy went up, with the inscription, "On the ashes of my campfire, this city is built." Around the site, rocks and cacti gave a western flavor.[192] The town formed the Southwest Historical Society in 1931, which operated a museum of sorts for some years, called "Beeson's corral."[193] When a steer head sculpture went up in 1932, the town celebrated with an "Old West day."[194]

It became even cornier and more mythological with the passage of time. A few local people complained about the kitsch, but most appreciated the tourist dollars. "Fakes may not be real history," a resident wrote, "but the visitors certainly lap them up." Outsiders wanted the West to be romantic according to their lights, and the local attractions would have to conform.[195]

Some of the worst of it was in the future in 1929, but the direction was there. Dodge City doubtless felt the pressure most, because few knew enough about many other towns in Western Kansas to have any expectations. But all realized that history was marketable for better or worse. Eastern newspapers in the fall of 1929 did some laughing at Dodge City for having a Billy Sunday rally and intimated that the town was trying thus to atone for its wicked past. No indeed, wrote the local press. "Why should Dodge City be ashamed of Boot Hill? Have we become so goody goody that the days of the primitive, elemental west offend our fine sense of right and wrong? The roistering, blood soiling, profanity reeking days of the cow trail were an integral part of the age. The West was no mail order concern. It was not built on upholstered lines."[196]

Historians since have shown that the cattle towns were not especially violent. Kansas had once taken pride in its moral reforms, including prohibition, which had arisen partly in repulsion at the tawdriness of its early era. But it was the "link with a rather unsavory past" and with the transient males that had populated it that "has done much to keep Dodge City in public interest."[197] Respectability did not sell. "This is Dodge City's famous Boot Hill, "read a sign erected in 1935, "burial ground of the six-shooting badmen."[198]

History and tourism would never bring in the income for Western Kansas that oil and gas did. But these shared the feature of being imports that created a more diverse economy at the expense of local initiative. Like the paved road and the consolidated school, they were invented elsewhere and imposed on a region that could hardly resist such firm national trends. It was ironic that even the local past should be held hostage to the perceptions of people living elsewhere.

Industrial combining, Western Kansas, 1928 (courtesy of Kansas State Historical Society)

The new developments changed the population of most counties in the region little in the decade. Exceptions were locations of larger towns and cities—Sedgwick County, where growth was driven by the development of the aircraft-building industry; Finney County, where Garden City remained a phenomenon; Ford County, where Dodge City was growing. Smaller towns sometimes grew modestly, but remained small. Goodland went from 2,700 population to 3,400; Larned from 2,900 to 3,500; and Colby from 1,200 to 2,300.[199] Valuation statistics were more impressive in their increase. Wheat thrived as a major industry. Kansas raised 177,633,000 bushels of wheat in 1929 while the entire eastern half of the United States raised only 167,249,000 bushels. The region west of Wichita accounted for 151 million of those bushels.[200] Since 1900, population in the forty-six counties west of the strict center line of the state had increased 60 percent, while the assessed valuation of the region had gone up 1,400 percent. Agricultural production for that far western region increased 500 percent.[201]

Diversity in the economy was greater than ever. Victor Murdock of Wichita wrote that Western Kansas in 1929 was reaching a time in its history "when agriculture will be merely incidental to industry." It was, he said, "witnessing the change from one great epoch to another. . . . Western Kansas is on the edge of a dream—the western line of smokestacks has come west and west and west until now it has reached the eastern part of the state and

I feel that Western Kansas is to become the peak in industry." The success of prairie people, Murdock thought, was due to "the linking of spiritual growth with material development," and now, provided as they were with cheap energy in the form of natural gas, they should have their finest opportunity.[202] The regional weather news at the end of the decade was of floods, not drought.[203] Wheat prices were over a dollar a bushel and the bushels were coming in.[204] "In former years," the editor at Hays remembered, "every temporary adversity, whether it was a drought, a severe winter, or some other uncontrollable cause, resulted in an exodus of residents. Those days are past."[205]

The atmosphere was heady. Alf M. Landon, an Independence oil man soon to be governor, said that the geology of Western Kansas was only now being discovered, and that all the territory west of the 6th principal meridian would be the next big oil-producing region of the Mid-Continent field.[206] Tri-motored airplanes operated by Universal Airlines, Inc., passed over Western Kansas in 1929 at waving altitudes. They were en route from Cleveland, Ohio, to Garden City, Kansas, where air-rail transcontinental passengers boarded the ATSF for the West Coast.[207] There were plans for a regional airline from Wichita to Dodge City, with landing fields every 30 miles and night travel lit by 2-million-candlepower electric beacons 10 miles apart.[208] Fred Fowler and James Woods of Ulysses, Kansas, both owned airplanes in 1929 and used them to survey their farms in the "Cimarron Desert" area. Fowler said he bought his with wheat profits and flew it to fishing spots.[209] At Great Bend, the skyline had a "novel electric sign" on top of the Nelson restaurant. After dark, a projector put advertising slides from twelve local merchants up, from seven to midnight each evening.[210]

Western Kansans, at the end of the 1920s, were sitting on the moon all right. The view was fine but the landscape was unfamiliar, and soon enough many of its novel features would either disappear or become liabilities.

9

A Stern Teacher

For Christmas 1929, Stanley Miner of Ness City, twelve years old, received a Lionel standard-gauge train, resplendent with brass trim and wheels highlighted in red. Probably his family ordered it through Miner's Cash Store, run by Stanley's grandfather, which had a window display of electric trains that season.[1] The boy's siblings and parents were there to watch him enjoy his new train as it clicked around its oval track set up on an oriental carpet purchased from Marshall Fields, Chicago. His sister, Margaret, had been married just a month earlier at that family home, wearing an eggshell satin gown, "amid banks of yellow and white chrysanthemums with ferns attractively arranged in baskets in the main living room."[2] Stanley regularly saw his name in the newspaper for getting good scores on school exams.[3]

However, things shortly turned bleak. The boy's father, Hal, a successful real estate dealer and loan broker, died early in January 1930 at age forty-seven of complications of diabetes. His death, wrote the newspaper, "shocked" the community, because Hal did not complain, "taking life as it came and always looking on the bright side of things." While "he had accumulated a great deal of the world's wealth in the short time he was with us, he was one of those who builded Ness county up to its present high agricultural standard by taking raw land and making it produce something of the world's goods."[4] That was a common story among the pioneer families of the region.

The funeral, with Masonic accompaniments that frightened Stanley, took place in a bitter cold wind. It was a bad day, and the beginning of a series of bad days as an era of drought and dust began. That was my family, and the story came down to me of how they comforted one another later by saying that, although Hal died young, at least he was spared living through the Great Depression. He did not have to witness, as did so many other Western Kansans, what Nature and outside forces, both of them cyclic and heartless, could do to regional adjustments and endemic optimism.

Later in that January in 1930, Henry Rein, fifty-five, one of the best-known cattlemen and farmers in Ness County, was found by his fourteen-year-old son in the barn, where he had hanged himself.[5] In November, John Brinkley, the controversial goat gland doctor and independent write-in candidate for governor, carried formerly solidly Republican Ness County.[6] Seventy miles east of Ness and a year later, the Great Bend Royalty company took out a full-page ad, headlined "The Last Chance." Oil investment, the company argued, offered the person of modest means a chance to participate in the resources of the earth and win a fortune. Thirty-two percent more people failed in farming than in the oil business, and a person could purchase a royalty unit for only $25.[7] Last chance indeed!

Western Kansans could chuckle at first about the stock market crash of 1929, arguing that the region was little affected by the speculations and overextensions of eastern corporations. However, the continued agricultural depression, exacerbated in the early 1930s by a weaker market for farm commodities and then the beginnings of a long-lasting drought, was something not to be ignored. Soil erosion was cumulative, and so was the psychological effect of heat, high winds, short crops, and low prices. Soon enough, Stanley Miner would be struggling to find his way the few blocks home from school, a wet handkerchief covering his face and the prairie light transformed by the sun's filtered path through mountains of suspended, blowing dust. Each year it became darker, odder, and more frightening, even for children who were not worried about making a living. Pat Rowley and his friends took water in coffee cans to try to help the bawling cattle stuck in rail cars on Wichita sidings on their way out of a region where there was not even grazing available anymore.[8] It was, many remembered, a kind of nightmare landscape, where it must have seemed that the bright hopes of a few years earlier were only an adumbration of this gloom, a trap for the naïve to make their suffering one day deeper for the memory of dreams turned sour. The stronger the dream, the more bitter was this dusty taste.

There were comforters, as always—exhorters to strength and action. Congressman Clifford Hope arranged in 1931 for every schoolroom in the region to receive a color poster of George Washington.[9] "This disaster comes," wrote a newspaperman at Dodge City in 1935, "if we sit by with dumb fatalism and do nothing about it." He emphasized that people of the region had experience with dry and windy weather. It was not "in the class of the cosmic ray or the interstellar elements." It could be a needed correction, a "stern teacher," who had visited before and would visit again.[10] It will rain, the editor at Ness City wrote. It always has.[11]

Maintaining that regional tradition of optimism, however, was not easy. It seemed almost that progressive Western Kansas was being shattered, bombed back by Nature into the more primitive state that the pioneers had struggled with the elements to survive. Irony piled on irony. Many farmers, unable to afford to run their tractors and combines, went back to using horses.[12] The oil in automobiles became a grinding compound, transformed by fine silting dust, which quickly ruined engines and brought mechanical travel to a halt even when visibility allowed some progress down the new paved roads.[13] Some people started constructing outbuildings of adobe or sod again to save money.[14] Prairie fires, thought nearly extinct, returned with a vengeance to the grazing areas that had been spared from dust, only to blow ash.[15] J. C. Hopper wrote Congressman Hope in 1935, reintroducing his plan of saving Western Kansas through damming the draws and summer fallow.[16] The *Ness County News* started printing Hopper's essays, almost exactly as it had in the 1890s.[17] The Nonpartisan League began again trying to organize in Western Kansas.[18] The grasshoppers and jackrabbits multiplied in abundance. A farmer in Scott County, having made his way through a dust storm, stopping several times, found a jackrabbit on his running board when he got home, as though the animal was seeking shelter like everyone else.[19] Even the rainmakers returned with their machines, schemes, and deceptive promises.[20] Western Kansans commonly blamed the dusty weather on Jupiter Pluvius, harking back to the capricious pagan pantheon to avoid associating the natural disaster with the presumably progressive Judeo-Christian God.[21]

Discouraging signs appeared early. Cheyenne Lake, in Barton County, which had reached a 50,000-acre extent and a 20-foot depth in places in the 1920s, went from a prime prospect for a federal wildlife preserve to muddy "bottoms" again. By July 1931, the Kansas Fish and Game Department was rescuing fish from the former massive lake before they flopped in inches of water. By that time, the lake covered fewer than 15,000 acres and could be waded everywhere by a short person.[22] In early September, Cheyenne Lake covered fewer than 100 acres.[23] That year, farmers stored a record wheat crop, bigger than the bumper crop of 1914, in farm bins or on the ground because of the low price of 30 cents a bushel.[24] Near Dighton, farmers in the summer of 1931 worked land so dry that "large clouds of dust drift for considerable distances behind their plows."[25] Greenleaf's Bakery at Scott City reduced the price of its loaves of bread to 5 cents in 1931, and made 3,600 of them a day.[26] At Larned, the Chamber of Commerce and local bankers and implement dealers proposed a debt holiday so that farmers would not be forced into bankruptcy "on the heels of the most prolific harvest in years."[27]

Soon enough, harvests too disappeared. A comparison of winter wheat yield statistics for 1931 and 1932, recorded side by side and county by county in the *Twenty-eighth Biennial Report of the State Board of Agriculture,* is a discouraging exercise, but it provides the merest suggestion of the shock to those trying to make a living on those dry plains. Ford County, for instance, went from 7,959,140 bushels of winter wheat harvested in 1931 to 1,907,289 in 1932, and from a value of $2,626,516.20 to $591,259.59. The decline was steeper further west. Grant County production went from 3,924,840 bushels to 251,235 bushels, and wheat income went from $1,255,948.80 to $80,295.20. Was there any way to plan for or to adjust to such a change?

Western Kansans, who had prided themselves on their independence and had resisted regulation by the Federal Farm Board in the 1920s, now found themselves back to the "Droughty Kansas" days of the 1890s, back to the reputation as beggars on the largesse of the rest of the country through government aid. When journalists came up with the moniker "Dust Bowl" to describe the worst-maligned region, eastern Kansas newspapers were quick to point out that their salubrious region had no part of it. It was only that curious western upland, which Topeka and Lawrence had never fully accepted, that was being so chastised. That was Western Kansas, an aberration, a scapegoat, not to be confused with Kansas proper.[28] It was a "busted Babylon," some said, and good riddance to it.[29]

As always, at base, it was a struggle with the weather and with its cycles, nonrespecting as they were of the plans of humanity. "Weather is like time," wrote a man in Tribune, "it has neither beginning or end. The weather may be beautiful or beastly, still it is weather."[30]

As late as 1929, there were complaints about too much rain. Ness County had had 5.65 inches in twelve hours in May of that year.[31] But, shortly, the observations were of a different type. There was dust in September.[32] In the spring of 1930 there was an estimate that hot winds were costing Kansas a million dollars a day in shriveled crops. "At a time when everybody is talking economy, why not do our bit by getting along without this big wind. . . . If we go on supporting this big hot wind in idleness and luxury it will eat us out of house and home."[33]

There was a feeling that it was temporary. There was talk about it having happened before, and that "hard times as well as good times may be influ-

1930s combine near Dighton (courtesy of Wichita State University Special Collections)

enced by a state of mind."[34] Sure, it had been a summer of 100-degree temperatures, but "brassy skies . . . return on schedule time and the whole play has to be re-enacted."[35] Remember, one editor reminded, "an atmospheric freak like this occurs only once in a lifetime."[36] Besides, the winter of 1930–31 was mild and there was lots of sunshine, regular Southern California–type weather, they said in Colby.[37]

Wheat prices in 1931 hovered around 25 to 30 cents a bushel. "We are going to be up against it this winter," said a farmer in Ford County, "if we have to pay everything that comes due." Merchants were not demanding credit payments, and banks were going easy on loans. A farmer usually had a cow and some chickens: "There's not much chance of anybody starving to death on a farm."[38]

Later in the year 1931 it turned very hot. It was 108 degrees in Colby in the last week in July. But local weather historians pointed out that it had been hotter. During the drought of 1911–13, there were several days in Colby that reached 111, and one hit 116.[39] Still, it boded ill for the fall planting. The nights were cool, but the days continued hot, far into September, with no rain at all. "That constant wind with its cloud of dust have been enough to try the patience of the oldest settlers."[40]

In 1932 there was more talk of dust, and more concern that the dry times were not going away soon. "The real estate that has been in circulation in Kansas the last week or so," wrote Jess Denious in April, "is a puzzle to visitors. The sleek, well manicured folk who stage walk from the Santa Fe Chief when it takes a breathing spell in our ornate union station area turn up their noses, gasp and expletively ask what Providence dispenses the canopy of dirt.

They rush for the newsstands where New York newspapers are sold. Then back to the train with a few more gasps and pertinent remarks about the climate that breeds dust storms."[41] Cars began to drive around in the daytime with the lights on, and people started to put wet blankets around their house windows. There were descriptions of dust clouds a hundred feet high.[42]

In 1933, there began a series of reports, which lasted for many years, of record-breaking temperatures, winds, and amounts of dust. In April 1933, wind at Dodge City reached 40 miles per hour. It drove gravel against peoples' homes as they "gasped for breath in the heavy air" and finished off the struggling wheat crop.[43] Late that month, Dodge had the headline "It Rains Mud When Shower Pierces Dirt." During a barometric low, "the atmosphere took on an eerie aspect as the dust obscured the slightly clouded skies and darkness descended." A high school janitor died of dust infection.[44] On May 22, there was a tornado at Liberal that caused $1 million in property damages and four deaths. The borders of that storm hurled a car 150 feet from the road near Garden City and killed one.[45] Other related weather resulted in fourteen deaths over the region. At Colby, "the most terrible and terrifying dust storm this vicinity ever saw rode the winds of a 50-mile gale out of the south." It brought a "stygian darkness at noon," with static electricity turning blades of windmills into balls of fire. Flowers "crumpled in the hand like dead and blow away like powder."[46] The wheat crop was the smallest in the twentieth century (248,000 bushels, compared with 3,611,790 bushels in 1931).[47]

The year 1934 started bleak. Warren Zimmerman of the *Liberal News* wrote Congressman Hope in January that, during a campaign for newspaper subscriptions going door-to-door, "we have found some things which have given us much concern and a lot of heartache. Most prominent of these is the despair and hopelessness that seems to confront so many. Crop prospects are heartbreaking right now. . . . Winds have already started their fatal work." The dust was "drifting like sand in places across highways east from Liberal like snow on a blustery day." Many homes were dependent on government programs. "I believe if I had to live on one of these Seward county farms these days, see my efforts blow away in the form of renewed sandstorms and dry weather for the third year I'd go 100 per cent crazy. For trying to run a little business there where we get a little money now and then is bad enough and heartsickening at that, but is heaven itself by comparison." Zimmerman had lived in the area for nearly thirty years, but "never have we faced such conditions." An old, hard-working subscriber said that he had sold two cows and a calf for $10 a few days earlier because they were too poor to kill and can

A large dust cloud rolling across the prairies, 1930s (courtesy of High Plains Museum, Goodland)

for living purposes and he had no food for them. A friend said he had never seen the section look so hopeless—"despair seeming to face them all."[48]

Details were scary. In Tribune, late in March, the temperature dropped 63 degrees in less than 24 hours, catching many outdoors and unaware.[49] "We have about given up all hopes of rain in this country," wrote a Garden City man to Hope that spring."[50] Wrote another: "Today is another one of those breathless hot windy days with the air full of dirt. . . . Streets are crowded with farmers and others today wondering what is going to happen to us. . . . Most of our people need help and don't know which way to turn."[51] The *Hays Daily News* in June commented that the drought was "assuming the proportions of a major catastrophe, and each day bringing higher temperatures with the approach of summer heightens the dire situation. . . . Small wonder, then, that some are moved to speculate on whether the great plains region may be destined to become a desert."[52] At Colby, the editor called it "this ungracious year of our Lord, 1934."[53]

The weather was no respecter of persons. Movie star Cary Grant was delayed at Syracuse, Kansas, in June 1934 while trying to drive his twelve-cylinder car across Kansas. He called the conditions "disgusting."[54] Day after day during that period, Kansas had the high temperatures in the nation.[55] It was 110 in Garden City early in July, 111 in Colby, and 114 in Great Bend.[56] Even at high altitude Goodland and Tribune, where it normally cooled down at night at least, temperatures never dropped below the upper seventies.[57]

Springs that had not failed in memory went dry, as did every stream.[58] Farmers harvested Russian thistle for feed.[59] At Gove City, the editor broke his promise not to mention the heat that year:

> But how in the hotel bill are you going to keep [from] thinking of the heat when everyone who steps through the door looks like he had just come out of a furnace room. . . . Tiny beads of perspiration, about the size of goose eggs, trickle down upon the typewriter keys as we proclaim to a red-eyed world that it's HOT. Hotter than we've ever seen it before and hotter than we ever want to see it again. Hotter than the shade of Sheol.[60]

It made a person "wonder if he shouldn't change his ways. Or his location."[61]

The experiment station records are dramatic for the 1930s. At Garden City, where the station had received over 31 inches of rain in 1928 and wheat yields in the late twenties averaged 30 bushels per acre, things turned rapidly.[62] The station's budget was cut so much that it had to combine its annual reports for 1932–37 into one report.[63] The Colby station had 24.78 inches of rain in 1930, 14.86 in 1932, 16.69 in 1933, and 7.37 in 1934. "All crop yields were low," the agent said, "and most crops were failures."[64] Tribune Experiment Station got 8.78 inches of rain in 1930 and was not impressed by the promises made by Kansas gubernatorial candidate Dr. J. R. Brinkley, who visited that year, promising a pond for every farm.[65] The station had over 11 inches of rain in June 1932—but this was too much at once, especially the 6-inch rain on June 3, which was accompanied by heavy hail. The rest of the year rain pretty much ceased.[66] In 1933, there was 17 inches of rain at Tribune, but the next year it was 7.76 inches—and the summer was the hottest ever. On July 14, and again on July 31, it was 107 degrees at Tribune. In 1935, the station got 8.83 inches of rain and again a lot of heat—twenty-four days of over 100 degrees.[67] In 1936, Tribune had 10.14 inches of rain, and in 1937, 11.85 inches—with all of these figures well below normal for the region.[68] It required "at least 18 inches of well-timed rain" to grow wheat, and the average for Western Kansas during the 1930s decade was just over 15 inches.[69]

Initially the solutions offered for the economic downturn were private and local. After 1933, they were increasingly public and federal. The psychological encouragement, the "hope-mongering," wore thin when year after year there were no crops and no money. The philosophy of toughness and self-reliance remained. "This is not time for people to look back," wrote a Scott City editor in 1934, "or to even hesitate about the future of this country. . . . Better still to take a hitch in our belt, a firm hold on the steering wheel, and face the future with a strong determination to go forward."[70] Perhaps the hard times would be a good thing. A writer in Garden City on New Year's Day 1931 put it this way:

> One trouble with 1930 was not with the year but with folks. . . . When people get back to living within their incomes, when every possible method of spending money is not embraced, when that which one has is made to do even if it is not the latest style or finest material or make, then folks will begin again to be in condition to enjoy some of the luxuries they are passing up today.[71]

The twenties had been "Rat-Riddled and Rotten," and it was time "the nation faced the prospect of getting over a delirious, but frightfully expensive joy ride."[72] True, some were considering suicide, but it was only a temporary insanity due to "physical lack of balance in their organic functions," which meant that their "mental vision becomes clouded and oppressive." A person with chronic melancholy was lucky to be married to someone cheerful, who could "come out smiling when misfortune strikes" and show the primacy of mind over matter.[73]

Battling adversity was good for the soul. "To those who have courage, sense and a determination to work," things would get better. That "class of parasites" whining about being oppressed should be ignored. Jess Denious at Dodge City wrote in 1931 that Western Kansans were fighters and that this was another fight. They knew the Depression was real: "We have heard it and seen it and felt it. We have even tasted the darn thing and it doesn't taste good." But he was proud of the reactions of people, "with the odds piled against them," and hopeful about progress that came from struggles with adversity. "It strikes me that no one ever would have come to western Kansas at all if he had merely been seeking an easy game. . . . Easy victories are no victories at all."[74] Hard conditions, he added, had created in Western Kansas "a hardy and sane and dependable race of men."[75] A man in Liberal wrote in 1932 in the same vein:

> Conditions are not pleasant in western Kansas, nor anywhere else we know of on earth today . . . but they are here and must be met in a brave way. . . . This is a period of battle, just as hard as a Meuse or Argonne, and the man who fights through it will come out bigger, better, and stronger for it all. . . . When some socialist or communist tells you the world is coming to an end and western Kansas is the worst spot on earth, tell him to jump in a lake.[76]

Editors suggested looking around at the beauty of sunsets, enhanced by the dust, and emphasizing the positive.[77] At Liberal, the official response to the

1933 tornado was to concentrate on the "triumph" of the community response and the rebuilding, not the pain of the disaster.[78] When L. E. Call, president of the Federal Land Bank in Wichita, told farmers at Hays that it was time to consider abandoning whole townships for agricultural purposes, residents said he lacked "horse sense." The land Call thought "useless" was assessed at more than $1 million, and 239 families paid local taxes on it. "Telling folks who are, in some cases, in desperate circumstances, to move off their farms and buy land somewhere else, passes the boundary line of utter lack of diplomacy and becomes the prattle of a fool."[79] Kansans had survived the 1890s, which, it was constantly emphasized in the early 1930s, were worse.[80] Western Kansans, Arthur Capper said, faced the drought with a "grim cheerfulness."[81] Wrote an editor in Gove City: "The Lord used his best clay when he moulded these Western Kansas farmers."[82]

Rhetoric aside, there were many private and individual means of coping. Frugality has been mentioned. Historian Pamela Riney-Kehrberg, in *Rooted in Dust*, documents a great number of innovations applied by people in southwestern Kansas.[83] Housewives swept and then re-swept, feeling a unity with others similarly threatened and saying they were "as happy as if they had good sense."[84] At Ellsworth, a reporter said that the Depression was bringing out the "inherent frugality" of people.[85] "They have hauled wood to burn in their stoves and their wives have cellars filled with canned fruits and vegetables." The *Hays Daily News* reported in October 1932, "No Fear Here."[86] There was talk about cities lowering taxes, turning off streetlights at night, and eliminating such luxuries as town health officers.[87] An issue of the *Liberal News* in 1931 was printed on paper made of cornstalks.[88]

Another coping mechanism was distraction. The trend in building and patronizing swimming pools continued. Larned had 1,126 paid admissions at its pool one July day in 1932.[89] By 1933, the federal government began helping to fund such projects, and many towns agitated for a "modern sanitary pool" to replace sandpits and swimming holes, to take peoples' minds off the heat and to provide a public works project for the unemployed.[90] In the fall of 1933, Great Bend voters approved, by a margin of three to one, a 200-by-100-foot pool that cost $21,000.[91] Sports were healthy. Kansans liked to brag about the exploits of miler Glenn Cunningham, "the Kansas flyer" from Elkhart, who regularly set world records.[92]

Western Kansans had mixed opinions about going to the movies on Sunday, drinking, smoking, and sex. The Women's Christian Temperance Union shut down a bathing beauty contest in Hays in 1930 and objected to gambling on the carnival grounds.[93] In 1931, Kansas began trying to enforce an

1868 "blue" law to stop Sunday movies.[94] There was a row in Barton County in 1931 over Sunday movie closings, with some saying that the movie was "a monument to the avarice and greed of man and shows to what length people will go for money." A sociologist quoted in the local press claimed that "the conclusion forced upon me is that more of the young people . . . are sex-wise, sex-excited and sex-absorbed than any other generation of which we have knowledge." He blamed movies.[95] However, many towns objected to any such restriction.[96] Movies were cheap and often the theaters were air conditioned.

Kansas was the archetypal prohibition state and kept its constitutional ban even after the rest of the country was released from all restrictions in 1933. But the legislature, led by what one newspaper called the "moron branch of the wet contingent," did come around to defining beer of 3.2 percent alcoholic content as not intoxicating and therefore as not covered by the general ban. There was the hope that beer sales would bring about revenue as well as distraction.[97] The flow was not heavy in Garden City, but the local paper reported that in the summer of 1933, before officially legal, enforcement was lax and that there were eight or ten places selling beer openly.[98] There were several cases of "jakeleg" paralysis reported among Wichita society women, who got the disease from drinking spiked punch at their bridge club. A few waded in sludge ponds at the local refineries in the hope of relieving the symptoms caused by illegal hard liquor of unregulated quality.[99] Legalization of 3.2 beer did not happen until 1937, however, and all attempts to repeal the general Kansas prohibition amendment failed.[100]

Cigarettes, banned in Kansas for a time in the teens and twenties, were much in evidence in the 1930s. Ads filled newspapers promising the ultimate distraction, and not only pleasurable, but safe. Cigarettes supposedly promoted weight loss ("When tempted to over-indulge, reach for a Lucky instead"), better romance ("My Sweetheart Smokes 'em"), and strength to survive ("They speak my language . . . and it's no 'namby-pamby' talk either").[101]

People professed to be shocked by a sex lecture given in Wichita in 1931, in which Professor Wayland Villiers demonstrated "the Law of Nature" with "living girl models," including one said to be the "healthiest specimen in America."[102] Newspapers ran pictures of scantily clad women in contests about who had the best back or legs. They were packed with silliness about the midget who married a 400-pound woman, the men who drove across America backwards, the shenanigans of "fan dancer" Sally Rand, the comments of young women who visited rising dictator Adolf Hitler, or the girl who could not stop yawning.[103]

It was all diversion, the imported unreality that had been distorting the view in Western Kansas for some years. The new $100,000 state lake in Scott County was beautiful, and building it employed some people, but it no more addressed the real problems of the region than the temporary escape provided by thinking about how Clyde Tombaugh of Burdett, having built his own telescope on a Kansas farm, went on to discover the planet Pluto.[104]

More significant as a private attempt to address the woes of regional agriculture was the move toward serious large-scale corporate farming. Many regarded the corporate trend as a positive development, including T. A. McNeal of the *Kansas Farmer*. In spring 1928, McNeal wrote an editorial about the Campbell Farming Corporation of Montana, which controlled 95,000 acres, with 47,000 acres of it planted to wheat and flax. It had large equipment and had succeeded in lowering the cost of farming. After citing the statistics, McNeal commented:

> This information is interesting and enlightening. Speaking of the farming industry as a whole, there are, in my opinion, two roads ahead; one is the road that leads to great corporation farms with efficient, scientific management, the other leads to a farming population with living conditions similar to those in France, where practically all the labor is performed by hand and with primitive tools. Under that system it will be idle to talk about agriculture controlling the market. Under the other system farming will become the greatest, the most scientific and most profitable as a whole of any business in the world.[105]

He added, "The business of agriculture is out of line with our present economic system." Individual farmers had innovated, "but the average farmer still is running his business in a haphazard way. He does not, and in many cases cannot, keep books showing what part of his plant is making money and what is losing."[106]

There were several major players in large-scale farming in Western Kansas in the early 1930s. A. D. Jellison operated the Kansas Farms Corporation in Junction City; R. H. Garvey ran the Mutual Farming Company with a base in Thomas County; John Baughman farmed on a large scale out of Liberal; Charles Sledd ran the Sledd Farm Corporation from Lyons; E. E. Fisher headed the Fisher Ranch Corporation in Greeley County; and John Bird headed the Wheat Farming Company, based in Hays.[107]

The Wheat Farming Company, formed by six Ellis County farmers in September 1927 with a capital of $150,000, got the most publicity. This was perhaps partly due to the fact that it was the first "dirt farmer" corporation in Kansas and partly that Bird owned a newspaper, the *Ellis County News*, and was an articulate lobbyist for his point of view.

"These men," the press reported, "felt that farmers must pool their interests and consolidate their efforts if they are to enjoy the success of business men."[108] Henry Ford in 1928 stated, "The wheat farming of the future will be done by big corporations, tilling large tracts of land by machinery, requiring little man power, and bringing to agriculture something of the system that is now used in other industry."[109]

There was plenty of evidence of the application of a system. Sledd, whose organization started early in 1926 with 30 men owning 300 acres of bottomland along Cow Creek, operated 1,500 acres of dryland wheat farms by 1928 and planned to expand to 20,000. Sledd was buying land at $70 to $90 an acre and thought he could farm wheat profitably even at a wheat price of 50 cents a bushel by farming on a large scale with big equipment. The corporation sold land to investors at cost, retaining a quarter of each section for itself. It provided a 30-horsepower caterpillar tractor, a five-bottom plow, a disc, two drills, and a combine for each section farmed. It then turned over 90 percent of the clear profits on the investor-owned land to the investor. It was definitely a business system, with expense- and profit-accounting rather than a family farm or tenant operation, as was traditional in the region.[110]

Garvey's Mutual Farming was a closely held corporation pooling the considerable (15,000 acres) holdings of Garvey himself; Joseph Geiger, a doctor in St. Joseph, Missouri; and W. D. Ferguson, a banker in Colby. The formation of the company in 1930 was unfortunate timing. Wheat and land prices were low, but Garvey noted that so were fuel, labor, and grocery prices. If the company could cut costs quickly and drastically enough, it could make a profit.[111] Mutual Farming employed a farm manager, Claude Schnellbacher, who coordinated the application and maintenance of machinery and labor over a substantial area.

Garvey believed in the method, but admitted to the challenge. "A great deal of industrial, agricultural, and financial history has been rewritten in the past couple of years," he commented to the corporation directors late in 1931. He had been "preaching worse conditions for the past year than I really thought they were but they are turning out far worse than I was preaching."[112] Although Garvey lived in Wichita, he emphasized that corporate farming was not "suitcase farming." It required a manager on the scene and careful attention to detail. "Like building any other successful business, farming requires constant, intensive work and management, and a life time is required to build a fine farm. It is not a hit or miss short time career" but needed people "who wish to own their farms, and have a grand passion for buying land."[113]

All the corporations emphasized that they were owned mostly by Kansans, that they farmed land where others had failed to make a profit, and that their profits inured to the benefit of Western Kansas communities. Their principal men were in contact with one another. Garvey, for instance, was an investor in the Wheat Farming Company, and in regular contact with Sledd and Jellison about their methods and their hopes.

The Wheat Farming Company was the most scientific. In 1929, its officers and foremen met at Colby with the staff of the experiment station there with a view to using the data that had been built up over the years. By then it controlled 33,000 acres of wheat in nine counties and would eventually operate over 70,000 acres. It had several superintendents, a shop foreman in charge of a machine shop in Hays, and a specialized foreman in charge of transportation and equipment. The common stock in 1928 paid a dividend of 11.5 percent. The company, Bird said, had resisted offers from New York and Chicago capitalists to expand, as it wished to get its methods right first. Its foremen would operate "as sort of a flying squadron going to stop leaks in the whole plan of defense where agricultural enemies are breaking through."[114] Scientific and business techniques would revolutionize the marketing of crops, as well as the maintenance of machinery and efficient and productive farming.[115] Bird felt the Kansas farmer, particularly when well organized and farming big acreages, could compete with anyone in the world. Kansas was flat, had low fuel costs, and Americans were mechanically minded. He pointed "to the development of power machinery as the final step in enabling the Kansas farmer with his high living standards, to compete with even the lowest priced laborer in other sections of the world." The company added 25,000 acres to its holdings in 1930 alone, confident that it could profit in any weather and market situation.[116] It owned four elevators by that time—and an airplane and thirty combines, which rolled through the fields "like a fleet of ships at sea."[117]

However, as Bird expanded, the political atmosphere for corporate farming in Kansas deteriorated. Its most active opponent was Harold McGugin of Coffeyville, who went to Congress in 1930 after a campaign that concentrated heavily on the dangers of corporate farming. The Kansas Farm Bureau joined in, although it thought that the farm corporation, along with the chain store, was probably inevitable. So did Senator Arthur Capper, who editorialized in his newspaper chain that the corporation was a "deadly peril in farming."[118]

McGugin wrote Governor Clyde Reed in March 1930 that the Kansas legislature must act to outlaw corporate farming even if it took a special session: "We must not let this thing go on another day." There had been only two Kansas farm corporations before the end of 1929—now there were five. "I know I am right in this matter." Jess Denious in Dodge City told McGugin that he thought corporation farming would destroy Western Kansas. "Loyalty to Kansas and loyalty to the Kansans, as I have known them," McGugin said, "compel me to do everything within my feeble power to stop this thing and stop it now. . . . Monopolization is running rampant in America. . . . It is taking away the last opportunity for the individual American citizen to be a free born independent American."[119] Perhaps farm corporations could make money with wheat selling at 28 cents a bushel, but the small family farmer could not, and it was that person who must be protected.[120]

Bills went forward in the spring of 1930 in the legislature to outlaw corporate farming, and between that time and the passage of such a bill in January 1931 there was a battle. Many Western Kansas newspapers supported farm corporations. The editor of the *Goodland News-Republic* thought purchase of large tracts over several counties minimized the danger of crop failure and that big machinery and hired labor was the way to go. "Western Kansas seems particularly adapted to this method of crop raising on account of the low price of land, and the great areas of level country, adapted to large scale operations." Systematic methods were cheaper.[121] The *Hays Daily News* saw it that way too. "Thoughtful farmers," its columns said, were for large farming, and copied the methods of the corporations to improve their family farms. Many farmers had formed voluntary associations to operate units of 2,000 acres or more. "The resulting economics have been startling." People had been advancing cooperation in farming for years, going back to the marketing pools of the 1920s, and this was just another way to cooperate. Corporations would not displace the efficient farmer, but only the inefficient one, and that would not hurt the community. "This is an era of cooperation. Organization is necessary in every line of human endeavor. If the farmer will not organize he must not be surprised to have someone else take the business from him. But we believe there is sufficient indication that the farmer has seen the trend of events and will place farming on a business basis."[122]

The companies had their own public relations campaign. Bird was a newspaperman and had been a Chamber of Commerce promoter in Hays for years. Garvey was an articulate and outspoken man who had himself owned a newspaper for a time. The Wheat Farming Company placed ads, headlined "Building the Foundation of Kansas Agriculture." "Agriculture," the ads went, "by far the biggest industry in the state, through minimum production costs together with maximum yields should and will become the most profitable industry in the state."[123] Another Wheat Farming Company ad, headlined "Agriculture of the Wheat Belt Can Help Itself," went, "However much wheat may have been overproduced, there has been a deplorable overproduction of Hell raising on the one hand, and too little constructive thinking on the other." Farming had changed since the early days of the Republic, when it was much as it was "in the time when Abraham came out of Ur of the Chaldees." A 160-acre farm, which once occupied the energies of a family, could now be farmed "by a sixteen-year-old boy in his spare moments." Agriculture had "ceased to be the Arcadian existence it formerly was."[124] The *Lyons News* ran ads from Sledd's headquarters. In a long piece called "Western Homesteaders Wheat Farming vs. Large Unit Farming," it argued for modern methods. There were testimonials from "power farmers" who had become rich, and comments that when diversified family farming was the rule "our towns came and went. Not only was the farmer bankrupt, but the merchant and bankers as well." If a person considered "safety, permanency, and yield" of importance in thinking of the future, he should consider shares in the Sledd Farm Corporation.[125]

Garvey was the most personal of the promoters, writing all his own ad copy in an autobiographical style. In December 1930, he wrote an ad called "Ruining the Country." Someone is always ruining the country, he commented. The Indians claimed the buffalo hunters spoiled it. The cattlemen said the homesteaders wrecked the cattle business. There was resistance to tractors. When the Wheat Farming Company bought 10,000 acres in Thomas County, nearly all of it distressed land under foreclosure, people complained. But the company raised 150,000 acres of wheat on that marginal land in 1930. Corporations owned less than 2 percent of the land in Thomas County, Garvey noted, and were doing a good job of farming.

> Yet some people claim that these corporations are ruining the country, but having heard claims of this kind so long and noting that production keeps increasing in Thomas, about all we believe of this is that a few of the inefficient will ruin themselves, but it will be a lesson in farming to the intelligent and diligent, and will help rather than ruin Thomas county. . . . No one except yourself owes yourself a living or a place to live, and the person who cannot adjust himself to changed conditions or his own circumstance, why the dinosaurs will get him if the goblins don't.[126]

But there was no lack of critics. One farmer wrote Governor Reed in the summer of 1930 that there were "sick men" behind corporate farming. The low price of wheat was "a final blow to the small wheat farmer and the one who is trying to make Kansas his home," and it did not help for the corporations to advertise that they could make a profit on such prices. It was a place for the Kansas legislature to "strike a blow."[127] The *Ness County News* asked its readers to "imagine the individual farmer being pushed aside when in competition with these monopoly concerns and these broad, fine farming lands, dotted here and there with shacks for temporary use by employees of the giant companies, and for filling stations of gas and oil used in operating large tracts."[128] The *Garden City Daily Telegram* editor thought it was another step in the trend that began with the mail order houses and discount stores. "There is one thing that this section doesn't need and that is more chain farms." The editor said the farm corporation would "inevitably depopulate any territory in which it operates, buy its farm equipment in car load lots, probably from some eastern supply house, cutting out the sale for the local implement dealer, and offer no inducement or aid in community, home, and school building."[129]

Congressman Hope studied the question in his usual careful manner. Sledd wrote to Hope, "I cannot see any other method that can possibly be used other than the corporation method, getting the equitable benefit for the farmer as against manufacturers of other items in the east." Sledd thought that in a few years "we corporations" would control enough of the production in the field to control the amount exported and aid the price. Sledd's letterhead contained the slogan "Mass Production Makes Greater Wheat Profits."[130] Hope responded that, "while I have not gotten as excited over corporation farming as some people," he had been concerned. For one thing, the corporation put new capital into an overcapitalized industry, with many investors who were not farmers. Also there was a social objection. "The American farm home has been the foundation of our social order ever since our nation was founded. It may be that we are entering a new phase of civilization and that the farm home is going to become extinct. I, for one, however, would certainly never want to do anything to accelerate any movement which may be going in that direction."[131] Hope made a list of advantages and disadvantages of farm corporations. The two columns were of about equal length, but the emotional arguments were on the negative side.[132]

Senator Capper was eloquent in opposition. In a radio address in September 1930, he said, "Kansas needs more citizens of the type that makes up the farmers of this state, not fewer citizens." Corporation farms, he thought, meant "the passing of the individual and independent farmer who no matter what the modernists and the cynics may say, has been the backbone of the civilization and government we have builded here in the United States of America." Anywhere there was a farm corporation there would be "no average farmer, no farm family, no farm home."[133]

The argument sometimes was personal. Bird debated McGugin in January 1931 before a realtors' convention in Dodge City. Bird said that corporate farming had contributed more than any other single factor to developing the Western Kansas wheat belt. The Wheat Farming Company operated land that others would not or could not operate "because of lack of power, lack of capital, of mortgage debt, chattel debt and because of broken morale among the owners and producers." The "continued and persistent efforts on the part of propagandists and self-seeking politicians and political fixers" to discourage the farmer did not help. "Political farming," he said, would do no good. The corporation would. McGugin responded, "Corporation farming is a challenge to the civilization we have known for centuries." It was a horrible prospect that the individual farmer, so loved by yeoman theorists from Thomas Jefferson forward, might be replaced by a poorly paid farmhand "working a few months a year and a tramp for the remaining nine months." The corporation might pay dividends, "but it is a social ravishment." The man who tilled the soil would be reduced to peonage. Self-preservation and patriotism demanded that the farm corporation in Kansas be stopped.[134] Farm corporations represented, McGugin thought, "the end of that fine agricultural civilization which has meant so much to the builders of America." The corporation was "destroying farm homes more effectually than could be done by a heartless invading army of vandals."[135]

Katherine O'Loughlin, of Hays, who was in the Kansas legislature in 1931 and later became a congresswoman, tried to slow the momentum toward outlawing farm corporations in Kansas. "You have heard about this great octopus that is depopulating the farms, vanquishing the little red school house and other terrible things," she said, but argued that it was not so.[136] Bird continued to make the same argument. He had lived in Western Kansas for twenty-three years, he said, and was hardly a grasping eastern capitalist. "You have been my friends and I have been your friend." Farming was changing. "The business of farming is not the little proposition that it used to be. When the boys went across the waters and into the Great War they saw things done in a large way. They drove tractors and trucks of 75 horsepower or more, and therefore they were not satisfied to come back to the kind of farming they left in 1915." But Bird was sometimes heckled, and O'Loughlin was overwhelmed.[137] The bill passed outlawing new incorporations, and ouster proceedings were instituted against existing farm corporations on the grounds that they had exceeded the powers of their charters. In the face of that, the Wheat Farming Company filed for bankruptcy in April 1931.[138] There was a similar ouster action against the Sledd Company.[139]

Garvey was comfortable with that. The corporation probably could never outdo the individual farmer while paying its overhead and promotional costs, he said, arguing that he had predicted the failure of the farm corporation all along. He formed a partnership with a cost-cutting manager to replace his own Mutual Farming Company and proceeded apace.[140] Bird, however, was deeply disappointed. "Five Years ago, and four years ago," he wrote Governor Harry Woodring in October 1931, "it seemed to me that real farm relief rested with those engaged in agriculture and would be accomplished by lower production costs, better average yields through better practices, the utilization of what had heretofore been wastes."[141]

One by one the corporations went. The Fisher Ranch Corporation, which had 7,000 acres of wheat and 1,500 acres of cattle grazing land, went bankrupt in the spring of 1932, about the last corporation to survive as an active operator. "Like many other questions," the editor in Tribune commented, "the human element was not taken into the equation." With the individual farmer, "there is little or no overhead for overseers, inspectors, efficiency experts or general managers. The individual farmer combines all these within himself."[142] That seemed to be the official explanation. However, the political intervention complicated the question of whether the farming corporations without political intervention could have survived and made good on their claim that they could make a profit even in a depression.

The corporate farm ousters opened the way for a public, governmental solution as all the private initiatives were found either unacceptable or ineffective and as the dusty, dry weather and the poor prices continued. Acceptance of a large government role in farming, however, took time. The initial reaction of Western Kansans to government solutions was embarrassment and hostility.

Had the day of the "self reliant pioneer" passed? Was there a citizenry that looked "more and more to the state to regulate everything" and that had become "soft and complacent?"[143] David Danbom's insightful study, *The Resisted Revolution*, makes the point that rural life in the early twentieth century was characterized by informality, individualism, localism, traditionalism, relative poverty, and almost no government influence beyond local schools and the post office. As self-reliant individuals, farmers "seldom perceived what government could do for them while always fearing what it might do to them."[144] Therefore, when the Hoover administration created the Federal Farm Board and when Secretary of Agriculture Arthur Hyde and

Farm Board head Alexander Legge made statements such as that "blind production" was the bane of agriculture, many farmers west of Wichita found the new scenario alien.[145]

The federal farm program started conservatively enough. A 1927 report by a group of businesspeople on the condition of U.S. agriculture documented that it had suffered since World War I and that government had not much cared. "Agriculture was left largely to the mercy of *laissez-faire*, while government support went to the building up of commercial and industrial enterprises."[146] President Hoover seemed determined to retain the individual initiative of farmers, and to have government play only a supportive role to voluntary associations. He said, in 1929, that government must not "undermine the freedom of our farmers and of our people as a whole by bureaucratic and governmental domination and interference." He viewed the farm problem as "part of a larger challenge of reconciling democratic and individual values with the technological and organizational imperatives of the twentieth century."[147] The Agricultural Marketing Act of 1929, which created the Farm Board, envisioned aiding farmers through loans to farmer-controlled cooperatives and creation of stabilization corporations to influence price through buying. However, after losing several hundred million dollars in the price crash between 1929 and 1931, the Farm Board began talking about acreage reduction and more direct federal regulation of land use.[148]

Acreage reduction was the proposal most frightening to regional farmers. Some places might do that, thought the regional press, but not Western Kansas. An editor in Hays wrote in the spring of 1930:

> An area such as Western Kansas, where[,] with power farming machinery[,] wheat can be produced as cheaply as it can anywhere else on earth, must remain in the grain growing business, for wheat is the major crop and it is "cash money.". . . The farm board's plea to sow less wheat out here of necessity must fall on deaf ears. Without its wheat production Western Kansas could return its lands to the Indians for use by them as a happy hunting grounds and gain something by the transaction, for to stay on without wheat would mean going into debt deeper and deeper each succeeding year.[149]

On another occasion, the editor commented, "Advising the farmers of Western Kansas to grow less wheat is hokum pure and simple and the farmer who lends an ear to such propaganda is swatting himself on the chin." The headline for that one was "Farmers Not Fools."[150]

Some people thought that if there were to be acreage reduction the government should be talking to corporate farmers about it. Corporate farming was "the theory of mass production applied to agriculture," and limiting corporate farming would do the most to limit the overall supply without hurting the family farmer. "Apparently the small wheat grower cannot longer compete successfully with the large grower of wheat," wrote one Kansan. "The plea of Mr. Hyde and Mr. Legge surely should not be made to the man who theoretically is doomed, but to the industrial wheat grower."[151] Others, however, thought corporate farming, too, should be left alone. It was just what was required to put farming on an equal footing with the rest of U.S. business, which was dominated by corporations using the latest scientific and business methods. There was no need for government to interfere.[152]

There was criticism directed also at the Kansas State Board of Agriculture, whose director, J. C. Mohler, advised wheat acreage reduction. A grain man at Hutchinson commented in 1930 that unless farmers put out their usual acreage, bankers would restrict their credit. Secretary Mohler, he jibed, "has been in the habit of placing his children on the state pay roll as soon as they are dry behind the ears," an option not available to Western Kansas farmers. "It seems as though he should be teaching the farmers how to raise more grain instead of trying to get them to quit work."[153]

Such dissenters against federal planning and regulation found a champion in the acerbic governor of Kansas, Clyde Reed. He spoke regularly against production limits. One man, commenting on a speech Reed made in Wichita in June 1930, wrote, "I am glad that you have the backbone and the nerve and the courage (it takes courage to oppose a set of numbskulls who are clothed with authority by our Government) to come up and deliberately state the facts." To offer a production curtailment plan to Western Kansans who had "braved the rigors of seasons, and have finally conquered it and made production of wheat possible" was "senseless, unreasonable," and "absolutely silly."[154] Were there not hungry people all over the world?[155] One friend wrote Reed that it would be better to hand out the wheat surplus to the poor than not to raise the grain. "This bugaboo of a surplus is more obnoxious to the farmer than tea in Boston harbor was to our forefathers during the revolution."[156]

It took nerve, most admitted, for Legge to come to Kansas to defend federal farm policy, but that is what he did. He participated in debates at Hays and Dodge City, called "Wheat Outlook" meetings, early in July 1930, with Secretary of Agriculture Hyde and Governor Reed on the platform with him. He was frank about his mission. Wasn't it an irony, Legge wrote Reed just before this event, that eastern investors were being solicited by Kansas farm corporations claiming they could raise wheat profitably with the price at 40 cents a bushel? Why should these eastern taxpayers support a government program to "aid producers so fortunately situated as these western wheat growers," unless there were some quid pro quo. It was time to stop record production. "Your wheat growers may be under the delusion that some Santa Claus may take over their wheat in any quantity they are able to produce, at a price satisfactory to them. And we feel they are due for a rather rude awakening." Reed's stance had only encouraged that delusion. If farmers in Kansas did not "make some reasonable adjustment" in wheat production voluntarily, they would have to "fight it out in a war of extermination."[157]

Hyde was plainspoken also but more diplomatic than Legge and Reed. "We are not here," he said, "to demand that you reduce your wheat acreage, but simply to give you the facts and let you do with them what you will. It is the steadfast opinion of you people that the prosperity of Kansas depends on wheat. We are not here to tear that down. We simply want to hang out the red lights as danger signals." He suggested a 25 percent acreage reduction in wheat.[158]

The event at Hays came on a hot July 9. About 1,500 people attended the proceedings at Sheridan Coliseum. Many more heard the broadcast on WIBW radio, the Capper station in Topeka, or read about it in extensive coverage by the press corps.[159] Legge was certain of his ground and minced no words. "The purpose of the meeting this afternoon," he said, "is to acquaint you farmers with a few facts which may be unpalatable."[160] His demeanor seemed to many listeners arrogant and indifferent. "He showed no desire whatever to be helpful or sympathetic," one noticed, saying at one point, "You're riding into a buzz saw . . . but it won't bother me any if the price goes to ten cents."[161] It did not help that Legge was a former executive of International Harvester, part of a cartel of manufacturers upon whom regional farmers were then heaping much blame.[162] "The Farmer today," wrote a Reed supporter, "and for years is a target for everybody to shoot at. He has absolutely no defense. Accepts what is offered him for his products and pays combination of trust prices for everything he buys. His worst enemy is the damnable Harvester Trust, with War prices still prevailing on farm machinery."[163] Someone overheard Legge saying later at his hotel: "We are going to get out of this town as quickly as we can!"[164]

That was a good strategy. One in the audience at Hays wrote Reed, "I sincerely believe that not since the . . . old turmoil populist days, has there occurred a debate or invasion of the state of foreign talent to cuss, scold or show Kansas the error of their ways, that has caused so much comment as the debate just concluded, and now as then, the enemy retreated with colors furled."[165] The two who had come from Washington, wrote a Hays editor, went out on a "long and brittle limb" and made a "happy day for the Democrats."[166] Reed was complimented for calling Legge's policy a "gospel of despair," and many agreed with the governor that the "whole socialistic marketing system" of the Hoover administration should be broken up.[167] A Ness County man asked for Legge's address. "I will send him a telegram and ask him to come out to Ness County and castrate all the bulls in Ness County and maybe they would have all us farmers where they would want us."[168]

There was a minority view that the Federal Farm Board was working with private pools and that farmers had to have some way of organizing to stabilize price and defeat the speculator.[169] But those opinions were scarce, and approval was limited to the marketing operations of the Farm Board, not suggestions to cut production. Most editorial opinion in Western Kansas by 1931 was that the Farm Board had been a "costly, ghastly mistake."[170] Clifford Hope, who had generally supported the Farm Board's marketing efforts, sent the agency a telegram in the summer of 1931: "Present price means ruin to this entire section, feeling against board most bitter."[171] Who was the chief enemy of agriculture? The *Garden City Telegram* confidently said it was "our own Federal Government."[172] Ray Garvey, in one of his ads at Colby, concluded, "The quicker all of us stop thinking about what the government is going to do for us, and settle down to our own economic destinies, the better off we will be."[173] Farmers in the western country, a state representative from Ransom wrote, had bought machines, and they had to pay for them.[174] A crowd of 20,000 at the Wheat Festival at Hutchinson, in September 1930, emphasized that they intended to "ride with wheat."[175]

There followed a period of silent suffering. A man came into the office of the *Garden City Telegram* in the fall of 1931. He was the father of five and "didn't have a thin dime, no work, no prospect of getting any." The editor gave him some change to buy breakfast, but ruminated about how long such private charity would be enough.[176] The abandoned southside schoolhouse in Garden City had by 1931 become a soup kitchen. The local poor fund was overdrawn from supplying it.[177]

The first political suggestion was to pare expenses and cut taxes, making local government less and not more active. Highway maintenance and building, for example, could go. U.S. Highway 40 through Western Kansas had been, according to a Plainville man, "a political football that has been more or less kicked around." Road groups advanced "a lot of hooey," and concrete roads were "a salve for various political ambitions" and not useful in the west. "Western Kansas needs slab highways like a cat needs six tails."[178] It needed the accompanying taxes even less. Various towns proposed debt holidays, since bill collectors were interfering with farm work.[179] County commissioners offered jobs chopping wood, dragging roads, and other tasks, with pay in vouchers for a local grocery, but their funds were limited and taxing for relief locally was out of the question.[180] Businesspeople's organizations, designed to raise funds for relief, could not bridge the gap.[181] Perhaps there should be ordinances against begging. People were holding out hats and selling pencils in the streets of Garden City, leading some locals to comment that most of them were better off than the people from whom they were begging, "with wheat at four for a dollar."[182] It was the same in Hays: "Good men, bad men, beggar men and thieves are pestering Hays and making life miserable for housewives." One morning in June 1932, fifteen strangers called on a single business, asking for work, something to eat, or both.[183]

There were some federal loans available, but not many were willing or able to take advantage of them. Under the Hoover plan, the borrower had to give an absolute first lien on all growing crops, and other lien holders had to waive their liens in favor of the federal loan security. This included a waiver by the landlord of his rent share. A second condition was that the borrower had to supply a sworn statement that he was completely without any other credit source and could not plant without the loan. Most were ashamed to make such a declaration, hoping instead to "wiggle along somehow."[184]

There were other ideas of how the government might help. Herb Fryback, writer of the "Cyclone Cellar" column in Colby, suggested early in 1932 that instead of appropriating billions to build a navy, the United States "should load high the decks of its war fleet with our surplus wheat, steam up some of the great rivers of the world and throw off this wheat in communities where the distress of the world has hit with greatest severity to feed jobless men, distressed mothers and hungry children. Just fool's fancy of course, but we can't help wondering."[185]

These solutions seemed weak. John Wasinger, who ran a garage at Victoria, Ellis County, wrote Governor Harry Woodring that he could not get a loan on his almost new building. Farmers could not pay what they owed him and his building was worth a fraction of what he had borrowed on it two years earlier. "I have not had a good night's sleep for weeks on account of this worry. There are eight of us in the family and what will happen to us?"[186] The governor could only advise Wasinger to see John Bird or some local friend in Hays, noting that his position was similar to that of many others.[187] "We who live out here in the wheat belt," wrote a man observing the 1931 harvest, "and see the actual conditions every day, can, I am sure, be pardoned for getting somewhat hysterical about the situation."[188]

Incumbents fared badly in elections. Katherine O'Loughlin, of Hays, who had received a J.D. degree from Chicago Law School in 1920, ran successfully for Congress in 1932.[189] Simon Fishman, a Jewish farmer from Tribune, defeated twelve-year incumbent state senator E. E. Frizell of Larned that same year.[190] Dr. John Brinkley got a considerable number of votes as a third party candidate for governor. Over 2,000 people turned out to hear him in Hugoton in 1932.[191] "We know he is a crook," said a supporter of quack doctor Brinkley, "but we have been voting so long for 'honest' men that we have decided to try a change and vote for a known crook and see what difference that will make."[192] Franklin Roosevelt could hardly have lost the national election that November. But throwing out the incumbents was not enough. The new politicians had to have a new approach.

The leader in Germany, Adolf Hitler, was certainly an orator, the editor at Hays commented in 1933, although not much to look at. The proof would be in the pudding. If Hitler succeeded in bringing Germany out of the depression, he would be regarded as great. If he failed, "he will be just another windjammer and demagogue, the by product of the most distressed period in the history of his country."[193]

With the election of Roosevelt and the implementation of the New Deal, there was a new acceptance in Western Kansas—an acceptance for these dark times anyway—of government planning and control. Perhaps the Federal Land Bank was not so bad and should be used more aggressively.[194] Perhaps Garden City should lobby Congress to resettle the unemployed from the east on irrigated plots in the Arkansas Valley of Western Kansas at federal expense.[195] Perhaps Barton County should push again for a federal game preserve at Cheyenne Bottoms, despite the fact that the lake was dry. Will Townsley, editor of the *Great Bend Daily Tribune*, wrote to Congressman Hope: "Just as water seeks a level so does business, so does agriculture. Kansas farmers as individuals say they don't want legislation, but collectively they pose as a united body demanding all kinds of government relief."[196] Local papers printed a cartoon showing a farmer at his plow, looking eastward toward a sunrise over Washington. The caption was, "Relief."[197]

Pride became dampened as conditions worsened. Joseph Shastid of Sublette wrote Clifford Hope in April 1933 that conditions in his district were "deplorable." Farmers could not afford gas for their cars and trucks and hitchhiked into town. People wanted to meet their obligations but could not. "All that these men ask is that the Government protect them until such time as they can make their payments."[198] A Dighton man said that everyone in his district, regardless of politics, was "plumb Nutty" about President Roosevelt.

Goodland, 1937 (courtesy of High Plains Museum, Goodland)

"If he would ask that every man in Kansas stand on his left ear and sing 'Abide with Me,' I am thoroughly convinced that fully 95 percent of the people would be ready to try it out once."[199]

When the Agricultural Adjustment Administration (AAA) bill passed in 1933 during the famous hundred days of legislation, that attitude of being willing to give it a try prevailed. A Dodge City editorial offered that the bill, providing for restrictions on acres planted (allotment), low interest loans, and commodity price subsidies, "has aroused new hopes throughout the country," and that there was little criticism of it. "The need of an economic improvement in the farm business is so pressing," the editor wrote, "and the hope that some new experiment might be helpful is shared by so large an element of the American public, that very few persons have been willing to interpose any objections to the provisions of the new bill." True, it did not solve the fundamental problem of the depression, and, true, eventually the farmer would chafe under the restrictions. But temporary relief was badly needed.[200] Congressman Hope, Republican to the core, felt the AAA was "a Godsend to our people to get some cash this fall when it looks like they might not have much other cash coming in."[201]

Western Kansas kidded about the forms and the bureaucracy connected with signing up for the new program.[202] But they signed up in droves. In Ford County, 90 percent of farmers signed AAA contracts at eight county centers on the first day they could. Nearly 1,200 farmers in the county, the news reported, "will be watching the mails for their contracts and later their three quarter of a million dollars of allotment money in the next few weeks."[203] Maybe it would work, maybe not, "but the men who have made a business of raising the largest wheat crops the Southwest ever has seen are playing ball with the government."[204]

Even ultraconservative Ray Garvey, after considerable debate, signed up his farms. "I never regretted not joining the Ku Klux Klan," he wrote, but "I hate like hell to miss this subsidy."[205] He agreed with a number of others that although he might not make the rules, or agree with them, one could not go it alone against all trends.[206]

By the end of the year 1933, and after some confusion concerning the rules, the AAA system was working smoothly. In Barton County, $250,000 in checks arrived in one week at the end of December. That, it was reported, "has been a real Santa Claus to the people of Barton County—a Christmas gift that has brought great blessings to many a grateful home. The distribution of this money has helped start the wheels of industry to moving to such a degree that 'what blesses one blesses all' becomes a practical reality."[207] In Thomas County, there were 1,450 separate contracts, and people awaited their checks with some anxiety. "There are taxes to be paid, automobile license tags to be got, coal and clothing for winter to be bought."[208]

There were those who worried about the long-term impact. A newspaper piece at Hays wondered if people were made of different stuff than their pioneer ancestors.

> Almost to a man we turned to the National Government for relief.
> Sick from a wild spree of high living, we asked for food; ragged, we
> asked for clothes. Those to some degree we have received, but in
> exchange we have paid a price. Today the National Government is
> in close contact with each individual citizen. It has the power to tell
> the producer how much he can produce, tell the laborer how many
> hours he can labor, tell the merchant at what price and under what
> conditions he can operate.

Would that end with the end of the Depression emergency, or would the change be permanent?[209] By the time there was a chance to vote again, in 1936, wrote the editor of the *Hays Daily News*, "there is no certainty that governmental bureaucracy by that time will not have such a suffocating hold on the country's throat that a majority can be mustered for the same reasons, in the main, that Germany today has no opportunity to express itself against Hitlerism."[210]

By the spring of 1934, some thought the honeymoon was over for the president in the region. "American voters are foolish sometimes," Hope wrote, "but they are not fools." People were tired of the New Deal, and "unless our Congress can check the present course of events, the present feeling will soon develop into a fanatical hatred." The trouble with the federal bureaucrats was that

> most of them are theorists who for the first time in their lives are having an opportunity to put some of their crazy theories into effect, and believe me they like it. They are having the time of their lives, and a lot of them haven't any more concern as to what is going to happen if their experiments fail than if they were trying their ideas out on a bunch of guinea pigs.[211]

One of Hope's constituents from Western Kansas wrote, "To an outsider it would seem that Washington has turned into a madhouse."[212] W. D. Ferguson wrote Garvey from Colby that he hoped the New Deal would "run out of letters before they get around to us and that may save us."[213]

There was laughter about the proposal for a tree belt across Western Kansas. Some could recall the forestation projects of the 1890s and those of the second decade of the twentieth century, all of which came to naught under the ravages of climate. Would people forsake their vacations to Colorado and California and roll down "scenic, shaded highways in Kansas?" Not likely.[214] It was another example of "chimerical hocus-pocus," that nevertheless brought "pork" to the region.[215]

Rexford Tugwell, the undersecretary of agriculture, who believed that government economic planning could reduce the wastefulness of capitalism, advanced the idea that much farmland in Western Kansas should be abandoned and the region returned to grass. At Hays, that idea was called "haywire" and was attributed to "the Washington nuthouse of college professors, the depths of whose ignorance no one has yet been able to plumb." Western Kansas needed aid, but that should not lead people to jump to the conclusion that it was now and forever economically worthless.[216] Was there not some way, a correspondent of Hope's wrote, to deport Tugwell to Russia?[217]

The year 1934 was a difficult one. In July, temperatures at Hays for six days running were 105, 110, 111, 107, 110, 108.[218] The evaporation rate at this temperature and altitude was such as to crush all hope of forests. Yet, doubtless, experts would be doing studies on the feasibility of growing them. "Isn't it fine," wrote a Pratt woman, "to be able to just say the word and it is done?" There was to be a million dollars set aside for a study of soil erosion in Haskell County, the woman noticed. "I am presuming that some youngster from the east who more than likely has never seen Kansas will be sent to tell us all about it."[219]

Civilian Conservation Corps project near Kalvesta, 1930s (courtesy of Wichita State University Special Collections)

Area residents, however, grasped at survival, whatever the program or its perceived merits. C. C. Isely at Dodge City started a housing project as part of the resettlement program.[220] Jess Denious of the same town organized a 4-H camp, using public works funds for its construction.[221] There were terracing projects to hold water and stop erosion.[222] Local young men in droves went to the Civilian Conservation Corps camps, which employed out-of-work men on public projects, and wrote home about the experience as though they had gone off to war.[223] Area politicians toyed with the idea of attracting federal money for major dam projects.[224] When there were cuts in the budgets for the experiment stations, Western Kansans protested.[225] When there was a government program proposed, Western Kansans applied for it. They built new auditoriums and new parks. They straightened some roads and paved others. They put up clubhouses and tennis courts. They remodeled schools and constructed flood control projects.[226] The only fear seemed to be "that some of these white rabbits that Mr. Roosevelt keeps pulling out of his hat will turn black when exposed for a time to the light of sensible inspection."[227]

John Stutz, Kansas director of public welfare, defended government intervention. Speaking in the fall of 1934, Stutz said that cooperation was a type of instruction in the possibilities of human beings. No disease was more damaging than worry and doubt, and there was no reason to worry over the inevitable. "We lament the drought, but we can't make it rain. All we can do is to do something about the effects of the drought. To stand up and scream day and night about there being no rain is not the way to ameliorate the effects of the drought."[228]

Still, there was no avoiding worry. The visitation of doom was painful, and not enough time had passed to give the suffering dignity. "Ashes to Ashes and Dust to Dust," a reporter in Dodge City quoted during a dust storm. "The women cried and the men folks cussed."[229] There was only the traditional humor and optimism on which to rely, but how long it would last was anyone's guess. Many felt that, given the horrors of the first half of the decade, the second half would be better. Surely 1934 was the bottom of the cycle and "we'll have a whale of a crop next year."[230] In that hope, this time, the locals were sadly mistaken.

10

Next Year Country

The years 1935 and 1936 were the nadir, the darkest days, literally and figuratively, for the Western Kansas region. It became hotter and colder, brighter and darker, than ever before. It was windy and dusty and depressing—as it had not been since the 1890s. The malevolent wildlife of those antique times, both the lepidopteran and the orthopteran varieties, came hopping and flying back again to add a special terror, as their legions ate the pitiful cereal remnant sun and hail had left to the farmer. Residents could appreciate the drama, could find in dust storms for a time some beauty and challenge, but were ultimately worn out by the unremitting pummeling they took.

Rainfall remained low and temperatures high. It had been 112 degrees in Tribune one day in July 1934, and for the whole year it had rained only 7.76 inches there, compared to an "average" of 17.03 inches.[1] Colby had had 6 inches and Garden City 9.4 inches, and there was no reserve of moisture.[2] The experiment station agent at Colby observed that the present drought was one of the most severe since climatic records started it 1888. Nineteen thirty-five was the fifth year of below average rainfall, and "the failure of wheat left thousands of acres unprotected by vegetative cover."[3]

The winter of 1934–35 was severe. It was 16 below zero at Ness City toward the end of January 1935.[4] By spring the weather varied but stayed bad. An editor reported in March that, during the previous week, "the weather man simply upset the cornucopia or whatever he uses and dumped everything he had on Kansas. There were dust storms, summer temperatures, thunderstorms, rains, snows, frigid temperatures, and tornadoes, all between Thursday morning and Sunday night."[5] Kansas, observed a man at Dodge City that terrible spring, never did anything half way. "Every once in a while we hear some farm folk long for the throb of activity in the cities. We always feel sorry for the powers of observation of those persons."[6] When there were a few lovely days in the fall, people could not believe it. "Those reared on the Kansas tradition ever are suspicious of fine weather. Their experience is that the weather they rave about is the harbinger of rough days."[7]

There was no relief the next year. The Colby Experiment Station superintendent noted "another year of failing crops and low appropriations" (rainfall was under 11 inches).[8] A Great Bend paper wrote numerous articles in July 1936 on the heat, thinking each one was surely an all-time spectacular. It was 112 degrees at three o'clock in the afternoon on July 17.[9] On July 24, it was 115 degrees.[10] The drought created disappointment and suffering. "Lacey, white clouds, sometimes of a darker hue, occasional flashes of lightning early in the evenings, stir hopes of rain." But the rain did not come, and the "stark, elemental and cruel" dryness prevailed.[11]

The signature feature, the one that made Western Kansas unwittingly and unwillingly famous, was the dust storm. "When the depression came along," wrote an editor, "we wondered what next. We soon found out; it was the dust storms."[12] They started early in 1935, raging in February, each successive storm advertised as the worst ever and probably the last such ever. At Larned, there was a "terrific" layer of dust everywhere late in February. "Street lights were useless in the dirt-laden atmosphere and motorists found that the headlights on their motor cars were of little value. It was worse than driving through a dense fog." Housewives kept busy with brooms; clerks at downtown stores swept the sidewalks, and window displays received a coating of fine silt.[13] At Tribune, they called that storm "fearful." It gave everything a strange "reddish hue" and buried optimism along with houses.[14] Unless people shook the pages of their newspapers often, they would be too covered with dust for Western Kansans to read about the rains in the eastern part of the state.[15]

But that was only a baby storm. In mid-March came a giant, weeklong, "blinding, choking" version of a black roller. People in Great Bend had trouble breathing while sleeping. Wind ran 30 to 40 miles per hour. "The dust drifted against obstructions and clung to homes like snow in a blizzard. Piles of dust were in evidence in every yard and on porches." Trains could not stay on schedule. People could not see across the court at the basketball tournament at Sheridan Coliseum in Hays. A restaurant there swept out 63 pounds of dust one morning. Chickens walked over 8-foot fences. People found milk bottles left on porches two-thirds filled with dirt, provided they could get their back doors open to look. The entire force of the *Great Bend Daily Tribune* had to work for hours to clean up the complex linotype machines sufficiently to get out their newspaper.[16] A man driving from Arkalon to Liberal said, "When you met a car with the lights on it looked like a couple of matches burning and you couldn't tell how far away it was."[17] The stores "resembled the old home place when the family returns from a summer's vacation. Every counter and shelf was tightly shrouded with curtains and covers." There was a "peculiar blue-white glow" in the air. At times, wires would crackle and spit sparks of electricity, and people felt shocks touching metal surfaces. "The density of dust cannot be described or even imagined."[18] A seven-year-old boy suffocated near Winona, lost and alone in the storm.[19]

That storm, wrote editor Denious at Dodge City, "was the double inlay, triple riveted, 18 carat, 100 percent proof sample about what can happen when we talk about taming the wind." The weather definitely was not "sedate, diplomatic, or circumspect. This is a country of superlatives. What Wichita, Kansas City or Des Moines would describe as the worst storm of the decade or century, doesn't satisfy the powers which control our storms." People would be talking for years, as they talked about the blizzard of '86, about 1935 when someone "upset the celestial dustpan."[20] Wrote the editor at Gove City, "Folks out our way have eaten so much dust and sand that every time they open their mouths some dirty remark is apt to drop out."[21]

People flocked to the air-conditioned demonstrator car on the ATSF railroad, where a mat of fine wool saturated with oil filtered the dust. "A lot of women seem to get pleasure out of telling everybody how many times they have cleaned their houses. It is reported that some of them are using words they have picked up from their husbands in describing the dust and others just indulge in extremely profane silences."[22] Commented a woman at Liberal, "If you can fix up some kind of house that will keep dirt out in this country, your fortune's made."[23]

At the end of March came another "worst yet" dust storm, with dust and snow falling together in some places and winds of nearly 50 miles per hour.[24] Area people noticed that the native wildlife was disappearing, and they had to defend against regular press reports that the country was going to desert.[25] Eastern reporters, said the *Scott County News*, had a "ten cent knowledge of the facts and a million dollar imagination. . . . If we are still optimistic we hope we will be pardoned. We have lived here all our life. This is our home and we are not ashamed of it."[26]

Then the storms came every week or two.[27] The visibility as far to the east as Wichita was reduced to less than 300 feet that April.[28] The superintendent at the Colby Experiment Station recorded twenty-one days of dust in March 1935 and twenty-three days in April:

> It is impossible to describe such a storm to one who has not experienced this condition. . . . It was impossible to see five feet ahead even though one's eyes were protected by goggles. . . . Living conditions for both man and beast were almost impossible. . . . On land where weeds were more scattered each weed soon became a mound of drifted dust. Some of the mounds were from five to eight feet in diameter and from one and one-half to three feet in height. In many cases weedy fence rows had the appearance of dikes as the fence was completely covered by dirt. . . . Implements would not scour in the dust piles and because traction was poor in them it was difficult to accomplish much tillage.[29]

In mid-April, dust buried the region again, with a strong wind from the west and bolts of lightning and thunder. It rained in some places amid the dust, and people were covered with mud. At Larned, surgical procedures at the hospital had to be cancelled as there was no way to keep the operating theater clean.[30] Hugoton called it a "terror." Several businesspeople there locked up their stores and went home.[31] At Goodland, the staff could barely get out the *News-Republic* and did so only because people "want a newspaper worse when all other contact with the outside world is cut off." The railroad there ran on slow orders and all highway travel stopped.[32] Hotels in the larger towns covered their windows with wet sheets, and marooned traveling salesmen tried to think how to pass the time. Farmers looked out on fields "covered with sand ridges that resembled ocean waves mysteriously fixed in place." Workers shoveled dirt off city streets.[33]

A correspondent of the *Ness County News* wrote an essay called "Anent the Dirt." He waxed poetic: "Here, in days gone by, the carnivorous prairie dogs made obeiscence [sic] to their liege lord, basking in the shadow of his ancient sun dial and the mournful coyotes sang in yappy jazz of the glories of this place that was, but is no more since the dust stirred up by a million I.H.C. tractors and aggravated by the playful western winds, settled down over the hapless baliwick [sic] of the sage of the shortgrass and blotted out his fair domain from the eyes of the curious."[34]

Indeed, the April storms, sudden and severe, made some think that not only had the end of that old pioneer world come, but the end of the world in general. People looked around "in awe and many of them in terror" through a blackness darker than midnight in which there were moments one could not see a hand in front of the face. People went into cellars, and "the

Dust drifts, Thomas County, 1935 (courtesy of Kansas State University Special Collections)

electricity snapped and popped on the windmill wire."[35] Laura Ingalls, attempting a transcontinental air speed record from Los Angeles to New York in a black monoplane, landed in eastern Colorado, forced down by dust.[36]

There could be a terrible beauty in it. At Hugoton, the editor described one of the April storms roiling up on the horizon 2,000 feet high. Out in front, the wind whipped a fine dust, "in contrast to a whirling mass of black silt and dirt in the background. . . . There were light and dark streaks in the wave in contrast to the blue of the sky and then a direct line along the bottom that designated which was earth and which was boiling mass." It seemed almost to "foam."[37] Robert Geiger, an Associated Press writer traveling in Western Kansas that April, described "black and saffron clouds of dusts, spectacularly menacing, intensely irritating to man and beast alike, choking, blowing out tender crops, and lasting without mercy for days."[38]

But the spectacle wore thin. By late April, an observer in Great Bend noted that it was the twenty-fourth severe dust storm since February, the latest iterations being "of such blackness and severity that they are almost incredible."[39] Local people didn't like the term "Dust Bowl" that was getting bandied about, calling it an "absurdity." Yet, in their heart of hearts, they doubtless saw the aptness of the phrase.[40] People developed hacking coughs, annoying headaches, and unusual infections.[41] They lost their interest in archaeology, "after digging ourselves, and our furniture, to say nothing of the chickens and young calves out of the dust."[42] Herb Fryback wrote that spring: "Western Kansas is a drab, hag-ridden area with little evidence of the spring season. Many feel that this whole area has returned to the primitive desert from whence it came, and many others openly advocate its desertion."[43] Jess Denious added, "Conditions in Western Kansas this season are so bad that it is a little difficult for us to determine at any particular time in which state we are located. . . . The only hope I can see is through rainfall and for some reason that one thing which we need so much seems to be withheld."[44]

The "saffron scourge" continued.[45] The drought in 1936 was more severe than the year before.[46] There were just over 10 inches of rain at Tribune, for example, and temperatures reached 108.[47] Wichita recorded 113.9 degrees on August 12, an all-time record for the city, and by September the city had received only 6.13 inches of rain for the year, compared with a normal for the period of over 22 inches.[48] "It is making life unbearable," wrote a Goodland editor. "It is not only ruining one crop, but crops for years to come."[49] Charles Scott, a newspaper editor at Iola, wrote Denious in March 1936, "The wind is blowing a gale and from my window I cannot see more than five or six blocks. I hesitate to think what it must be out in your stricken country."[50]

The remaining years of the decade remained severe, full of dust and cracks in the baking soil. The Garden City Experiment Station superintendent recorded and classified dust storms. There were seventy-seven there in 1937. Seven of these the station classed as very bad, twenty-two as bad, and forty-eight as "dusty."[51] The superintendent at the Tribune Experiment Station reported that he gave up on his flower garden in 1937.[52] The year 1939 at that station was "one of the most severe ever experienced in Western Kansas." Rainfall was 9.79 inches, or over 7 inches below the thirty-two year average. Only a little over 6 inches fell during the growing season, compared with an average of about 13 inches. There were thirty days of temperatures over 100 degrees, with two days topping out at 107. It was 105 one day in September there, an all-time high for the time and place, and it was 78 on a day in December, another record. There were eighty dust storms at Garden City in 1939. It was small comfort that only two were rated "very bad."[53] It was not until 1940 that the experiment stations in general were able to report a near normal year for Western Kansas crops. There were only three days of visible dust that year at Tribune. Even so, wheat in many places averaged fewer than 10 bushels per acre that year.[54]

The suffering for some was extreme. The vague disease of "dust pneumonia" was never well documented as a health threat, but the privations of people without money or prospects were well enough known, both to officials administering Kansas relief and to the sufferers' neighbors in Western Kansas. In April 1935, there was a conference of agricultural college representatives at Garden City, where they got a firsthand look at the dust and the menace to "health and well-being" that it represented. There was little feed for livestock. Soil was eroding, and nothing was growing on what remained.[55] Listing might help, but the federal subsidy for encouraging that was insufficient to pay the real costs of farmers.[56] A man in Scott County noticed that the wind was uncovering Indian artifacts, causing him to imagine what the country must have been like when the Native Americans held sway there. "The Indian LIVED," he commented, "and the white man who thinks we are better off is foolish."[57]

The Kansas Emergency Relief Committee had paid for the building of 2,000 farm ponds and the drilling of 6,540 wells in Kansas, but it was too little.[58] John Stutz, the efficient administrator of the KERC, reported that relief needs were greatly in excess of the ability of local communities to give it, and consequently the federal government had distributed nearly $75 million in federal money to care for 400,000 individual Kansans. The old poor farm system had been supplanted by the federal agencies, which had more than "a tub of lard and a sack of beans" to offer. The federal relief organization in Kansas had made, by 1935, 300,000 comforters, sheets, pillowslips, and blankets and had manufactured 25,000 mattresses. It canned 13 million cans of beef and made 50,000 leather coats from the hides of thin cattle bought from impoverished farmers. It created 105 county relief organizations.[59]

When the Agricultural Adjustment Administration (AAA) came under attack in 1935, many in Western Kansas defended it. "The attitude of the farmers is certainly not hard to understand," went one editorial. "Beset by droughts, floods, dust storms and common prices below the cost of production, hundreds of thousands of farmers have been able to keep going . . . only through the government aid they received from the AAA."[60] The worry was that relief would become a habit, a part of the culture that would outlast hard times. Young people, thought an observer in Hays, had "lost that vital spirit of self-confidence and self-reliance that is so necessary to fight the battle of life."[61]

There were harrowing stories. Governor Alf Landon got a report from Graham County in August 1935 noting that the drought was "more appalling than it has been heretofore." There was a small amount of feed, "but other crops and even gardens are rapidly becoming a thing of the past along with morale and 'the will to do.'" Crops, private business, and government aid were all, according to this correspondent, "in an extremely leaky boat." He concluded, "The picture is black and the horizon uninterrupted."[62]

A female relief worker from the same county confirmed this. "Now I spend my days writing to irate grocers and interviewing discouraged, outraged farmers who justly feel they have been deceived." Over a third were ineligible for work relief. "They feel there is real cause for alarm; if the government does not do something for them a great many of them are facing actual starvation."[63] It was no different in Wallace County. Anna Enlow, the Poor Commissioner there, wrote that the farmers "do not wish to *borrow* for living expenses. . . . They desire the same privilege of working for a living as is given the man in the urban area. . . . If these farmers will not borrow and cannot work, then it will devolve upon the counties to care for them and the counties are already carrying a very heavy burden and do not have funds sufficient for this purpose."[64]

In 1936 and 1937, there were a number of mass meetings in Western Kansas with resolutions forwarded to Topeka and Washington. At Scott City, in February 1936, four hundred farmers from twenty western counties passed thirteen resolutions, urging legislation that "will enable farmers to adjust supply and demand by legal means with something like the same effectiveness with which American industry adjusts supply and demand—but with provisions safe-guarding farmer control and also safeguarding consumer welfare against extending adjustment into scarcity."[65] In March 1937, a similar gathering of southwest Kansas farmers passed resolutions highlighting "the grave state of emergency" due to "continued wind soil erosion." Temporary measures, they wrote, were appreciated but inadequate:

> We know that the outside world is not fully awakened to the fact that our wind swept plains are a problem of vital importance to the whole United States, and that conditions are very rapidly becoming worse. These conditions may be best illustrated by comparing the great floods of the east to a man stricken with a violent illness, and the dust bowl to a man with cancer. The first action is swift, causes excitement and results are obtained immediately or forever lost. The latter action is just as dangerous and as sure of destruction as the first, if not properly handled.[66]

E. D. Cooper, a partner with large landowner John Baughman, urged drastic action "before the situation gets entirely beyond human power to control."[67] A land company owner at Elkhart wrote, "I have talked with many farmers and the situation is truly desperate in these parts, as a last resort the morale of the people is breaking, and of course you know the next thing these counties will be evacuated."[68] Members of the county commission reported: "Things in Haskell County are at a standstill."[69]

There was some moving out. In the 1930s, Kansas had a net loss in total population, the only decade in its history for which that was true.[70] Paul Sears published his classic *Deserts on the March* in 1935, suggesting that agriculture on the plains had been a bad ecological idea, and that the wages of hubris were now being gathered.[71] The 1936 Farm Security Administration film, *The Plow That Broke the Plains*, came to similar conclusions.[72] The prevailing opinion in Western Kansas, however, was that people would stick it out, and historians have confirmed that they largely did.[73] "There will be no exodus from the high plains. Dodge City, Garden City, Liberal and hundreds of other important towns will not revert to range. The high plains evolution cannot back track and if it could, the huge investments in these states would prohibit it. . . . The prairie folk have faith in the land no matter if it is restless. . . . Quitters don't build empires."[74]

But it might be literally whistling in the wind. Mamie Fay of Pratt wrote Clifford Hope in the spring of 1935: "This is an interesting tho' uncomfortable time to live. So many old-new plans are being tried again. These dust storms have gotten me almost scared. I can see now a thing that has always been a mystery to me and that is why there were no human remains in the dust buried cities of the old world." She thought Kansans were too independent to substitute "bread and butter" for principles. Still, "perhaps we are coming to the end of an age and the old earth has gotten tired of her position and is resting herself a little by shifting her position."[75]

A galling part of the general malaise was plagues of grasshoppers and jackrabbits. Some thought the latter were cute, but residents of the region cared for neither of the beasts, nor for their rapid reproduction rates and voracious appetites. Grasshoppers were present in over fifty species.[76] In Seward County, in the summer of 1936, hoppers covered the grounds and the walks and converged on all the greenery of the county.[77] At Scott City, they swarmed around electric lights, and pedestrians could not take a step without crunching the bodies on the sidewalk.[78] Sometime seagulls migrated to help, but the weapon of choice against hoppers was poison, which often had to be put out every few days.[79]

That could be dangerous, not only to birds and small children, but even to grown men. Fred Ficken, age twenty-nine, a resident of Gove County, was working on his car on a hot day in 1938 when he drank from what he thought was a water jug near the house. The grasshopper poison was odorless, and his first warning came when the acid burned his mouth. He spat violently, but some had already gone down his throat. He had studied chemistry, knew the antidote, and called for his mother and aunt to bring eggs and milk. He consumed half a dozen eggs and a large quantity of milk, vomiting several times. But the poison had penetrated his vital organs and it was a long way to town. The doctor noted that even one drop of the poison was fatal. The victim died on the operating table at Scott City.[80]

Far more publicized than grasshoppers were jackrabbits. They were the topics alternately of humor and scorn. On the one hand, there were funny postcards of "jackalopes" with antlers attached and of huge rabbits saddled and ridden away. Colby residents could joke that there was fear the rabbits would get together and attack a town.[81] Humorist Lee Larabee could talk about the man who lost his mules in a rabbit drive because people could not tell the difference between them and the enormous jacks.[82] On the other hand, statistics on how much rabbits ate, and observations that they were eating gardens and trees in towns, as well as any crop that emerged, were taken seriously.[83] Farmers, one wag quipped, had not raised a thing in two years: "Only the rabbits and Russian thistles have thrived."[84]

There had always been rabbit hunts. But the innovation at the beginning of 1935 was to institute enormous rabbit drives. Thousands of residents walked in lines to collect rabbits inside v-shaped fences erected at county expense and then waded in with clubs to dispatch the critters.[85] It seemed therapeutic to them, a "brand new sport," and a sort of bonding experience as well.[86] "Old and young men, women and children had lots of fun on these drives," wrote a reporter. "They were armed with sacks and clubs of various sorts and sizes, which were swung madly and at times hurled at the rabbits. The war whoops and yelling would increase when a rabbit tried to break the line."[87] Observers further east found this behavior bizarre.

The numbers both of hunters and the hunted illustrated the extent of the problem. There were 6,000 rabbits killed in a single drive around Garden City early in 1935, and that sort of take was not unusual.[88] There were several huge hunts. One at Dighton in February 1935 had 10,000 citizens killing between 30,000 and 50,000 rabbits.[89] There were 15,000 killed in one hunt near Scott City.[90] The granddaddy of them all, to be held near Kalvesta in March 1935 with an expectation of killing 100,000 rabbits in a day, was postponed so often by dust storms that the plan was abandoned.[91] A typical hunt, like the one at Gove City in January 1935, drew 2,000 people corralling about 2,500 rabbits.[92] Less than that result was considered a failure. Sometimes the carcasses sold for a few cents apiece to feed to hogs. One man at Great Bend tried turning the livers into a product, Ben Turner's Little Giant Fish Bait, at 25 cents a tin, but had few sales.[93] Usually the bodies were simply plowed under.[94]

Was it brutal? Not at all, said the locals:

Rabbit drive, Scott County, 1935 (courtesy of Wichita State University Special Collections)

Ten thousand Kansas farmers can't be wrong, although the families of 50,000 jackrabbits killed this week in the western part of the state might have the opposite point of view. . . . Kansas farmers have been chasing jackrabbits since plow shares first turned the virgin sod in days long since gone by. Fathers, sons and hired men still take to the war on a traditional enemy as a boy turns to the old swimming hole. These hardy descendents of sturdy race are not likely to abandon a favorite and useful pastime until the last jack has gone to his reward, neither he nor others of his kind to return to destroy the luscious grain.[95]

One local philosopher wrote that anyone who objected to clubbing rabbits to death should be told a thing or two. It might seem to someone who "has never been pestered by the furry scamps" that it was wrong to hit them, but when a woman's garden was scratched by chickens the normally mild-mannered woman would wring their necks with a vengeance and the family would have chicken for dinner. The rabbit was a similar fundamental threat to the farmer where he lived.[96] Reporting on a drive at Scott City, the local press commented it was "real sport" and also "excellent exercise extending from medium to violent, with the violent predominating. . . . War whoops of the weirdest nature rend the air. Clubs of all kinds and makes, some sandpapered down and finely finished, others roughly hewn from willow or hedge, are swung madly by the crusaders, as they urge the jacks on to the promised land."[97] If the humane society in Lawrence objected to their methods, why not have one huge last drive and push all the jacks to eastern Kansas where "people in the cities there can build pens and feed them."[98] Meanwhile it was suggested that people might mount horses and kill rabbits with polo clubs rather than broomsticks. It would be a fine thing for the Movietone News.[99]

The peak of the rabbit hunt mania seemed to be confined to the bleak spring of 1935, with much less publicity afforded to drives thereafter. Farmers reported that the drives did not seem to reduce the numbers much, and people complained they had not the leisure to form 20-mile-long lines and spend their Sundays marching around the countryside.[100] Rabbits died of starvation after a time, or suffocated from dust, as did the fish in the shallow streams.[101] Lawrence Svobida suggested in his Dust Bowl memoir that in 1936 the rabbits became too numerous for the drive method to be effective and the region turned to mass poisonings. Maybe the sport went out of it too, and it got to be grim work, this up-close killing. But newspapers and magazines covered the hunts while they lasted, and, like the unusual and atypical everywhere, served to characterize culture in the Dust Bowl.[102] "Kansas," a reporter wrote, "seems to have fallen heir to the unfavorable publicity concerning all sorts of plagues and afflictions."[103]

Pride was muted in Western Kansas, but it was still there—that "unconquerable spirit" so long talked of.[104] Residents were depressed and cursed their "God-forsaken country" and "hole of a town"—but resented their critics elsewhere and refused to move out.[105]

Even William Allen White came in for some drubbing when, in April 1935, he wrote an editorial about lazy people in Western Kansas. It might have taken courage to be a pioneer in that region, White commented, but it took very little work, either physically or mentally. "In any case, there is no logic or sense in maintaining [the Western Kansas farmer] at public expense, when both his dust storms and his occasional surplus crops constitute a public nuisance." Western editors called that a "gross misapprehension," and said they had little spare time to feel sorry for themselves.[106]

But with typical Kansas self-deprecation, they blamed themselves a little. They said that this time was a "check" and that in the long run it might be good:

> It struck us hard, we could not believe it. Someone else must stop, not us. We continued to grow grain, but what were we to do with it? The eastern manufacturers sold us the big machines. It was great to drive them, and we continued night and day until the bins were

full and there was no place to dump, then the crisis came. We still had the spirit of the pioneer and refused to hear. But nature stepped in and we were forced to stop and listen. It has been a bitter dose. For four years we charged and recharged and we will charge again. We have lost and lost again. Every time we have come back again with a more determined effort to go over the top and win. . . . The easterners liked our stories [of the dust storms] and we said a little too much. We could use a lot of government aid for our people and we poured on the power and gave the picture a bad looking front. We have suffered from our own folly. We have damaged our country with publicity of unpleasant things.[107]

The thing to do, wrote an editor at Hugoton, was to forget the New Deal agencies and get down to individual working out of salvation at one's home place. Kansas had always had winds, storms, and dust. Newspapers had always had people behind on their subscriptions, and the region had always had illusory booms. Underneath it was something unromantic, something day-to-day, that worked, and in that people should have "faith." A woman at Tribune noted, "We live in hopes even though we may die in despair." The land was still there. "It is all right to play, but business is not a plaything. To succeed you and I must think business, dream business, do business. We must work."[108] Whether "Black Friday" had been a real event or referred to Robinson Crusoe's servant did not matter: best to forget about it.[109]

The success of that approach would depend on realism and pragmatism, both of which were among the "stern lessons" that these times, and indeed the whole history of Western Kansas, should have taught. "We have to take things as they are and make the best of them," said a Tribune citizen in 1935. That, commented his local editor, was what had made the region work. "Western Kansas is such a great country because the people here have taken things as they are and have tried to do the best they can. There are certain facts or realities of nature and human beings that seemingly defy change. Many Western Kansas people realize this and do not waste time complaining, grumbling, and trying to butt down a stone wall with their heads." Things were not in a total funk. All they needed was rain.[110]

There was much comment about this regional attitude, which conditions had proved was no fluke. J. F. Jarrell, of the Santa Fe railroad, wrote, "The people who settled southwestern Kansas were pretty high-caliber folks," and their character seemed strengthened by adversity.[111] Similar sentiments came from Harold Duryea, who wrote a guest editorial in November 1935 for the *Southwest Daily Times* at Liberal:

One always runs the risk of being accused of lapsing into sentimental drivel when he begins to write enthusiastically of the courage and morals of a people who live cheerfully under the adverse circumstances of an economic depression such as we have witnessed in recent years, but the consistent high level of courage, good cheer, and freedom from bitterness which characterizes the disposition of the people of the southwest is so genuine that it can be written of at any length without bringing discredit upon those who appreciate it. . . . Surrounded by bigness they are lifted above pettiness and have large and enduring perspectives. Being able to see so far across the land, they are furnished with another dimension in vision which treats time in a manner proportionate to the space and they look ahead to developments which assure better things to come.[112]

There was a deep and abiding "sanity" about the place, foreign reporters often noticed. A dust storm could induce panic and create wild theories and talk of deserts. One eastern reporter wired back to New York the headline, "New Yorker Is Awed and Shocked in the Fog of a Dust Storm—Rides 200 Miles on Train through Blinding Murk That Chokes and Kills All Animal and Plant Life and Dunes and Ravages a Once Rich Land."[113] But local people had better balance. "Wind erosion can't be cured in thirty minutes," a reporter at Garden City wrote. "It will take more than a few rainy days to stop the dust storms. But it needn't take a century either."[114] The most common comment heard in those dark days of 1935 and 1936 on the Kansas High Plains was, "Won't it be fine if it rains?"[115]

The power of positive thinking, combined with self-discipline and realism, could indeed accomplish great things. At the bottom, Western Kansas set about waiting for and working for the turn—the glorious "next year" they were always imagining.

There are endless small examples. For example, Mary Dyck, living in Hamilton County in far western Kansas on a 1,200-acre farm, started a diary in 1936 when she was fifty-two years old.[116] Her comments written in the third person about "Mo," her name for herself, are down-to-earth and a guide for coping, devised by a woman of considerable strength and optimism. "South wind," she wrote in November, "dust flying considerable. . . . Baked Bread & Churned, was home all alone in after noon. Very blue & clowdy day fir Mo, her heart was busted. . . . Wind is singing a sad tune."[117] Or again: "Wind blew fierce all night long, whistled, sang sad tunes. . . . Doors

. . . banged, also squeeked most of the Night."[118] Mary had menopausal headaches, she used up hand lotion she could not afford, trying to keep her hands from cracking, and the static electricity in the air often interfered with the reception on her favorite radio programs.[119] But she insisted on enjoying "Betty and Bob" on the radio amid the darkest and dustiest days.[120] While she swatted stinging flies, she was also able to record and appreciate the fine days. And she kept fighting and cleaning and cooking. "Mo made 3 Pumpkin pies," she wrote in October 1938; "washed Lamp globes and cleaned house. She got the Cows milked & fed the calf and also took care of the Hens. . . . Bob [on the radio] kissed his Betty dear while being in her cell in jail."[121] Fiction and romance blended seamlessly with the everyday. When Hitler's speeches began to be broadcast in snippets on the radio, Mary could understand the German, but even that did not throw her.[122]

Others coped by the discipline of keeping farm accounts. Reading these in hindsight is rather pitiful. The Leslie Linville family lived in Logan County and received farm account books, at first from the Farm Bureau and later from the Farm Security Administration. There were eight in the family: Leslie, 34; Bertha, 34; Richard, 10; Walter, 9; Maxine, 8; Harold, 7; Louise, 6; Norman, 6. Their income was miniscule and their expenses equally so. In 1937, for instance, total farm expenses were $580.89, with a rather heavy $92.57 going to maintain their car, a 1934 Chevrolet coach. Household supplies were cut to the bone. That category amounted to only $1 to $3 a month, or $27.00 for the year. Food was $17 to $30 a month, or $281.53 a year for the family. Clothing was $58.86, broken down carefully by month. The personal expenditures category was only $12.64 for the entire year. They sold eggs for 13 cents a dozen, barley for 30 cents a bushel, and cream for a bit over 5 cents a pound. More usefully, they consumed products of their cows and hens and vegetables from their garden themselves and subsisted as rural people have for thousands of years. They were buying a cream separator in 1937 on time payments of $11 a month, and their income was not doing much for their debt. They owed $2,553 at the beginning of the year, almost $2,000 of that in Farm Security Administration loans, and $2,123.04 at the end of it. They had $40 in unpaid doctor's bills, $30 in past-due rent, and $40 in past-due interest. Their total household inventory was valued at $258, and they had a net worth of a bit over $1,000. And this was a fairly substantial farmer, with 365 acres of owned land planted to wheat, that magical cash crop of the 1920s.[123]

There was grudging appreciation of the federal presence. "Wheat allotment checks came in mighty handy during the past few years," wrote a Liberal newspaper in 1936.[124] By the time the constitutionality of the AAA was challenged in 1936, it had invested $2 million in Gray County and nearly the equivalent of that in many other Western Kansas counties.[125] When Franklin Roosevelt visited Kansas in October 1936, 15,000 people turned out to see him in Wichita, and a large crowd turned up for his twenty-minute train stop in Dodge City.[126]

Western Kansas, however, was not exactly rolling in wealth from federal sources. A Garden City newspaper estimated late in 1937 that twenty-seven western counties had received $44,479,670 from various federal programs, distributed over 183,297 square miles. When eastern newspapers drastically underestimated the population of this region at 23,000, it appeared that every person had gotten enough "to move to an expensive resort." That was an error. Actual population for the twenty-six westernmost and least populous counties in Kansas at that time was over 125,000. That would mean about $350 per person in federal spending up to 1937. "Still, it is a lot of money. We are grateful."[127] Simon Fishman of Tribune debated anti–New Dealer Dan Casement of Manhattan in 1936, arguing that, having lost markets, "we need a farm bill like a child needs its mother."[128]

There remained, however, a strong undercurrent of resentment at the bureaucracy and the dependence its existence implied. Price Davis of Liberal expressed the view of many when he wrote Clifford Hope in 1935 that farmers needed to farm, not be diverted into other sorts of relief programs such as building roads. "If everyone was put to work in the fields we would be getting something rather than importing a lot of stuff, sending money out of the county, and then printing more money." It was time, he said, to get the farmers "off this monkey business and back as self respecting citizens."[129] People were like animals in some respects, wrote another Hope correspondent. "You can crowd an animal about so far and have him cowed but if you go too far, he will resist and when he does, all H– can't put the fear in him."[130] The real cause of the Dust Bowl, wrote a third, "is the unnatural, insane, wasteful, God-defying policy of the RAW-Dealers . . . in buying off our farmers to *plow up* and *let be idle*, MILLIONS OF ACRES of productive Western farm lands. . . . LET THE FARMERS ALONE *to run their own business* is our prayer."[131] Mamie Fay of Pratt, one of Hope's constant and most articulate advisors, said that it was terrible for proud descendants of pioneers to have to take an oath of poverty to get a pittance from Washington. "The trifling, inefficient, careless are made wards of a paternal government," while the man suffering from circumstances beyond his control "but who still wishes to maintain his self respect must grovel for a job."[132] It was a shame, wrote a Sterling man, that "this good country of ours should be made to tolerate all these leeches and their foolishness." If crops were close to normal, Western Kansans "would be glad to tell the Government to mind its own business."[133]

The "junket method" of whirlwind visits by federal officials to the dusty region, hoping to manage it by "remote control," would not do. Wrote the *Dodge City Globe*: "That is the weakness of a government that shows a tendency to become more bureaucratic and centralized. Its contact with the people is not direct." There were too many outside agents coming from Washington:

> Every county seat has two or three and in the large towns the federal staff is larger than the county government. . . . This effort to project Washington into every farmstead in America has required a clerical routine that from the standpoint of red tape makes the army's military channels appear tapeless. . . . Running the farm from Washington is an expensive and doubtful method even if the men in charge of the new enterprise knew anything about it.[134]

There were regular complaints about each individual program. When the Civilian Conservation Corps camp near Dodge City complained about its people not being able to buy drinks in town, a regional editor characterized it as "a piece of audacity that goes beyond the intelligence of the average man. . . . Maybe the time has come when folks should be kicked out on their pants and compelled to hunt jobs as their daddies and granddaddies did!"[135] The resettlement program for moving people off marginal lands was called the most "asinine" of "countless silly, impractical ideas."[136] The shelterbelt plan of planting trees was characterized as "an alluring and expensive undertaking that under scrutiny proved impracticable." It was an example of a federal government that "is always on the way but so often doesn't know where it is going."[137] Nine Western Kansas counties voted down soil conservation districts when proposed in 1937.[138] Even the reorganized AAA received criticism. The farmer, said a Ness man, should not have to "swallow an AAA pill every time somebody tells him to."[139] There was discomfort about those who seemed to prefer farming the government to farming the land.[140] The New Deal, wrote a Western Kansas observer in 1939, had created a $40 million debt and "changed the whole complexion of this section. . . . If the people of Brownell, McCracken and Alexander could kidnap some of the government officials and hold them here until after a dust storm maybe things would be changed."[141] In 1936, Jess Denious wrote:

> The most active and vocal choristers of a new deal in social planning, agriculture and everything else are invited to look over in Ford county. . . . They've developed the Washington idea of suspended animation—they will not bat an eyelid until the document properly initialed, signed and sealed is delivered to them. . . . They've given

up trying to do anything on their own because they have discovered less trouble and worry in having the government do it.

It did not have to be that way. Western Kansas farmers were good conservationists, Denious wrote. Their self-interest dictated it. "We had good farming before congress started saving the farmer in mass production style."[142] Wouldn't it be grand if political "adjustment" would end and the region "would get up enough spunk to solve its own problems?"[143]

Clifford Hope, while sympathetic, disagreed with the more cynical assessment of government's role. He was not of the opinion that government owed everyone a living, nor did he support any form of socialism. But, he wrote in the dusty days of 1935, "there is no question that this thing is going to plague us for years to come and yet, frankly, I don't know what would have happened if we had not set up the relief system which has been in effect." Perhaps it could have been left to local initiative, "but our experience in Western Kansas . . . amply demonstrates that there are situations where the local governments cannot possibly meet the demands which are made for relief."[144]

There was solidarity, however, in responding to what were seen as unfair calumnies on the region. The film *The Plow That Broke the Plains*, made by filmmaker Pare Larentz as part of the attempts of Rexford Tugwell's Resettlement Administration to bring information to the American people, increased resentment against Tugwell and his ilk. Its portrayal of overambitious farmers creating a wasteland was seen by Western Kansas farmers as pure propaganda for Tugwell's resettlement program. "This film isn't a fair picture and will arouse resentment in the prairie area. Its purpose is to belittle the men and women who carved a grain growing empire in the southwest and by implication they are classed as freebooters."[145] Although they had to admit that Tugwell's "gloomy forebodings" just might come true eventually "unless intelligent action is taken to combat the effects of recurrent droughts," regional residents were more enthusiastic about the "farming machine," invented by C. T. Peacock of Arriba, Colorado, for conserving moisture than they were for resodding and resettlement.[146] Over 3,000 people, many from Western Kansas, made a pilgrimage to Peacock's farm in August 1936.[147]

The alternative theory in Western Kansas was that there had long been cyclic "dust bowls" and that the "chiseling hoofs and snorting tractors" were not responsible for this regional manifestation of Nature. It was necessary always to think in the long run, and "in the long run there is something to be said for the optimists." The farmer could not go against Nature. "He cannot get out of the Great Plains more than Nature has put in. If he tries to reap the fruits of a decade in a single year he runs the grave danger of ruining himself and his land." Still, if people would "season their optimism with science" and be patient, they need not abandon mechanized wheat farming as something the 1930s had proved impractical forever.[148] Hundreds attended a farm leaders' conference at Liberal in January 1937 with the purpose of creating "permanent stabilization" through responsible private action on scientific lines.[149] Tarzan, the ape man, was carrying out his funny paper exploits in 1937 in an airplane.[150] There was reason to believe that the farmer could adapt also to the promise and the limits of modernity.

Western Kansas responded to views that were uninformed or simplified in the press. A certain eastern reporter, junketing at the Dust Bowl in 1937, had "developed a queer attitude as to geography and peculiarities of geographical sectors," maybe dating back to the *Wizard of Oz* and the last great dust period. He was surprised. "Instead of finding wind whipped farmhouses teetering under the elements and pastures studded with the bleaching bones of starved cattle, he was amazed to see farmhouses, green wheat fields, paved highways, tree bordered lands, and small towns with busy stores and traffic snarls." His account was in contrast to that written by a *New York Times* reporter, who had published a "pernicious story" after having inspected the dust area from a Pullman window—he "dressed up the yarn with dramatic phraseology." It might be fun for readers to hear of great cracks in the earth and visibility less than a block. "His story was more colorful than the lamentations of a Hebrew prophet," a Dodge City editor wrote, but "he missed the facts almost every paragraph."[151] Maybe those who thought the desert had already obliterated Elkhart and was moving in on Liberal should visit the tractor shows in Western Kansas. Despite the tabloid reporting, "this vast farming region has not quit."[152]

Galling beyond most all other national pieces was the *Collier's* article of 1937, entitled "Land Where Our Children Die." That got response from editors all over the Plains, the most-quoted being the countereditorial in the *Amarillo Daily News*, entitled "Thou Shalt Not Bear False Witness." *Collier's* was known for distortion, the newspaperman said, but this article went the limit. It described people of the High Plains as "insane, drug addicts, parents of 'unnatural' children, given to homicidal fury especially during dust storms, racketeers, political beggars and thieves, hysterical cowards, and incompetent farmers." Drugstores supposedly ran out of sedatives after dust storms. This was "entirely fiction . . . and could have been made just as ghastly if he [the *Collier's* writer] had never left his own smug office."[153]

Congressman Hope, at a joint meeting of the Garden City civic clubs at the Hotel Warren, called Walter Davenport, the writer of the *Collier's* piece, "a first class liar. . . . It will be a long time before I believe anything I read in *Collier's* again."[154]

As sufferers from the dust of the 1890s had ruminated on the lessons that were learned, or should have been learned, from the excesses of the boom days of the 1880s, so sufferers in the 1930s harked back to the 1920s and even earlier to the "golden age" of the World War I years. And the lesson, now as then, was moderation. The region need not be so bipolar in its hopes and fears, only realistic in its expectations and chary of overblown promises—political, mechanical, social, or scientific. "Any man who has watched the ups and downs of Western Kansas entertains no illusions about that country," wrote an observer in Topeka. "It can never be made what is called a sure crop country, but if cultivated in the right way it will sustain a moderate population." There was no more reason to curse the wind than to try to empty an ocean with a spoon.[155] Wrote Secretary of Agriculture Henry Wallace in the spring of 1939: "The task of building and keeping the prosperity is the responsibility of the sound farmers who have stayed through prosperity and through hard times. They have learned their lesson and will not likely forget it."[156] There was hope that this cycle had passed and that it would be remembered. Wrote an editor in Colby in 1937: "The Devil is Sick."[157]

They worried, though. Many Western Kansas towns were in the mountain time zone, cut off by more than climate and culture, it seemed, from the rest of the state.[158] Consolidation of railroads, elimination of local lines, and the introduction of the diesel-electric locomotive eliminated many of the stops that had supported regional towns.[159] Some of the modern distractions backfired, too. A fourteen-year-old, Bobby Strouse, drowned in the Garden City municipal pool in 1937 when he got stuck in the heavy pressure of an outtake pipe. He and a friend wanted to know how it felt to go up into the pipe.[160] It was an awful thing, the local editor wrote, "terrifying even to think about," perhaps even worse than the dangers of the old swimming hole.[161] No one could foresee, of course, that Herbert Clutter, the county agent for Finney County in 1937, would in twenty years be murdered with his whole family in their farmhouse in rural Holcomb by drifters acting on a jailhouse rumor. Truman Capote's account, *In Cold Blood*, would forever disabuse readers of any security they felt about the small Western Kansas town where people could leave their doors unlocked.[162]

They did know times were changing—maybe for the better economically but never to return to the old ways. Santa Fe westbound number seven no longer stopped at Garden City. Instead it kicked off the mail "to an uncer-

Roadside cabins, Stockton, Rooks County, 1939 (courtesy of Wichita State University Special Collections)

tain fate," while racing by at full throttle.[163] Slower transcontinental trains and schedules disappeared, in favor of the California Limited, extra-fare, diesel streamliner set. The more leisurely trains were "sacrificed to speed," in a time when front-page news was of the 347 miles-per-hour done on the Bonneville Salt Flats and of innovations in big city society, which were aped all along the track.[164] Ultramodern chain stores sold groceries cheaper, and the old 1920s' concern about the decline of mom-and-pop, local-taxpaying stores had been muted as the protest wore out.[165] Great Bend's population was up 1,563 in one year between June 1937 and June 1938, signaling the end of the worst times.[166] What did it matter that people showed, as one Western Kansas editor noted, "A 12-Year-Old Intelligence," in panicking at the radio program "War of the Worlds?"[167] So what if a man dressed as Santa Claus drifted out to sea and died when parachuting from an airplane in a stunt?[168] The world was daffy over the racehorse Seabiscuit beating his archrival War Admiral, not the price of wheat.[169]

Then there was the war, coming inexorably and inevitably, pushing out the bit of local news that had not already been displaced by the fast-breaking domestic stuff from the Associated Press wire. With the whole of western civilization under threat, it hardly mattered, even to Western Kansans, that their form of rural, small-community, agricultural civilization was threatened too. It was happenstance, beside the point, as Hitler spewed invectives.

Area people were concerned about Hitler and the trends he represented. The *Hays Daily News* commented in the fall of 1938 that there was great tension. The masses of population had no grievances, but here was one man who was making the most of the media star system. The ambition of this man, "a onetime paperhanger, whose intelligence quotient rates low indeed, is about to embroil the world in a war on the outcome of which it is hazardous to speculate."[170] Early in 1939, people tracked and killed a "roving monster wolf" through the snow in the Saline River hills, a huge beast with a gray head and a black body.[171] Would that other threats that faced regional people were so direct and so easily countered.

In 1939, Hollywood came to Dodge. It was an event devotedly desired by the people there, a direction they had been heading, in their concern with tourism as a business, for a decade or more. Warner Brothers shot a few scenes of its epic *Dodge City* in the actual Western Kansas environs of the historical events upon which this film was loosely based. Dodge promoters convinced the studio to hold the world premiere of the movie at Dodge City, and the town went all out to make the most of it. "One must certainly hand it to Dodge City," wrote rival Hays. "It certainly has capitalized on its early-day period when it was a hang-out for card sharps and a sprinkling of bad men. Tourists may see, free, of course, a bogus graveyard at the edge of the business center of the city where no dead men lie buried. There once was a 'boot hill' at Dodge but it was too inconveniently located for 'historical' purposes."[172] The Great Bend newspaper editor said, tongue in cheek, that he could not wait "to see 2 gun Jess Denious with a flowing beard and in chaps, sombrero boots and spurs." The studio built a brand-new Front Street for Dodge City at a cost of $57,000. It was three blocks long, and there was a lot of sentiment in Dodge for purchasing it after the filming was done and substituting it for the much-changed original.[173]

Forty film personalities showed up for the premiere. People in the town grew beards, and an estimated 100,000 people from the area thronged the streets of Dodge City.[174] *Life* magazine covered it.[175] Editor Denious wrote that no real event of the cowboy day "was strong enough to project into the moving picture era."[176] "The glamour school has no standing in strict history," but it was good for the tourist business.[177] History had to be spectacular to compete with present-day events.[178] There was a perceived need to put "more punch into our historical background."[179] The Technicolor *Wizard of Oz* appeared the same year, and, though editor Rolla Clymer of the *El Dorado Times* was livid about the distortions of Kansas in that film, the papers in Hutchinson suggested that it was fun being kidded about those myths.[180] The premiere of the movie, *Dodge City*, took place on April Fools' Day, 1939.

The World Premiere at Dodge City, 1939 (courtesy of Kansas State Historical Society)

Nature could still be mean, it seemed—with drought and flood alternating. On the morning of August 18, 1938, the problem on the Rock Island railroad bridge over the Cimarron River near Arkalon, Kansas, was flood. The fast freight, "Gold Ball," pulling a train of twenty-nine cars, plunged off the damaged bridge that morning and into the river, killing only one but throwing a considerable scare into the railroad and into area residents.[181] The spectacle of huge engine 5036 crashing, in the middle of the night, into swollen waters, despite electric signals and the most modern equipment, was terrifying.[182]

The solution was reassuring, although it came from afar. The railroad, already recovered from the Depression and long frustrated by the several crossings of the unpredictable Cimarron, proposed immediately to employ 300 men to build a $1.4-million steel bridge, the like of which had never before been seen in Western Kansas.[183] When it was dedicated in March 1939, the "Streamline Bridge," mounted on four art deco concrete pillars, was a wonder indeed.[184] There were five steel spans, each 255 feet long, which allowed trains to pass over the river at a height of 100 feet above the water, without even slowing down.[185] Shortly it got the nickname, "Samson of the

Cimarron." Even in rusting ruin at the approach of a new century, it remained something to behold.

"Who Said They Never Come Back?" went a 1939 headline at Liberal. "Farmers Have Joined Together in a Great Fight, and Have Won over Dust and Drought."[186] A few days later came the headline "Land That Was Robbed Forgives and Forgets."[187] The year 1938 had been a relatively good one. "During 1938 we have all worked, we have planned, we have eaten more or less regular meals and had somewhat near sufficient sleep." Western Kansas, one sloganeer put it, was "The Land of Now." Even more so, residents thought, it was the land of tomorrow, of next year or the year after. People had learned to remember, and not so much with nostalgia as with selective pragmatism—they had been through "the toughest years" and had found hope intact:

> It is the land of eternal hope. A few who have weakened, who have lost hope, who have ceased to thrill at the vast possibilities of this country, have gone. But many more have come to take their places. Many more, who will carry on the traditional attitude of faith, the traditional outlook of hope. And therein lies the secret of the happy years. . . . For happiness is largely a state of mind, and if the attitude and outlook are wrong, no set of outside circumstances, regardless of how ideal, can bring happiness.[188]

Western Kansas, wrote a resident of Hays, had been in a war, maybe since the first settlers moved to that semiarid region, but certainly since the middle 1920s, and most certainly in the dusty thirties. The world war approaching could bring the worst of times and the best of times for the region. It could be an economic boom, as World War I had been. Residents could not foresee the vast airfields that would come to the High Plains for bomber training during the war, but they could well enough predict an increase in wheat prices that would be a wonderful concomitant to the increasing rainfall of a turning weather cycle. They were gamblers. They had been and they would be. Maybe perfect security would be the greatest bore of all. "Gambling on a war may seem like a sordid business," one analyst wrote, "but the farmer himself, it is well to keep in mind, is fighting a war for his own existence and his fight for a right to live, in the final analysis, is on a par with that of great masses of people in European nations who are destined to live or die in their struggle for self-preservation."[189] Jess Denious commented that, in a day when security seemed to be the holy grail of economic quest, no matter how extravagant the price, the durability of the prairie folk may commend study. The hard winter wheat area is carrying on without lamentation or undue pessimism. . . . No one will say that business is as good as normal because it is far from that but no one can say truthfully that the Southwest has thrown in the towel. The battle goes on under inconvenient circumstances it is true but the battle goes on. [Western Kansas was built by] determined men and women . . . leaders in every line who refuse to take the path of discouragement. Such an area is certain to survive and do great things and to reap larger harvests.[190]

Western Kansas had, wrote William Allen White, always been an interesting place, filled with "raw courage" and individualism. It would be wonderful if someone would write a book about it, he said, but unfortunately the constant struggle, the "grim fight" to keep a footing, left little time for recorded reflection.[191] Seven years of drought, wrote the editor at Hays, "and trials that torture the souls of men and women only spur Western Kansas on to greater efforts. Its people know better days will come. Until then, they will take their beatings standing up and without flinching."[192]

Conclusion:
A Harvest of Understanding

Western Kansas, wrote secretary F. D. Coburn of the State Board of Agriculture in 1911, had been "persistently misunderstood and misrepresented by those unacquainted with it." Some living within the region, as well as many outside it, had "brought themselves to believe it is a wide expanse of desolation without any future of consequence." Coburn, however, felt that the region had "scarcely started toward the useful destiny it will meet" when newcomers learned the lessons pioneers had already absorbed about adaptation and patience.

"It takes time," he wrote, "to develop a country, especially when new and strange conditions are encountered. . . . While western Kansas is admittedly different from other localities having greater rainfall, the fact that it is different is neither to its discredit or detriment. Each region has its uses much as each individual who finds he has his niche." There was one fact, Coburn wrote, "that looms as conspicuously as a piece of black court plaster on a fair woman's face," and that was that people who had been in Western Kansas for years were at least comfortable financially and not rarely wealthy. He thought that was because they had patience and open minds and were "conducting their affairs in the ways best calculated to bring returns each year, regardless of the season."[1]

Adaptation was a constant theme from the start and returned to at each crisis. "We have tried to beat nature out there for twenty years," a Topeka editor said of Western Kansas in 1897,

> and at the show down nature has always held four aces while the settler has exhibited a diminutive pair of deuces.

It is time to let common sense have a show. All talk about putting all that country under irrigation, or half of it, or even a tenth part of it, is attenuated moonshine, and on the other hand the man who waits for the climate to change, and the rain belt to move west to Colorado, will still be waiting when the angel, standing with one foot on the Gulf of Mexico and the other on the abandoned additions to Wichita, shall proclaim . . . "That time was, time is, but time shall be no more." If the people of western Kansas will follow nature instead of entertaining a fool notion that they are smarter than she is, the problem will be nearly solved and that section of the state will enter on an era of permanent prosperity with a firm grip on the tail of destiny.[2]

There was a strong element in the region of what English poet Edmund Spenser had called "Mutability." Change was a feature of all human life. But most everyone is uncomfortable with violent and sudden change, change that gives no time to adjust, nor obvious reason to try. Western Kansas taught the lessons of mutability more clearly than most places, since it was not obviously or consistently one kind of place or another. The weather could be devilish to the point of profanity one day, with winds that residents joked "blew the cistern out of the ground."[3] The next day might break so achingly lovely that Plains towns could imagine themselves as health resorts. The mutability by days was echoed in the mutability by decades and by centuries, and, if the dendrochronologists, paleontologists, and geologists are to be trusted, by millennia. Living was good in the good years, one man recalled later, but, unfortunately, good years came on an average of one out of three or four years. When the bad years contributing to the "average" piled up in succession, "the homestead family was in serious trouble."[4]

Amid such variation, there is always the natural human desire for stability, for control. That natural desire was regularly enhanced by the introduction of brand-new elements—mechanical, agricultural, economic, political—into the mix. It was like the old joke about the economics professor, who, when asked why he never modified his exams, said that he kept the same questions but from time to time changed the answers.

A country like Western Kansas—filling up in a latter day and puffed up with the pride of the modern—might be excused for being badly fooled by Nature, even repeatedly. It might be excused for being optimistic about the next time, to the point of bullheadedness. Wrote one who penned essays to describe it: "It is a beautiful country—an embryonic poem—a picture still lacking a few delicate touches—a romance with the last chapter yet unwritten—gorgeous in its native grandeur, but destined to be more beautiful when time, and the conscious energies of the people, shall have solved the mighty problems of its higher and more perfect civilization."[5]

Perhaps those early pioneers whose dreams had come crashing down had just been unlucky—or overreached their limited powers a little. After all, they did not have electric pumps, and automobiles, and diesel engines, and combines, and power farming, and oil and gas fields, and state experimental farms, and regional colleges, and local cantatas, and a host of other things the twentieth century brought. And perhaps even the reverses of the twentieth century were the result of accidental, temporary factors or just bad luck, rather than a fundamentally flawed approach. Perhaps in the long run the faithful would be rewarded for applying the lessons of civilization to the shortgrass. "Pays Better Than Being an Indian," a long-time resident commented in 1903.[6]

But there was no guarantee that the artificial world would remain—would be allowed to remain—just because determined people had laid it down. A writer at Liberal in far southwest Kansas explained in 1898 that children needed to be educated about the bumpy rides of recent history or they would believe that "like the sky, the creek, the graveyard hill, the town was 'always there,' and never did begin."[7] Or, it might be added, lest they believe it never could end.

Western Kansas changed dramatically between 1890 and 1940, and there are critics who think the change was for the worse. But whether it is called progress or nonsustainable illusion, the pattern that developed was not the result of theory but of practice—not the imposition of Nature solely, nor the hubris of humans. Rather it was the result of interaction between human civilization and the dictates of Nature over several prairie weather cycles and through national developments of significant import.

An example is the emergence of wheat as the dominant crop. People in the region and state were not unaware of the potential problems of monoculture. The constant suggestions to practice diversified farming and the regular and deep suspicions of large-scale and corporate commercial wheat farmers were not too different in tone in 1910 from that of critics of the decline of the self-sufficient family farm and the destruction of rural community in 2005. The "dam the draws" and dry farming advocates of the early twentieth century certainly presaged the environmental, minimum-impact thinkers of recent times. The advocates of large-scale irrigation, on the other hand, shared much with high capital, high-tech, big government thinkers who are still active in proposing agricultural solutions globally. They too proposed alternatives to wheat—alfalfa, potatoes, sugar beets, truck gardening.

Dryland farming was widely adopted. Sugar beets and irrigation gained some purchase. Government subsidy did become permanent. However, every alternative to wheat as a dominant crop failed, and the failure worked itself out in history and in economics. People, however visionary they may be in the short term or as individuals, are highly practical in the long term and en masse. History imposes what in modern slang would be called a "reality check," and it does it not in months or over millennia, but in the decades that constitute the change in generations living in a region.

The lesson on farming in twentieth-century Western Kansas was that one should farm wheat, and mostly dryland wheat. This choice was tested over and over, through the vagaries of weather, market, science, and technology—decade after decade. Wheat always survived and its scope always expanded. It was never before or since as profitable as in the World War I "golden age." However, even in the Dust Bowl, it was wheat that worked—hybrid wheat maybe, farmed on a larger scale with machinery—but still wheat.

Western Kansas lost much of its autonomy over the years of the early twentieth century. But that was not something wholly imposed but rather partly chosen by residents who were tired of being thought of and thinking of themselves as isolated rural hayseeds. Regional residents wanted automobiles, and combines, and radios, and colleges, and waterworks, and telephones, and mail order goods, as much as foreign corporations wanted to provide them. They did not relish being on the "edge of the world" and were as influenced by consumer culture and by the desire for money profits and what they would buy as anyone else. It can be argued that it is urban academics who are most nostalgic for the prairie, the old-time farm, and rural town life, especially when they do not have to face the diphtheria epidemics, experience the boredom, or smell the manure. Western Kansas people in the twentieth century agreed with the concept of "industrial farming," loved to use mechanical power in their work to make it both more efficient and easier, and accepted enthusiastically the idea that farming was or should be a business, not a folkway.

One could say there was a battle between centralization and decentralization and that centralization prevailed. Western Kansas farmers could rant about the tax-eaters and good roads advocates in Topeka. They could talk about secession. They could vote Populist. But these bright colors of regional individuality faded in the great wash of standardization and lost out to the advantages of conformity.

There has been plenty of criticism of these trends from academics and analysts, particularly pointing out the dire impact of overexpansion, high capital, and dependency. Deborah Fitzgerald, in her study of the industrial ideal in 1920s agriculture, speaks of an imposed pattern of modernism that was based on an analogy that did not apply well to farming. She characterizes the transition in technical and scientific innovation in farming— the arrival of tractors, hybrid seeds, pesticides, and electrification on the twentieth-century farm—as "often unnerving." When a farmer bought a tractor, "he tacitly adopted a host of other practices and entered into a new set of relationships." These relationships made him less self-sufficient than before. Industrialization also required "recalibration" of a host of relationships among families and communities. It connected farmers with bankers, college professors, and good roads advocates, distant both geographically and culturally, in a new way. "In general," she points out, "the process of industrialization was promoted not by the artisans themselves, but by the financiers and business owners whose interests were primarily economic." Standardization, mechanization, and scale were the key, and agriculture by 1910 "was beginning to look like the last great nest of chaos in American productive enterprise."[8]

Hal Barron has a similar take on the broader social impact. "The emergence of large-scale organizations and the centralization of power" in the rural Midwest in the early twentieth century, he writes, was paralleled by "the expansion of a consumer economy and the development of a consumer culture," which affected farmers by challenging "their identities as producers and their assumptions about the moral superiority of rural life by introducing new standards of value that were defined and embodied in material possessions that emanated from and reflected urban culture."[9]

Such thinking goes back to the Kansas Populists of the 1890s. William Peffer wrote, in his 1891 book, *The Farmer's Side: His Troubles and Their Remedy*, that there was an irony in the fact that the industrialized farm had not seemed to benefit the farmer as much as others. "He plows and sows and reaps with machines. A machine cuts his wheat and puts it in a sheaf, and steam drives his threshers. He may read the morning paper while he plows, and sit under an awning while he reaps." Yet dust and depression damaged him still, as always.[10]

The outlook of avoidable exploitation is common too among contemporary observers of the Kansas agricultural and political system. Wendell Berry and Wes Jackson, both of whom have deep experience with Kansas, regard modern commercial agriculture as a nonsustainable disaster and see its precursor changes as mistakes. Naturally, the Kansas Farm Bureau, the

Kansas Chamber of Commerce, and the average Rotary speaker at luncheon meetings across the state see things differently. As has been made clear, I have a foot in both camps. My family has owned wheat farms in Western Kansas, has bought and sold wheat farms there, and has even been an agent for eastern capital in making those sometimes burdensome, sometimes helpful, mortgage loans. Yet I am a professor, too, and a part of that cosmopolitan perspective. Ultimately, however, conclusions should not be a matter of background or philosophy any more than of race or religion. They should follow from communicated research, though they may not exhaust the possibilities or even adequately characterize the significance of the historical facts for every reader.

It is often argued that the economic benefits are not worth the social costs. Thomas Frank, in his 2004 best-selling book, *What's the Matter with Kansas?*, could talk about Garden City, a land out of the range of his cell phone, as the center of a kind of third-world country. It was "the other end of the world," where they did not have a Dean & DeLuca deli as graced Overland Park, hard on Kansas City. He argues, "There are ranchers aplenty but few rugged individualists out here anymore; today Garden City and Dodge City are caught on the steel hooks of economic logic as surely and as haplessly as are the cows they hack so industriously apart." He complains about how slaughterhouses "routinize" and de-skill work, everything driven by cost, while the countryside is a "showcase of industrialized agriculture," characterized by "gigantic rolling irrigation devices" rather than "picturesque old windmills." It was a place full of trash, he thought, a "post-Apocalyptic suburb of death," and nearly devoid of people except for low-wage immigrants.[11]

The "steel hooks of economic logic" is a happy phrase, if a bit pejorative. Some of what Frank observes in Garden City belongs to a later period than this book, when the feedlot, re-decentralized packing, and the corporate hog farm were the panaceas to save Western Kansas from redesertification and depopulation. But they were just the latest manifestations of a familiar challenge-and-response dance with Nature, which was at base characterized by the balanced common sense for which Kansans were known. Like the earlier changes, these were grafted onto an already sound enough economy as a hoped-for supplement, not as a replacement for the ubiquitous wheat farmer. Every spate of new-style development in Western Kansas since the 1860s has been accompanied by controversy—and followed by a drought and depression and by suggestions that the area was through and should be returned to grass, the bison, or the Indians. It was all a familiar refrain to the families of the pioneers. Perhaps someday it would be true. But perhaps also there would come the "next year" utopia of which they had so long dreamed. Meanwhile, there was a living to be made in that place.

The "man from Thomas County," who became wealthy after sticking it out through the poor years and adding to his property, was both an icon and a reality. To pay for land in Western Kansas with a single wheat crop was by no means rare. It happened, and it happened not just to a few, here and there, or once in a while. A person willing to take a reasonable risk had a genuine chance to win in Western Kansas. Despite reverses, the region usually thrived economically and often produced beautifully, which was a pleasure in any market. As much of the world starved, there was pride in being one of the greatest food-producing regions in the world.

Harry Mason, in his memoir of Western Kansas, *Life on the Dry Line*, thinks that perhaps there was a class division involved with progressive attitudes. "Farmers who were oriented toward the town life, that is, who felt more fulfilled in a suit than in overalls, were more likely than others to concentrate on winter wheat as a crop, relegating egg gathering, milking and other barnyard enterprises to women." Be that as it may, he reports that most people in his region were "captives of the American Dream. That dream, in WaKeeney, was to be realized by planting and harvesting progressively larger acreages of hard red winter wheat." The contemporary critics worried, Mason wrote in 1994, that farms were becoming factories. Strange that they should notice so late. "The farm has been becoming a factory for a long time."[12]

There was moving out at some times. The 1890s and the 1930s had almost equal regional percentages of outflow, corresponding with a peak in media rhetoric about return to the desert and the need for grass and diversified farming. There was moving in at others, in fact in every other decade before 1940, and it was no coincidence that there were in these times a great many machinery ads and new hybrid varieties of wheat. While some southwestern Kansas counties lost 20 to 50 percent of their populations in the dusty decades, landowners even then were much more likely to stay than tenants. And these counties gained 100 to 300 percent in population in the recovery decade of 1900–1910. They were, Riney-Kehrberg observes, people with "rising expectations," to whom it was "easy to speak in terms of prospects rather than limitations." They had, one of them pointed out, a "stubborn adaptability."[13]

No matter how many successful dissertations, articles, and books may be based on contrary assumptions, the conclusion of this regional history must be that change in history is not sudden, coming on the wings of a fresh book or a new president, nor is it uniform nationally or even statewide. People are not prescient. They can therefore be—and are—swallowed up in unexpected reverses. But neither are they reckless with the basis of their living. They are slow and cautious when moving into the unknown, and the line forward is never a "straight" one. The fierce intracounty struggles that a narrow focus can reveal show the tenuousness of generalizing even about a subregion like Western Kansas and warn how easy it is to be led astray by confusing word with deed, law with practice, or one place with another.

The long view and big picture perspective of Geoff Cunfer in his 2005 book, *On the Great Plains: Agriculture and Environment*, applies here. Cunfer has used census data and GIS mapping to show land use on the Great Plains over more than a century. One of his detailed case studies is of Rooks County, Western Kansas. In a nutshell, his conclusion is that whatever the cultural atmosphere, the technology, or the politics of the moment, in the long run, people do not manipulate or control Nature on the Great Plains. It chastens them and restricts them. And, over many spaces and individual stories, land use is consistent and sustainable. There was stability between 1920 and 2000, when it can be argued that the experimenting was done and the education had taken place. In other words, Great Plains residents have been environmentalists on purpose or in spite of themselves, because that is the only way to survive there. There has been a pattern of "embrace and farewell," as ideas and people come and go, but the basics, so mutable in the short term, have a kind of immutability in the long term with which no one can tamper fundamentally.

The lessons are matters of fact and unavoidable. That Lawrence Svobida failed at wheat farming in Meade County had more to do with Meade County than with Svobida as a farmer or the 1930s as an era. Meade County, Clark County, and the Gypsum Hills of Barber County are mostly in grass in the twenty-first century, just as are the extensive Flint Hills area in eastern Kansas. All these were farmed for small grains once, but weather and economics taught that their best use was pasture. Wrote an editor at Hutchinson in 1931: "Farmers, for all the cries of the commentators, are still pretty independent and will plant just about as much wheat as they think is wise from an income standpoint."[14] He added that it was clear that "after digesting these endless arguments and parading panaceas," the proper use of the land was "still a problem for each individual farmer out where the plow is handier if not mightier than the spoken word."[15]

Scholars can agree on that pragmatic learning process and its real stakes. Elliott West applies Liebig's law to the Plains, namely that whether the resident be a nomadic Indian or a power farmer, there are limits imposed by the environment at its most challenging over a period of decades. All are fooled temporarily by mutability, but all learn in the end, or leave, or die.[16] "Agriculture," Cunfer writes, "is the central realm in which human beings negotiate daily with the living and nonliving forces of the environment." That negotiation becomes their history.[17]

People in Western Kansas did often arrive with certain inappropriate cultural assumptions. They also loved their region and thought of farming as a romantic folkway as well as a business. "The harvest is the thing," wrote one observer watching it in 1931, just as it had always been.

> Drive out into the country at dusk and see the golden fields, enclosed in the graceful black frame that is made by the cottonwoods around a field's edge, all topped with a dome that is as peaceful a blue as exists anywhere in the world. Look at these fields, half close your eyes, relax, drink in their beauty. Then, try to think of the Federal Farm Board and International Wheat Conference. Just try to think of them.[18]

That romance was a part of the famous regional stubbornness and optimism, but then there was the voice of pragmatism and experience along beside. They did learn things. It is the continuity of the past that makes history useful to planning and can make it a sound support to the otherwise forlorn. Western Kansans particularly learned lessons from unusually good times, like the 1880s boom and the 1914–18 golden age, followed by unusually bad times, such as the dust bowls of the 1890s and the 1930s.

Newspapers reflected extensively on these lessons of the lovely days mixed with the hard knocks, and the main reflections were of patience, hope, and temperance. "Those people who have lived on the prairie for any length of time," wrote Helen Havely Fowler of Dodge City in 1930, "quite often confess a great fondness for that prairie, for if the dominant impression of the mountains is vividness, that of the prairie is serenity." But the peace was not the peace of the dead, but of the optimistic:

> In every way the prairie seems to partake of the prodigious and illimitable. It seems to be in touch with immeasurable things; it is prodigal in all its doings; it can help feed the whole world. . . . The prairie dreams of future wonders of convenience, beauties, and bounties for her children. . . . The prairie has the wisdom and tolerance of age and the charm of youth. It seems to find nothing to make a commotion about.[19]

The high prairie environment gave dignity to the sufferings and strivings of its inhabitants. It connected them with the elemental and the ancient, whether they looked down in the day or up at night. These people were determined in a biblical sense to bring order out of chaos and not to be dominated by senseless plants or dumb animals. But they perceived too that excess pride went before a fall, and that the overextended were easily cut off.

They were not gullible, or some exotic breed. One of the attractions of the region is that even its severest critics regard it as a kind of heartland, as typical America. If people in Western Kansas were excited by machines in 1910, or turned toward Washington in the 1930s, it did not make them unique. They shared much with other Americans of their time—sharing more and more as the twentieth century with its mass media evolved—but they always put a distinctly local twist onto these translations to their ground. They were foolish and wise, strong and weak, alternately and at the same time. Yes, a mob of two hundred took a fifty-three-year-old man out of the Cheyenne County jail at St. Francis, in the spring of 1932 and hanged him to a tree. He had confessed to strangling eight-year-old Dorothy Hunter, and some were not going to wait for the judicial process, any more than they had in 148 previous lynchings in Kansas.[20] But the lynchers drove cars and could repair a tractor or follow the wheat export market. And they were as determined about their own proper destiny as they were convinced of the fate that must meet the "degenerate." They made choices and they lived with the consequences. "The story of the development of Western Kansas," said a writer for *Kansas Farmer* in 1928, looking back over recent history,

> is one of the most dramatic in history. It is a story of great adventure, of blasted hopes, of magnificent courage, of mingled idealism, selfishness and dishonor, or roseate dreams unfulfilled, of bright prospects of happiness and financial success suddenly changed to darkness and despair. It is a story of mingled comedy and tragedy; of the building of the structure of modern civilization, but a structure marred by corruption, blackened by the soot of shame and splotched with human blood.[21]

People learn the wrong lessons and are fooled, but usually not a second time. They can be stubborn but seldom foolish, hopeful but not crazy. Reverses, especially when they could be carefully studied and the direction appropriately modified, were not a reason to give up the entire enterprise. Wrote an editor in Ellis County in 1925: "We are a great family striving for a higher destiny."[22]

In 1936, an editor in Tribune talked about the influence of the drought on the regional character in a way that could apply as well to the whole historical experiment in the region. Hopes of rain, he said, had not been realized, but "hope, faith, and courage are not destroyed, no matter how stark, naked, elemental and cruel the drouth may make things appear." Challenges, when they did not destroy, made those people who were temperamentally suited stronger—to strike out, to conquer "again and again, no matter what adversities may confront them." When one caught "the pattern of the whole thing," it was "amazing." Unusual climate in Western Kansas had attracted and bred unusual people, "fearless" people, "who will go on plowing, sowing, and in time harvesting golden grain being richly repaid for past hardships and disappointments. And when there is no grain, crops shrivel under a scorching sun, and cattle become lean as they vainly seek feed, there is a harvest of understanding, sympathy, courage and abiding faith. Yes it is a great country."[23]

Notes

Preface

1. Speech of Jess Denious to Kansas Author's Club, n.d. [1939], Jess Denious Papers, box 14, Kansas State Historical Society (hereafter KSHS).

2. *Ness County News*, Jan. 5, 1895.

3. *Walnut Valley Standard*, quoted in *Garden City Herald*, Apr. 27, 1895.

4. *Dodge City Daily Globe*, Dec. 26, 1935.

5. Otto Trevelyan, *The Life and Letters of Lord Macauley* (2 vols.; New York: Harper and Bros., 1877), 1: 99.

6. Orientation is best found by referring to Homer Socolofsky and Huber Self, *Historical Atlas of Kansas* (Norman: University of Oklahoma Press, 1972). The most useful map here is no. 2, entitled "Latitude and Longitude of Kansas." Good reference sources for obscure towns are Robert W. Baughman, *Kansas Post Offices, May 29, 1828–August 3, 1961* (Topeka: Kansas State Historical Society, 1961), and John Rydjord, *Kansas Place Names* (Norman: University of Oklahoma Press, 1972).

7. *Globe-Republican* (Dodge City), Nov. 25, 1892; *Hays City Sentinel*, Dec. 6, 1892.

8. *Ashland Clipper*, Nov. 7, 1912.

9. See William Least Heat-Moon, *PrairyErth* (Boston: Houghton Mifflin Company, 1991), for a good example of what can be done with an intensive study of a single Kansas county.

10. Pamela Riney-Kehrberg, ed., *Waiting on the Bounty: The Dust Bowl Diary of Mary Knackstedt Dyck* (Iowa City: University of Iowa Press, 1999), 24.

Introduction: Blood Ties

1. *Ness County News*, May 12, 1928.

2. Ibid., Aug. 8, 15, 1896.

Chapter 1. Foreclosed

1. See Thomas Averill, "Oz and Kansas Culture," *Kansas History* 12 (Spring 1989): 2–12. For the debate among historians on the significance and symbolism of the book, see

Ranjit Dighe, ed., *The Historian's Wizard of Oz: Reading L. Frank Baum's Classic as a Political and Monetary Allegory* (Westport, Conn.: Praeger, 2002).

2. *Wichita Eagle* in *Ness County News*, Dec. 28, 1889.

3. White editorial in *Emporia News*, Aug. 19, 1895, in Russell Fitzgibbon, ed., *Forty Years on Main Street* (New York: Farrar and Rinehart, 1937), 73.

4. *Ness County News,* Apr. 20, 1889.

5. Ibid., June 22, 1889.

6. Ibid., July 13, 1889. For a fuller description, see Craig Miner, *West of Wichita: Settling the High Plains of Kansas* (Lawrence: University Press of Kansas, 1986), 227–29.

7. See, for example, *Ness County News*, Oct. 5, 1889.

8. Ibid., Aug. 30, 1890.

9. Ibid., July 25, 1891.

10. Thanks to Ben Hruska, a graduate student at Wichita State University, for compiling these overall figures. Huber Self, *Environment and Man in Kansas: A Geographical Analysis* (Lawrence: Regents Press of Kansas, 1978), 83. Detailed county population statistics may be found in the *Biennial Reports of the Kansas State Board of Agriculture,* published by the Kansas Department of Agriculture, Topeka, through these years. Absent these compilations, the finest tuning one could do would be to use a combination of federal and state census data, which provides material only every five years (1885, 1890, 1895, 1900) and therefore misses both the 1887–1888 population peak for most of these counties and the 1897–1898 trough.

11. *WaKeeney World* in *Alliance Echo* (Sharon Springs), Aug. 1, 1890.

12. *Colby Free Press*, Jan. 2, 1890.

13. An example at Atwood is described in *Hays City Sentinel*, Dec. 5, 1893.

14. *Hays City Sentinel*, quoted in *Western Times* (Sharon Springs), Aug. 17, 1893.

15. *Oberlin Herald* in *Colby Free Press*, Sept. 11, 1890.

16. *Lawrence Gazette* in *Hays City Sentinel*, Nov. 6, 1894.

17. James Humphrey and others to Lyman Humphrey, Jan. 17, 1891, Lyman Humphrey Papers, 27-05-02-05, KSHS.

18. Mrs. E. R. Holloway to Lyman Humphrey, Jan. 18, 1891, ibid., 25-05-03-05.

19. J. D. Smith to Lyman Humphrey, Feb. 20, 1892, ibid., 27-05-02-04.

20. T. S. O'Blenis to L. E. Lewelling, July 1, 1894, Lorenzo Lewelling Papers, 27-05-04-06, KSHS.

21. *Colby Free Press*, Sept. 1, 1892.

22. *Topeka Daily Capital*, Nov. 28, 1893, in County Clippings files, Scott County clippings, KSHS, vol. 1.

23. Mrs. Susan Orcut to L. D. Lewelling, June 29, 1894, Lorenzo Lewelling Papers, 27-05-04-06, KSHS.

24. *Colby Free Press*, June 7, 1894.

25. *Hays City Sentinel*, Sept. 4, 1894.

26. *Alliance Echo* (Sharon Springs), Apr. 10, 1891.

27. W. O. Meier in *Alliance Echo* (Sharon Springs), Feb. 6, 1891.

28. *Western Times* (Sharon Springs), Mar. 25, 1891, quoting *Russell Record*.

29. Ibid., Apr. 8, 1891.

30. Memoirs of Bonnie Bailey Vaughn, *Scott City News-Chronicle*, Apr. 28, 1960, County Clippings files, Scott County clippings, KSHS, vol. 1.

31. *Western Times* (Sharon Springs), Mar. 10, 1892.

32. Ibid., May 3, 1892.

33. Vaughn memoirs, May 26, June 2, June 9, 16, 23, Aug. 25, 1960, County Clippings files, Scott County clippings, KSHS, vol. 1.

34. *Smith County Journal* in *Colby Free Press*, Feb. 22, 1894.

35. *Colby Free Press*, May 10, 1894.

36. *Garden City Herald*, Sept. 19, 1896.

37. Vaughn memoirs, June 16, 23, Aug. 18, 1960, County Clippings files, Scott County clippings, KSHS, vol. 1.

38. *Western Times* (Sharon Springs), Dec. 1, 1892.

39. *Alliance Echo* (Sharon Springs), July 24, 1891.

40. Ed Blair in *Manhattan Republic*, quoted in *Kinsley Graphic*, Aug. 9, 1901.

41. Self, *Environment and Man*, 52, 57–58.

42. *Topeka State Journal*, Apr. 12, 1906, in County Clippings files, Sherman County clippings, KSHS, vol. 1.

43. *Seventh Biennial Report of the Kansas State Board of Agriculture*, 239; *Eighth Biennial Report of the Kansas State Board of Agriculture*, 289.

44. *Colby Free Press*, June 24, 1926.

45. *Irrigation Age* in *Garden City Herald*, Apr. 27, 1895.

46. For a careful account of some of these crop years, see James Malin, *Winter Wheat in the Golden Belt of Kansas: A Study in Adaptation to Subhumid Geographical Environment* (Lawrence: University of Kansas Press, 1944), 144–46. Malin's book is filled with insight on the history of wheat growing.

47. *Garden City Herald*, July 10, 1897.

48. *Hays City Sentinel*, Apr. 10, 1894.

49. *Globe-Republican* (Dodge City), Sept. 2, 1891.

50. *Hays City Sentinel*, Sept. 4, 1894.

51. Sis to [Katy], July 27, 1910, Hansen-Bales Family Papers, box 2, Kansas Collection, University of Kansas.

52. *Colby Free Press*, Feb. 27, 1890.

53. *Globe-Republican* (Dodge City), Feb. 15, 1895.

54. *Kansas City Star*, n.d. [1903], County Clippings files, Ellis County clippings, KSHS, vol. 1: 102–4.

55. Vaughn memoirs, Aug. 18, 1960, County Clippings files, Scott County clippings, KSHS, vol. 1.

56. *Colby Free Press*, Apr. 18, 1895.

57. *Garden City Herald*, June 1, 1895.

58. Ibid., Apr. 20, 1895.

59. *Johnson City Journal* in *Garden City Herald*, Apr. 20, 1895.

60. *Garden City Herald*, May 2, 1896.

61. *Emporia Gazette*, quoted in *Liberal News*, Dec. 14, 1922.

62. *Liberal News*, Feb. 13, 1896.

63. The easiest way to get at this is the compilation "Twenty Years of Kansas Agriculture," published in *Twelfth Biennial Report of the Kansas State Board of Agriculture*, 1901, following p. 872.

64. *Hays City Sentinel*, May 26, 1891.

65. *Kansas Farmer*, Jan. 11, 1893.

66. *Hays City Sentinel*, May 24, 1892.

67. The various issues of the *Biennial Reports of the Kansas State Board of Agriculture* contain all these statistics, as well as the farm production numbers for the rest of the state.

68. *Kansas Farmer*, Feb. 10, 1892.

69. Ibid., Sept. 24, 1890.

70. *Great Bend Register* in *Liberal News*, Feb. 15, 1894.

71. *Goodland Republic* in *Colby Free Press*, May 24, 1894.

72. *Colby Free Press*, Nov. 20, 1894.

73. *Garden City Herald,* Nov. 16, 1895.

74. *Hays City Sentinel*, July 21, 1891.

75. *Kansas Breeze* in *Garden City Herald*, Aug. 24, 1895.

76. *Hugoton Hermes* in *Garden City Herald*, Dec. 17, 1896.

Chapter 2. Fooled

1. *Colby Free Press*, Feb. 25, 1892.

2. *Kansas Farmer*, Feb. 18, 1891.

3. *Liberal News*, Jan. 28, 1897.

4. *Globe-Republican* (Dodge City) in *Liberal News*, Dec. 17, 1896.

5. *Liberal News*, Dec. 17, 1896.

6. *Garden City Herald*, Mar. 10, 1894. For earlier talk of "rain follows the plow," see Miner, *West of Wichita*, 38–51. See also David Emmons, *Garden in the Grasslands: Boomer Literature of the Central Great Plains* (Lincoln: University of Nebraska Press, 1971), and Malin, *Winter Wheat*.

7. Allen Ecord, "Life on a Homestead in Western Kansas, 1880 to 1910," typescript, 1980, KSHS, 37.

8. *Liberal News*, June 3, 1897.

9. *Wichita Eagle* in *Liberal News*, Dec. 10, 1896.

10. *Ness County News*, May 17, 1890.

11. Ibid., May 24, 1890.

12. Vaughn memoirs, June 23, 1960, County Clippings files, Scott County clippings, KSHS, vol. 1.

13. Judge A. J. Abbott in *Aurora* (July 1894), quoted in *Garden City Herald,* Oct. 20, 1894.

14. Quoted in *Liberal News,* Feb. 24, 1898.

15. Ibid., May 25, 1899.

16. Clark Spence, *The Rainmakers: American 'Pluviculture' to World War II* (Lincoln: University of Nebraska Press, 1980), 1–2, 4, 8, 52–59.

17. Thearie and Cooper to Lyman Humphrey, May 14, 1889, Lyman Humphrey Papers, 27-05-04-04, KSHS.

18. Michael Cahill to Lyman Humphrey, May 12, 1890, ibid.

19. Spence, *The Rainmakers*, 60–76; *Globe Republican* (Dodge City), June 2, 9, 1893.

20. *Globe-Republican* (Dodge City), June 2, 1893.

21. *Larned Chronoscope*, July 3, 1891.

22. *Salina Journal*, Sept. 29, 1893.

23. *Garden City Herald*, May 26, 1894.

24. *Salina Journal*, Dec. 10, 1891.

25. *Colby Free Press*, Oct. 15, 1891.

26. *Hays City Sentinel*, June 27, 1893.

27. *Goodland Republic* in *Colby Free Press*, May 24, 1894.

28. *Garden City Herald*, May 26, 1894.

29. Vaughn memoirs, May 5, 1960, in County Clippings files, Scott County clippings, KSHS, vol. 1.

30. Spence, *The Rainmakers*, 77.

31. *New York World* in *Garden City Herald*, Nov. 13, 1896.

32. A good recent overview is Gene Clanton, *Populism: The Humane Preference in America, 1890–1900* (Boston: Twayne, 1991). For the "sour grapes" view, see Richard Hofstadter, *The Age of Reform* (New York: Alfred Knopf, 1955).

33. *Mail and Breeze* in *Liberal News*, Jan. 7, 1897.

34. *Hays City Sentinel*, July 7, 14, 1891.

35. Memoirs of Bonnie Bailey Vaughn, July 21, 1960, in County Clippings files, Scott County clippings, KSHS, vol. 1.

36. *Colby Free Press*, Oct. 29, 1891.

37. *Larned Chronoscope*, July 18, 1890.

38. *Colby Free Press*, Oct. 6, 1892.

39. W. R. Christy to L. D. Lewelling, Dec. 28, 1894, Lorenzo Lewelling Papers, 27-05-04-06, KSHS.

40. Isaac Mulholland to L. D. Lewelling, Aug. 18, 1894, ibid.

41. A. M. McDonald and others to L. D. Lewelling, July 3, 1893, ibid.

42. J. S. Blount to L. D. Lewelling, July 26, 1894, ibid.

43. An example of such a charge is J. L. Merrit to C. H. Robinson, Apr. 27, 1890, Lyman Humphrey Papers, 27-05-03-04, KSHS.

44. R. M. Harris to L. D. Lewelling, Aug. 7, 1893, Lorenzo Lewelling Papers, 25-05-04-06, KSHS.

45. E. C. Prather to Executive Council of Kansas, Aug. 14, 1893, ibid.

46. A. H. Cox to L. D. Lewelling, July 15, 1893, ibid.

47. Mrs. E. R. Holloway to L. U. Humphrey, Jan. 28, 1891, Lyman Humphrey Papers, KSHS.

48. *Larned Chronoscope*, May 2, 1890.

49. *Western Times* (Sharon Springs), Aug. 17, 1893.

50. *Larned Chronoscope* in *Liberal News*, Nov. 1, 1894.

51. *Hugoton Hermes* in *Liberal News*, Feb. 13, 1896.

52. *Ness County News*, Oct. 24, 1891.

53. *Garden City Herald*, Nov. 16, 1895.

54. *Salina Journal*, Oct. 5, 1894.

55. Kate Field, "A Kansas Cyclone," quoted in *Larned Chronoscope,* Mar. 13, 1891.

56. *Ness County News,* Aug. 1, 1891.

57. For very graphic accounts, see *Salina Journal,* Sept. 15, 1892, Apr. 21, 1893.

58. *Salina Journal,* Apr. 28, 1893.

59. Committee Petition to L. D. Lewelling, May 18, 1893, Lorenzo Lewelling Papers, 27-05-04-06, KSHS.

60. See, for example, the account of the lynching of J. G. Burton, John Gay, and William Gay at Russell as recounted in *Hays City Sentinel,* Jan. 16, 1894.

61. *Hays City Sentinel,* June 18, 1895.

62. *Colby Free Press,* May 3, 1894.

63. James Hurst to L. E. Lewelling, May 11, 1894, Lorenzo Lewelling Papers, 27-05-04-06, KSHS.

64. *Salina Journal,* May 11, 1894.

65. Ibid., May 18, 1894.

66. A collection of primary documents on the robbery is in Microbox 373, train robbery records, KSHS. The reward poster of June 10, 1893, is a guide to perception.

67. *Emporia Gazette* in *Garden City Herald,* Sept. 28, 1895.

68. *Salina Journal,* Feb. 9, 1894.

69. *Larned Chronoscope,* Oct. 17, 1890.

70. *Hays City Sentinel,* Oct. 28, 1890.

71. *Salina Journal,* May 5, 1892.

72. Typed memo, Edmund Morrill Papers, n.d. [1895], 27-05-05-07, KSHS.

73. *Hays City Sentinel,* Aug. 26, 1890.

74. Quoted in *Liberal News,* Feb. 20, 1896.

75. *Salina Journal,* Nov. 10, 1893.

76. Ibid., Mar. 27, 1896.

77. *Hays City Sentinel,* Nov. 28, 1893.

78. *Alliance Echo* (Sharon Springs), Dec. 12, 1890.

79. *Johnson City Journal* in *Globe-Republican* (Dodge City), Jan. 7, 1897.

80. P. F. Vessels in *Liberal News,* Dec. 24, 1896.

81. *Garden City Herald,* Jan. 25, 1896.

82. *Ness County News* in *Garden City Herald,* Dec. 26, 1896.

83. *Hugoton Hermes* in *Liberal News,* Nov. 3, 1898.

84. *News-Lever* (Scott City), Dec. 17, 1896.

85. For Murdock's thinking, see James Malin, *Power and Change in Society* (Lawrence, Kans.: Coronado Press, 1981).

86. J. K. Barnd to Marshall Murdock, Jan. 26, 1892, Victor Murdock Papers, Library of Congress, container 9.

87. J. A. Arment to Marshall Murdock, Jan. 28, 1892, ibid.

88. E. W. Ober, Salina, to Marshall Murdock, May 3, 1892, ibid.

89. *Globe-Republican* (Dodge City), Dec. 2, 1892.

90. Ibid., Nov. 25, 1892; W. R. Hopkins in *Garden City Herald,* Jan. 9, 1897.

91. *Ness County News,* Mar. 9, 1895.

92. *Ness County News* in *Garden City Herald,* Dec. 26, 1896.

93. *Ness County News,* Feb. 27, 1897.

94. *Garden City Herald,* Aug. 17, 1895.

95. Ibid., Jan. 25, 1896.

96. Ibid., June 1, 1895.

Chapter 3. The Edge of the World

1. *Salina Journal,* July 17, 1896.

2. Judge A. J. Abbott in *Aurora* (July 1894), quoted in *Garden City Herald,* Oct. 20, 1894.

3. William Allen White, quoted in *Liberal News,* Dec. 14, 1922.

4. *Ness County News,* Dec. 30, 1899.

5. *Hays City Sentinel,* Mar. 26, 1895.

6. Quoted in *Garden City Herald,* Dec. 9, 1905.

7. *Emporia Republican* in *Globe-Republican* (Dodge City), Apr. 29, 1891.

8. *Ness County News,* Jan. 4, 1890.

9. *Dighton Herald* in *Garden City Herald,* May 22, 1897.

10. *Garden City Herald,* May 26, 1900.

11. Ibid., July 28, 1906.

12. *American Wool and Cotton Reporter* in *Globe-Republican* (Dodge City), Sept. 30, 1892.

13. *Larned Chronoscope,* Apr. 24, 1891.

14. *Kansas Farmer,* Nov. 29, 1893.

15. John Knox of Topeka made an extensive analysis of the reasons for the boom and bust, including this railroad factor, in *Kansas Farmer,* May 24, 1893.

16. *Colby Free Press,* Nov. 14, 1907.

17. *Ness County News,* Apr. 20, 1901.

18. Ibid., Sept. 21, 1901.

19. Ibid., Jan. 21, 1911.

20. Fred Hazelton to C. W. Cline, Mar. 19, 1899, Kansas Town & Land Company Papers, box 2, KSHS.

21. E. T. Guymon to C. W. Cline, May 4, 1899, ibid.

22. May 4, 1900, box 5, ibid.

23. May 15, 1900, ibid.

24. Thomas Leonard to C. W. Cline, July 2, 1900, box 6, ibid.

25. E. W. Cline to R. G. Holaday, May 29, 1901, box 8, ibid.

26. *Globe-Republican* (Dodge City), Nov. 26, 1896, Feb. 25, Sept. 30, 1897, Dec. 9, 1898.

27. *Topeka Journal,* Feb. 23, 1898, County Clippings files, Ford County clippings, KSHS, vol. 1.

28. *Kansas City Star,* Sept. 7, 1902, ibid.

29. *Liberal News,* May 3, 1906, Feb. 21, 1907.

30. Socolofsky and Self, *Historical Atlas of Kansas,* 36.

31. Miner, *West of Wichita,* 194.

32. *Eighth Annual Report of the Board of Railroad Commissioners for the Year Ending December 1, 1890, State of Kansas* (Topeka: State Publishing House, 1890), viii, 150, 195.

33. *Eighteenth Report of the Board of Railroad Commissioners, State of Kansas, for the Year Ending November 30, 1904* (Topeka: George A. Clark, State Printer, 1904), 50.

34. Miner, *West of Wichita,* 191.

35. For the Orient, see Arthur Stillwell, *Cannibals of Finance: Fifteen Years' Contest with the Money Trust* (Chicago: Farnum, 1912), and John Kerr and Frank Donovan, *Destination Topolobampo: The Kansas City, Mexico and Orient Railway* (San Marino, Calif.: Golden West Books, 1969).

36. These developments may best be studied using the Kansas map collection at Special Collections, Ablah Library, Wichita State University, or a similar collection. The best maps for this purpose are the official railroad maps published by the Kansas Board of Railroad Commissioners. Maps produced by national companies are sometimes of uncertain dating and accuracy. The *Annual Reports of Board of Railroad Commissioners, Kansas, 1883–1910,* have further information on the companies.

37. *Garden City Herald,* Sept. 11, 1913, June 24, 1915; *Tiller and Toiler* (Larned), Oct. 16, 1914.

38. *Kansas Farmer,* Oct. 11, 1893.

39. For White's thinking on this issue, see especially Edward Agran, *Too Good a Town: William Allen White, Community, and the Emerging Rhetoric of Middle America* (Fayetteville: University of Arkansas Press, 1998).

40. *Republican* (Hays), Feb. 29, 1908.

41. James Forsythe, *The First 75 Years: A History of Fort Hays State University, 1902–1977* (Topeka: Josten's Yearbook Company, 1977), 3, 6, 9, 16. For the military history of the fort, see Leo Oliva, *Fort Hays: Keeping Peace on the Plains* (Topeka: Kansas State Historical Society, 1980).

42. For an overview of the struggle for the soldiers' home, see Leo Oliva, *Fort Dodge: Sentry of the Western Plains* (Topeka: Kansas State Historical Society, 1998), 106–8. A college use was proposed by the Methodists for this fort reservation also.

43. J. D. Barker, Henry Booth, Ira Collins to Lyman Humphrey, Dec. 11, 1889, Lyman Humphrey Papers, 27-05-02-05, KSHS.

44. *Republican* (Hays), Apr. 6, 1898.

45. Ibid., Jan. 21, 1899.

46. *Russell Record* in ibid., Dec. 23, 1899.

47. For Wichita, see Craig Miner, *Uncloistered Halls: The Centennial History of Wichita State University* (Wichita: Wichita State University Endowment Association, 1995).

48. *Salina Journal,* Nov. 19, 1891.

49. *Globe-Republican* (Dodge City), May 23, 1892.

50. Ibid., Apr. 12, 1895.

51. Ibid., Feb. 9, July 27, Sept. 21, 1894, May 24, 1895.

52. Ibid., Feb. 27, 1896; *Kansas City Star,* Sept. 7, 1902, in County Clippings files, Ford County clippings, KSHS, vol. 1.

53. *Republican* (Hays), Mar. 22, June 28, 1902.

54. George Clothier, "How Seed Breeding Should Be Conducted in Kansas," in *Republican* (Hays), Aug. 19, 1899.

55. Earl Teagarden, comp., "History of the Kansas Extension Service from 1868 to 1964," 3 vols., typescript, Special Collections, Kansas State University, 1: 27–38.

56. *Topeka Capital* in *Republican* (Hays), Nov. 16, 1907.

57. Major histories of Kansas State Agriculture College and Kansas State University (KSAC and KSU) are Julius Willard, *History of the Kansas State College of Agriculture and*

Applied Science (Manhattan: Kansas State College Press, 1940), and James Carcy, *Kansas State University: The Quest for Identity* (Lawrence: Regents Press of Kansas, 1977).

58. Teagarden, "History of the Kansas Extension Service," 1: 15.

59. *Republican* (Hays), Dec. 21, 1901.

60. Ibid., Dec. 21, 1901, Aug. 9, 1902.

61. *Kansas Farmer*, Dec. 19, 1901.

62. *Republican* (Hays), Feb. 22, 1902.

63. Ibid., Aug. 2, 9, 1902.

64. William Phillips, *History of the Agricultural Research Center—Hays: The First 100 Years,* Kansas State University Agricultural Experiment Station and Cooperative Extension Service Bulletin SB663 (Manhattan: Kansas State University, 2001).

65. *Republican* (Hays), Dec. 14, 1901, Aug. 9, 1902.

66. Annual Reports, typescript, Garden City Experiment Station, 1908, Special Collections, Kansas State University.

67. Annual Report, Tribune Experiment Station, 1913, ibid.

68. Annual Report, Colby Agricultural Experiment Station, 1914, ibid.

69. Annual Report, Garden City Experiment Station, 1914, ibid.

70. For the history of the movement, see classic studies by Mary Hargreaves, *Dry Farming in the Northern Great Plains, 1900–1925* (Cambridge: Harvard University Press, 1957), and *Dry Farming in the Northern Great Plains: Years of Readjustment 1920–1990* (Lawrence: University Press of Kansas, 1992).

71. *Republican* (Hays), Feb. 10, 1900.

72. *Garden City Herald*, July 29, 1905.

73. *Hutchinson News* in *Liberal News*, Feb. 4, 1909.

74. *Hill City Republican* in *Ness County News*, Jan. 14, 1911.

75. R. H. Faxon to George Hodges, Aug. 15, 1914, George Hodges Papers, 27-07-03-04, KSHS.

76. Frank Blackmar, ed., *Kansas,* 4 vols. (Chicago: Standard Publishing Company, 1912), 3: 496.

77. *Ness County News*, Nov. 14, 1908.

78. Ibid., Nov. 21, 1908.

79. Ibid., Nov. 28, 1908.

80. Ibid., Jan. 2, 1909.

81. *Scott City Chronicle* in *Ness County News*, Apr. 24, 1909.

82. H. B. Walker to J. W. Lough, Nov. 25, 1915, Arthur Capper Papers (as governor), 27-08-01-06, KSHS.

83. J. W. Lough to Arthur Capper, Nov. 30, 1915, ibid.

84. *Southwest Daily Times* (Liberal), Sept. 30, 1960, in County Clippings files, Seward County clippings, KSHS, vol. 2.

85. Ibid., Oct. 1, 1960.

86. Ibid., Oct. 5, 1960.

87. *Kansas City Star*, Sept. 10, 1911, in County Clippings files, Meade County clippings, KSHS.

88. *Republican* (Hays), Sept. 21, 1907.

89. *Salina Journal*, Mar. 17, 1893.

90. Ibid., Mar. 17, 1893.

91. *Ness City Sentinel* in *Liberal News*, Apr. 20, 1893.

92. *Kinsley Graphic*, Mar. 15, 1895.

93. *Globe Republican* (Dodge City), Feb. 6, 1896.

94. Ibid., Feb. 20, 1896; Kirke Mechem, ed., *The Annals of Kansas*, 1886–1925, 2 vols., 1: 212; *Globe Republican* (Dodge City), Oct. 26, 1899.

95. *Garden City Herald*, Aug. 28, 1897.

96. *Ness County News*, Mar. 26, 1898.

97. *Meade Globe* in *Liberal News*, Oct. 14, 1897.

98. *Ness County News*, May 19, 1898.

99. Quoted in *Garden City Herald*, Feb. 4, 1909.

100. *Kansas Farmer*, July 25, 1894.

101. *Colby Free Press*, Aug. 30, 1894.

102. *Salina Journal*, Aug. 17, 1894.

103. *Tiller and Toiler* (Larned), July 24, 1908.

104. *Garden City Herald*, May 13, 1909.

105. *Kansas Farmer*, Dec. 31, 1890; Clyde Hyder, *Snow of Kansas: The Life of Francis Huntington Snow* (Lawrence: University Press of Kansas, 1953), 191–94.

106. *Ness County News*, Dec. 13, 1890.

107. *Garden City Herald*, Sept. 9, 1893.

108. Ibid., Oct. 28, 1893.

109. An account of an early coursing meet in the region is *Salina Journal*, Oct. 29, 1891.

110. *Garden City Herald*, Jan. 1, 1898.

111. Ibid., Dec. 28, 1911.

112. *Colby Free Press*, Jan. 3, 1895.

113. *Scott Chronicle* in *Ness County News*, Dec. 30, 1911.

114. *Santa Fe Monitor* in *Liberal News*, Aug. 5, 1897.

115. *Republican* (Hays), Apr. 7, 1900.

116. Ibid., Apr. 28, 1900.

117. M. C. Buffington in *Ness County News*, May 19, 1900.

118. *Ness County News*, June 2, 1900; *Republican* (Hays), Apr. 13, 1901.

119. *Garden City Herald*, Mar. 30, 1901.

120. *Colby Free Press*, May 22, 1902.

121. *Ness County News*, Mar. 7, 1903.

122. *Topeka Capital* in *Garden City Herald*, June 15, 1901.

123. *Garden City Herald*, June 27, 1896.

124. Ibid., Sept. 10, 1904.

125. *Kinsley Graphic*, Dec. 3, 1897; *Garden City Herald*, July 30, 1904; *Ness County News*, July 21, 1906.

126. *Garden City Herald*, Sept. 16, 1905.

127. *Kinsley Graphic*, July 7, 1899.

128. *Garden City Herald*, Aug. 6, 1904.

129. On second thoughts concerning the coyote, see ibid., Feb. 2, 1901.

130. Ibid., May 11, 1901, Jan. 6, 1906.

131. *Globe Republican* (Dodge City), Oct. 5, 1899.

132. *Osborne Farmer* in *Republican* (Hays), July 7, 1900.

133. *Ness County News*, Jan. 20, 1900.

134. *Garden City Herald*, Feb. 7, 1903.

135. Ibid., Feb. 2, 1901.

136. Bessie Wilder, *Government Agencies of the State of Kansas, 1861–1956* (Lawrence: University of Kansas Publications, 1957); *Kansas Farmer*, Jan. 5, 1905.

137. Martin Allen to Lyman Humphrey, Sept. 1, 1889, Mar. 31, 1890, Lyman Humphrey Papers, 27-05-02-05, KSHS.

138. *Kansas Farmer*, Apr. 9, 1890.

139. Martin Allen to Lyman Humphrey, Aug. 25, 1890, Lyman Humphrey Papers, 27-05-02-05, KSHS.

140. *Ness County News*, Jan. 21, 1899.

141. *Globe-Republican* (Dodge City), June 20, 1892.

142. Ibid., June 20, 1892, Feb. 24, 1893.

143. Ibid., June 20, 1892.

144. G. W. Bartlett to E. N. Morrill, July 26, 1896, Edmund Morrill Papers, 27-05-05-02, KSHS.

145. *Garden City Herald*, May 16, 1903.

146. The history of boom ditch irrigation is discussed in Miner, *West of Wichita*, 172–88.

147. *Report of the Board of Irrigation Survey and Experiment for 1895 and 1896 to the Legislature of Kansas* (Topeka: Kansas State Printing Company, 1897), 5.

148. Donald Pisani, *Water, Land, and Law in the West: The Limits of Public Policy, 1850–1920* (Lawrence: University Press of Kansas, 1996), 181–82.

149. A fine study of the Arkansas River issues is James Sherow, *Watering the Valley: Development along the High Plains Arkansas River, 1870–1950* (Lawrence: University Press of Kansas, 1990).

150. *Garden City Herald*, Oct. 24, 1894.

151. *Colby Free Press*, Sept. 19, 1889.

152. *Report of the Board of Irrigation Survey and Experiment for 1895 and 1896*, 5.

153. *Larned Chronoscope*, July 24, 1891.

154. *Garden City Herald*, Sept. 2, 1893.

155. J. W. Gregory to L. U. Humphrey, Sept. 25, 1891, Lyman Humphrey Papers, 27-05-03-06, KSHS.

156. *Hays City Sentinel*, June 23, 1891.

157. *Larned Chronoscope*, June 5, 1891.

158. Ibid., June 3, 1892.

159. *Colby Free Press*, Oct. 11, 1894.

160. *Larned Chronoscope*, Mar. 13, 1896.

161. *Kansas City Times* in *Garden City Herald*, Sept. 30, 1893.

162. Wilder, *Government Agencies*, 69–70; *Garden City Herald*, Mar. 2, 1895.

163. *Kansas Farmer*, Mar. 13, 1895.

164. *Report of the Board of Irrigation Survey and Experiment for 1895 and 1896*, 9.

165. *Grant County Republican* in *Garden City Herald*, Jan. 19, 1895.

166. H. W. Daul [?] to E. N. Morrill, Feb. 19, 1895, Edmund Morrill Papers, 27-05-05-07, KSHS.

167. *Garden City Herald*, June 15, 1895.

168. Wm. Sutton to E. N. Morrill, June 24, 1895, Edmund Morrill Papers, 27-05-05-02, KSHS.

169. *Republican* (Plainville) in *Hays City Sentinel*, July 2, 1895.

170. Wm. Sutton to E. N. Morrill, Jan. 27, 1896, Edmund Morrill Papers, 27-05-04-02, KSHS; *Liberal News*, Apr. 30, 1896.

171. *Garden City Herald* in *Globe-Republican* (Dodge City), Jan. 4, 9, 1896.

172. *Globe Republican* (Dodge City), Jan. 7, 1897; Wilder, *Government Agencies*, 69.

173. *Republican* (Hays), May 15, 1897.

174. *Larned Chronoscope*, Sept. 26, 1890.

175. *Kansas Farmer*, Apr. 12, 1892.

176. *Bird City News* in *Colby Free Press*, Apr. 11, 1892.

177. *Globe-Republican* (Dodge City), Mar. 3, 1892.

178. *Ness County News*, Oct. 3, 1903.

179. E. G. Buff in *Ness County News*, July 28, 1900.

180. *Colby Free Press*, Aug. 30, 1906.

181. Jarvis Bloostem in ibid., Sept. 9, 1897.

182. Wayne Wingo, *A History of Thomas County, Kansas, 1884–1964* (n.p.: n.d., privately printed), 33–34. Wingo's book was based on his master's thesis at Ft. Hays State University in 1964.

183. *Hays City Sentinel*, July 21, 1891.

184. Ibid., June 23, 1891.

185. *Larned Chronoscope*, Sept. 11, 1891.

186. *Globe Republican* (Dodge City), May 2, 1892.

187. Ibid., May 2, 1892.

188. Ibid., Dec. 16, 1892; *Kansas City Star* in *Garden City Herald*, Sept. 22, 1894.

189. *Globe-Republican* (Dodge City), Feb. 2, 1894.

190. Ibid., Jan. 21, 1897. There is material on Fike in Wingo, *History of Thomas County*.

191. *Globe-Republican* (Dodge City), June 10, 1897.

192. *Colby Free Press*, June 1, 1899.

193. *Republican* (Hays), Dec. 21, 1901.

194. Ibid., July 20, 1905.

195. *Kansas Farmer*, Oct. 19, 1892.

196. *Logan Republican*, June 8, 1961, in County Clippings files, Phillips County clippings, KSHS.

197. *Topeka Capital*, in ibid., Feb. 20, 1896.

Chapter 4. Deus Ex Machina

1. *Ness County News*, Mar. 22, 1902.

2. *Larned Chronoscope*, Aug. 5, 1898.

3. An example of the accident genre is *Globe-Republican* (Dodge City), Feb. 28, 1907.

4. Ibid., May 3, 1906.

5. Ibid., June 21, 1906.

6. *Larned Chronoscope*, May 13, 1898.

7. *Liberal News*, Apr. 25, 1907.

8. *Larned Chronoscope,* Nov. 9, 1900.

9. *Garden City Herald*, Jan. 2, 1897.

10. Ibid., Oct. 6, 1894.

11. Ibid., Oct. 5, 1895.

12. *Kansas Farmer*, Oct. 31, 1894.

13. *Garden City Herald*, Oct. 12, 1895.

14. *Colby Free Press*, May 5, 1910.

15. *Hays Republican*, Dec. 5, 1908.

16. *Colby Free Press*, June 17, 1915.

17. *Garden City Herald,* Apr. 20, 1901.

18. *Colby Free Press*, Dec. 9, 1909, Jan. 10, 1910, Sept. 14, 1911.

19. Again the statistics come from the *Biennial Reports of the Kansas State Board of Agriculture* and were compiled by Ben Hruska.

20. A. B. McDonald, "Big Country Merchants: A. A. Doerr of Larned, Kansas," *Country Gentleman* 85, no. 39 (Sept. 25, 1920), 15. This article is based on an interview with Doerr, who was one of the most successful regional marketers of farm machinery.

21. *Colby Free Press,* Feb. 17, 1916.

22. Alpha Hansen to "Kitten" [Kate Hansen], Dec. 29, 1907, Hansen-Bales Family Papers, box 2, Kansas Collection, University of Kansas.

23. Alpha Hansen to "Kitten," Feb. 16, 1908, Mamma to Katy, Apr. 21, 1908, in ibid.

24. *Topeka Journal* in *Ness County News*, May 19, 1900.

25. *Colby Free Press*, Dec. 7, 1916.

26. *Ellis County News*, May 20, 1916.

27. Ibid., Sept. 30, 1916.

28. *Liberal News*, Sept. 18, 1902.

29. *Garden City Herald*, May 21, 1904.

30. *Tiller and Toiler* (Larned), *Feb. 14, 1907.

31. *Colby Free Press*, Apr. 18, 1907.

32. *Ness County News*, Aug. 10, 1907.

33. *Garden City Herald*, Dec. 17, 1908.

34. *Topeka State Journal* in *Liberal News*, May 5, 1910.

35. *Tiller and Toiler* (Larned), July 24, 1908.

36. Ibid., July 31, 1908.

37. Charles Harger in *Saturday Evening Post*, quoted in *Kansas Farmer*, Apr. 24, 1909.

38. *Kansas Farmer*, Apr. 24, 1895.

39. *Larned Chronoscope*, Mar. 6, 1896.

40. *Kansas Farmer*, Nov. 23, 1899.

41. *Wichita Beacon*, May 9, 1900 [or 1901], County Clippings files, Barton County clippings, KSHS.

42. Douglas Harvey, "Creating a 'Sea of Galilee': The Rescue of Cheyenne Bottoms Wildlife Area, 1927–1930," *Kansas History* 24 (Spring 2001): 4. Harvey's master's thesis, entitled "'Drought Relief Efforts Delayed by Rain:' The History of the Cheyenne Bottoms

Wildlife Area" (Wichita State University, Department of History, 2000), well documents the difficulties of the "all natural" theory of water control and use.

43. *Kansas Farmer*, July 14, 1898.

44. An excellent overview of the legal issues is Robert Irvine, "The Waterscape and the Law: Adopting Prior Appropriation in Kansas," *Kansas History* 19 (Spring 1996): 22–35.

45. *Garden City Herald*, May 28, 1904.

46. See Sherow, *Watering the Valley*, particularly chapter 6, "The Contest for the 'Nile of America': *Kansas v. Colorado*, 1890–1910," pp. 103–19. The Colorado development of the Arkansas River can be traced in Lawrence MacDonnell, *Reclamation to Sustainability: Water, Agriculture, and the Environment in the American West* (Niwot: University Press of Colorado, 1999), 13–49.

47. *Globe-Republican* (Dodge City), Feb. 18, Apr. 1, Sept. 2, Dec. 2, 1909. For the earlier history of the Eureka Canal, see Miner, *West of Wichita*, 182–83. For the ditch boom in general, see Anne Marvin, "'A Grave-Yard of Hopes': Irrigation and Boosterism in Southwest Kansas, 1880–1890," *Kansas History* 19 (Spring 1996): 36–51.

48. *Globe-Republican* (Dodge City), Sept. 9, Dec. 2, 1909.

49. Mechem, ed., *Annals of Kansas*, 2: 145.

50. *Kansas Farmer*, Apr. 11, 1907.

51. *Topeka Capital*, June 18, 1911, County Clippings files, Meade County clippings, KSHS.

52. *Kansas Farmer*, Apr. 23, 1903.

53. *Topeka Capital*, Mar. 22, 1908, County Clippings files, Finney County clippings, KSHS.

54. *Globe Republican* (Dodge City), Aug. 18, 1904.

55. T. Lindsay Baker, "Blowin' in the Wind: Windmill Manufacturing and Distribution in Kansas," *Kansas History* 19 (Spring 1996): 6, 8, 10, 12–13.

56. *History of Finney County, Kansas*, 2 vols. (Garden City, Kans.: Finney County Historical Society, 1950), 1: 139, 182.

57. James Tomayko, "Irrigation Technology and the Development of Southwest Kansas," (Ph.D. diss., College of Humanities and Social Sciences, Carnegie-Mellon University, 1980), 73, 77.

58. *Garden City Herald*, Feb. 20, 1904.

59. *Larned Chronoscope*, Mar. 23, 1893; *History of Finney County*, 1: 146, 211.

60. *Kansas Farmer*, Dec. 17, 1903; *Garden City Herald*, June 20, 1903.

61. Among many accounts, see especially Pisani, *Water, Land, and Law in the West.* Chapter 3, pp. 38–49, discusses the shift to federal initiative in the Progressive Era. For the historiography of the water issue in Kansas, see James Sherow, "The Art of Water and the Art of Living," *Kansas History* 25 (Spring 2002): 52–71.

62. *Globe-Republican* (Dodge City), Dec. 5, 1901.

63. J. G. Haney to W. J. Bailey, Aug. 1, 1903, Willis Bailey Papers, 27-06-01-07, KSHS.

64. F. Dumont Smith to W. J. Bailey, Aug. 22, 1903, ibid.

65. *Globe-Republican* (Dodge City), Dec. 10, 1903.

66. *Garden City Herald*, Dec. 12, 1903.

67. Ibid., Dec. 31, 1904.

68. Ibid., Jan. 16, 1904.

69. *Globe-Republican* (Dodge City), Feb. 25, 1904.

70. *Garden City Herald,* Jan. 23, 1904.

71. *Saturday Evening Post,* in ibid., Feb. 27, 1904.

72. *Globe-Republican* (Dodge City), May 19, 1904.

73. The Reclamation Service until 1907 was under the auspices of the U.S. Geological Survey and was the ancestor of the Bureau of Reclamation, which was later relocated to the Department of the Interior. See William Warne, *The Bureau of Reclamation* (New York: Praeger Publishers, 1973), 27.

74. *Kansas City Journal* in *Garden City Herald,* Sept. 3, 1904.

75. *Garden City Herald,* Oct. 8, 1904.

76. Ibid., Apr. 1, 8, 22, 1905.

77. Tomayko, "Irrigation Technology," 82–83.

78. *Liberal News,* Apr. 27, 1905.

79. *Wichita Eagle* in *Garden City Herald,* Sept. 16, 1905.

80. *Hays Republican,* May 27, 1905.

81. For the sorghum industry in Western Kansas, see Miner, *West of Wichita,* 185–88, 227–29; and Homer Socolofsky, "The Bittersweet Tale of Sorghum Sugar," *Kansas History* 16 (Winter 1993–1994): 276–89.

82. *Kansas City Journal* in *Larned Chronoscope,* Aug. 19, 1892.

83. James Shortridge, *Cities on the Plains: The Evolution of Urban Kansas* (Lawrence: University Press of Kansas, 2004), 203.

84. *Kansas Farmer,* Dec. 1, 1899, Jan. 3, 1901; Mechem, *Annals of Kansas,* 1: 92.

85. *Garden City Herald,* Dec. 15, 1900.

86. Ibid., Dec. 22, 1900.

87. *Kansas Farmer,* Dec. 26, 1901.

88. Mechem, *Annals of Kansas,* 1: 356; *Kansas Farmer,* Dec. 26, 1901.

89. *Garden City Herald,* Dec. 28, 1901.

90. *Globe-Republican* (Dodge City), Dec. 5, 1901.

91. *Garden City Herald,* Dec. 28, 1901.

92. *Kansas Farmer,* Aug. 14, 1902.

93. *Topeka Daily Capital* in *Garden City Herald,* June 10, 1905.

94. *Kansas Farmer,* Dec. 26, 1901.

95. *Garden City Herald,* Jan. 7, 1905.

96. Ibid., Sept. 16, 1905.

97. *Fourteenth Biennial Report of the Kansas State Board of Agriculture,* 1905, 654.

98. *Lakin Investigator* in *Garden City Herald,* Dec. 14, 1904; *Fourteenth Biennial Report of the Kansas State Board of Agriculture,* 660.

99. *Syracuse Journal* in *Garden City Herald,* Jan. 7, 1905.

100. *Garden City Herald,* Mar. 11, 1905.

101. Ibid., July 22, 1905.

102. Ibid., Aug. 5, 1905.

103. Ibid., Nov. 11, 1905.

104. *Kansas Farmer,* Nov. 16, 1905.

105. *Garden City Herald,* Dec. 9, 1905.

106. Ibid.

107. *Kansas Farmer,* Mar. 22, 1906.

108. *Garden City Herald*, Apr. 21, 1906.

109. Ibid., June 2, Sept. 8, 1906.

110. Ibid., Sept. 8, 1906.

111. *Hutchinson News* in *Garden City Herald*, Nov. 22, 1906.

112. *Garden City Herald*, Sept. 8, 22, 1906.

113. Ibid., Nov. 24, 1906, Apr. 11, 1907; *Kansas Farmer*, Nov. 29, 1906.

114. *Garden City Herald,* Nov. 29, 1906.

115. Ibid., Feb. 16, 1907.

116. *Kansas Farmer*, Mar. 28, 1907.

117. *Sixteenth Biennial Report of the Kansas State Board of Agriculture, 1909*, 968–69.

118. *Garden City Herald,* Dec. 7, 1911.

119. Ibid., Jan. 20, 1916.

120. Shortridge, *Cities on the Plains,* 203.

121. An excellent and near-unique account of this phenomenon in the secondary literature is Henry Avila, "Immigration and Integration: The Mexican American Community in Garden City, Kansas, 1900–1950," *Kansas History* 20 (Spring 1997): 22–37.

122. *Garden City Herald,* Apr. 11, 1907.

123. Avila, "Immigration and Integration," 27, 39.

124. *Garden City Herald,* June 17, 1920.

125. Ibid., Nov. 4, 1920.

126. Ibid., Nov. 30, 1922, May 7, June 4, 1925, Sept. 16, 1926.

127. Ibid., Mar. 22, 1928.

128. *Larned Chronoscope* in *Garden City Herald*, May 24, 1924.

129. *Garden City Herald,* May 18, 1907.

130. *News-Chronicle* (Scott City), Aug. 5, Dec. 2, 1910.

131. Ibid., Nov. 3, 1911.

132. Ibid., May 22, 1914.

133. Ibid., Aug. 17, 1907.

134. *Garden City Herald*, Dec. 9, 1905.

135. *Globe-Republican* (Dodge City), Nov. 22, 1906.

Chapter 5. "Hustle or Rot"

1. *Kansas Farmer*, Oct. 30, 1909. An excellent source for broad context on many of these issues is Hal Barron, *Mixed Harvest: The Second Great Transformation in the Rural North, 1870–1930* (Chapel Hill: University of North Carolina Press, 1997). For Country Life specifically, see William Bowers, *The Country Life Movement in America, 1900–1920* (Port Washington, N.Y.: Kennikat Press, 1974).

2. The resistance pattern is documented in Ronald R. Kline, *Consumers in the Country: Technology and Social Change in Rural America* (Baltimore: Johns Hopkins University Press, 2000). A summary is on page 9.

3. Barron, *Mixed Harvest*, 9, 11.

4. Ibid., 193. For the nineteenth-century origins of consumer culture in rural areas, see David Blanke, *Sowing the American Dream: How Consumer Culture Took Root in the Rural Midwest* (Athens: Ohio University Press, 2000).

5. *Kansas Farmer,* Aug. 28, 1910.

6. Ibid., June 18, 1910.

7. Ibid., July 9, 1910.

8. *Ashland Clipper,* Nov. 7, 1912.

9. R. H. Faxon to Walter Stubbs, Oct. 14, 1911, Walter Stubbs Papers, 27-06-06-07, KSHS.

10. *Larned Chronoscope,* Feb. 1, 1907.

11. *Globe-Republican* (Dodge City), Nov. 25, 1909.

12. Ibid., Jan. 6, 1910, Nov. 22, 1906.

13. For natural gas, see *Globe-Republican* (Dodge City), July 2, 1908.

14. *Hutchinson News* in *Garden City Herald,* Aug. 13, 1898.

15. *Garden City Herald,* June 11, 1898; *History of Finney County,* 1: 170.

16. *Garden City Herald,* Mar. 24, 1900.

17. Ibid., May 12, 1900.

18. Ibid., June 1, Aug. 3, 1911.

19. Ibid., May 26, 1900.

20. Ibid., May 23, 1903.

21. *Kansas City Star* in *Garden City Herald*, Jan. 11, 1902.

22. *Ness County News,* Dec. 22, 1900, Sept. 16, 1905.

23. Ibid., June 15, 1901, June 20, 1905.

24. Ibid., Feb. 2, 9, Mar. 9, Sept. 28, 1901.

25. Ibid., Aug. 15, 1903.

26. Ibid., June 6, 1903.

27. Ibid., June 14, 1903, Feb. 13, 1904.

28. Harold Miner to Mabel Pinkney, Aug. 11, 1907, author's collection.

29. *Ness County News,* Feb. 20, 1904.

30. Ibid., May 14, 28, 1904.

31. Ibid., July 30, 1904.

32. Ibid., Nov. 5, 1904.

33. Ibid., Feb. 17, 1906.

34. Ibid., Sept. 28, 1907.

35. Ibid., Nov. 9, 1907.

36. Ibid., Mar. 28, 1908.

37. Ibid., May 30, 1908.

38. Ibid., Jan. 9, 1909.

39. Ibid., Feb. 13, 1909.

40. Ibid., Mar. 5, 1910.

41. Ibid., July 1, 1911.

42. Ibid., July 1, 1911.

43. Ibid., July 8, 22, 1911.

44. Ibid., Dec. 11, 1911.

45. *Colby Free Press,* Sept. 28, Oct. 12, 1905, Feb. 15, 1906.

46. Ibid., Feb. 13, 1908. Population figures come from the *Biennial Reports of the Kansas State Board of Agriculture.* Craig Miner, *Harvesting the High Plains: John Kriss and the Business of Wheat Farming, 1920–1950* (Lawrence: University Press of Kansas, 1998), 65.

47. *Colby Free Press,* Jan. 10, June 30, Dec. 29, 1910.

48. Ibid., Dec. 9, 1909.

49. *Larned Chronoscope,* Mar. 17, 1893.

50. *Tiller and Toiler* (Larned), Oct. 12, 1908.

51. *Republican* (Hays), June 22, 1901.

52. Ibid., Apr. 16, Aug. 12, 1904.

53. Ibid., Sept. 17, 1904.

54. Ibid., June 15, 1907.

55. *Liberal News,* Dec. 14, 1905.

56. Ibid., Aug. 23, 1906.

57. Ibid., July 8, 1909.

58. *Garden City Herald,* Feb. 7, 1903.

59. *Salina Journal,* Sept. 18, 1892.

60. Ibid., Jan. 4, 1895.

61. Ibid., Mar. 8, 1895.

62. *Hays City Sentinel,* Feb. 12, 1895.

63. Ibid., Apr. 23, 1895.

64. *Hays Daily News,* Jan. 31, 1954, County Clippings files, Ellis County clippings, KSHS.

65. *Liberal News,* June 4, 1908.

66. Mamma to children, Jan. 19, 1904, Hansen-Bales Family Papers, Kansas Collection, University of Kansas.

67. *Republican* (Hays), Dec. 5, 1903.

68. Ibid., Sept. 21, 1907.

69. *Garden City Herald,* Feb. 13, 1897.

70. Ibid., Mar. 19, 1898.

71. *Republican* (Hays), June 27, Sept. 19, 1908.

72. *Garden City Herald,* Jan. 28, July 8, 1909.

73. Ibid., Nov. 9, 1907, Feb. 11, 1909.

74. Ibid., Apr. 22, 1905.

75. *Ellis County News,* Nov. 20, 1919.

76. *Hays Daily News,* Apr. 11, 1965, County Clippings files, Ellis County clippings, KSHS.

77. Letterhead in Albert Doerr Papers, box 9, KSHS.

78. McDonald, "Big Country Merchants: A. A. Doerr of Larned, Kansas," 15, 24; *Larned Chronoscope,* May 13, 1898.

79. A. A. Doerr to Emerson Manufacturing Company, Oct. 12, 1903, Albert Doerr Papers, KSHS.

80. Grace to ?, Mar. 3, 1909, ibid.; *Tiller and Toiler* (Larned), Feb. 4, 1910.

81. James Lund to A. A. Doerr, Feb. 17, 1912, Albert Doerr Papers, KSHS.

82. *Tiller and Toiler* (Larned), Feb. 4, 1910.

83. Biographical information on Doerr is from the typescript finding aid to the Albert Doerr Papers, KSHS.

84. W. G. Clugston, "A Storekeeper Who Studies Farmers' Wants," *American Magazine* 92, no. 1 (July 1921): 61.

85. *Tiller and Toiler* (Larned), June 4, 1908.

86. *Ness County News*, Oct. 31, Nov. 14, 1891, Aug. 10, Sept 7, 1895, Aug. 25, 1900, Oct. 3, 1903.

87. Ibid., Sept. 21, 1895.

88. Ibid., Sept. 19, 1896, Jan. 24, 1903.

89. Ibid., July 31, 1897.

90. Ibid., Feb. 17, 1900.

91. Ibid., June 18, Sept. 3, 1904.

92. Ibid., Apr. 8, 1911.

93. Harold Miner to Mabel Miner, Mar. 10, 1907, author's collection.

94. *Ness County News*, June 30, 1900.

95. Ibid., Oct. 3, 1903.

96. Ibid., Feb. 15, 1902.

97. Ibid., Aug. 15, 1903.

98. Ibid., Apr. 16, 1910.

99. This information comes from a group of letters in the author's possession from Hal Miner to Mabel Pinkney written while they were courting in 1907. W. D. Miner was my great-grandfather and Hal Miner was my grandfather.

100. Harold Miner to Mabel Miner, Feb. 17, 1907, author's collection.

101. Ibid., Mar. 24, 1907.

102. Ibid., Mar. 17, 1907. With a week to go in the month Miner estimated the firm's gross sales of land for that month alone at over $32,000. Ibid., Mar. 21, 1907.

103. Ibid., Mar. 28, 1907.

104. Ibid., Mar. 17, 1907.

105. Ibid., Aug. 1, 1907.

106. *Globe-Republican* (Dodge City), Sept. 5, 1907.

107. *Garden City Herald*, Apr. 6, 1898.

108. Ibid., May 11, 1901.

109. *Santa Fe Republican* in ibid., Mar. 25, 1905.

110. *Garden City Herald*, May 21, 1898.

111. Ibid., Aug. 20, 1898.

112. Ibid., Apr. 22, 1899.

113. Ibid., May 21, 1898.

114. *Republican* (Hays), July 7, 1900.

115. *Globe-Republican* (Dodge City), July 10, 1902.

116. *Colby Free Press*, July 18, 1901.

117. Ibid., Feb. 14, 21, 1907.

118. Ibid., Nov. 15, 1915.

119. *Liberal News*, July 6, 1899.

120. *La Crosse Republican* in *Ness County News*, Mar. 10, 1900.

121. *Garden City Herald*, Nov. 16, 23, 1901.

122. Ibid., Nov. 30, 1901.

123. Ibid., Mar. 29, Dec. 27, 1902, July 25, 1903.

124. Ibid., July 15, 1909.

125. See Samuel Crumbine, *Frontier Doctor* (Philadelphia: Dorrance, 1948); and Linda Hemmen, "Out of the Darkness, Into the Light: The Transformation of the Kansas State

Board of Health, 1885–1925" (master's thesis, Department of History, Wichita State University, 2003).

126. *Garden City Herald*, Aug. 25, 1906.

127. *Ness County News*, Sept. 2, 1905, Aug. 14, 1909.

128. Mrs. E. S. Harner in *Garden City Herald*, Mar. 14, 1903.

129. *Syracuse News* in *Garden City Herald*, Apr. 29, 1899.

130. *Kansas City Star*, Aug. 27, 1911, County Clippings files, Ellis County clippings, KSHS.

131. *Republican* (Hays), May 27, 1905.

132. *Kinsley Mercury* in *Garden City Herald*, Apr. 12, 1902.

133. *Globe-Republican* (Dodge City), July 18, 1895. For background, see Robert Haywood, *Victorian West: Class and Culture in Kansas Cattle Towns* (Lawrence: University Press of Kansas, 1991).

134. *Globe-Republican* (Dodge City), Apr. 22, 1909.

135. *Garden City Herald*, July 1, 1909.

136. *Ness County News*, June 17, 1899. This reference was from a letter written by my great-uncle John, serving in Manila, to his parents, and was quoted in the newspaper. Therefore it must have been acceptable language in middle-class families of moral and Christian reputation.

137. Ibid., Jan. 26, 1901.

138. *Liberal News*, June 6, 1907.

139. Mamma to children, Sept. 11, 1899, Hansen-Bales Family Papers, Kansas Collection, University of Kansas.

140. *Kinsley Graphic*, Aug. 30, 1901.

141. Ibid., Nov. 22, 1900.

142. *Liberal News*, Sept. 17, 1908.

143. Ibid., Sept. 16, 1909.

144. *Hutchinson News* in *Globe-Republican* (Dodge City), Aug. 22, 1901.

145. *Globe-Republican* (Dodge City), Oct. 23, 1902.

146. *Kansas City Journal*, Mar. 14, 1901, in County Clippings files, Ellis County clippings, KSHS.

147. *Topeka Capital*, Oct. 27, 1901, in ibid.

148. *Globe-Republican* (Dodge City), Oct. 22, 1903.

149. *Garden City Herald*, Aug. 23, Nov. 29, 1902, Nov. 11, 1909; *Kinsley Graphic*, Aug. 13, 1901.

150. Emory Lindquist, *Bethany in Kansas: The History of a College* (Lindsborg, Kans.: Bethany College, 1975), 154, 159.

151. *Republican* (Hays), Dec. 8, 1900.

152. Ibid., Apr. 16, Dec. 24, 1904.

153. Ibid., Feb. 2, 1907.

154. Alpha Hansen to Kitten, Oct. 28, 1906, Hansen-Bales Family Papers, Kansas Collection, University of Kansas.

155. Olive Thomas to Alpha Hansen, June 25, 1907, ibid.

156. Sissy to Kitten, Nov. 24, 1907, ibid.

157. Alpha Hansen to Kitten, Dec. 9, 1907, ibid.

158. Ibid., Dec. 15, 1907.

159. Ibid., Dec. 29, 1907.

160. Ibid., Jan. 5, 1908.

161. Ibid., Jan. 19, 1908.

162. Ibid., Sept. 4, 1910.

163. Harold Miner to Mabel Pinkney, Feb. 24, 1907, author's collection.

164. Program, May 30, 1907, author's collection.

165. *Kansas City Journal* in *Ness County News*, Feb. 7, 1903.

166. *Ness County News*, Oct. 24, Nov. 28, 1903.

167. Ibid., Mar. 12, 1904.

168. Ibid., Dec. 23, 1905.

169. Ibid., Jan. 20, 1906.

170. Ibid., Apr. 21, 1906.

171. Ibid., Feb. 27, 1906.

172. Ibid., June 5, 1909.

173. *Garden City Herald*, Apr. 21, 1906.

174. *Ness County News,* Aug. 4, 1906, Mar. 23, 1907.

175. *Globe-Republican* (Dodge City), Apr. 21, 1898.

176. *Tiller and Toiler* (Larned), Dec. 20, 1907.

177. Ibid., Apr. 17, 1908.

178. *Liberal News*, Oct. 31, 1901.

179. Ibid., Mar. 19, 1908.

180. *Ashland Clipper,* Aug. 12, 1912.

181. Ibid., Nov. 21, 1912.

182. Ibid.

183. *Republican* (Hays), Nov. 19, 1904.

184. Ibid., June 6, 1908.

185. *Kansas City Star*, June 9, 1912, in County Clippings files, Edwards County clippings, KSHS.

186. *Larned Chronoscope*, Oct. 31, 1902.

187. Ibid.

188. *Ellis County News-Republican,* May 9, 1914.

189. *Globe-Republican* (Dodge City), Jan. 9, 1902.

190. *Kinsley Mercury* in *Globe-Republican* (Dodge City), Jan. 9, 1902.

191. *Larned Chronoscope*, Oct. 9, 1903.

192. *Hays Daily News*, Feb. 2, 1965, in County Clippings files, Ellis County clippings, KSHS; *Republican* (Hays), Oct. 13, 1906.

193. *Hays Daily News*, June 25, 1967, in County Clippings files, Ellis County clippings, KSHS.

194. *Salina Journal*, Apr. 30, 1896.

195. *Globe-Republican* (Dodge City), Dec. 29, 1904.

196. Ibid., Mar. 30, 1905.

197. *Western Kansas World*, Mar. 4, 1954, County Clippings files, Trego County clippings, KSHS.

198. *Garden City Herald*, Mar. 25, 1909.

199. Ibid., July 22, 1905.

200. Ibid., Oct. 14, 1909.

201. Ibid., Mar. 25, 1909.

202. Ibid., Dec. 16, 1915.

203. *Liberal News*, Mar. 2, 1907.

204. *Belleville Telescope*, Mar. 17, 1905.

205. *Kansas Farmer*, Mar. 30, 1912.

206. *Larned Chronoscope*, June 13, 1902, Mar. 2, 1906.

207. *Kinsley Mercury* in ibid., Oct. 23, 1903.

208. *Ellis County News-Republican* (Hays), Aug. 2, Oct. 4, 1913.

209. *Kansas City Star*, Dec. 30, 1945; *Kansas City Times*, Dec. 10, 1948; *Rush County News*, Apr. 13, 1961, County Clippings files, Rush County clippings, KSHS.

210. *Garden City Herald*, July 29, 1915.

211. Ibid., May 21, 1910.

212. Ibid., May 23, 1910.

213. *Tiller and Toiler* (Larned), Oct. 28, 1910.

214. Ibid., Nov. 11, 1910.

215. Ibid., Dec. 16, 1910.

216. *Republican* (Hays), Feb. 14, 1903.

Chapter 6. The Golden Age

1. Annual Reports, typescript, Garden City Experiment Station, 1908, Special Collections, Kansas State University.

2. Annual Report, Garden City Experiment Station, 1914, ibid.

3. Annual Report, Tribune Experiment Station, 1913, ibid.

4. Annual Report, Colby Experiment Station, 1914, ibid.

5. *Kansas City Star*, June 5, 1913, in County Clippings files, Thomas County clippings, KSHS.

6. *Colby Free Press*, June 5, 1913.

7. *Kansas City Star*, June 5, 1913, in County Clippings files, Thomas County clippings, KSHS.

8. *Colby Free Press*, Sept. 18, 1913.

9. Ibid., Mar. 26, 1914.

10. *Topeka Daily Capital*, July 10, 1913, ibid.

11. *Kansas City Star*, July 12, 1914; *Kansas City Journal*, Aug. 4, 1915, ibid.

12. Annual Reports, typescript, Colby Experiment Station, 1914, Special Collections, Kansas State University.

13. Annual Report, Tribune Experiment Station, 1913, ibid.

14. Ibid., 1914.

15. Annual Report, Garden City Experiment Station, 1914, 1915, ibid.

16. Phillips, *History of the Agricultural Research Center—Hays: The First 100 Years*, 9–10.

17. *Tiller and Toiler* (Larned), Sept. 20, 1912.

18. J. K. Freed to G. Hodges, July 15, 1913, George Hodges Papers, 27-07-03-03, KSHS.

19. *Tiller and Toiler* (Larned), May 21, 1915.

20. *Kansas Farmer*, Nov. 15, 1913.

21. Ibid., Jan. 3, 1914.

22. *Dodge City Daily Globe*, May 18, 1928.

23. *Kansas Farmer*, Apr. 4, 1914.

24. Ibid., July 4, 1914.

25. *Garden City Herald*, June 2, 1906.

26. Ibid., May 9, 16, 1903.

27. Ibid., May 23, 1903, Feb. 16, 1906.

28. Royal Kellogg, *Forest Planting in Western Kansas* (Washington, D.C.: Government Printing Office, 1904), 9–14, 19, 24, 48.

29. *Garden City Herald*, Aug. 18, 1906.

30. Ibid., June 2, 1906.

31. *Tiller and Toiler* (Larned), Mar. 19, 23, June 2, Oct. 27, Nov. 24, 1911.

32. Ibid., Oct. 27, 1911.

33. *Garden City Herald*, Feb. 22, 1908.

34. Ibid., Sept. 1, 1906.

35. Ibid., Apr. 11, 1908.

36. Ibid., July 22, 1909.

37. Ibid., Oct. 28, 1909.

38. Ibid., June 23, 1910.

39. Ibid., Aug. 25, 1910.

40. Ibid., Jan. 14, 1915.

41. Ibid., Jan. 23, 1919; *Tiller and Toiler* (Larned), Oct. 29, 1915.

42. *Twenty-first Report of the Board of Railroad Commissioners, State of Kansas, for the Years Ending November 30, 1909, and November 30, 1910* (Topeka: State Printing Office, 1910), 430, 530; *Garden City Herald*, Mar. 16, 1907.

43. *Garden City Herald*, Apr. 20, Nov. 18, 1907.

44. Ibid., May 25, 1907.

45. Ibid., May 2, 1908.

46. *News-Chronicle* (Scott City), Nov. 12, 1908.

47. *La Junta Tribune* in *Garden City Herald*, May 21, 1908.

48. *Twenty-first Report of the Board of Railroad Commissioners, State of Kansas, for the Years Ending November 30, 1909, and November 30, 1910*, 430–31; *Scott County News*, Nov. 12, 1908.

49. *Garden City Herald*, Sept. 3, 1908.

50. *Globe-Republican* (Dodge City), Aug. 20, 1908.

51. *Garden City Herald*, Oct. 15, 1908.

52. *Globe-Republican* (Dodge City), June 10, 1909.

53. Ibid., Nov. 25, 1909.

54. *Garden City Herald*, Aug. 26, 1909.

55. Ibid., Dec. 30, 1909.

56. *News-Chronicle* (Scott City), Mar. 11, 1910.

57. *Larned Chronoscope* in ibid., Aug. 12, 1915.

58. *Garden City Herald*, Aug. 17, 1916.

59. *Garden City Herald*, Dec. 17, 1908.

60. T. Hankins in *Ness County News*, Apr. 6, 1907.

61. *Ness County News*, Nov. 2, 1907.

62. Lee Berglund, *Wheat Belt Route: Wichita Northwestern, the Story of a Dust Bowl Railroad* (David City, Nebr.: South Platte Press, 1998), 7–9.

63. *Tiller and Toiler* (Larned), Sept. 31, 1915.

64. Ibid., Mar. 23, 1917.

65. *Second Biennial Report of the Public Utilities Commission, State of Kansas, December 1, 1912, to November 30, 1914* (Topeka: Kansas State Printing Office, 1915), 110, 121–22, 146.

66. *Third Biennial Report of the Public Utilities Commission, State of Kansas, December 1, 1914, to November 30, 1916* (Topeka: Kansas State Printing Plant, 1917), 268.

67. *Fourth Biennial Report of the Public Utilities Commission, State of Kansas, December 1, 1916, to November 30, 1918* (Topeka: Kansas State Printing Plant, 1918), 212, 224–25.

68. *Tiller and Toiler* (Larned), May 14, 1915.

69. Ibid., May 28, 1915, Jan. 21, 1916.

70. *Globe-Republican* (Dodge City), Dec. 18, 1902.

71. *Dodge City Reporter*, Feb. 15, 1901; *Globe-Republican* (Dodge City), Feb. 5, 1903.

72. *Liberal News,* Feb. 5, 1903.

73. *Globe-Republican* (Dodge City) in *Liberal News*, Dec. 25, 1902.

74. *Wichita Eagle* in *Liberal News*, May 2, 1901.

75. *Globe-Republican* (Dodge City), Nov. 30, 1905.

76. Ibid., May 24, 1906.

77. Ibid., Oct. 25, 1906; ibid. in *Liberal News*, Dec. 25, 1902.

78. *Globe-Republican* (Dodge City), Dec. 6, 1906.

79. Ibid., Apr. 29, 1909.

80. Ibid., June 24, 1909.

81. *Garden City Herald* in *Liberal News*, Apr. 21, 1910.

82. *Liberal News*, Aug. 19, 1912.

83. E. P. Ripley to W. D. Hines, June 16, 1909, Atchison, Topeka and Santa Fe Railroad Archives, New York Executive Department Files, RR 34.5, KSHS.

84. H. D. Hines to E. P. Ripley, July 1, 1909, ibid.

85. Gardiner Lathrop to E. P. Ripley, July 9, 1909, ibid.

86. Walker Hines to E. P. Ripley, July 14, 1909, ibid.; Walker Hines to Mr. Linn, Oct. 29, 1909, ibid.

87. E. P Ripley to Walker Hines, Jan. 6, 1910, ibid. Jobes's biography comes from William Connelley, *History of Kansas: State and People*, 5 vols. (Chicago and New York: American Historical Society, 1918): 4: 2181–82.

88. E. P. Ripley to Walker Hines, Feb. 1, 1910, Atchison, Topeka and Santa Fe Railroad Archives, New York Executive Department Files, RR 34.5, KSHS.

89. Ibid., July 13, 1910.

90. E. T. Cartlidge to E. J. Engel, Feb. 19, 1915, ibid.

91. E. J. Engel to D. L. Gallup, Feb. 23, 1915, ibid.

92. C. B. Mason to David Gallup, Mar. 1, 1915, ibid.

93. *Dodge City Daily Globe*, Feb. 8, 1912.

94. E. J. E. [Engel] to Ripley, Feb. 23, 1916, Atchison, Topeka and Santa Fe Railroad Archives, New York Executive Department Files, RR 34.5, KSHS.

95. E. P. Ripley to Walker Hines, Mar. 11, 1916, ibid.; *Topeka Capital*, Dec. 14, 1924, County Clippings files, Haskell County clippings, KSHS.

96. *Wichita Eagle*, Sept. 30, 1906, County Clippings files, Morton County clippings, KSHS.

97. *Topeka Journal*, Oct. 7, 1907, ibid.

98. Willard Mayberry in *Elkhart Tri-State News*, Sept. 8, 1950, ibid.

99. *Elkhart Tri-State News*, Sept. 15, 1950, ibid.

100. *Kansas City Times,* Dec. 18, 1936; *Dodge City Daily Globe*, May 1, 1969, County Clippings files, Haskell County clippings, KSHS.

101. *Topeka Journal*, Sept. 8, 1923, County Clippings files, Stanton County clippings, KSHS.

102. *Topeka Journal*, Dec. 8, 1922, ibid.

103. Ibid., May 31, 1912.

104. These insights come from George Ham and Robin Higham, eds., *The Rise of the Wheat State: A History of Kansas Agriculture, 1861–1986* (Manhattan, Kans.: Sunflower University Press, 1987), particularly from Oliver Bidwell and William Roth, "The Land and the Soil," 1–6, and E. G. Heyn, "The Development of Wheat in Kansas," 41, 48.

105. *Medicine Lodge Cresset* in *Larned Chronoscope*, June 2, 1905.

106. *Larned Chronoscope*, Aug. 25, 1905.

107. Ham and Higham, *Rise of the Wheat State*, 51–53.

108. *Kansas City Journal* in *Garden City Herald,* May 1, 1907.

109. *Saturday Evening Post* in *Garden City Herald*, Feb. 27, 1904.

110. Ham and Higham, *Rise of the Wheat State*, 43, 51–53.

111. Ibid., 45–46.

112. *Republican* (Hays), July 8, 1905.

113. *Kansas Farmer*, May 11, 1912.

114. Thomas Isern, "Wheat Explorer the World Over," *Kansas History 23* (Spring/Summer 2000): 14–15, 19, 23–25. A good short biography of Carleton is in *Great Bend Daily Tribune*, Dec. 24, 1926.

115. The classic work on early crop adaptation is Malin, *Winter Wheat*.

116. *Ashland Clipper*, July 3, 1913.

117. C. W. Miller to George Hodges, July 14, 1914, George Hodges Papers, 27-07-03-03, KSHS.

118. *Colby Free Press*, Mar. 18, 1915.

119. *Hays Republican*, May 18, 1907.

120. *Topeka Capital* in *Republican* (Hays), Nov. 16, 1907.

121. *Kansas Farmer*, June 8, 1910.

122. Helen Harris, "Agriculture and Fort Hays State University," *Kansas History 9* (Winter 1986/1987): 165–68.

123. *Kansas Farmer*, Aug. 31, 1912.

124. Ibid., Mar. 1, 1913.

125. Ibid., July 6, 1912.

126. *Dodge City Daily Globe*, Aug. 1, 1912.

127. Ibid., Sept. 14, 1913.

128. Robert M. Wright, *Dodge City: The Cowboy Capital and the Great Southwest* (Wichita: Wichita Eagle, 1913), 330, 333.

129. M. G. Blackman, "Best Methods for West," *Dodge City Daily Globe,* Mar. 8, 1913.

130. *Dodge City Daily Globe,* Oct. 28, 1912.

131. *Ellis County News* (Hays), Mar. 21, 1914.

132. Harris, "Agriculture and Fort Hays State University," 165–68.

133. *Tiller and Toiler* (Larned), Jan. 21, 1916.

134. Barton Curie in *Country Gentleman,* quoted in ibid., Mar. 10, 1916.

135. *Western Kansas News* in *Colby Free Press,* Jan. 4, 1917.

136. Harry Mason, *Life on the Dry Line: Working the Land, 1902–1944* (Golden, Colo.: Fulcrum Publishing, 1992), 34, 45.

137. *Kansas City Journal* in *Larned Chronoscope,* June 23, 1905.

138. *Tiller and Toiler* (Larned), May 14, 1915.

139. Ibid., Apr. 7, 1916.

140. *Kansas City Star,* Nov. 20, 1910, in County Clippings files, Sedgwick County clippings, KSHS.

141. *Ellis County News* (Hays), July 31, 1915.

142. *Dodge City Daily Globe,* Jan. 14, 1915.

143. Forsythe, *The First 75 Years,* 32–33.

144. *Ellis County News* (Hays), Mar. 21, 1914.

145. Ibid., Aug. 14, 1915.

146. Ibid., Nov. 20, 1915.

147. Ibid., Mar. 29, 1917.

148. Ibid., May 15, 1919.

149. Ibid., Apr. 24, 1919; *Colby Free Press,* May 15, 1919.

150. W. H. Kerr to Arthur Capper, Jan. 13, 1915, Arthur Capper Papers (as governor), 27-08-01-04, KSHS.

151. The daily newspaper information is from *Dodge City Daily Globe,* Dec. 12, 1913. *Liberal News,* Apr. 10, 1913, contains the Baughman information. The rest of the paragraph is gleaned from numerous articles in papers all over the region. The auto noise ordinance is from *Liberal News,* Sept. 3, 1914. Mrs. Minnie Johnson Grinstead of Liberal was an example of a serious political candidate, even making a bid for the U.S. Senate in 1914. See *Liberal News,* Mar. 2, 1914, July 4, Oct. 31, 1918. Finney County's historical society is documented in *Garden City Herald,* Apr. 16, 1914. Its municipal light plant issue can be followed in *Garden City Herald,* Sept. 23, Oct. 21, 1915, Mar. 2, 16, 1916.

152. *Liberal News,* Sept. 20, 1917.

153. Ibid., Sept. 27, 1917.

154. *Tiller and Toiler* (Larned), July 11, 1913.

155. Karl Schletzbaum, "Early Motorcycle Racing in Kansas, 1910–1922" (master's thesis, Department of History, Wichita State University, 2002), 36, 41, 44, 61, 63–66, 72, 97.

156. *Garden City Herald,* Sept. 13, 1917.

157. *Weekly Kansas Chief* in *Colby Free Press,* Aug. 29, 1918.

158. *Country Gentleman,* quoted in *Colby Free Press,* Nov. 27, 1919.

159. *Salina Union* in *News-Chronicle* (Scott City), Dec. 8, 1915.

160. *News-Chronicle* (Scott City), Apr. 5, 1916.

161. Ibid., Sept. 27, Oct. 11, 1916.

162. Ibid., Jan. 31, 1917.

163. Ibid., May 16, 1917.

164. *Garden City Herald*, June 7, 1917.

165. Tom McNeal, quoted in *Colby Free Press*, July 19, 1917.

166. *Colby Free Press*, Dec. 11, 1919.

Chapter 7. A Storm of Readjustment

1. J. C. Hopper in *Ness County News*, June 30, 1917.

2. Ibid., May 19, 1917.

3. Ibid., Apr. 28, 1917.

4. *Ness County News*, Jan. 26, 1918.

5. W. G. McAdoo to Arthur Capper, Jan. 6, 1917, Arthur Capper Papers (as senator), Jan. 6, 1917, 27-08-02-06, KSHS.

6. Statement of Arthur Capper, n.d. [1917], Arthur Capper Papers (as governor), box 32, KSHS.

7. John Baughman ad in *Liberal News*, May 17, 1917.

8. *Colby Free Press,* July 5, 1928.

9. Ibid., July 12, 1917.

10. *Dodge City Daily Globe*, July 12, 1920.

11. Ibid., Sept. 2, 1918.

12. *Ellis County News* (Hays), July 19, 1917.

13. Dan Callahan, President, Federal Land Bank, Wichita, to Arthur Capper, Oct. 23, 1917, Arthur Capper Papers (as governor), 27-08-02-06, KSHS.

14. *Hutchinson News*, Dec. 18, 1917, in ibid., Dec. 18, 1917, 27-08-02-05.

15. *Great Bend Daily Tribune*, Mar. 13, 1920.

16. *Ellis County News* (Hays), Apr. 11, 1918.

17. Joel Mitchell, Plainville, to Arthur Capper, Jan. 23, 1918, Arthur Capper Papers (as governor), 27-08-04-04, KSHS.

18. C. D. Hestwood in *Liberal News*, Jan. 24, 1918, enclosed in John Boles to Arthur Capper, Jan. 24, 1918, 27-08-04-03, ibid.

19. *Goodland Republic*, Dec. 4, 18, 1919.

20. A. M. Hopper to Henry Allen, Jan. 17, 1919, Henry Allen Papers, 27-09-02-03, KSHS.

21. *Goodland Republic*, Jan. 30, 1919.

22. *Colby Free Press*, Jan. 16, 1919.

23. *Liberal News*, Apr. 5, 1917; *Great Bend Daily Tribune*, Apr. 27, 1920; *Liberal News,* Apr. 5, 1917.

24. *Great Bend Daily Tribune*, Apr. 27, 1920.

25. *Liberal News,* Nov. 15, 1917.

26. Joseph Cratts in *Ness County News*, June 2, 1917.

27. *Goodland Republic*, Apr. 11, 1918.

28. *Colby Free Press*, Mar. 21, 1917.

29. Ibid., May 9, 1918.

30. E. Wyant to Arthur Capper, Oct. 29, 1918, Arthur Capper Papers (as governor), 27-08-04-03, KSHS.

31. Mrs. Ruth Connell to Arthur Capper, Nov. 30, 1918, 27-08-04-02, ibid.

32. *Ellis County News* (Hays), Oct. 17, 1918.

33. Jack Danciger to Arthur Capper, Jan. 18, 1916, Arthur Capper Papers (as governor), 27-08-02-02, KSHS.

34. Petition, Jan. 4, 1916, ibid.

35. *Dodge City Daily Globe,* Mar. 30, 1915.

36. John Barry, *The Great Influenza: The Epic Story of the Deadliest Plague in History* (New York: Viking, 2004), 4, 92–94, 169–70.

37. *Goodland Republic*, Oct. 10, 1918.

38. Ibid., Oct. 17, 24, 1918.

39. *Dodge City Daily Globe*, Nov. 29, 1918. The anecdotal information comes from ibid., Feb. 2, Apr. 11, Dec. 24, 1917, Dec. 7, 1918.

40. *Great Bend Daily Tribune* in *Liberal News*, June 10, 1920. See Craig Miner, *Kansas: The History of the Sunflower State, 1854–2000 (Lawrence: University Press of Kansas, 2002),* 236–46, for an overview of the atmosphere.

41. *Ellis County News* (Hays), June 6, 1918.

42. *Great Bend Daily Tribune*, June 2, 1922.

43. *Liberal News*, Jan. 13, 1921.

44. *Colby Free Press*, Feb. 5, 1920.

45. *Dodge City Daily Globe,* July 22, 1916.

46. Ibid., Apr. 23, 1918.

47. Robert Morlan, *Political Prairie Fire: The Nonpartisan League, 1915–1922* (Minneapolis: University of Minnesota Press, 1955), 1, 19, 22, 123, 277. See also Theodore Salutos and John Hicks, *Agricultural Discontent in the Middle West, 1900–1930* (Madison: University of Wisconsin Press, 1951), 149–218. The secondary accounts of the League hardly mention Kansas.

48. *Dodge City Daily Globe*, May 4, 1918.

49. *Ness County News*, July 17, 1920.

50. *Colby Free Press,* Feb. 24, 1918.

51. T. A. Case to Arthur Capper, Mar. 12, 1918, Arthur Capper Papers (as governor), 27-08-03-02, KSHS.

52. M. L. Amos to Arthur Capper, Mar. 23, 1919, ibid.

53. Broadside, n.d. [1911], Milton Amos Papers, box 1, Kansas Collection, University of Kansas.

54. Clipping, Mar. 9, 1918; Letter, J. L Cross to Arthur Capper, Feb. 27, 1918, Arthur Capper Papers (as governor), 27-08-03-02, KSHS.

55. S. M. Millsack, Goodland, to Arthur Capper, Mar. 25, 1918, Elmer Peterson, Wichita, to Arthur Capper, Apr. 25, 1918, Arthur Capper Papers (as governor), 27-08-03-02, KSHS.

56. *Dodge City Daily Globe*, May 11, 1918.

57. *Ellis County News* (Hays), Apr. 25, 1918.

58. *Dodge City Daily Globe*, May 4, 1920.

59. Ibid., June 18, 1920.

60. Ibid., June 7, 1920.

61. *Great Bend Daily Tribune,* June 9, 1920.

62. Ibid., June 14, 18, 1920.

63. Ibid., June 26, 1920.

64. Ibid., Mar. 12, 1921.

65. *Hutchinson News*, Mar. 13, 1921.

66. *Great Bend Daily Tribune*, June 21, 1920.

67. Ibid., Jan. 21, 1921.

68. Ibid., Mar. 14, 1921.

69. Ibid., June 1, 1921.

70. Ibid., Mar. 7, 1922.

71. *Kansas Farmer*, July 3, 1920.

72. Ibid., July 24, 1920.

73. Ibid., Feb. 14, 1920.

74. A good overview of conditions is found in Salutos and Hicks, *Agricultural Discontent*.

75. *Goodland Republic*, Oct. 30, 1919.

76. *Great Bend Daily Tribune*, Jan. 31, 1922.

77. *Dodge City Daily Globe*, Apr. 14, June 24, 1921.

78. *Twenty-fourth Biennial Report of the Kansas State Board of Agriculture,* 1925, 129.

79. *Dodge City Daily Globe*, July 21, 1923.

80. Ibid., Aug. 14, 1923.

81. *Twenty-fourth Biennial Report of the Kansas State Board of Agriculture,* 570–71; *Dodge City Daily Globe*, Sept. 4, 1929. The latter source documents that in 1929 Western Kansas raised over 151 million bushels of wheat of the 177 million raised for the entire wheat state.

82. *Great Bend Daily Tribune,* Nov. 15, 1923.

83. Arthur Evans in *Denver Post*, quoted in *Colby Free Press*, July 26, 1923.

84. *Dodge City Daily Globe*, Oct. 12, 1923.

85. Ibid., Dec. 22, 1922; *Twenty-fourth Biennial Report of the Kansas State Board of Agriculture,* 570–71.

86. *Dodge City Daily Globe*, Oct. 17, 1923.

87. Ibid., July 21, 1923.

88. Ibid., July 26, 1923.

89. Ibid., Feb. 7, 1921.

90. Ibid., Dec. 1, 1920.

91. Ibid., Oct. 5, 1920.

92. Ibid., Dec. 6, 1920.

93. *Great Bend Daily Tribune*, Jan. 14, 1922.

94. *Goodland Republic*, Apr. 15, 1920.

95. Ibid., Jan. 29, 1920.

96. *Kansas Farmer*, Dec. 20, 1919.

97. Ibid., May 30, 1925.

98. These statistics are based on the tables in the *Biennial Reports of the Kansas State Board of Agriculture*.

99. A convenient place to study these trends is the foldout chart opposite page 282 in *Twenty-Ninth Biennial Report of the Kansas State Board of Agriculture* (Topeka: Kansas State Printing Plant, 1935). This tracks production and value of wheat for twenty years. The call for acreage reduction is seen in *Dodge City Daily Globe*, Nov. 3, 1923, among other places. Comparison to national production is in *Dodge City Daily Globe*, Dec. 18, 1923.

100. *Goodland Republic*, May 13, 1926.

101. *Hugoton Hermes*, July 4, 1930.

102. H. M. Bainer in *Hugoton Hermes*, Dec. 5, 1930.

103. *Cimarron County News* in *Hugoton Hermes*, May 2, 1930.

104. Annual Reports, typescript, Colby Experiment Station, 1918, Special Collections, Kansas State University.

105. Ibid., 1919.

106. Ibid., 1921, 1923–1927.

107. Annual Report, Garden City Experiment Station, 1922, ibid.

108. Ibid., 1928.

109. Annual Report, Tribune Experiment Station, 1918, 1922, 1925–1926, ibid.

110. *Stockton Review* in *Colby Free Press*, Aug. 30, 1917.

111. *Goodland Republic*, Oct. 2, 1919.

112. *Dodge City Daily Globe*, Oct. 7, 1924.

113. Ibid., Nov. 30, 1925.

114. *Hugoton Hermes*, May 26, 1926.

115. Ibid., June 4, 1926.

116. Ibid., July 30, 1926.

117. Ibid., July 2, 1926.

118. *Goodland News-Republic*, Aug. 26, 1926.

119. *Dodge City Daily Globe*, Oct. 23, 1923.

120. *Great Bend Daily Tribune*, Feb. 24, 1922.

121. *Garden City Herald*, Feb. 26, May 27, 1920.

122. Ibid., Mar. 25, Apr. 8, 22, May 27, 1920.

123. *Dodge City Daily Globe*, Dec. 20, 1920; *Kansas Farmer*, Oct. 2, 1920.

124. *Dodge City Daily Globe*, Nov. 8, 1923.

125. Ibid., Dec. 20, 1923.

126. Ibid., May 4, 1920, May 24, 1921.

127. *Great Bend Daily Tribune*, June 30, 1921.

128. *Colby Free Press*, July 12, 1923.

129. *Dodge City Daily Globe*, May 26, June 12, 1925.

130. Ibid., May 15, 1926.

131. *Ness County News*, July 5, 12, 1919.

132. *Great Bend Daily Tribune*, May 4, 1921.

133. Ibid., May 12, 1922.

134. *Garden City Herald*, May 28, 1925.

135. *Globe-Republican* (Dodge City), Mar. 19, 1896.

136. The phrase is from *Colby Free Press*, June 20, 1901.

137. *Dodge City Daily Globe*, June 6, 1921.

138. *Tiller and Toiler* (Larned), Sept. 2, 1920.

139. *Country Gentleman* in *Tiller and Toiler* (Larned), May 19, 1921.

140. *Tiller and Toiler* (Larned), July 5, 1923.

141. Michael Grant, *Down and Out on the Family Farm: Rural Rehabilitation in the Great Plains, 1929–1945* (Lincoln: University of Nebraska Press, 2002), 16.

142. Quoted in *Great Bend Daily Tribune*, Mar. 18, 1927.

143. *Kansas Farmer*, Jan. 31, 1920.

144. Ibid., Feb. 22, 1919.

145. Ibid., Feb. 7, 1920.

146. Thomas Isern, *Custom Combining on the Great Plains: A History* (Norman: University of Oklahoma Press, 1981), 11.

147. *Great Bend Daily Tribune*, July 20, 1926.

148. Ibid., June 13, 1927.

149. Thomas Isern, *Bull Threshers and Bindlestiffs: Harvesting and Threshing on the North American Plains* (Lawrence: University Press of Kansas, 1990), 174.

150. *Colby Free Press,* Apr. 4, 1929.

151. *Dodge City Daily Globe,* June 16, 1927.

152. *Ness County News*, Jan. 29, 1921.

153. *Great Bend Daily Tribune,* May 16, 1927.

154. Ibid., July 1, 1920.

155. A. A. Doerr speech, Sept. 21, 1920, Albert Doerr Papers, box 9, KSHS.

156. An example is in *Tiller and Toiler* (Larned), Apr. 22, 1920.

157. W. Ed Williams to A. A. Doerr, July 9, 1927, Albert Doerr Papers, box 9, KSHS.

158. Typescript of Doerr speech, Jan. 11, 1932, box 28, ibid.

159. Clugston, "A Storekeeper Who Studies Farmers' Wants," 61.

160. MacDonald, "Big Country Merchants," 15.

161. Isern, *Custom Combining,* 14.

162. *Hugoton Hermes*, Feb. 20, 1925.

163. *Liberal News*, Apr. 30, 1925.

164. *Hugoton Hermes*, June 4, 1926.

165. *Ellis County News* (Hays), June 24, 1926.

166. *Liberal News*, June 7, 1928.

167. *Dodge City Daily Globe*, Mar. 3, 1931.

168. Ibid., May 18, 1928, Mar. 4, 1929.

169. *Ness County News*, Feb. 15, 1930.

170. *Dodge City Daily Globe,* Mar. 5, 1930.

171. *Kansas Farmer*, Oct. 19, 1925.

172. Orville Kile, *The Farm Bureau through Three Decades* (Baltimore: Waverly Press, 1948), 24, 35–36, 45, 47.

173. Salutos and Hicks, *Discontent*, 255.

174. *Kansas Farmer*, Sept. 11, 1920.

175. Thomas Van Sant, *Improving Rural Lives: A History of Farm Bureau in Kansas, 1912–1992* (Manhattan, Kans.: Sunflower University Press, 1993), 26, 32–33.

176. *Great Bend Daily Tribune*, June 20, 1921.

177. *Tiller and Toiler* (Larned), June 23, 1916.

178. Ibid., Apr. 1, 1920.

179. *Dodge City Daily Globe*, Jan. 10, 1918.

180. *Ellis County News* (Hays), Feb. 12, 1920, Dec. 29, 1921.

181. *Dodge City Daily Globe*, Dec. 16, 1922.

182. Ibid., Feb. 2, 1921.

183. *Goodland News-Republic*, Dec. 16, 1926.

184. *Goodland Republic,* Apr. 20, 1922.

185. *Dodge City Daily Globe,* Feb. 16, 1921.

186. *Ness County News,* Dec. 27, 1924.

187. Ibid., Jan. 29, 1921, June 17, 1922.

188. Ibid., May 29, 1920.

189. Ibid., Dec. 29, 1923.

190. Marilyn Holt, *Linoleum, Better Babies, and the Modern Farm Woman, 1890–1930* (Albuquerque: University of New Mexico Press, 1995), 46–47, 120–21.

191. *Tiller and Toiler* (Larned), Nov. 22, 1923.

192. *Ness County News,* Nov. 1, 1924.

193. *Tiller and Toiler* (Larned), Mar. 22, 1928.

194. Cooperative Extension Service, Historical Files, Report of County Agent Leader, Feb. 5–Mar. 3, 1917, U91.7, University Archives, Special Collections, Kansas State University.

195. Ibid., Mar. 1917.

196. Ibid., August 1917.

197. Annual report for Barton County, Apr.–Sept. 1918, ibid.

198. Ibid., Nov. 20, 1919–Apr. 21, 1920.

199. For the broad role of the Farm Bureau in cooperatives, see Barron, *Mixed Harvest,* 141–49.

200. Salutos and Hicks, *Discontent,* 273, 290.

201. *Great Bend Daily Tribune,* Oct. 14, 1920.

202. Ibid., Oct. 27, 1920.

203. Ibid., Oct. 30, 1920.

204. *Kansas Farmer,* Dec. 11, 1920.

205. Ibid., May 28, 1921.

206. Ibid., Apr. 16, 1921.

207. Ibid., Oct. 20, 1920.

208. *Kansas Farmer,* Oct. 30, 1920.

209. *Great Bend Daily Tribune,* Apr. 20, 1921.

210. Ibid., Apr. 29, 1921.

211. *Colby Free Press,* Mar. 6, 1924.

212. *Dodge City Daily Globe,* Mar. 17, 1924.

213. *Kansas Farmer,* Apr. 16, 1921.

214. Ibid., Nov. 20, 1920.

215. *Dodge City Daily Globe,* July 22, 1921.

216. *Tiller and Toiler* (Larned), Jan. 17, 1924.

217. Ibid., Feb. 7, 1924.

218. *Great Bend Daily Tribune,* July 7, 1922, July 17, 1923.

219. *Dodge City Daily Globe,* Apr. 25, 1921.

220. *Great Bend Daily Tribune,* Aug. 21, 1924.

221. Ibid., Sept. 16, 1924.

222. Ibid., Nov. 7, 1924.

223. *Goodland Republic,* May 15, 1924.

224. J. B. Brown in *Goodland Republic*, Mar. 20, 1924.

225. *Hutchinson News,* Nov. 11, 1922.

226. *Great Bend Daily Tribune,* Oct. 26, 1922.

227. Ibid., July 17, 1923.

228. Ibid., Nov. 8, 1924.

Chapter 8. Sitting on the Moon

1. For a history of the trains, see Constance Menninger, "The Gospel of Better Farming according to Santa Fe," *Kansas History* 10 (Spring 1987): 43–66. Social context about the impact of the trains on women is found in Holt, *Linoleum,* 26–28, 146–47.

2. E. W. Houx to C. W. Campbell, Jan. 19, 1922, Atchison, Topeka and Santa Fe Railroad Archives, Agricultural Development and Publicity Office, Correspondence and Clippings Files, RR 402, KSHS; Menninger, "Gospel," 44.

3. *Kinsley Mercury,* May 4, 1922, Atchison, Topeka and Santa Fe Railroad Archives, Agricultural Development and Publicity Office, Correspondence and Clippings Files, RR 408, KSHS.

4. Memo, n.d., Atchison, Topeka and Santa Fe Railroad Archives, Agricultural Development and Publicity Office, Correspondence and Clippings Files, RR 402, KSHS. Most of the manuscript material on the 1925 Special is in folders 7–8, RR 402.

5. ? to F. C. Fox, July 11, 1925, ibid.; ? to Bruce Hunter, July 14, 1925, ibid.

6. Sam Pickard to Frank Jarrell, July 9, 1925, ibid.

7. Frank McDonald to Frank Jarrell, July 13, 1925, ibid.; *St. John News,* July 30, 1926, RR 409, ibid.

8. *Great Bend Daily Tribune,* July 24, 1925, ibid.

9. Hockaday's insanity is documented in *Great Bend Daily Tribune,* Oct 12, 13, Nov. 21, 1925.

10. *Ness County News,* July 4, 1925.

11. *Concordia Kansan,* July 23, 1925, Atchison, Topeka and Santa Fe Railroad Archives, Agricultural Development and Publicity Office, Correspondence and Clippings Files, RR 402, KSHS.

12. W. H. Simpson to J. F. Jarrell, May 20, 1925, ibid.

13. ? to H. M. Bainer, July 10, 1925, ibid.

14. *Kansas City Weekly Star,* Aug. 5, 1925, *Topeka Capital,* June 17, 1923, RR 409, ibid. Menninger, "Gospel," 50–51, 53. The extensive Kansas clippings files kept by the railroad provide a social study in themselves. They fill most of RR 409, Atchison, Topeka and Santa Fe Railroad Archives, Agricultural Development and Publicity Office, Correspondence and Clippings Files, KSHS.

15. *Lincoln Sentinel,* July 23, 1923, RR 409, ibid.

16. *Hutchinson Herald,* July 23, 1925, *Kansas City Journal,* Aug. 1, 1925, ibid.

17. *Hutchinson Herald,* July 25, 1925, ibid.

18. *Great Bend Daily Tribune,* July 23, 24, 1925, ibid.

19. *Pratt Tribune,* July 28, 1925, *Wichita Beacon,* July 31, 1925, ibid.

20. *Hutchinson News,* July 21, 1925, ibid.

21. *Hutchinson News,* July 28, 1925, ibid.

22. ? [Frank Jarrell] to Edward Chambers, Aug. 5, 1925, RR 402, ibid.

23. Clipping, n.d., Clifford Hope Papers, box 50, folder 31, KSHS.

24. *Garden City Herald*, July 27, 1926, Atchison, Topeka and Santa Fe Railroad Archives, Agricultural Development and Publicity Office, Correspondence and Clippings Files, RR 410, KSHS.

25. *Topeka Capital*, July 28, 1926, ibid.

26. *Dodge City Globe*, July 23, 1926, ibid.

27. *Hugoton Hermes*, June 21, 1935.

28. *Goodland Republic*, June 11, 1925.

29. For summaries of the issue, see Miner, *Kansas*, 261–66; and Paul Sutter, "Paved with Good Intentions: Good Roads, the Automobile, and the Rhetoric of Rural Improvement in the *Kansas Farmer*, 1890–1914," *Kansas History* 18 (Winter 1995–1996): 284–99.

30. *News-Chronicle* (Scott City), Feb. 8, 1922.

31. *Dodge City Daily Globe*, Feb. 16, 1917.

32. *Garden City Herald*, Feb. 15, 1918.

33. Mason, *Life on the Dry Line*, 152.

34. *Garden City Herald*, Oct. 21, 1920.

35. Ibid., Feb. 22, 24, 1917.

36. Ibid., Feb. 15, 1918.

37. *Great Bend Daily Tribune*, Apr. 14, 1920.

38. *Colby Free Press*, Mar. 23, 1922.

39. P. L. Jackson in *Ness County News*, Oct. 14, 1922; *Ellis County News* (Hays), May 27, 1926.

40. *Hugoton Hermes*, Oct. 2, 1925.

41. Ibid., Oct. 30, 1925.

42. *Kansas Union Farmer*, quoted in *Great Bend Daily Tribune*, Nov. 3, 1925.

43. *Colby Free Press*, Dec. 31, 1925.

44. *Dodge City Globe*, Oct. 8, 1925.

45. *Ellis County News* (Hays), Aug. 16, 1928.

46. Ibid., May 27, 1926.

47. *Goodland News-Republic*, Feb. 21, 1929.

48. *Liberal News*, Jan. 12, 1928.

49. T. C. Wilson in ibid., Dec. 8, 1927.

50. The Highway 40 arguments are detailed in *Colby Free Press*, Dec. 17, 1925.

51. *Goodland News-Republic*, Mar. 7, 1929.

52. *Christian Science Monitor* in *Colby Free Press*, Mar. 17, 1921.

53. *Garden City Herald*, Aug. 26, 1920; *Ellis County News* (Hays), Sept. 2, 1920.

54. *Kansas Farmer*, Dec. 11, 1920.

55. *Dodge City Daily Globe*, Jan. 6, 1921.

56. *Colby Free Press*, Nov. 24, 1921.

57. E. H. Benson to Jonathan Davis, Jonathan Davis Papers, Jan. 30, 1924, 26-09-04-07, KSHS.

58. *Colby Free Press*, Mar. 23, 1922.

59. *Garden City Herald*, Dec. 20, 1923.

60. *Liberal News*, Jan. 15, 1925.

61. *Ellis County News* (Hays), Mar. 29, 1928.

62. *Dodge City Daily Globe*, Feb. 9, 1927.

63. *Great Bend Daily Tribune*, Mar. 9, 1927.

64. Typescript, n.d. [1927], Clifford Hope Papers, box 50, folder 32, KSHS.

65. *Great Bend Daily Tribune*, Feb. 10, 1927.

66. *Ellis County News* (Hays), Feb. 21, 1929.

67. *Great Bend Daily Tribune*, Mar. 16, 1927.

68. *Dodge City Daily Globe*, June 9, 1928.

69. *Ellis County News* (Hays), Feb. 28, 1929.

70. Ibid., Mar. 15, 1928.

71. *Ness County News*, Mar. 16, 1922.

72. *Great Bend Daily Tribune*, Feb. 7, 1925.

73. *Tiller and Toiler* (Larned), Dec. 3, 1925.

74. *Ness County News*, Dec. 4, 1926.

75. [A. A. Doerr] to Otho Mooney, Nov. 28, 1921, Albert Doerr Papers, box 9, KSHS.

76. *Officer's Reports, The Western Retail Implement & Hardware Association to the Thirty-Fifth Annual Convention,* box 28, ibid.

77. A. A. Doerr to Jonathan Davis, Jan. 24, 1924, box 35, ibid.

78. A. A. Doerr to H. J. Hodge, July 26, 1928, box 27, ibid.

79. Otho Mooney to A. A. Doerr, Feb. 7, 1929, ibid.

80. *Tiller and Toiler* (Larned), Mar. 14, 1929.

81. Otho Mooney to A. A. Doerr, Aug. 28, 1929, Albert Doerr Papers, box 9, KSHS.

82. [A. A. Doerr] to Otho Mooney, Aug. 19, 1929, ibid.

83. Speech, "Putting Personality into Business," n.d. [mid-1920s], box 27, ibid.

84. *Tiller and Toiler* (Larned), Dec. 26, 1929, Feb. 6, 1930.

85. Ibid., Sept. 19, 1929.

86. *Ness County News*, Feb. 19, 1927.

87. W. A. White, quoted in *Tiller and Toiler* (Larned), June 16, 1916.

88. For early AP wire service presence in Western Kansas, see *Great Bend Daily Tribune*, July 22, 1927.

89. For Duplex installations, see *Dodge City Daily Globe*, Dec. 10, 1917; *Great Bend Daily Tribune,* Feb. 22, 1924. For Liberal's consolidation and new Kelly press, see *Liberal News*, Aug. 7, 14, 21, 1924.

90. *Liberal News*, May 2, 1929.

91. Ibid., Apr. 11, 1929.

92. *Goodland Republic*, Dec. 11, 1924.

93. For the Crème-O-Milk plant at Larned, see *Topeka Capital*, Sept. 24, 1922; *Tiller and Toiler* (Larned), Mar. 29, Nov. 1, 1923. A history of the increasingly capital-intensive Garden City public utilities may be found in *Garden City Herald*, Mar. 25, 1926. Airport pieces are *Goodland Republic*, Sept. 1, 1927; *Garden City Herald*, Nov. 3, 1927, Jan. 26, June 6, 1928; *Dodge City Daily Globe*, Oct. 22, 1928.

94. For a general history of Western Kansas oil and gas development, see Craig Miner, *Fire in the Rock: A History of the Oil and Gas Industry in Kansas, 1855–1976* (Wichita: Kansas Independent Oil and Gas Association, 1976); Craig Miner, *Discovery: Cycles of Change in the Kansas Oil and Gas Industry, 1860–1987* (Wichita: Kansas Independent Oil and Gas

Association, 1987). See also the excellent analysis of the impact of oil and gas on towns in the section, "Oil and Gas Cities of Central and Southwestern Kansas," in Shortridge, *Cities on the Plains*, 196–201.

95. *Great Bend Daily Tribune*, Feb. 20, Mar. 20, 1923.

96. *Garden City Herald*, Feb. 20, 1919.

97. *Ness County News*, July 22, 1922.

98. *Liberal News*, July 28, 1921.

99. *Hugoton Hermes*, Dec. 23, 1927.

100. Miner, *Fire in the Rock*, 75–77.

101. Shortridge, *Cities on the Plains*, 198, 200.

102. The statistics come from the *Biennial Reports of the Kansas State Board of Agriculture*.

103. *Dodge City Daily Globe*, Apr. 26, 1929.

104. Miner, *Fire in the Rock*, 80.

105. *Great Bend Daily Tribune*, Mar. 5, 1923.

106. *Liberal News*, Mar. 30, Apr. 6, 1922.

107. *Hugoton Hermes*, Apr. 4, 1930.

108. Ibid., Dec. 20, 1929.

109. Ibid., Mar. 21, 1930.

110. Ibid., Mar. 28, 1930.

111. Ibid., June 20, 1930.

112. Ibid., Oct. 24, 1930.

113. Ibid., Dec. 12, 1930.

114. Ibid., Feb. 20, 1931.

115. *Great Bend Daily Tribune*, Mar. 28, 1921.

116. *Hutchinson News*, Apr. 3, 1922.

117. *Dodge City Daily Globe*, Feb. 19, 1920.

118. *Goodland Republic*, Sept. 21, 1922.

119. *Ellis County News*, Dec. 13, 1923; *Garden City Herald*, Dec. 1, 1927.

120. For Clifford Hope's biography, see Cliff Hope Jr., *Quiet Courage: Kansas Congressman Clifford R. Hope* (Manhattan, Kans.: Sunflower University Press, 1997).

121. W. E. Brown to Clifford Hope, Feb. 21, 1926, Clifford Hope Papers, box 50, KSHS.

122. *Garden City Herald*, Oct. 23, 1924, Feb. 25, 1926.

123. Ibid., Aug. 5, 1926.

124. R. F. Mirick to Clifford Hope, Apr. 29, 1927, Clifford Hope Papers, box 50, KSHS.

125. *Tiller and Toiler* (Larned), Aug. 17, 1922.

126. *Dodge City Daily Globe*, Sept. 5, 1922.

127. *Liberal News*, Aug. 31, 1922.

128. Ibid., Sept. 7, 1922.

129. Ibid., Sept. 14, 1922.

130. *Goodland Republic*, Oct. 26, 1922.

131. Ibid., Apr. 9, 1925.

132. *Dodge City Daily Globe*, Jan. 4, 1923.

133. *Kansas Farmer*, Sept. 16, 1922.

134. *Ness County News*, Dec. 1, 1923.

135. Ibid., Dec. 8, 1923.

136. *Liberal News*, June 12, 1924.

137. Charles H. McBrayer, Grand Dragon, Realm of the Kansas Knights of the Ku Klux Klan, in *Ness County News*, Nov. 1, 1924.

138. *Tiller and Toiler* (Larned), Oct. 8, 1925.

139. Ibid., Sept. 2, 1926.

140. *Ness County News*, Dec. 8, 1923.

141. Ibid., Jan. 5, 1924.

142. Mrs. Eva Murphy in *Goodland Republic*, Feb. 7, 1924.

143. *Dodge City Daily Globe,* Mar. 29, 1923.

144. Ibid., Feb. 22, 1917.

145. *Liberal News*, July 16, 1931.

146. *Garden City Herald*, Apr. 22, 1920.

147. *Ness County News*, Apr. 25, 1925.

148. Ibid., Oct. 28, 1922.

149. *Goodland Republic*, Aug. 21, 1924.

150. *Liberal News*, Jan. 15, 1925.

151. *Garden City Herald*, Mar. 26, 1925.

152. Ibid., May 7, 1925.

153. *Dodge City Daily Globe*, Apr. 4, 1925.

154. Ibid., June 9, 1925.

155. *Great Bend Daily Tribune*, Apr. 11, 1921.

156. Ibid., Apr. 6, 1925.

157. *Ellis County News* (Hays), July 19, 1923.

158. Ibid., June 12, 1924.

159. Ibid., Jan. 15, 1925.

160. Movie ad in *Great Bend Daily Tribune*, Nov. 14, 1921.

161. *Great Bend Daily Tribune,* Mar. 20, 1925.

162. *Ellis County News* (Hays), Apr. 26, May 10, 1928.

163. *Dodge City Daily Globe*, Apr. 8, 1929.

164. *Garden City Herald*, Oct. 30, 1924.

165. An example is *Great Bend Daily Tribune,* Sept. 23, 1925.

166. *Goodland Republic*, Dec. 16, 1926.

167. Ibid., Nov. 29, 1928. Some great later impressions of the pool are in Holly Clifford Hope, *Garden City: Dreams in a Kansas Town* (Norman: University of Oklahoma Press, 1988), 27–28. She remembered it as "too big" and very cold.

168. *Garden City Herald*, July 20, Aug. 10, 1922.

169. *Great Bend Daily Tribune,* July 18, 1927.

170. *Garden City Herald*, Jan. 3, 10, 1924.

171. *Liberal News,* Aug. 31, 1922.

172. Ibid., June 19, 1924.

173. Ibid., June 2, 1927.

174. *Tiller and Toiler* (Larned), June 18, 1931.

175. *Hugoton Hermes*, Sept. 11, 1925.

176. For a history with excellent photographs, see Mal Elliott, *Perry Maxwell's Prairie Dunes* (Chelsea, Mich.: Sleeping Bear Press, 2002).

177. *Liberal News*, Sept. 22, 1921.

178. Ibid., Oct. 21, 1926.

179. *Tiller and Toiler* (Larned), June 22, 1922.

180. *Ellis County News* (Hays), Feb. 25, 1926; *Kansas City Journal-Post*, Feb. 14, 1926, County Clippings files, Ellis County clippings, KSHS, vol. 1.

181. *Kansas City Star*, Oct. 16, 1927, County Clippings files, Ellis County clippings, KSHS, vol. 1.

182. *Dodge City Daily Globe*, Oct. 10, 1927.

183. Ibid., Mar. 23, 1927.

184. *Great Bend Daily Tribune*, May 25, 1912.

185. *Hutchinson News,* Aug. 22, 1921.

186. *Dodge City Daily Globe*, Oct. 11, 1922.

187. *Great Bend Daily Tribune*, Aug. 31, 1923.

188. *Tiller and Toiler* (Larned), Nov. 12, 1925.

189. *Ellis County News* (Hays), Nov. 21, 1929.

190. *Dodge City Daily Globe*, Feb. 4, 1927.

191. Kevin Britz, "'Boot Hill Burlesque': The Frontier Cemetery as Tourist Attraction in Tombstone, Arizona, and Dodge City, Kansas," *Journal of Arizona History* 44 (Autumn 2003): 215.

192. Ibid., 217–19.

193. Ibid., 219; *Dodge City Daily Globe*, Sept. 13, 1933.

194. *Dodge City Daily Globe,* May 9, 1932.

195. Britz, "Boot Hill," 226–27, 239–40.

196. Quoted in *Hugoton Hermes*, Oct. 4, 1929.

197. *Dodge City Daily Globe*, May 21, 1929.

198. Britz, "Boot Hill," 224.

199. Study of the *Biennial Reports of the Kansas State Board of Agriculture* yields running population and crop statistics.

200. *Dodge City Daily Globe*, Sept. 4, 1929.

201. *Ellis County News* (Hays), May 16, 1929.

202. Ibid., May 23, 1929; *Great Bend Daily Tribune*, May 25, 1929.

203. *Great Bend Daily Tribune,* July 16, 1929.

204. Ibid., July 17, 1929.

205. *Ellis County News* (Hays), May 16, 1929.

206. Ibid., June 4, 1929.

207. *Great Bend Daily Tribune,* June 14, 1929.

208. Ibid., Dec. 14, 1928.

209. Ibid., July 12, 1929.

210. Ibid., Oct. 24, 1928.

Chapter 9. A Stern Teacher

1. *Ness County News*, Dec. 14, 1929. Some details in this section come from the author's conversations with his father.

2. *Ness County News*, Nov. 30, 1929.

3. See, for example, ibid., Mar. 8, 1930.

4. Ibid., Jan. 11, 1930.

5. Ibid., Jan. 25, 1930.

6. Ibid., Nov. 8, 1930.

7. *Great Bend Daily Tribune*, Jan. 9, 1931.

8. This information comes from interviews with Stanley Miner and Patrick Rowley by the author.

9. *Great Bend Daily Tribune,* Sept. 4, 1931.

10. *Dodge City Daily Globe*, Mar. 4, 1935.

11. One of many examples is *Ness County News*, Apr. 6, 1932.

12. *Garden City Daily Telegram*, Sept. 7, 1931; *Tiller and Toiler* (Larned), June 1, 1933.

13. *Great Bend Daily Tribune,* Apr. 15, 1935.

14. *Goodland News-Republic* in *Greeley County Republican*, Feb. 23, 1933; *Goodland News-Republic,* Feb. 8, 1933; *Great Bend Daily Tribune*, Aug. 4, 1934.

15. *Goodland News-Republic*, Mar. 1, 1933; *Great Bend Daily Tribune*, Aug. 4, 1934.

16. J. C. Hopper to Clifford Hope, Feb. 16, 1935, Clifford Hope Papers, box 50, KSHS.

17. J. C. Hopper series in *Ness County News*, Nov. 4, 1933, and in many other issues in surrounding months.

18. *Garden City Daily Telegram*, July 14, 1931.

19. *News-Chronicle* (Scott City), Apr. 13, 1933.

20. Alexander Roy to Harry Woodring, May 26, 1932, Harry Woodring Papers, 27-10-07-04, KSHS.

21. See, for example, *Garden City Daily Telegram*, June 28, 1935.

22. *Great Bend Daily Tribune*, July 16, Aug. 6, 1931.

23. Ibid., Sept. 9, 1931.

24. Ibid., July 11, 15, 1931.

25. Ibid., July 31, 1931.

26. *News-Chronicle* (Scott City), Sept. 17, 1931.

27. *Great Bend Daily Tribune*, July 10, 1931.

28. The Kansas City papers were strong on this. See an account, for example, in *Liberal News*, Apr. 15, 1935.

29. *Dodge City Daily* Globe, Apr. 29, 1932; *Liberal News*, Feb. 7, 1935.

30. *Greeley County Republican* (Tribune), Mar. 10, 1932.

31. *Ness County News*, May 18, 1929.

32. Ibid., Sept. 21, 1929.

33. *Emporia Gazette* in *Hays Daily News*, Apr. 24, 1930.

34. *Garden City Daily Telegram*, Aug. 28, 1930.

35. *Topeka Capital* in *Liberal News*, Aug. 13, 1930.

36. *Emporia Gazette* in *Hays Daily News*, Aug. 20, 1930.

37. *Colby Free Press*, Feb. 25, 1931.

38. *Dodge City Daily Globe*, July 20, 1931; *Garden City Daily Telegram*, July 29, 1931.

39. *Colby Free Press,* July 29, 1931.

40. *Ness County News*, Oct. 3, 1931.

41. Denious quoted in *Greeley County Republican* (Tribune), Apr. 21, 1932.

42. *Great Bend Daily Tribune*, May 21, 1932.

43. *Garden City Daily Telegram*, Apr. 13, 1933; *Hays Daily News*, Apr. 13, 1933.

44. *Dodge City Daily Globe*, Apr. 29, 1933.

45. *Garden City Daily Telegram*, May 23, 1933. A fine account is Pamela Riney-Kehrberg, "Tragedy as Triumph: Liberal, Kansas, and Its 1933 Tornado," *Kansas History* 21 (Summer 1998): 88–101.

46. *Colby Free Press*, May 24, 1933.

47. *Goodland News-Republic*, June 14, 1933.

48. Warren Zimmerman, Liberal, to Clifford Hope, Jan. 31, 1932, Clifford Hope Papers, box 50, KSHS.

49. *Greeley County Republican* (Tribune), Mar. 22, 1934.

50. J. L. Horlacher to Clifford Hope, Apr. 22, 1934, Clifford Hope Papers, box 50, KSHS.

51. Jess Bennett to Clifford Hope, May 12, 1934, ibid.

52. *Hays Daily News*, June 1, 1934.

53. *Colby Free Press*, June 6, 1934.

54. *Garden City Daily Telegram*, June 19, 1934.

55. *Great Bend Daily Tribune*, June 29, 1934.

56. *Garden City Daily Telegram*, July 9, 1934; *Great Bend Daily Tribune,* July 14, 1934; *Colby Free Press*, July 18, 1934.

57. *Great Bend Daily Tribune*, July 16, 1934.

58. *Garden City Daily Telegram*, July 19, 1934.

59. *Gove County Republican-Gazette* (Gove City), Aug. 23, 1934.

60. Ibid., July 19, 1934.

61. Ibid., Aug. 9, 1934.

62. Annual Reports, typescript, Garden City Experiment Station, 1929, Special Collections, Kansas State University.

63. Ibid., 1937.

64. Annual Reports, Colby Experiment Station, 1921, 1932, 1933, 1934, ibid.

65. Annual Report, Tribune Experiment Station, 1931, ibid.

66. Ibid., 1932.

67. Ibid., 1933, 1934, 1935.

68. Ibid., 1936, 1937.

69. Pamela Riney-Kehrberg, *Rooted in Dust: Surviving Drought and Depression in Southwestern Kansas* (Lawrence: University Press of Kansas, 1994), 23.

70. *News-Chronicle* (Scott City), Feb. 1, 1934.

71. *Garden City Daily Telegram*, Jan. 1, 1931.

72. *Great Bend Daily Tribune,* Jan. 5, 1935.

73. *Greeley County Republican* (Tribune), Apr. 7, 1932.

74. Speech of Jess Denious to Rotary Club, Nov. 23, 1931, Jess Denious Papers, box 14, KSHS.

75. Denious speech to Farm Bureau, Aug. 4, 1932, ibid.

76. *Liberal News*, June 4, 1932.

77. Examples of sunset articles are *Greeley County Republican* (Tribune), June 16, 1934, and Apr. 21, 1932, quoting a Dodge City editorial.

78. This is the theme of Riney-Kehrberg, "Tragedy as Triumph."

79. *Hays Daily News*, May 11, 1934.

80. *Great Bend Daily Tribune*, Aug. 11, 1934.

81. Speech, 1933, Arthur Capper Papers (as senator), box 51, KSHS.

82. *Gove County Republican-Gazette* (Gove City), Dec. 20, 1934.

83. Riney-Kehrberg, *Rooted in Dust*. She describes her unique focus on p. 3.

84. Ibid., 37.

85. *Ellsworth Reporter* in *Great Bend Daily Tribune*, Jan. 1, 1932.

86. *Hays Daily News*, Oct. 28, 1932.

87. *Liberal News*, Aug. 4, 8, 12, 1932.

88. Ibid., July 15, 1931.

89. Ibid., July 21, 1932.

90. *Great Bend Daily Tribune*, June 27, 1933.

91. Ibid., July 25, Sept. 7, 1933.

92. *Dodge City Daily Globe*, Jan. 3, 1934.

93. Ibid., Apr. 24, July 12, 1930.

94. *Hays Daily News*, June 8, 1931.

95. *Great Bend Daily Tribune*, Apr. 4, 1931.

96. *Garden City Daily Telegram*, May 9, 1931.

97. *Great Bend Daily Tribune*, May 26, 1932.

98. *Garden City Daily Telegram*, July 27, 1933.

99. *Hays Daily News*, Apr. 28, 1930; *Great Bend Daily Tribune*, Apr. 15, 1930.

100. Robert Bader, *Prohibition in Kansas: A History* (Lawrence: University Press of Kansas, 1986), 224, 229.

101. *Hays Daily News*, July 1, 1930; *Dodge City Daily Globe*, Sept. 9, 1931; *Garden City Daily Telegram*, Sept. 10, 1931.

102. Mary Doherty to Harry Woodring, Aug. 20, 1931, Harry Woodring Papers, 27-10-07-02, KSHS.

103. *Great Bend Daily Tribune*, Dec. 5, 18, 1934.

104. *Hays Daily News*, Mar. 19, 1930; *Dodge City Daily Globe*, June 6, July 12, 1930; *Greeley County Republican*, May 26, 1932.

105. *Kansas Farmer*, May 12, 1928.

106. Ibid., July 28, 1928.

107. The most complete account is an early one, Emy Miller, "Corporation Farming in Kansas" (master's thesis, Department of History, University of Wichita, 1933). For Garvey, see also Miner, *Harvesting the High Plains*.

108. *Great Bend Daily Tribune*, Sept. 3, 1927.

109. Ibid., Apr. 6, 1928.

110. Ibid., Apr. 30, 1928.

111. R. H. Garvey to W. D. Ferguson, Mar. 20, 1930, Ray Hugh Garvey Papers, box 1, KSHS.

112. R. H. Garvey to Directors of Mutual Farming Corporation, Dec. 16, 1931, ibid., box 3.

113. Garvey Land Company ad in *Colby Free Press*, Jan. 31, 1931.

114. *Ellis County News* (Hays), May 9, 1929. An account of Kansas corporate farming and its political fate is in Miner, *Kansas*, 278–86.

115. *Goodland News-Republic*, July 17, 1929.

116. *Ness County News*, Feb. 1, 1930.

117. Miner, *Kansas*, 278; *Hays Daily News*, May 30, 1930.

118. Francis Schruben, *Kansas in Turmoil: 1930–1936* (Columbia: University of Missouri Press, 1969), 62.

119. Harold McGugin to Clyde Reed, Mar. 3, 1930, Clyde Reed Papers, 27-10-03-04, KSHS.

120. Schruben, *Kansas in Turmoil*, 62.

121. *Goodland News-Republic*, Mar. 5, 1930.

122. *Hays Daily News*, May 29, 1930.

123. Tear sheet from *Topeka Daily Capital*, Apr. 12, 1930, Clifford Hope Papers, box 50, KSHS.

124. J. S. Bird in *Hays Daily News*, July 8, 1930.

125. Clipping from *Lyons Daily News*, Apr. 29, 1930, Clifford Hope Papers, box 50, KSHS.

126. Garvey Land Company ad in *Colby Free Press*, Dec. 11, 1930.

127. Elmer Stocking to Clyde Reed, July 7, 1930, Clyde Reed Papers, 27-10-03-05, KSHS.

128. *Ness County News*, Oct. 4, 1930.

129. *Garden City Daily Telegram*, Nov. 29, 1930.

130. Charles Sledd to Clifford Hope, Nov. 3, 1930, Clifford Hope Papers, box 50, KSHS.

131. Clifford Hope to Charles Sledd, Nov. 10, 1930, ibid.

132. List, not dated, folder 36, ibid.

133. *Kansas Farmer*, Sept. 13, 1930.

134. *Hays Daily News*, Jan. 6, 1931.

135. *Garden City Daily Telegram*, Jan. 23, 1931.

136. *Hays Daily News,* Feb. 3, 1931.

137. Ibid., Jan. 31, 1931.

138. *Garden City Daily Telegram*, Apr. 20, 1931; *Great Bend Daily Tribune*, Apr. 27, 1931; Schruben, *Kansas in Turmoil*, 62–63.

139. *Hays Daily News*, May 11, 1931.

140. Garvey Land Company ad entitled "We Told You So," *Colby Free Press*, May 6, 1931; Miner, *Harvesting the High Plains*, 76–78.

141. J. S. Bird to Harry Woodring, Oct. 14, 1931, Harry Woodring Papers, 27-10-07-02, KSHS.

142. *Greeley County Republican* (Tribune), May 26, 1932.

143. *Newton Journal* in *Ellis County News*, Mar. 1, 1928.

144. David Danbom, *The Resisted Revolution: Urban America and the Industrialization of Agriculture, 1900–1930* (Ames: Iowa State University Press, 1979), 16–17.

145. *Hays Daily News*, Jan. 27, 1930.

146. *The Condition of Agriculture in the United States and Measures for Its Improvement: A Report by the Business Men's Commission on Agriculture* (New York: National Industrial Conference Board, 1927), 7.

147. David E. Hamilton, *From New Day to New Deal: American Farm Policy from Hoover to Roosevelt, 1928–1933* (Chapel Hill: University of North Carolina Press, 1991), 28, 66.

148. Good summaries of the politics may be found in Gilbert Fite, *American Agriculture and Farm Policy since 1900* (New York: Macmillan, 1964), 12–13; Theodore Salutos, *The American Farmer and the New Deal* (Ames: Iowa State University Press, 1982), 28–33; and

Murray Benedict, *Farm Policies of the United States, 1790–1950: A Study of Their Origins and Development* (New York: Twentieth Century Fund, 1953), 239–42.

149. *Hays Daily News*, Mar. 13, 1930.

150. Ibid., Apr. 3, 1930.

151. Ibid., June 20, 1930.

152. Walter Layton to Alexander Legge, July 2, 1930, Clyde Reed Papers, 17-10-03-05, KSHS.

153. Ralph Russell to Clyde Reed, Apr. 18, 1930, ibid., 27-10-03-04.

154. James Gifford to Clyde Reed, June 21, 1930, ibid., 27-10-03-05.

155. Edgar Corse to Clyde Reed, July 7, 1930, ibid.

156. George Whitson to Clyde Reed, July 8, 1930, ibid.

157. Alexander Legge to Clyde Reed, June 26, 1930, ibid., 27-10-03-01.

158. *Kansas Farmer*, July 19, 1930.

159. *Hays Daily News*, July 8, 1930; *Great Bend Daily Tribune*, July 12, 1930.

160. *Hays Daily News*, July 9, 1930.

161. Ibid., July 10, 1930.

162. Frank Caldwell to Clyde Reed, July 9, 1930, Clyde Reed Papers, 27-10-03-05, KSHS.

163. H. F. Disque to Clyde Reed, July 10, 1930, ibid.

164. *Plainville Times* in ibid., July 11, 1930.

165. T. Wagstaff to Clyde Reed, July 14, 1930, Clyde Reed Papers, 27-10-03-05, KSHS.

166. *Hays Daily News*, July 10, 1930.

167. Frank Donahue to Clyde Reed, July 12, 1930, Clyde Reed Papers, 27-10-03-05, KSHS. E. H. Taylor to Clyde Reed, July 17, 1930, ibid., 27-10-03-01, details a survey by *Country Gentleman* magazine on opposition to acreage reduction.

168. H. R. Murdock to Clyde Reed, July 19, 1930, ibid., 27-10-03-01.

169. A thoughtful article of this type is in *Ness County News*, Dec. 5, 1930.

170. *Garden City Daily Telegram*, June 12, 1931.

171. Ibid., July 3, 1931.

172. Ibid., Nov. 15, 1930.

173. *Colby Free Press*, Feb. 11, 1931.

174. W. A. Doershlag to Harry Woodring, Apr. 14, 1931, Harry Woodring Papers, 27-11-01-05, KSHS.

175. *Baltimore Sun* in *Hays Daily News*, Sept. 4, 1930.

176. *Garden City Daily Telegram*, Sept. 5, 1931.

177. Ibid., Sept. 10, 1931.

178. John Ford in *Hays Daily News*, June 2, 1931.

179. *Great Bend Daily Tribune*, July 10, 1931.

180. *Garden City Daily Telegram*, Oct. 16, 1931.

181. Ibid., June 14, 1932.

182. Ibid., July 14, 1931, Apr. 8, 1932.

183. *Hays Daily News*, June 27, 1932.

184. *Colby Free Press*, Mar. 16, 1932.

185. Ibid., Mar. 30, 1932.

186. John Wasinger to Harry Woodring, Oct. 6, 1931, Harry Woodring Papers, 27-10-07-04, KSHS.

187. Harry Woodring to John Wasinger, Oct. 20, 1931, ibid.

188. W. A. Doershlag to Harry Woodring, July 31, 1931, Harry Woodring Papers, 27-11-01-05, KSHS.

189. *Hays Daily News*, July 16, 1932.

190. *Greeley County Republican* (Tribune), Aug. 4, 1932.

191. *Hugoton Hermes*, Oct. 7, 1932.

192. *Greeley County Republican* (Tribune), Sept. 15, 1932.

193. *Hays Daily News*, Feb. 1, 1933.

194. J. W. Berryman to Arthur Capper, Feb. 3, 1933, Clifford Hope Papers, box 50, KSHS.

195. *Great Bend Daily Tribune*, Feb. 10, 1933.

196. Will Townsley to Clifford Hope, Feb. 13, 1933, Clifford Hope Papers, box 50, KSHS.

197. *Garden City Daily Telegram*, Mar. 21, 1933.

198. Joseph Shastid to Clifford Hope, Apr. 5, 1933, Clifford Hope Papers, box 50, KSHS.

199. W. T. Caldwell to Clifford Hope, May 1, 1933, ibid.

200. *Dodge City Daily Globe*, May 5, 1933.

201. Clifford Hope to S. S. Alexander, June 20, 1933, Clifford Hope Papers, box 50, KSHS.

202. *Great Bend Daily Tribune*, Aug. 12, 1933.

203. *Dodge City Daily Globe*, Aug. 18, 1933.

204. Ibid., Aug. 18, 1933.

205. R. H. Garvey to W. D. Ferguson, Aug. 24, 1934, Ray Hugh Garvey Papers, box 4, KSHS.

206. *Tiller and Toiler* (Larned), Sept. 2, 1933.

207. *Great Bend Daily Tribune*, Dec. 20, 1933.

208. *Colby Free Press*, Dec. 20, 1933.

209. *Hays Daily News*, Mar. 17, 1934.

210. Ibid., Aug. 29, 1934.

211. Clifford Hope to J. R. Hickok, Mar. 30, 1934, Clifford Hope Papers, box 50, KSHS.

212. A. L. Jacobson to Clifford Hope, May 10, 1934, ibid.

213. W. D. Ferguson to R. H. Garvey, Jan. 3, 1934, Ray Hugh Garvey Papers, box 6, KSHS.

214. *Garden City Daily Telegram*, July 24, 1934; *Hays Daily News*, July 24, 1934.

215. *Hays Daily News*, Aug. 27, 1934.

216. Ibid., Sept. 7, 1934.

217. William Elliott to Clifford Hope, Feb. 26, 1934, Clifford Hope Papers, box 50, KSHS.

218. *Hays Daily News*, July 28, 1934.

219. Mamie Fay to Clifford Hope, July 23, 1934, Clifford Hope Papers, box 50, KSHS.

220. C. C. Isely to Robert Laubengayer, June 6, 1933, Alfred Landon Papers, 27-11-04-03, KSHS; C. C. Isely to Clifford Hope, Feb. 26, 1934, Clifford Hope Papers, box 50, KSHS.

221. Jess Denious to M. H. Does, Oct. 4, 1933, Jess Denious Papers, box 1, KSHS.

222. Jess White to Alf Landon, June 15, 1933, Alfred Landon Papers, 27-11-04-03, KSHS.

223. *Hays Daily News*, July 20, 1933; *Tiller and Toiler* (Larned), Sept. 7, 1933.

224. Mrs. Matilda Atteberry to Alf Landon, Aug. 28, 1933, Alfred Landon Papers, 27-11-04-03, KSHS.

225. J. L. Horlacher to Clifford Hope, Jan. 20, 1934, Clifford Hope Papers, box 50, KSHS; *Colby Free Press*, Mar. 14, 1933.

226. Report of Civil Works projects, May 13, [1934], Alfred Landon Papers, 27-11-04-03, KSHS.

227. U. G. Balderston, Dodge City, to Clifford Hope, Feb. 7, 1934, Clifford Hope Papers, box 50, KSHS.

228. Speech, "The Public Welfare Administration of Kansas," Sept. 22, 1934, Alfred Landon Papers, 27-11-04-04, KSHS.

229. *Dodge City Daily Globe*, Feb. 22, 1935.

230. *Great Bend Daily Tribune*, June 7, 1934.

Chapter 10. Next Year Country

1. *Greeley Country Republican* (Tribune), Jan. 2, 1935.

2. *Colby Free Press*, Mar. 27, 1935. Annual Reports, typescript, Garden City Experiment Station, 1932–1937, Special Collections, Kansas State University; Annual Report, Tribune Experiment Station, 1935, ibid.

3. Annual Report, Colby Experiment Station, 1935, ibid.

4. *Ness County News*, Jan. 26, 1935.

5. *Kansas City Times* in *Greeley County Republican* (Tribune), Mar. 7, 1935.

6. *Dodge City Daily Globe*, Mar. 21, 1935.

7. Ibid., Oct. 2, 1935.

8. Annual Reports, typescript, Colby Experiment Station, 1935, Special Collections, Kansas State University.

9. *Great Bend Daily Tribune*, July 17, 1936.

10. Ibid., July 24, 1936.

11. *Greeley County Republican* (Tribune), July 30, 1936.

12. *Ness County News*, Sept. 28, 1935.

13. *Tiller and Toiler* (Larned), Feb. 28, 1935.

14. *Greeley County Republican* (Tribune), Feb. 28, 1935.

15. Ibid., Mar. 14, 1935.

16. *Great Bend Daily Tribune*, Mar. 16, 1935.

17. *Liberal News*, Mar. 20, 1935.

18. *Ness County News*, Mar. 23, 1935.

19. *Hays Daily News*, Mar. 16, 1935; *Great Bend Daily Tribune*, Mar. 20, 1935; *Dodge City Daily Globe*, Mar. 20, 1935.

20. *Dodge City Daily Globe*, Mar. 18, 1935.

21. *Gove County Republican-Gazette* (Gove City), Mar. 21, 1935.

22. *Great Bend Daily Tribune*, Mar. 21, 1935.

23. *Liberal News*, Mar. 20, 1935.

24. *Great Bend Daily Tribune*, Mar. 30, 1935.

25. Ibid., Apr. 2, 1935; *Dodge City Daily Globe*, Apr. 5, 1935.

26. *Scott County News* in *Dodge City Daily Globe*, Apr. 5, 1935.

27. Good descriptions of the 1935 storms were recorded by Meade County farmer Lawrence Svobida in his 1940 book, *An Empire of Dust*. This was reprinted in 1986 by the University Press of Kansas as *Farming the Dust Bowl: A First-Hand Account from Kansas*. See particularly pp. 118–37.

28. *Wichita Eagle*, Apr. 11, 1935.

29. Annual Reports, typescript, Colby Experiment Station, 1935, Special Collections, Kansas State University.

30. *Tiller and Toiler* (Larned), Apr. 11, 1935.

31. *Hugoton Hermes*, Apr. 12, 1935.

32. *Goodland News-Republic*, Apr. 10, 1935.

33. *Great Bend Daily Tribune*, Apr. 12, 1935.

34. Q. E. Becker in *Ness County News*, Apr. 13, 1935.

35. *Liberal News*, Apr. 15, 1935.

36. Ibid., Apr. 17, 1935.

37. *Hugoton Hermes*, Apr. 19, 1935.

38. *Great Bend Daily Tribune*, Apr. 15, 1935.

39. Ibid., Apr. 23, 1935.

40. *Hays Daily News*, Apr. 26, 1935.

41. *Hugoton Hermes,* May 3, 1935.

42. *Dodge City Daily Globe*, May 4, 1935.

43. *Colby Free Press*, May 1, 1935.

44. Jess Denious to Wilber Denious, Apr. 16, 1935, Jess Denious Papers, box 1, KSHS.

45. *Garden City Daily Telegram*, Mar. 17, 1936.

46. Schruben, *Kansas in Turmoil*, 158.

47. Annual Reports, typescript, Tribune Experiment Station, 1936, Special Collections, Kansas State University.

48. *Wichita Eagle*, Sept. 1, 1936.

49. *Goodland News-Republic*, May 5, 1936.

50. Charles Scott to Jess Denious, Mar. 26, 1936, Jess Denious Papers, box 2, KSHS.

51. Annual Reports, typescript, Garden City Experiment Station, 1932–1937, Special Collections, Kansas State University.

52. Annual Report, Tribune Experiment Station, 1937, ibid.

53. Annual Report, Garden City Experiment Station, 1939, ibid.

54. Annual Report, Tribune Experiment Station, 1940, ibid.

55. W. E. Grimes to Alf Landon, Apr. 23, 1935, Alfred Landon Papers, 27-11-04-03, KSHS.

56. Pawl Switzer to Alf Landon, Apr. 26, 1937, ibid.

57. *News-Chronicle* (Scott City), June 20, 1935.

58. Press Release, KERC, June 24, 1935, Alfred Landon Papers, 27-11-04-03, KSHS.

59. "Three Years of State Public Service in Kansas," by John Stutz, June 24, 1935, ibid.

60. W. G. Clugston in *Kansas City Journal Post,* quoted in *News-Chronicle* (Scott City), Aug. 15, 1935.

61. *Hays News*, quoted in ibid., Nov. 23, 1935.

62. Eri Hulbert memo, Aug. 2, 1935, Alfred Landon Papers, 27-11-04-03, KSHS.

63. Memo from Mrs. Forrester, Aug. 10, 1935, ibid.

64. Anna Enlow to Alf Landon, Aug. 21, 1935, ibid.

65. Resolutions, Feb. 29, 1936, 27-11-04-02, ibid.

66. H. S. Carothers, Leoti, to Walter Huxman, Mar. 3, 1937, Walter Huxman Papers, 27-11-05-04, KSHS.

67. E. D. Cooper to Walter Huxman, May 24, 1937, ibid.

68. Carl McClung to Walter Huxman, May 7, 1937, ibid.

69. County Commissioners to Walter Huxman, June 15, 1937, ibid.

70. Schruben, *Kansas in Turmoil*, 217.

71. Paul Sears, *Deserts on the March*, 4th ed. (Norman: University of Oklahoma Press, 1980).

72. Donald Worster, *Dust Bowl: The Southern Plains in the 1930s* (New York: Oxford University Press, 1979), 96.

73. The Dust Bowl scholarly literature has much statistical information on persistence or lack thereof, varying quite a lot by county, but constituting by no stretch a mass exodus, except in those areas where the federal government was buying land as part of the resettlement program. See particularly Riney-Kehrberg, *Rooted in Dust*, and Donald Worster, *Dust Bowl*. Whether they *should* have stayed or not is the subject of a deeper debate.

74. *Dodge City Daily Globe*, July 31, 1936.

75. Mamie Fay to Clifford Hope, May 10, 1935, Clifford Hope Papers, box 50, KSHS.

76. Annual Reports, typescript, Garden City Experiment Station, 1939, Special Collections, Kansas State University.

77. *Southwest Daily Times* (Liberal), July 15, 1936.

78. *News-Chronicle* (Scott City), July 16, 1936.

79. Annual Reports, typescript, Tribune Experiment Station, 1936, Special Collections, Kansas State University; *Southwest Daily Times* (Liberal), Oct. 16, 1936.

80. *Gove County Republican-Gazette* (Gove City), June 9, 1938.

81. Miner, *Harvesting the High Plains*, 65–66.

82. Larabee's hyperbole may be found in *Great Bend Daily Tribune*, Feb. 21, 1935; *Liberal News*, Feb. 26, 1935; and in many other places.

83. *Colby Free Press*, Nov. 28, 1934.

84. *Hays Daily News*, Jan. 17, 1935.

85. *Gove County Republican-Gazette* (Gove City), Jan. 10, 1935.

86. *Colby Free Press*, Dec. 19, 1934.

87. *Greeley County Republican* (Tribune), Jan. 17, 1935.

88. *Great Bend Daily Tribune*, Jan. 4, 1935.

89. Ibid., Feb. 13, 1935.

90. *Greeley County Republican*, Jan. 31, 1935.

91. *Tiller and Toiler* (Larned), Mar. 14, 1935.

92. *Gove County Republican-Gazette* (Gove City), Jan. 17, 1935.

93. *Great Bend Daily Tribune*, Mar. 11, 1935.

94. *Colby Free Press*, Dec. 19, 1934.

95. *Wichita Beacon*, quoted in *Hugoton Hermes*, Feb. 22, 1935.

96. *Gove County Republican-Gazette* (Gove City), Feb. 7, 1935.

97. *News-Chronicle* (Scott City), Jan. 10, 1935.

98. *Liberal News*, Feb. 7, 1935; *Gove County Republican-Gazette* (Gove City), Feb. 21, 1935.

99. *Liberal News*, Mar. 6, 1935.

100. *News-Chronicle* (Scott City), Mar. 14, 1935.

101. *Ness County News*, May 4, 1935.

102. Svoboda, *Farming the Dust Bowl*, 172, 175.

103. *Garden City Daily Telegram*, July 31, 1931.

104. *Hugoton Hermes*, May 3, 1935.

105. *Gove County Republican-Gazette* (Gove City), June 13, 1935.

106. *News-Chronicle* (Scott City), Mar. 14, 1935.

107. *Hugoton Hermes*, June 21, 1935.

108. Ibid., June 21, 1935; *Greeley County Republican* (Tribune), Aug. 29, 1935.

109. *News-Chronicle* (Scott City), Mar. 26, 1936.

110. *Greeley County Republican* (Tribune), July 28, 1935.

111. *Hugoton Hermes*, Oct. 11, 1935.

112. Harold Duryea in *Southwest Daily Times* (Liberal), Nov. 16, 1935.

113. *Garden City Daily Telegram*, Mar. 25, 1937.

114. Ibid., Feb. 26, 1937.

115. *Gove County Republican-Gazette* (Gove City), Mar. 5, 1936.

116. Riney-Kehrberg, ed., *Waiting on the Bounty*, 14.

117. Ibid., 33.

118. Ibid., 35.

119. Ibid., 42, 46, 51.

120. Ibid., 56.

121. Ibid., 150.

122. Entries for 1939, ibid.

123. "Family Farm Record Book, United States Department of Agriculture, Farm Security Administration," 1937, in Leslie Linville Papers, box 1, folder 18, Special Collections, Wichita State University.

124. *Southwest Daily Times* (Liberal), Jan. 7, 1936.

125. Ibid., Aug. 7, 1936.

126. Ibid., Oct. 13, 1936.

127. *Garden City Daily Telegram*, Oct. 9, 1937.

128. *Tiller and Toiler* (Larned), Feb. 6, 1936.

129. Price Davis to Clifford Hope, Mar. 24, 1935, Clifford Hope Papers, box 50, KSHS.

130. Dr. W. D. Howard to Clifford Hope, Apr. 12, 1935, ibid.

131. Clinton Clough to Clifford Hope, Apr. 18, 1935, ibid.

132. Mamie Fay to Clifford Hope, May 10, 1935, ibid.

133. A. L. Jacobson to Clifford Hope, May 11, 1935, ibid.

134. *Dodge City Daily Globe*, Aug. 18, 1936.

135. *Great Bend Daily Tribune*, Dec. 18, 1936.

136. *Garden City Daily Telegram*, May 28, 1936.

137. *Kansas City Star*, in *Great Bend Daily Tribune*, June 2, 1936.

138. *Garden City Daily Telegram*, Nov. 3, 5, 1937.

139. *Ness County News*, June 2, 1938.

140. *Garden City Daily Telegram*, Sept. 3, 1938.

141. *Great Bend Daily Tribune*, June 24, 1939.

142. *Dodge City Daily Globe*, Feb. 18, Apr. 10, 1936.

143. Ibid., Aug. 20, 1935.

144. Clifford Hope to Mamie Faye, May 29, 1935, Clifford Hope Papers, box 50, KSHS.

145. *Dodge City Daily Globe*, June 11, 1936.

146. *Garden City Daily Telegram*, Aug. 11, 1936; *Southwest Daily Times* (Liberal), July 26, 30, Aug. 2, 1936.

147. *Southwest Daily Times* (Liberal), Aug. 23, 1936.

148. *Hays Daily News*, Aug. 12, 1936.

149. *Southwest Daily Times* (Liberal), Jan. 17, 1937.

150. Ibid.

151. *Dodge City Daily Globe*, Mar. 23, 1937.

152. Ibid., Apr. 12, 1937.

153. *Southwest Daily Times* (Liberal), Sept. 13, 1937.

154. *Garden City Daily Telegram*, Sept. 15, 1937.

155. *Topeka Daily Capital* in *Southwest Daily Times* (Liberal), Dec. 27, 1937.

156. *Garden City Daily Telegram*, Mar. 25, 1939.

157. *Colby Free Press*, June 2, 1937.

158. *Garden City Daily Telegram*, Dec. 23, 1936.

159. Ibid., Mar. 22, Apr. 9, 1938.

160. *Garden City Daily Telegram*, Sept. 2, 1937.

161. Ibid., Sept. 3, 1937.

162. Ibid., Sept. 10, 1937, contains some of Clutter's advice. For the murder and aftermath, see Miner, *Kansas*, 350–52.

163. *Garden City Daily Telegram*, May 22, 1938.

164. *Southwest Daily Times* (Liberal), Aug. 30, 1938.

165. *Great Bend Daily Tribune*, Oct. 27, 1939.

166. Ibid., June 2, 1938.

167. Ibid., Oct. 31, 1938.

168. Ibid., Dec. 24, 1937.

169. Ibid., Nov. 2, 1938.

170. *Hays Daily News*, Sept. 23, 1938.

171. Ibid., Jan. 17, 1939.

172. Ibid., Feb. 4, 1939.

173. *Great Bend Daily Tribune*, Dec. 14, 1938.

174. *Southwest Daily Times* (Liberal), Mar. 22, 1939.

175. *Hays Daily News*, Apr. 15, 1939.

176. *Dodge City Daily Globe*, Feb. 25, 1939.

177. Ibid., Apr. 19, 1939.

178. Ibid., July 28, 1939.

179. Ibid., June 25, 1937.

180. *Hays Daily News*, Aug. 9, 1939.

181. Sara Keckeisen, "The Samson of the Cimarron," *Kansas Heritage* 11 (Summer 2003): 18–20.

182. *Southwest Daily Times* (Liberal), Aug. 18, 1938.

183. Ibid., Nov. 8, 1938.

184. Ibid., Mar. 15, 1939.

185. Keckeisen, "Samson of the Cimarron," 21.

186. *Southwest Daily Times* (Liberal), Jan. 15, 1939.

187. Ibid., Jan. 22, 1939.

188. Ibid., Jan. 1, 1939.

189. *Hays Daily News*, Aug. 15, 1938.

190. *Dodge City Daily Globe*, Aug. 9, 1939.

191. *Hays Daily News*, Dec. 6, 1938.

192. *Hays Daily News*, Dec. 26, 1938.

Conclusion: A Harvest of Understanding

1. F. D. Coburn in *Topeka Mail and Breeze,* quoted in *News-Chronicle* (Scott City), Nov. 17, 1911.

2. *Topeka Mail and Breeze* in *News-Lever (Scott City)*, Jan. 7, 1897.

3. *Liberal News*, June 1, 1899.

4. Ecord, "Life on a Homestead in Western Kansas," 38.

5. J. S. Painter (editor of *Garden City Herald*), "Southwest Kansas," *Collections of Kansas State Historical Society* 4 (1890): 286.

6. *Kansas City Star*, Sept. 23, 1903, County Clippings files, Ellis County clippings, KSHS, vol. 1.

7. *Wichita Eagle* in *Liberal News*, Mar. 17, 1898.

8. Deborah Fitzgerald, *Every Farm a Factory: The Industrial Ideal in American Agriculture* (New Haven: Yale University Press, 2003), 5–6, 24–26, 28.

9. Barron, *Mixed Harvest*, 155–56.

10. W. A. Peffer, *The Farmer's Side: His Troubles and Their Remedy* (New York: Appleton and Company, 1891), 5.

11. Thomas Frank, *What's the Matter with Kansas?: How Conservatives Won the Heart of America (New York: Henry Holt, 2004)*, 41–43, 54–55.

12. Mason, *Life on the Dry Line*, 59, 69.

13. Riney-Kehrberg, *Rooted in Dust*, 139–64, 180. Riney-Kehrberg's southwest Kansas population tables are on pp. 189–96.

14. *Hutchinson News,* Apr. 17, 1931.

15. Ibid., May 29, 1931.

16. Elliott West, *Contested Plains: Indians, Goldseekers, and the Rush to Colorado* (Lawrence: University Press of Kansas, 1998), 91.

17. Geoff Cunfer, *On The Great Plains: Agriculture and Environment* (College Station: Texas A&M University Press, 2005), ix, 8, 236–38. See Svobida, *Farming the Dust Bowl;* and for the Flint Hills pattern, see Joseph Hickey, *Ghost Settlement on the Prairie: A Biography of Thurman, Kansas* (Lawrence: University Press of Kansas, 1995).

18. *Hutchinson News,* June 27, 1931.

19. *Dodge City Daily Globe*, Mar. 3, 1930.

20. *Hutchinson News,* Apr. 18, 1932.

21. *Kansas Farmer*, Apr. 21, 1928.

22. *Ellis County News* (Hays), Nov. 5, 1925.

23. *Greeley County Republican* (Tribune), July 30, 1936.

Bibliography

ARCHIVES

Author's Collection

Harold Miner/Mabel Pinkney letters, 1907

Kansas State Historical Society

Atchison, Topeka & Santa Fe Railroad Archives
New York Executive Department Files
Agricultural Department and Publicity Office, Correspondence and Clippings Files
Microbox 373, train robbery records
Henry Allen Papers
Willis Bailey Papers
Arthur Capper Papers (as governor)
Arthur Capper Papers (as senator)
Jonathan Davis Papers
Jess Denious Papers
Albert Doerr Papers
Ray Hugh Garvey Papers
Edward Hoch Papers
George Hodges Papers
Clifford Hope Papers
Lyman Humphrey Papers
Walter Huxman Papers
Kansas Town & Land Company Papers
Alfred Landon Papers
Lorenzo Lewelling Papers
Edmund Morrill Papers
Benjamin Paulen Papers
Payne Ratner Papers
Clyde Reed Papers

William Stanley Papers
Walter Stubbs Papers
Harry Woodring Papers

Kansas State University, Special Collections

Annual Reports, typescript, Agricultural Experiment Stations
Cooperative Extension Service, Historical Files
Reports of Farm Bureau County Agents

Library of Congress

Victor Murdock Papers

University of Kansas, Kansas Collection

Milton Amos Papers
Hansen-Bales Family Papers

Wichita State University, Special Collections

Leslie Linville Papers
Victor Murdock Papers (microfilm from Library of Congress)

NEWSPAPERS

County Clippings files, Kansas State Historical Society, for all sixty counties of region
    (multiple volumes)
Alliance Echo (Sharon Springs), 1890–1891
Ashland Clipper, 1911–1914
Belleville Telescope, 1904–1906
Colby Free Press, 1890–1940
Dodge City Daily Globe, 1911–1940
Dodge City Reporter, 1901
Ellis County News-Republican (Hays), 1912–1914
Ellis County News (Hays), 1915–1929
Garden City Daily Telegram, 1929–1940
Garden City Telegram, 1906–1929 (early title varies)
Garden City Herald, 1890–1929
Globe-Republican (Dodge City), 1891–1910
Goodland Republic, 1918–1926
Goodland News-Republic, 1926–1939
Gove County Republican-Gazette (Gove City), 1934–1940
Great Bend Daily Tribune, 1920–1940
Greeley County Republican (Tribune), 1917–1940
Hays City Sentinel, 1890–1895
Hays Daily News, 1929–1940
Hugoton Hermes, 1910–1937
Hutchinson Herald, 1930

Hutchinson News, 1922–1924, 1931–1932
Kansas Farmer, 1890–1924
Kinsley Graphic, 1890–1901
Larned Chronoscope, 1890–1906
Liberal News, 1892–1935
Ness County News, 1890–1940
News-Chronicle (Scott City), 1903–1940 (early title varies)
News-Lever (Scott City), 1892–1903
Republican (Hays), 1895–1912
Salina Journal, 1890–1896 (title varies)
Scott City Republican, 1893–1896
Southwest Daily Times (Liberal), 1935–1940
Tiller and Toiler (Larned), 1907–1940 (daily after 1934)
Western Times (Sharon Springs), 1890–1891

ARTICLES

Averill, Thomas. "Oz and Kansas Culture." *Kansas History* 12 (Spring 1989): 2–12.

Avila, Henry. "Immigration and Integration: The Mexican American Community in Garden City, Kansas, 1900–1950." *Kansas History* 20 (Spring 1997): 23–37.

Baker, T. Lindsay. "Blowin' in the Wind: Windmill Manufacturing and Distribution in Kansas." *Kansas History* 19 (Spring 1996): 6–21.

Britz, Kevin. "'Boot Hill Burlesque': The Frontier Cemetery as Tourist Attraction in Tombstone, Arizona, and Dodge City, Kansas." *Journal of Arizona History* 44 (Autumn 2003): 211–42.

Clugston, W. G. "A Storekeeper Who Studies Farmers' Wants." *American Magazine* 92, no. 1 (July 1921): 61.

Ecord, Allen. "Life on a Homestead in Western Kansas, 1880 to 1910." Typescript, 1980, KSHS.

Harris, Helen. "Agriculture and Fort Hays State University." *Kansas History* 9 (Winter 1986/87): 164–74.

Harvey, Douglas. "Creating a 'Sea of Galilee': The Rescue of Cheyenne Bottoms Wildlife Area, 1927–1930. " *Kansas History* 24 (Spring 2001): 2–17.

Irvine, Robert. "The Waterscape and the Law: Adopting Prior Appropriation in Kansas." *Kansas History* 19 (Spring 1996): 22–35.

Isern, Thomas. "Wheat Explorer the World Over. " *Kansas History* 23 (Spring/Summer 2000): 12–25.

Keckeisen, Sara. "The Samson of the Cimmaron." *Kansas Heritage* 11 (Summer 2003): 18–21.

MacDonald, A. B. "Big Country Merchants: A. A. Doerr of Larned, Kansas." *Country Gentleman* (Sept. 25, 1920): 15, 24.

Marvin, Anne. "'A Graveyard of Hopes': Irrigation and Boosterism in Southwest Kansas, 1880–1890." *Kansas History* 19 (Spring 1996): 36–51.

Menninger, Constance. "The Gospel of Better Farming According to Santa Fe." *Kansas History* 10 (Spring 1987): 43–66.

Painter, J. S. "Southwest Kansas." *Collections of Kansas State Historical Society* 4 (1890): 281–86.

Riney-Kehrberg, Pamela. "Tragedy as Triumph: Liberal, Kansas, and Its 1933 Tornado." *Kansas History* 21 (Summer 1998): 88–101.

Sherow, James. "The Art of Water and the Art of Living." *Kansas History* 25 (Spring 2002): 52–71.

Socolofsky, Homer. "The Bittersweet Tale of Sorghum Sugar." *Kansas History* 16 (Winter 1993–1994): 276–89.

Sutter, Paul. "Paved with Good Intentions: Good Roads, the Automobile, and the Rhetoric of Rural Improvement in the *Kansas Farmer*." *Kansas History* 18 (Winter 1995–1996): 284–99.

Teagarden, Earl, comp. "History of the Kansas Extension Service from 1868 to 1964." 3 vols. Typescript, Kansas State University, Special Collections.

BOOKS

Agran, Edward. *Too Good a Town: William Allen White, Community, and the Emerging Rhetoric of Middle America*. Fayetteville: University of Arkansas Press, 1998.

Annual Reports of Board of Railroad Commissioners, Kansas, 1890–1915.

Bader, Robert. *Prohibition in Kansas: A History*. Lawrence: University Press of Kansas, 1986.

Barron, Hal. *Mixed Harvest: The Second Great Transformation in the Rural North, 1870–1930*. Chapel Hill: University of North Carolina Press, 1997.

Barry, John. *The Great Influenza: The Epic Story of the Deadliest Plague in History*. New York: Viking, 2004.

Baughman, Robert. *Kansas Post Offices, May 29, 1828–August 3, 1961*. Topeka: Kansas State Historical Society, 1961.

Benedict, Murray. *Farm Policies of the United States, 1790–1950: A Study of Their Origins and Development*. New York: Twentieth Century Fund, 1953.

Berglund, Lee. *Wheat Belt Route: Wichita Northwestern, the Story of a Dust Bowl Railroad*. David City, Nebr.: South Platte Press, 1998.

Berry, Wendell. *The Art of the Commonplace: The Agrarian Essays of Wendell Berry*. Washington, D.C.: Counterpoint, 2002.

Biennial Reports of the Public Utilities Commission, Kansas, 1915–1918.

Biennial Reports of the State Board of Agriculture, Kansas, 1885–1940.

Blackmar, Frank, ed. *Kansas*. 4 vols. Chicago: Standard Publishing Company, 1912.

Blanke, David. *Sowing the American Dream: How Consumer Culture Took Root in the Rural Midwest*. Athens: Ohio University Press, 2000.

Bowers, William. *The Country Life Movement in America, 1900–1920*. Port Washington, N.Y.: Kennikat Press, 1974.

Carey, James. *Kansas State University: The Quest for Identity*. Lawrence: Regents Press of Kansas, 1977.

Clanton, Gene. *Populism: The Humane Preference in America, 1890–1900*. Boston: Twayne, 1991.

The Condition of Agriculture in the United States and Measures for Its Improvement: A Report by the Business Men's Commission on Agriculture. New York: National Industrial Conference Board, 1927.

Connelley, William. *History of Kansas: State and People*. 5 vols. Chicago and New York: American Historical Society, 1918.

Crumbine, Samuel. *Frontier Doctor*. Philadelphia: Dorrance, 1948.

Cunfer, Geoff. *On the Great Plains: Agriculture and Environment*. College Station: Texas A&M University Press, 2005.

Danbom, David. *The Resisted Revolution: Urban America and the Industrialization of Agriculture, 1900–1930*. Ames: Iowa State University Press, 1979.

Dighe, Ranjit, ed. *The Historian's Wizard of Oz: Reading L. Frank Baum's Classic as a Political and Monetary Allegory*. Westport, Conn.: Praeger, 2002.

Elliott, Mal. *Perry Maxwell's Prairie Dunes*. Chelsea, Mich.: Sleeping Bear Press, 2002.

Emmons, David. *Garden in the Grasslands: Boomer Literature of the Central Great Plains*. Lincoln: University of Nebraska Press, 1971.

Fite, Gilbert. *American Agriculture and Farm Policy since 1900*. New York: Macmillan, 1964.

Fitzgerald, Deborah. *Every Farm a Factory: The Industrial Ideal in American Agriculture*. New Haven: Yale University Press, 2003.

Fitzgibbon, Russell, ed. *Forty Years on Main Street*. New York: Farrar and Rinehart, 1937.

Forsythe, James. *The First 75 Years: A History of Fort Hays State University, 1902–1977*. Topeka: Josten's Yearbook Company, 1977.

Frank, Thomas. *What's the Matter with Kansas?: How Conservatives Won the Heart of America*. New York: Henry Holt, 2004.

Grant, Michael. *Down and Out on the Family Farm: Rural Rehabilitation in the Great Plains, 1929–1945*. Lincoln: University of Nebraska Press, 2002.

Ham, George, and Robert Higham. *The Rise of the Wheat State: A History of Kansas Agriculture, 1861–1986*. Manhattan, Kans.: Sunflower University Press, 1987.

Hamilton, David. *From New Day to New Deal: American Farm Policy from Hoover to Roosevelt, 1928–1933*. Chapel Hill: University of North Carolina Press, 1991.

Hargreaves, Mary. *Dry Farming in the Northern Great Plains, 1900–1925*. Cambridge: Harvard University Press, 1957.

———. *Dry Farming in the Northern Great Plains: Years of Readjustment, 1920–1990*. Lawrence: University Press of Kansas, 1992.

Haywood, Robert. *Victorian West: Class and Culture in Kansas Cattle Towns*. Lawrence: University Press of Kansas, 1991.

Heat-Moon, William Least. *PrairyErth*. Boston: Houghton Mifflin Company, 1991.

Hickey, Joseph. *Ghost Settlement on the Prairie: A Biography of Thurman, Kansas*. Lawrence: University Press of Kansas, 1995.

History of Finney County, Kansas. 2 vols. Garden City, Kans.: Finney County Historical Society, 1950.

Hofstadter, Richard. *The Age of Reform*. New York: Alfred Knopf, 1955.

Holt, Marilyn. *Linoleum, Better Babies, and the Modern Farm Woman, 1890–1930*. Albuquerque: University of New Mexico Press, 1995.

Hope, Cliff, Jr. *Quiet Courage: Kansas Congressman Clifford R. Hope*. Manhattan, Kans.: Sunflower University Press, 1997.

Hope, Holly. *Garden City: Dreams in a Kansas Town*. Norman: University of Oklahoma Press, 1988.

Hyder, Clyde. *Snow of Kansas: The Life of Francis Huntington Snow*. Lawrence: University Press of Kansas, 1953.

Isern, Thomas. *Bull Threshers and Bindlestiffs: Harvesting and Threshing on the North American Plains*. Lawrence: University Press of Kansas, 1990.

———. *Custom Combining on the Great Plains: A History*. Norman: University of Oklahoma Press, 1981.

Kellogg, Royal. *Forest Planting in Western Kansas*. Washington, D.C.: Government Printing Office, 1904.

Kerr, John, and Donovan Frank. *Destination Topolobampo: The Kansas City, Mexico, and Orient Railway*. San Marino, Calif.: Golden West Books, 1969.

Kile, Orville. *The Farm Bureau through Three Decades*. Baltimore: Waverly Press, 1948.

Kline, Ronald R. *Consumers in the Country: Technology and Social Change in Rural America*. Baltimore: Johns Hopkins University Press, 2000.

Lindquist, Emory. *Bethany in Kansas: The History of a College*. Lindsborg, Kans.: Bethany College, 1975.

MacDonnell, Lawrence. *Reclamation to Sustainability: Water, Agriculture, and the Environment in the American West*. Niwot: University Press of Colorado, 1999.

Malin, James. *Power and Change in Society*. Lawrence, Kans.: Coronado Press, 1981.

———. *Winter Wheat in the Golden Belt of Kansas: A Study in Adaptation to Subhumid Geographical Environment*. Lawrence: University of Kansas Press, 1944.

Mason, Harry. *Life on the Dry Line: Working the Land, 1902–1944*. Golden, Colo.: Fulcrum Publishing, 1992.

Mechem, Kirke, ed. *The Annals of Kansas, 1886–1925*. 2 vols. Topeka: Kansas State Historical Society, 1954, 1956.

Miner, Craig. *Discovery: Cycles of Change in the Kansas Oil and Gas Industry, 1860–1987*. Wichita: Kansas Independent Oil and Gas Association, 1987.

———. *Fire in the Rock: A History of the Oil and Gas Industry in Kansas, 1855–1976*. Wichita: Kansas Independent Oil and Gas Association, 1976.

———. *Harvesting the High Plains: John Kriss and the Business of Wheat Farming, 1920–1950*. Lawrence: University Press of Kansas, 1998.

———. *Kansas: The History of the Sunflower State, 1854–2000*. Lawrence: University Press of Kansas, 2002.

———. *Uncloistered Halls: The Centennial History of Wichita State University*. Wichita: Wichita State University Endowment Association, 1995.

———. *West of Wichita: Settling the High Plains of Kansas*. Lawrence: University Press of Kansas, 1986.

Morlan, Robert. *Political Prairie Fire: The Nonpartisan League, 1915–1922*. Minneapolis: University of Minnesota Press, 1955.

Oliva, Leo. *Fort Dodge: Sentry of the Western Plains*. Topeka: Kansas State Historical Society, 1998.

———. *Fort Hays: Keeping Peace on the Plains*. Topeka: Kansas State Historical Society, 1980.

Peffer, W. A. *The Farmer's Side: His Troubles and Their Remedy*. New York: Appleton and Company, 1891.

Phillips, William. *History of the Agricultural Research Center—Hays: The First 100 Years*. Manhattan: Kansas State University, 2001.

Pisani, Donald. *Water, Land, and Law in the West: The Limits of Public Policy, 1850–1920*. Lawrence: University Press of Kansas, 1996.

Report of the Board of Irrigation Survey and Experiment for 1895 and 1896 to the Legislature of Kansas. Topeka: Kansas State Printing Company, 1897.

Riney-Kehrberg, Pamela. *Rooted in Dust: Surviving Drought and Depression in Southwestern Kansas*. Lawrence: University Press of Kansas, 1994.

———, ed. *Waiting on the Bounty: The Dust Bowl Diary of Mary Knackstedt Dyck*. Iowa City: University of Iowa Press, 1999.

Rydjord, John. *Kansas Place Names*. Norman: University of Oklahoma Press, 1972.

Saloutos, Theodore. *The American Farmer and the New Deal*. Ames: Iowa State University Press, 1982.

Saloutos, Theodore, and John Hicks. *Agricultural Discontent in the Middle West, 1900–1930*. Madison: University of Wisconsin Press, 1951.

Schruben, Francis. *Kansas in Turmoil, 1930–1936*. Columbia: University of Missouri Press, 1969.

Sears, Paul. *Deserts on the March*. 4th ed. Norman: University of Oklahoma Press, 1980. First published in 1935.

Self, Huber. *Environment and Man in Kansas: A Geographical Analysis*. Lawrence: Regents Press of Kansas, 1978.

Sherow, James. *Watering the Valley: Development along the High Plains Arkansas River, 1870–1950*. Lawrence: University Press of Kansas, 1990.

Shideler, James. *Farm Crisis, 1919–1923*. Berkeley: University of California Press, 1957.

Shortridge, James. *Cities on the Plains: The Evolution of Urban Kansas*. Lawrence: University Press of Kansas, 2004.

Snyder, Ralph. *We Kansas Farmers*. Topeka, Kans.: F. M. Steves and Sons, 1953.

Socolofsky, Homer, and Huber Self. *Historical Atlas of Kansas*. Norman: University of Oklahoma Press, 1972.

Spence, Clark. *The Rainmakers: American 'Pluviculture' to World War II*. Lincoln: University of Nebraska Press, 1980.

Stillwell, Arthur. *Cannibals of Finance: Fifteen Years' Contest with the Money Trust*. Chicago: Farnum, 1912.

Svobida, Lawrence. *Farming the Dust Bowl: A First-Hand Account from Kansas*. Lawrence: University Press of Kansas, 1986.

Van Sant, Thomas. *Improving Rural Lives: A History of Farm Bureau in Kansas, 1912–1992*. Manhattan, Kans.: Sunflower University Press, 1993.

Warne, William. *The Bureau of Reclamation*. New York: Praeger Publishers, 1973.

West, Elliott. *The Contested Plains: Indians, Goldseekers, and the Rush to Colorado*. Lawrence: University Press of Kansas, 1998.

Wilder, Bessie. *Government Agencies of the State of Kansas, 1861–1956*. Lawrence: University of Kansas Publications, 1957.

Willard, Julius. *History of Kansas State College of Agriculture and Applied Science*. Manhattan: Kansas State College Press, 1940.

Wingo, Wayne. *History of Thomas County, Kansas, 1884–1964*. N.p.: privately printed, n.d.

Worster, Donald. *Dust Bowl: The Southern Plains in the 1930s*. New York: Oxford University Press, 1979.

Wright, Robert M. *Dodge City: The Cowboy Capital and the Great Southwest.* Wichita: Wichita Eagle, 1913.

THESES AND DISSERTATIONS

Harvey, Douglas. "'Drought Relief Delayed by Rain': The History of the Cheyenne Bottoms Wildlife Area." M.A. thesis, Wichita State University, Department of History, 2000.

Hemmen, Linda. "Out of the Darkness, Into the Light: The Transformation of the Kansas State Board of Health, 1885–1925," M.A. thesis, Department of History, Wichita State University, 2003.

Miller, Emy. "Corporation Farming in Kansas." M.A. thesis, Department of History, University of Wichita, 1933.

Schletzbaum, Karl. "Early Motorcycle Racing in Kansas, 1910–1922." M.A. thesis, Department of History, Wichita State University, 2002.

Tomayko, James. "Irrigation Technology and the Development of Southwest Kansas." Ph.D. diss., College of Humanities and Social Sciences, Carnegie-Mellon University, 1980.

Index